Crime and Economics

Crime and Economics provides the first comprehensive and accessible text to address the economics of crime within the study of crime and criminology.

The economics of crime is an area of growing activity and concern, increasingly influential both to the study of crime and criminal justice and to the formulation of crime reduction and criminal justice policy. As well as providing an overview of the relationship between economics and crime, this book poses key questions such as: What is the impact of the labour market and poverty on crime? Can society decrease criminal activity from a basis of economic disincentives? What forms of crime reduction and methods of reducing re-offending are most cost beneficial? Can illicit organised crime and illicit drug markets be understood better through the application of economic analysis?

For those interested in economic methods, but without previous economic training, this book also provides an accessible overview of key areas such as cost–benefit analysis, econometrics and the debate around how to estimate the costs of crime.

This book will be key reading for undergraduate and postgraduate students of criminology and economics and those working in the criminal justice system including practitioners, managers and policy-makers.

Kevin Albertson is Acting Head of the Department of Economics at Manchester Metropolitan University.

Chris Fox is Professor of Evaluation in the Department of Sociology at Manchester Metropolitan University.

Crime and Economics

An introduction

Kevin Albertson and Chris Fox

Routledge
Taylor & Francis Group

LONDON AND NEW YORK

First published 2012
by Routledge
2 Park Square, Milton Park, Abingdon, Oxon, OX14 4RN

Simultaneously published in the USA and Canada
by Routledge
711 Third Avenue, New York, NY 10017

Routledge is an imprint of the Taylor & Francis Group, an informa business

British Library Cataloguing in Publication Data
A catalogue record for this book is available from the British Library

Library of Congress Cataloging in Publication Data
Albertson, Kevin, 1963–
    Crime and economics : an introduction / Kevin Albertson and
    Chris Fox. — 1st ed.
    p. cm.
    1. Crime—Economic aspects. I. Fox, Chris, 1973– II. Title.
    HV6030.A43 2011
    364.01—dc22
    2011003447

ISBN: 978–1–84392–843–0 (hbk)
ISBN: 978–1–84392–842–3 (pbk)
ISBN: 978–0–20381–304–1 (ebk)

Typeset in Times New Roman
by Swales & Willis Ltd, Exeter, Devon

MIX
Paper from
responsible sources
FSC
www.fsc.org   FSC® C004839   Printed and bound in Great Britain by the MPG Books Group

Kevin would like to thank his valued
colleagues in the Department of Economics at
Manchester Metropolitan University for their
support and encouragement and for bearing
with him while he ran ideas past them over
endless cups of coffee.

Chris would like to thank everyone at
Manchester Metropolitan University with
whom he has worked over the last three years.
He dedicates this book to Emma, with love.

Contents

Figures

Tables

1   Introduction

Why crime and economics?

Why do we need a book on crime and economics? At first glance the reader might wonder what economics can bring to the study of crime. As Levitt and Miles point out:

> The casual observer might expect that economics has little to contribute to the understanding of criminal activity. Economics is a discipline seemingly concerned with market-based transactions in which parties act purposefully to realize the benefits of exchange. In contrast, many criminal acts, such as homicide and theft, are inherently nonconsensual, even coercive. Moreover, many crimes appear to be acts of impulse or emotion rather than the kind of rational decision making associated with market behavior.
>
> (Levitt and Miles 2006: 147)

However, as Levitt and Miles go on to show, this is to take too narrow a view of economics and what it has to offer. Over recent years, the 'reach' of economics has grown. In their best-selling book, *Freakonomics*, Levitt and Dubner (2005: 14) write economics is 'the hidden side of . . . everything'. As an applied social science, the tools economists wield have been applied to subjects ranging from: obesity (Chou *et al.* 2004); to sport (Morley and Thomas 2005, for example); and climate change (for example, Nordhaus 2007; Stern 2007); to name but a few.

Over recent years economists have played an increasing role in research and policy on crime, crime reduction and criminal justice. This has taken many forms. Following Gary Becker's landmark 1968 article, economic debate on crime in the 1970s concentrated in particular on developing economic theories of criminal behaviour and the effect of criminal justice sanctions. The improvement of data available through the criminal justice system has allowed economists to use their favoured forms of analysis in this field. Economists have undertaken cost–benefit analyses of crime reduction and criminal justice interventions, estimated the costs of different types of crime and contributed to the development of criminal justice policy. And anyway, it's fun, isn't it? What we wonder is: why isn't economics *more* prominent in criminology courses and why are economists not more prominent in the development of criminal justice policy?

Why isn't economics more prominent in the study of crime?

Looking first at the teaching of criminology in universities, we would argue that there is more economics in most criminology courses than most students (and, sometimes, their lecturers) realise. Take the standard introduction to criminological theory which crops up in the early stages of most undergraduate and taught postgraduate criminology degrees. Such modules will often take a chronological approach and trace the origins of criminology back to the Enlightenment. There we are introduced to the 'classical' thinkers who first turned their attention to crime and laid some of the foundations for the modern discipline of criminology; writers such as Beccaria and Bentham. However, what is not always made clear is that these were writers on the political economy, some of whom also laid important foundations for the modern discipline of economics.

Working through the nineteenth century and into the twentieth century the typical criminology student is introduced to a variety of theorists ranging from Durkheim to Marx, from Merton to Shaw and McKay. Writers such as these were all, to greater or lesser extents, concerned with economics. In the development of criminology as a discipline, key theorists returned repeatedly to the economic dimensions of crime. In the late 1970s and 1980s a distinctly economic theory of crime – Rational Choice theory – became increasingly influential in criminological theory as well as crime reduction policy-making.

One of the principal tenets of economics, as we shall see, is that specialisation improves the range of outcomes available. It would be true to say that this has applied to the disciplines of Economics and Sociology/Criminology, which have sometimes specialised to the point of no longer communicating. Another economic principle, however, is 'gains from trade'. It is clear both disciplines have much to learn from each other.

Why isn't economics more prominent in criminal justice policy-making?

Until fairly recently, economists and economics have not tended to be prominent in the development of criminal justice policy. Reflecting on the situation in the USA in the mid 1990s, there might have been some truth in DiIulio's rather patronising observation that:

> As crime has risen to the top of the nation's domestic policy agenda, so has the need for a body of policy-relevant knowledge about crime, for theoretical ideas and empirical findings that can be translated into popular discourse and carved into public laws. To be frank, the professional criminologists, sociologists, political scientists, law professors, public management specialists and self-styled practitioner-scholars who have dominated the field are incapable of meeting this challenge. They generally lack the quantitative and formal modelling skills necessary to shed new light on old controversies or provide analytically compelling answers to methodologically complicated questions.

In my view, therefore, criminal justice is a field that needs to be conquered by economists.

(DiIulio 1996: 3)

However, in the last 10 years or so things have changed. Take penal policy as an example. Concern on both sides of the Atlantic about the inexorable rise in prison populations has increasingly drawn on economic arguments. In the UK, Patrick (now Lord) Carter's first review of the criminal justice system (Carter 2003) drew on economic concepts both to understand the problem (a demand-led system) and to propose solutions (an overall approach to sentencing which would better match supply and demand to improve cost-effectiveness). More recently, in a speech in 2007, Lord Philips, the Lord Chief Justice, drew on economic thinking when he noted that:

> If you decide to lock up one man for a minimum term of 30 years, you are investing £1 million or more in punishing him. That sum could pay for quite a few surgical operations or for a lot of remedial training in some of the schools where the staff are struggling to cope with the problems of trying to teach children who cannot even understand English.
>
> (Philips 2007: 6)

Recently, Kenneth Clarke, Lord Chancellor and Secretary of State for Justice has asked:

> how do we actually go about improving the safety and protecting the property of honest citizens in the most cost effective way?
>
> (Clarke 2010: unnumbered)

The solution proposed by the 2010 UK Coalition Government seems to be one which is explicitly 'economic'. For example, 'payment by results' is proposed as one of the key tools in reforming criminal justice services:

> The principle of incentivising performance through payment by results, with success based on the absence of re-offending, should be introduced for prisons, the providers of community sentences and the providers of rehabilitation programmes – whether in the public, private or voluntary sector. With devolved responsibilities and new incentives, we can create a revolution in how offenders are managed, and drive down re-offending.
>
> (Conservative Party 2009: 49)

Thus, the Coalition Government proposes that rehabilitation services would be paid for in part according to how successful they were at reducing re-offending. A basic tariff is paid to cover their costs and an additional tariff paid if targets to reduce re-offending are met. In delivering this, they quote the 'Peterborough Social Impact Bond' as a promising model (Clarke 2010).

In the USA, concern over rising prison numbers has also increasingly been framed in economic terms. Recently, the PEW Center on the States (2008: 3) reported:

> Three decades of growth in America's prison population has quietly nudged the nation across a sobering threshold: for the first time, more than one in every 100 adults is now confined in an American jail or prison.
>
> (PEW Center on the States 2008: 3)

However, the Center was also concerned with rising prison costs, which were reported to have 'exploded' from $10.6 billion in 1987 to $44 billion in 2007; a 315 per cent jump (ibid.). Some of the most innovative approaches to tackling these issues have also drawn on economics. Take, for example, the Justice Reinvestment movement which uses economic analysis to model the potential savings in criminal justice budgets that can be achieved by investing in the most cost-effective interventions. This process of moving some expenditure from prisons to more progressive, community-based crime reduction measures will, it is expected, reduce the long-term demand for prison places.

Thus, to return to DiIulio's observation from the mid-1990s, writing in 2010 we can now say, with a degree of confidence, that a 'conquest' of criminal justice policy by economists is no longer necessary. What we have seen over the last decade is that the application of quantitative techniques more familiar, in the UK at least, to economists than criminologists has added further weight to the argument that criminologists and economists can do more together than we are able to apart.

The need for a book on crime and economics

It is surprising, despite the important relationship that exists between economics and crime, and, increasingly, between economists and criminologists, that to date no publication has attempted a comprehensive survey of crime and economics. Two publications of which the current authors are aware are: Winter's (2008) *The Economics of Crime: An Introduction to Rational Crime Analysis*; and Fielding *et al.*'s (2000) *The Economic Dimensions of Crime*. We have found Winter's publication useful in shaping our own thinking on the economics of crime and cite it at several points in the following, but we hope our book goes beyond Winter's work to provide a more wide-ranging and in-depth analysis. Fielding *et al.*'s book, an edited collection, is comprised of some classic essays on crime and economics with some contemporary essays by influential academics in the field. Again, we have found this an informative book and reference essays from it at several points. However in places the essays in Fielding *et al.* are likely to be inaccessible to a reader without a background in economics and much has happened in this field since it was published.

There are also a number of edited collections and textbooks which cover some of the issues we address in this book and again we are indebted to them for the insight they have given us. These include chapters by Reiner on 'Political economy, crime and criminal justice' and by Levi on 'Organized crime and terrorism' in Maguire *et al.*'s (2007) *The Oxford Handbook of Criminology* and Hale's chapter on 'Economic marginalization, social exclusion, and crime' in Hale *et al.* (2009) *Criminology*. Finally, from the field of popular science we must also acknowledge Levitt and Dubner's (2005) *Freakonomics*, several chapters of which make accessible to a wide audience a number of Levitt's influential studies on crime and crime reduction.

For whom is this book written?

This book has been written for two main groups of people. The first group are undergraduate and postgraduate students studying crime and economics. We recognise that those students might either be criminologists making their first foray into the world of economics or vice versa and therefore we have written this book assuming neither a previous understanding of criminology nor of economics. The second main group of people for whom this book is written is made up of those working in the criminal justice system, whether as practitioners, managers or policy-makers, and who are increasingly being asked to think about the economic dimensions of crime, crime reduction and criminal justice.

Finally, we hope that this book will be of interest to readers from around the world. Most studies that we cite are from the UK and USA and our own research has been undertaken primarily in the UK. However, many important developments in this area have taken place in other countries and, where possible, we cover these as well.

What do we mean by crime and economics?

Before we go too much further we should say something about what we understand by crime and economics.

Crime

There is a vibrant debate among criminologists and policy-makers about the nature of crime. For criminologists this argument ranges from: debates about the reliability of crime statistics; to whether or not the experiences and perceptions of individual victims and offenders can ever be fully understood by others (be they researchers or police officers). Criminologists have also begun to compare the relative harm that results from activities such as polluting the environment or neglecting to protect the safety of workers to more 'traditional' understandings of crime, such as burglary. For policy-makers, the debates range from: discussions about the relative importance of tackling 'anti-social behaviours' such as littering and noisy neighbours; concerns about the way in which certain individuals and communities seem to bear a disproportionate burden of crime; to differing views on the relative threats to society posed by transnational organised crime and terrorism. At points in this book – and where economists have something to add – we touch on these debates. For instance, economists have devised various methods for placing a monetary value on different types of crime and have contributed to debates about the relative harms posed to society by organised crime, terrorism and illicit drugs markets; and, at a theoretical level, economists have put forward particular conceptions of crime and criminality which have important implications for development of criminal justice policy. Nevertheless we recognise that the debate around how to define crime is one which is too broad and sophisticated for us to seek to engage fully.

Economics

The study of economics arises from the scarcity of resources. Wherever there is scarcity individuals and society must decide how to divide them up. Thinking specifically about crime, Levitt and Miles (2006) argue that four characteristics distinguish the economic approach to the study of crime from that of other social sciences. These characteristics are:

1.   an emphasis on the role of incentives in determining the behaviour of individuals, whether they are criminals, victims, or those responsible for enforcing the law;
2.   the use of econometric approaches that seek to differentiate correlation from causality in nonexperimental settings;
3.   a focus on broad, public policy implications rather than evaluation of specific, small-scale interventions; and
4.   the use of cost–benefit analysis as the metric for evaluating public policies.

While we do not entirely agree with their third point, these characteristics are useful for helping to outline a theoretical and a methodological project that encompasses most economic work in relation to crime, crime reduction and criminal justice.

What this book covers

It might appear at first sight that this book is written for disparate groups – undergraduate students in two disciplines and criminal justice practitioners – however, we believe this adds to the strength of our approach. Economics students will benefit from the application of their core skills to real-world examples and criminologists from the insights economics can bring. Thus we begin by taking no knowledge as given, only the intelligence and interest of the reader. In the first section of the book – Chapters Two, Three and Four – we introduce the basic tools and concepts of the discipline of economics and how they are used in the explanation and analysis of crime and criminal behaviour. Policy recommendations are suggested to which we return in the applied/empirical chapters of the book.

Chapter Two is by far the most economically focused of the book. Before the reader can appreciate the application of the tools of economics (the viewpoint of an economist) it is necessary briefly to describe what these may be. Economics arises because there are only limited resources available to us; it is the study of how to make the best use of those resources. Often economics is confused with other disciplines – with, for example, accounting or business – however, economics is a much broader discipline than this. It seeks nothing less than to describe the way that humans, as individuals, as collectives, as businesses, as charities, as nations and societies and indeed across the planet, interact with each other and with the world. Economics doesn't necessarily claim to be the oldest human profession; it does, however, predate any profession for the simple reason that all actions undertaken with any aforethought to improve one's circumstances fall within the scope of economics. Indeed, one of the strengths of economics is that a lot of it, once considered appropriately, would seem to involve little more than the informed application of common sense.

In Chapter Two we look at the common-sense principles which underlie every society: the gains from specialisation, which of course lead to the concepts of trading and the market. Economists assume humans have a particular enjoyment from, for example, consumption – if we did not, why would we engage in it? This enjoyment is commonly termed 'utility'. In general humans are interested in improving their own utility. However, arising from specialisation and trade come a new set of problems, the problems of dealing with other humans and their (potentially) conflicting interests and values. What might make us better-off might leave other people worse off. While human society can produce and consume much greater amounts per capita than any of us could on our own, this very society can only exist if there are structures and codes to which we adhere. If these structures and codes are transgressed, inefficiency will result. Why is it then that humans have such difficulty in adhering to these structures? Whither temptation? We show that economic principles can explain this.

The seminal article on criminality from an economic perspective is the work of Becker (1968) which we discuss at length in Chapter Three. Two of the basic problems which are of interest to economists are 'which actions are likely to improve utility?' and 'how much of that action should be carried out?' Because each action undertaken has a cost as well as a benefit, humans as individuals, and as societies, get to choose how to utilise scarce resources. Becker considers these questions from the point of view of a society which wishes to minimise the costs arising from criminal behaviour. These costs are not only the direct losses which result from crime, but also the costs of determining the culprit and the punishment imposed. Becker's model, which has formed the foundation for much of the analysis of crime which follows, allows us to consider: which is the more efficacious of the two actions, detection and punishment; and how should society respond to increasing severity of crime and the costs of the criminal justice service (the costs of punishment and so on). The efficient society will be likely to model its criminal justice policy on the ideas presented by Becker.

A similar problem is considered by Ehrlich (1973). However Ehrlich considers the issue from the perspective of the potential criminal. One of the most basic units of resource, the time available, is considered and the best use of this resource weighed so as to maximise the pay-off to the individual decision-maker. The obvious link with a more sociological consideration of criminality arises from the attributes of the potential offender: issues such as level of education, gender, rate of time preference, etc., all reflect on the level of satisfaction to be gained from criminal (as opposed to legal) behaviour, and thus on the choice of the mix of activities which will be undertaken.

Both Becker and Ehrlich, and indeed all work which builds on theirs, consider that both society and individuals behave in ways which are amenable to explanation qualitatively (descriptively) and quantitatively (mathematically). Such explanations are often grouped together by the use of the term 'models'. A model of human behaviour is an explanation of the drivers and level of a particular activity. However, in order to build such models, and bearing in mind that different individuals may have very different perceptions, social scientists such as economists and criminologists assume choices are approached in a uniform way. This approach is summed up by Rational Choice theory, the discussion of which forms the basis of Chapter Four.

Early consideration of Rational Choice is sometimes little more than tautological – it is observed this or that action is undertaken, therefore this or that action must be rational. However, the theory goes beyond such simple observations. The *raison d'être* of Rational Choice theory is to predict how actions may change and adapt as a result of changes in the cost and benefit balance and the incentive structures which are available. Thus, we might not be able accurately to explain why such-and-such an individual prefers illegal to legal activities (or why they prefer tea to coffee), however, we can predict how they will behave if the expected return from their activities changes.

If it is indeed taken as a working hypothesis that potential criminals are rational, responding to incentive structures in a way likely to maximise their own utility, it follows that societies may alter behaviour in predictable ways by changing the incentive structure in operation in the economy. However, there is a distinction which may be made between decisions at higher levels (or meta-levels) , such as the decision whether or not to engage in criminal activities per se, and the choice over which activities to undertake. Similarly, the state of mind of individuals, whether angry or calm for example, can be modelled using Rational Choice. It may be the (seemingly) irrational actions undertaken by individuals when angry are not easily modelled; however, the decision to *become* angry may be modelled.

Having described in economic terms why people commit crime, and how society might respond efficiently, we go on to consider in Chapter Five the impact of poverty and labour market conditions on people's choices. The application of economic principles suggest poverty and the labour market might influence an individual's choice about whether or not to engage in crime; they might also influence the individual's choice about which crimes to commit.

Our starting point in Chapter Five is a consideration of different criminological theories which address the possible links between the state of the economy and the level of crime. Not surprisingly, many criminological theories have at least touched upon this relationship. An understanding of these theories can help us develop an insight into how prevailing economic conditions may lead an individual to choose a criminal lifestyle. We move on to consider whether there is statistical evidence to support such theories. Chapter Five is thus the first chapter where the empirical evidence researchers and economists have assembled is examined. Straight away we encounter some of the challenges which will recur in later chapters which examine other areas of empirical evidence. For example, how should we define 'employment' and 'unemployment'? In answering this question economists distinguish between voluntary and involuntary unemployment. Empirical data on the changing nature of unemployment over recent decades also alerts us to the changing nature of the labour market. So, for example, more women are economically active in paid employment today than in the past. Also, recent decades have seen an increase in part-time employment. Another challenge we touch on in Chapter Five is the issue of causality. We cannot, for example, automatically assume that unemployment causes crime. Certainly, at the individual level, the opposite might be true.

As Becker (1968) makes clear, all criminal justice systems have a trade-off to make between the cost of an intervention and the benefits to be realised. Becker's model is, however, theoretical. Thus it wasn't long before economists started to carry out empirical studies to test his theories. Chapters Six and Seven look in more detail at the most common empirical approaches economists use in studying crime and crime reduction.

Early empirical work following Becker's 1968 paper relied on econometric[1] studies. Indeed, much of the empirical evidence we have on the relationship between poverty, unemployment and crime comes from econometrics. Econometrics in essence is a tool kit of analytical and statistical methods designed to quantify the impact of economic relationships. As such it generally involves making use of large, pre-existing data sets, often ones that are generated by the criminal justice system through its management structures and processes. Econometricians take large sets of data, for example trends in crime and unemployment, and examine the relationships which exist between them. However, econometric studies have their limitations. In particular, the results of such analyses will be dependent on exactly which data sets are included and exactly which statistical techniques are applied.

Often an econometric study is the only option, perhaps because the subject being studied is in the past or because the cost of gathering bespoke data would be prohibitive. However, because of the limitations that are associated with econometric studies, where possible, economists prefer to use cost–benefit analysis (CBA) to evaluate the efficiency of different approaches to reducing or preventing crime. In a CBA data is gathered on the costs of delivering an intervention, estimates are made of the impact that the intervention achieved, and a value is then put on the benefits associated with achieving that impact. It is then possible to estimate what return is achieved by investing in a particular intervention, normally expressed in a cost–benefit ratio. Undertaking a CBA is not always straightforward. Challenges include the difficulties of estimating the impact of an intervention and different methods for capturing the costs of interventions.

Many of the challenges encountered in undertaking a CBA in the criminal justice sector are not distinct to criminal justice policy, but are also encountered when economists undertake CBAs in areas such as health policy or the education sector. However, one area that presents particular challenges is that of estimating the cost of crime and hence the benefits of avoiding crime. For this reason, and to do justice to the extensive literature on the subject, we devote the whole of Chapter Seven to a discussion of how to estimate the costs of crime. Some costs of crime are relatively easy to estimate. If you have your car broken into it is relatively easy to estimate the cost of the damage to the car. Your local garage will provide you with a quote for the repair and this is a market valuation of the damage. However, if you are a victim of a mugging, estimating the cost of the physical and psychological harm you suffer is more difficult. Different approaches have been used over the years. Early attempts in the UK drew on previous research on road traffic accidents and tried to draw parallels with injuries sustained as a result of crime victimisation. In the USA a number of 'willingness-to-pay' studies have been undertaken in which the public have been questioned about their willingness either to pay to avoid, or receive compensation for, crime. Latterly, researchers have drawn on health economics to develop what are arguably more sophisticated understandings of the costs of crime to individual victims.

For any readers who feel apprehensive at talk of research, statistics and data: *don't panic*! We don't make any assumptions about prior knowledge of statistics or research methods. This is not a methods textbook and so we try to explain concepts in accessible, non-technical language using practical examples.

In Chapters Eight to Eleven we apply our understanding of economic theory and methods to different areas of crime and criminal justice. Our choice of areas is informed by those we thought would be of most interest to students of both disciplines and those where economic analysis either has made, or has the potential to make, the most decisive contributions to the development of criminal justice policy.

Chapters Eight and Nine consider economic contributions to reducing crime. Chapter Eight looks at crime reduction, which, in simple terms covers interventions that individuals, organisations and the state make to reduce the likelihood of crime occurring in the first place. Chapter Nine is concerned with measures taken, primarily by the state, to reduce the likelihood of offenders committing further offences.

Crime reduction covers a broad array of activities ranging from different approaches to policing through the use of 'situational crime prevention' (measures which reduce opportunities for crime in specific locations) to interventions that seek to influence the early development of those at risk of going on to commit crime. In all of these areas the use of cost–benefit analysis provides insight into which interventions are most efficient. Economics has also made a particular contribution to the development of situational crime prevention, which draws its theoretical justification from Rational Choice theory. Rational Choice theory emphasises the importance of choice to criminal involvement or criminality. However, according to this theory, *opportunity* is central to understanding the potential criminal's decision-making process at a specific criminal event. Situational crime prevention therefore focuses on the reduction of opportunity.

In Chapter Nine we move on to consider interventions designed to reduce the likelihood of convicted offenders re-offending. We look in detail at the economics of (what has been described as) the 'prisons crisis': the result of substantial increases in the numbers being incarcerated. The economic evidence suggests continued increases in prison populations are not sustainable. Economic theory also contributes to our understanding of the rationale for the use of punishment. We go on to consider work undertaken by economists to estimate the impact and efficiency of different interventions. Attempts to estimate the impact of custody have involved the use of econometric studies and there are also a number of cost–benefit analyses that have been undertaken of different custodial and community sentences. However, this is an area where the available evidence is quite limited and so there is still much work to do. We conclude Chapter Nine by looking in detail at the concept of 'Justice Reinvestment' which makes explicit use of economic concepts and evidence to try and develop more efficient criminal justice systems. Evidence from the USA on the implementation of Justice Reinvestment is promising. Implementation in the UK is still at an early stage, but momentum is building.

The focus in Chapters Ten and Eleven is primarily on organised crime. Chapter Ten is devoted specifically to a discussion of organised crime and the contribution economics has made to our understanding of it. Chapter Eleven looks in more detail at illicit drugs. These chapters are obviously complementary as organised crime is often implicated in the trade in illicit drugs.

We start Chapter Ten by recognising that the study of organised crime is to some extent limited by a relative lack of empirical data. Presenting a concise overview is made harder because of the contested nature of organised crime. There is fierce debate not only about the nature of organised crime – what is it, how 'organised' is it, etc., – but also about its prevalence and impact. We start the chapter by considering different definitions of organised crime used by different countries, the United Nations (UN) and the European Union (EU). We go on to consider the harm organised crime causes and note that threat assessments undertaken in different countries are often inconsistent. A number of theoretical models of organised crime are considered – all of which, to some extent, draw on economic concepts. As we look in more detail at the relationship between organised crime and legitimate business, and organised crime and the state, economic principles are particularly helpful in explaining the extent of such illicit enterprises. What emerges is an understanding of organised crime that has relatively little in common with popular media images (such as 'The Godfather'), but is every bit as troubling. In Chapter Two we discussed how society requires social structures and codes if it is to work efficiently. We also started to explore how transgression of these will lead to inefficiency. At a very abstract level this is a basic account of how crime can be harmful to society. For a much more practical example, the reader is directed to the discussion in Chapter Ten of the harm organised crime, and the corruption with which it is usually associated, can do to society. The corruption of state officials reduces certainty and leads to inequity; this in turn has a detrimental impact on the efficiency of markets.

Chapter Eleven provides several examples of how an informed analysis of organised crime contributes to our understanding both of drugs markets and of policy options for tackling them. We could have written a whole book on drugs and economics. Covering this ground in only one chapter has therefore been challenging. Essentially Chapter Eleven is in two parts. One part concentrates on supply in illicit drug markets and the other on drug consumption (demand). Economists have played an important part in our understanding of both the supply and demand for illicit drugs. Our examination of illicit drugs markets draws parallels between the operation of legal commodities markets, such as for tea or coffee, and the production and supply of illicit drugs. Analysis of illicit drug production, processing and supply chains reveals how profitable drugs markets are when compared to comparable licit markets. This goes some way to explaining the resilience of drugs markets to law enforcement activities. However, while profit margins in wholesale drugs markets are high, the same cannot be said of the profits made by street dealers. An economic analysis of illicit drugs markets suggests a number of law enforcement approaches which are more likely (or less) to be effective in achieving society's objectives. While an economic analysis suggests that the 'war on drugs' is probably unwinnable, it also suggests strategies such as asset confiscation might have some effect on wholesale drugs markets and that a 'harm reduction' approach to the policing of local, street-level drugs markets also has some potential.

If economics is to be a useful tool in explaining the supply and consumption of illicit drugs we must assume that drug consumers exercise some degree of rational choice. At first sight, this might seem counter-intuitive; however, economists have developed theories of 'rational addition' that, to some extent, are supported by the (limited) evidence available about the choices drug takers make. Through the use of cost–benefit analysis economists have also made important contributions to assessing the efficiency of different approaches to reducing the demand for drugs. We look at a range of strategies including educating the public about drugs, providing drug treatment to those addicted to drugs and harm reduction strategies such as needle exchange.

We close Chapter Eleven by considering the case for and against legalising drugs. The debate on drug legalisation has many dimensions to it, but some of the most compelling arguments for legalisation are undoubtedly economic ones. Those draw on evidence about the harms associated with drug consumption, crime committed to fund drug use and violence associated with illicit drug markets. This is combined with analysis of the economics of drug markets and the ways in which prohibition 'distorts' the operation of the market. Ironically such distortions may further encourage that which society would actually prefer to discourage, organised criminal enterprise.

In sum, then, it has been said, 'to know all is to forgive all'.[2] Most economists would certainly not go so far as to say they know all; however they can contribute enough – through theory, applications and policy analyses – to be able to comment on: what are the issues; what is the trade-off between different policy options; and what is likely to be most effective.

2 A brief introduction to economic theory

In the sweat of thy face shalt thou eat bread.

(Genesis 3:19*a*)

Introduction

In this chapter we provide a short explanation of some of the key ideas and concepts economists have developed to help explain the social world. Economics is a large discipline and so we have had to be selective in what we include. We have therefore concentrated on the concepts that have the most relevance to later chapters in this book and these are covered largely by providing an overview of microeconomics.[1] Microeconomics is the branch of economics that examines how rational individuals work in the market place to allocate limited resources. In later chapters the concepts we cover here, such as rationality, supply and demand, incentives, margins and public goods, will all crop up regularly. Our starting point in writing this chapter is that the reader has no previous knowledge of economics. However, we hope readers with a previous knowledge of economics will bear with us in the early stages of this chapter because, once we have introduced some basic economic concepts, we will start to sketch out some ideas of what economics might bring to the study of crime and the criminal justice system, ideas that we will develop in much more detail in Chapters Three and Four.

The origins of economic thought

The early origins of economic thought

The word 'economics' comes from the Greek, *oikonomikos*, literally household management and, along with philosophy and politics (with which it is pretty much inextricably linked), it is one of the oldest streams of human thought. The need for economics arises from scarcity. As Robbins (1945: 15) writes, 'Here then is the unity of subject of Economic Science; the forms assumed by human behaviour in disposing of scarce means'. Because resources are not limitless, economics seeks to make the best use of what is available. In order to see how economists suggest it is best to achieve this, there are several foundations of economic thought on which we must build. We expand on these further below. In brief: the wealth of a society comes from co-operation and specialisation. More goods and services may be produced for a given level of resource if every person specialises in what they are best at. However, for specialisation to succeed as a viable economic system, trade is needed. If trade is to succeed, law and order is required. Thus, application of economics ranges from the 'balancing the books' approach of early economic thought, to the creation of wealth, welfare, sustainability and law and order.

Economists, therefore, are generally concerned with the most efficient use of the limited resources which are available. By efficient, what is meant is that no greater level of human satisfaction could be achieved at the same or a lower use of resources. Economic thought seeks not only to maximise human satisfaction – often termed 'utility' – in the short term, but to maximise it across any relevant time period. For example, Joseph of Egypt (Genesis 41), whose policy to store grain during years of good harvests so the country would survive years of lean harvests, was implementing what is now called a counter-cyclical economic policy. Such an approach is still as sound today as it was then (it is to be much regretted this example was not followed during the first decade of the twenty-first century).

Early economic thinkers did not consider their subject a stand-alone discipline. Two of the earliest, Chanakya[2] and Aristotle, writing independently two millennia ago, are typical in that they saw economics as part of state-craft overall. In the *Arthashastra* ('Science of Material Gain' or 'Science of political economy' in Sanskrit) Chanakya considered (amongst many other topics) what we would call economics as a part of the welfare and collective ethics of a society in general. In order for a state to thrive, Chanakya argued, law and order must be maintained.[3]

To Aristotle also, as with many later economic philosophers, economic thought was bound up intrinsically with ethics. In Aristotle's *Nicomachean Ethics*, he discusses (amongst other things) the amount which should be paid for a good when it is differently valued by different agents. This presupposes the existence of 'gains from trade' on which the theory of markets relies. Similarly Aristotle argued the purpose of production was consumption up to the limit of satiation. This assumes one of the main tenets of consumer theory; enjoyment of a good or service generally declines with the amount already consumed.

The Romans, recognising the benefits of trade, also saw justice and economic welfare as enjoying a symbiotic relationship. Justinian (from whom we derive the word 'justice') went so far as to give one of the principles of fair trade as '*tantum bona valent, quantum vendi possunt*' ('goods are worth as much as they can be sold for'). Sometimes, however, these amounts may not be self-evident.

Similarly, Ibn Khaldûn of Tunisia (1332–1406) saw economic theory as inextricably linked with history. In *Muqaddimah*, Ibn Khaldûn elaborates theories of production, value, distribution and cyclical growth/decay which collectively form a framework for his consideration of, and explanation for, history.

Thus economics is not at its heart a stand-alone discipline. We have seen it has been inextricably linked with philosophy, justice, the study of society, national wealth and prestige from its beginnings. More recently, however, economists have begun to follow their own advice and to specialise.

Modern economic thought

Modern economic philosophers trace their consideration of economics as a separate discipline to Adam Smith, whose aptly titled *The Wealth of Nations* was published in 1776. Smith writes, in book IV:

> Political œconomy, considered as a branch of the science of a statesman or legislator, proposes two distinct objects: first, to provide a plentiful revenue or subsistence for the people, or more properly to enable them to provide such a revenue or subsistence for themselves; and secondly, to supply the state or commonwealth with a revenue sufficient for the public services. It proposes to enrich both the people and the sovereign.
>
> (Smith 1776: IV.I.1)

Smith notes the increased level of production which resulted from division of labour in the pin manufacturing industry. This results, he conjectures, from improvement in a labourer's skill due to specialising in a specific task and the associated improvement in tools which may be employed. Smith is not, of course, the first to notice this. In *The Republic*, Plato takes it as self-evident that 'all things are produced more plentifully and easily and of a better quality when one man does one thing which is natural to him . . . and leaves other things' (Plato, *The Republic*: XVI – Socrates – Adeimantus).

Smith coins the (much overused) phrase 'the invisible hand' of the market to describe how all may benefit from specialisation and trade. In *The Theory of Moral Sentiments*, he writes: people

> are led by an invisible hand to make nearly the same distribution of the necessaries of life, which would have been made, had the earth been divided into equal portions among all its inhabitants, and thus without intending it, without knowing it, advance the interest of the society.
>
> (Smith 1759: IV.I.10)

This advancement in society results, not from any imposed plan, but from the self-interest of all. In *Wealth of Nations* he writes:

> It is not from the benevolence of the butcher, the brewer or the baker, that we expect our dinner, but from their regard to their own self interest. We address ourselves, not to their humanity but to their self-love, and never talk to them of our own necessities but of their advantages.
>
> (Smith 1776: I.2.2)

The market

> [T]hey will need a market-place, and a money-token for purposes of exchange.
>
> (Plato, *The Republic*: Book II Socrates – Adeimantus)

As we have seen, a nation's economic prosperity is enhanced through specialisation in the production of goods and services. However, in order to eat, the tailor must be sure he can trade with the baker and, in turn, the baker must be able to trade with the tailor if he is to be clothed. Thus increasing economic prosperity depends on the functioning of markets where such trades may take place. By utilising specialisation and trade, all agents may produce and consume more from a given set of time and materials than would result if each became a Jack-of-all-Trades.

In practice, of course, bilateral trade or barter is uncommon, and indeed reduces the possibilities for specialisation; the baker's need for a new suit is likely to arise less frequently than the tailor's need for a loaf of bread. In order for markets to operate smoothly, therefore, we require an agreed medium of exchange; to wit, money. Traditionally such media might be, for example: a fixed weight of grain; stone; or a precious metal (the Pound Sterling was originally so-called as it was set to be equal to a pound weight of silver). Generally money became a simple token of socially recognised value.

Markets

The theory of markets, at its most basic level, considers the demand for and supply of a single good or service and how valuable it is in terms of the agreed medium of exchange. Thus there are three unknown levels to be set in the market: the amount supplied to the market, the amount demanded and the price at which trades take place. Economists, with an eye to efficiency, prefer to use as few letters as possible for any given concept, so let us write the level of supply as simply s, demand as d and the price as p.

The relationship between demand and price

As we have seen one characteristic of consumption of a good or service is that the consumer will eventually become satiated with it. Consider, for example, the enjoyment one might gain from eating chocolate cake. If a customer buys a slice of cake and eats it, we might assume there is a certain level of enjoyment or satisfaction derived from this. If, however, the customer continues to eat more and more cake, their enjoyment level per slice will diminish. There may come a point, in fact, when the continued eating of cake will actually decrease their overall well-being and enjoyment. In short, there will be a point at which the demand for cake will be satiated.

As the enjoyment level per slice of cake declines where more cake has already been eaten, it is not unreasonable to suppose the customer will be prepared to pay less for each subsequent slice. There is, in general then, a relationship between the demand for a good or service, d, and the price the consumer is prepared to pay, p.[4] Because of satiation, it is reasonable to suppose agents will be prepared to pay a higher price per slice if little is consumed. Thus relatively higher prices are associated with little demand and relatively lower prices indicate relatively greater demand. In short, the amount demanded depends on the price: demand is negatively related to price per unit from the consumer's point of view.

The relationship between supply and price

Similarly, we may consider the baker's decision to supply cake to the market. It is not unreasonable to assume the production of cake requires some effort, for which the baker must be compensated. By producing more cake, the baker is giving up time which might be spent in leisure. We may assume leisure itself is something with which the baker may become satiated. Therefore we see, the less time for leisure the baker has after work, the more highly they will value that leisure. In order to motivate a baker to produce a relatively greater amount of cake (and thereby take relatively less leisure) they must be paid a relatively greater amount of money. As the price of cake varies, the baker will produce at different levels.[5] Indeed, given the preceding discussion, it is reasonable to suppose relatively higher prices will be required to motivate relatively higher cake production. Similarly, as the price of cake increases, and let us suppose the price of bread does not, there will be an incentive for the baker to produce more of the former and less of the latter. Again we see an increase in the price of cake (other things being equal) will lead to an increase in production. In short, the amount supplied depends on the price: supply is positively related to price per unit.

The relationship between supply and demand

Both the supply and demand relationships may be illustrated by means of a simple figure. As we have seen, demand may be expected to decline as the price increases, while, independently of this, supply may be expected to rise as price increases. To illustrate these we represent the values of price along the vertical axis and the quantities which might be demanded and supplied along the horizontal axis (see Figure 2.1).

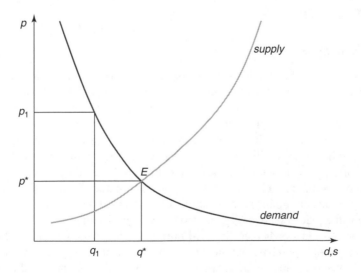

Figure 2.1 Supply and demand.

The point at which the representations of supply and demand meet, i.e. where the amount to be sold exactly equals the amount to be bought is called the equilibrium point, labelled E on the diagram. At the price p^*, we see an amount q^* is traded.

Profits and utility

Now we have determined how much is traded and at what price, we may consider what each side (the consumer and producer, also referred to as 'economic agents') obtains from the transaction. The return to the producer is the profit; which is to say the amount received for the good or service less the cost of production. This may (and generally will) be quantified in terms of the medium of exchange: money. What the consumer receives is not so easily quantifiable. If, for example, we consider the example given above of a quantity of chocolate cake traded; what is the value of this cake to the consumer? We might be tempted to answer p^*, but this is not necessarily the case; in fact the value to the consumer of q^* units of cake is generally greater than the price paid.

To see why the consumer values the cake more highly than the price paid, consider the amount q_1. The consumer would have been prepared to pay p_1 for this quantity of cake; the values (q_1, p_1) are on the curve which represents demand. Now, the value placed on q_1 units of cake must be at least p_1 or the consumer would not have been prepared to pay this amount. At the equilibrium, however, we see they have been able to purchase the q_1 units, and more besides, at a lower price than p_1. In other words, they were not asked to pay their full valuation for the q_1 units. Hence there is a distinction between the price paid for a good or service and the value of that good or service to the consumer. The value is called the 'utility' of the good or service to the consumer. If an item has greater utility to a buyer, they are generally prepared to pay a higher price, but that does not mean they *have* to pay the higher price.

Analysis of the margin

We have now established the value or utility to the consumer of the purchase of q^* pieces of cake is not necessarily equal to the price paid, p^*. What, then, does p^* represent? To answer this we must make use of another tool of economics, the concept of the 'margin'. Suppose, for example, our cake-munching consumer has just purchased q_1 units of cake at the equilibrium price p^*: we might like to consider whether they will have eaten enough cake, or whether they will purchase more. This consideration of the next step (the purchase of an additional amount of the commodity or, in the case of the producer, the manufacture of an additional amount of the commodity) is an example of analysis of the margin.

The value placed on eating q_1 units of cake is p_1. Having eaten these units the consumer considers whether they will purchase another unit of cake. This additional (marginal) purchase will take place if the consumer's utility increases as a result. Given the principle of satiation discussed above, the value of the marginal unit – the next piece of cake beyond q_1 – will be less than p_1 (the consumer values the next unit less as they are getting to the point where they are 'full' of cake). However, so long as the value of the marginal unit of cake is greater than the price at which cake is offered, p^*, the consumer will make an additional purchase. In this way they will carry on eating cake until equilibrium, E, at which point the value of the marginal unit is exactly equal to the price. Hence we see the price paid for q^* units of cake is not the value to the consumer of q^* units, it is the value of the final unit traded; the q^{*th} unit.

We may also consider analysis of the margin from the side of the producer: we see from the demand and supply curves shown above, the amount the producer would ask to produce q_1 units of cake is less than the market price, p^*. Hence they will increase production until the cost of producing the marginal unit exactly equals the price received. This occurs at the point E. At equilibrium, therefore, the production cost of the q^{*th} unit exactly equals the value of the q^{*th} unit to the consumer.

Opportunity costs, incentives and disincentives

All well and good so far; we have considered a single market for a single good or service. However, in reality such market transactions do not exist in isolation. If the producer were not making cake, they might be baking bread, or reading a book – if the consumer did not spend all their money on cake, they might purchase a cup of tea. As economic resources (income, raw materials and time) are finite, each decision made in the economy will have a cost over and above that explicitly represented in the market. The cost is the forgone opportunity to do or buy something else. This additional cost is defined as (lost) opportunity cost. An economic agent balances the cost and value they may gain from a transaction against the cost and value of alternative transactions which must be forgone.

It is not only the monetary cost of a transaction and the forgone opportunity to purchase something else which influence decisions. There are also matters of taste, fashion, etc. Economists tend to group all such factors together and label them 'incentives' or 'disincentives'. Through the use of incentives and disincentives, policy-makers may interfere in markets. For example, the health warning on packets of cigarettes and the recent ban on smoking in public places are disincentives to smoke tobacco. Such factors influence agents' decisions, but they have no specific monetary cost, hence the need to consider these separately from the actual price paid for the good.

Ceteris paribus *and the 'Law of Unintended Consequences'*

In any given economic transaction, we have seen there is often a very large number of considerations which affect agents' decisions. Not only the cost of each good and associated incentives, but the cost and incentive structure of all other goods, the purchase of which may be affected through this transaction. If we wish completely to understand consumers' (or producers') choices, it seems we must allow for all of these. However, such an approach is impractical. As an economist would say, the marginal cost (in terms of temporal resources) of analysing fully even a single consumer is greater than the marginal benefit. To allow for this, an assumption is often made which allows the focus of analysis to be narrowed to smaller systems: *ceteris paribus*, literally 'other things unchanged'. In practice, economic sub-systems may be analysed with all other variables – those not explicitly in the sub-system under consideration – assumed to be held constant and therefore factored out of the analysis.

The down-side of assuming *ceteris paribus* is the so-called 'Law of Unintended Consequences'. If the system analysed is too small, some factors which certainly should have been considered may be overlooked. Often the very result which was looked for in the application of policy initiatives, for example, may turn out to be reversed once all factors are taken into account. This may occur in situations where the policy implemented to achieve a worthwhile goal distorts the incentive structure of society and creates an unwanted (or unintended) side effect. As an example of this, consider government tax revenue. Although governments may like to believe tax revenues may be raised without limit, it is possible for an increase in taxes actually to reduce, rather than increase, government revenue. This concept, suggested by Khaldûn, was popularised by Arthur Laffer (1940–) and summarised in the so-called Laffer curve (Laffer 2004); see Figure 2.2.[6]

Suppose government revenue (let us denote this G) is represented on a vertical axis – higher means more money government can spend – and the tax rate, t, runs from zero to 100 per cent along a horizontal axis. Clearly, when $t = 0$, $G = 0$; the government can increase revenue by increasing the tax rate. This is shown by the left-hand side of the curve, where the tax rate is less than t^*. As t rises to t^*, the increase in taxes will create a disincentive to work and economic agents will refrain from earning all they might have. Some may even decide to emigrate to

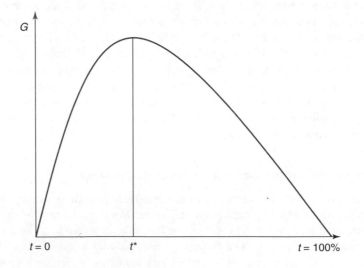

Figure 2.2 The Laffer curve (Laffer 2004).

countries where the tax regime is less of a burden. Although government revenue rises, overall the level of income in the economy is reduced.

If the tax rate increases beyond t^*, the decline in income in the economy becomes so great, government revenue is reduced. Further increases in t lead to the government taking a larger and larger slice of a smaller and smaller cake until, at $t = 100$ per cent, no taxable income is generated; agents will cease to work if the government takes all the income they might make (or perhaps they might revolt). Thus, seeking to increase tax revenue might have the unintended consequence of reducing it.

Of course, the Law of Unintended Consequences is not limited to economics – it may be observed in any situation where a change in a sub-system being analysed brings about a change in agents' behaviour in a wider system. For example, the law introduced in the UK in 1981 to make it compulsory for motorists to wear seat-belts understandably made drivers feel safer. This brought about a change in the incentive structure of motoring; the safety of the driver and passengers is, after all, something which is weighed up in choosing whether to, and how to, drive. As a consequence, drivers began to drive a little less carefully, secure in the knowledge the seat-belt would protect them from harm. It has been suggested that there is no compelling evidence that seat-belt legislation has made Britain's roads safer (Adams 1982). The legislation has, of course, made crashes safer (ibid.).

Rationality and attitudes to risk

Having considered the costs (including opportunity costs) and benefits of each transaction they may undertake, we assume economic agents will act in their own best interests. This is what is known as the assumption of rationality. If any agent acts against their own interests (for example: a consumer not increasing their utility to the maximum possible; or a producer not maximising their profits), that agent is irrational.

However, given the huge, potentially infinite, amount of information economic agents must retain in order accurately to judge, not just the value of their transactions, but the opportunity cost of consumption or production of a good or service relative to all other goods or services, it is not unreasonable to ask whether markets will ever operate as efficiently and rationally as economists are wont to assume they do. Indeed, agents are likely to have complete information only about some aspects of the economy, and must form expectations about what they do not know. In the context of this uncertainty and the formulation of expectations, the objective of producers and consumers is weakened slightly: we assume rational consumers will maximise their *expected* utility, and rational producers to maximise their *expected* profits. If there is no systematic bias in the way agents form their expectations, we say those expectations are rational.

However, analysis of agents' expectations does indeed indicate there is persistent bias in their decisions. For example, many people buy UK National Lottery tickets, although they are well aware the probability of winning a life-changing amount of money is very close to zero; approximately 1 in 14,000,000. Similarly we observe insurance contracts in which the probability of having to make a claim is very low, and agents who take out such contracts clearly expect the insurance companies to make a profit, implying those who take out their insurance will make, on average, a loss. Does such behaviour contradict rationality? In order to answer this, we must consider agents' attitude to risk.

To illustrate attitudes to risk, suppose a game is to take place as follows: a coin is tossed; it is known it is a fair coin in the sense that the two results Heads (H) and Tails (T) are equally likely. If H is observed a prize of £100 is given; if T is observed the game is over. Clearly if the game were to be played a very large number of times, players would receive £100 half of the time and so the expected value of the game is, on average, £50.

Now suppose the game varies so as to allow the probability of winning to be any value between zero and one. For example, suppose two coins are tossed and the player wins if two Hs are observed; in this case the long-run expected value of the game to the player is £25, as they will win one time in four. Alternatively, if two coins are tossed, and the player will win *unless* two Ts are observed, the expected value of the game is £75, as the player wins three times out of four.

A risk-neutral player will value any such game according to the long-run average return from playing. As the probability of winning varies between zero and one, so the risk-neutral valuation of the game varies along a line from zero to £100, as shown in Figure 2.3.

We have seen that an agent completely neutral with regard to risk will value at £50 a single game in which there is a 50 per cent probability of winning £100. This and all other risk-neutral valuations are represented by the set of points which make up the straight diagonal line. Consider another agent, averse to risk, who will have a lower valuation of the game. A risk-averse agent may consider a game in which there is a 50 per cent probability of winning £100, and a 50 per cent

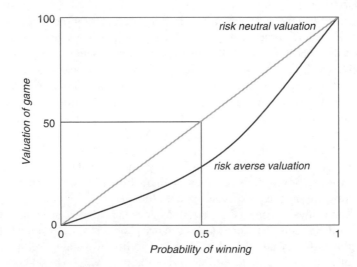

Figure 2.3 Attitudes to risk.

probability of winning nothing, to be worth, for example, £30. Such a person would be indifferent between £30 with complete certainty and £100 with probability of one half. Thus the set of valuations of a risk-averse agent will be below that of a risk neutral agent. The difference between the two sets of valuations is not irrational; it is merely the cost the risk-averse agent is prepared to pay to avoid risk.

Conversely, others may prefer risk. Such a one may well be prepared to pay more than the long-run average return to play the game once.

In practice, agents may be both risk averse and risk seekers depending on the circumstances. An agent may display risk-averse behaviour in deciding to insure their property and display risk seeking behaviour in deciding to gamble. The agent is prepared to pay to avert the risk, however small, of being homeless, and to pay for the hope, however small, of winning a large amount of money.

Efficiency

In analysing a market as above, we often assume the system is operating *efficiently*, which is to say the consumer is spending their money in such a way as to maximise their enjoyment (utility) given their budget; and similarly the producer is providing as much of the good or service as is possible from a given level of inputs. In other words, there is no wastage of resources. If a market is efficient, no agent can improve their situation (increase their utility or output) without some other agent becoming worse off. This is also known as Pareto Optimality. On the other hand, if a situation exists in which at least one agent can improve their situation, without leaving anyone else worse off, the system is Pareto inefficient or sub-optimal.

Market inefficiency

Although economics is often portrayed as an amoral discipline, which is to say, neither defining nor commenting on either 'right' or 'wrong', many economists have indeed wrestled with the concepts of morality[7], beginning with the pragmatic observation that, if Pareto improvement is possible, it cannot be un-ethical to pursue it. In other words, an agent may, with a clear conscience, seek to improve their position so long as they do no harm to anyone else's position. Conversely, we may pragmatically question agents' actions if they reduce the overall level of well-being in society. Here we consider several examples of individual or group economic activity that reduce overall societal welfare. We present these in the context of market inefficiency as the one thing on which all economists agree is that it is 'wrong' to waste resources.

Rent-seeking behaviour

This term, introduced by Krueger (1974), does not refer to the payment made by an agent to the owner for the use of physical capital (land or buildings, etc.), but to the misuse of market or political power in such a way as to allow some agents to accumulate benefits resulting from market inefficiencies. For example, lobby groups may often wish to have trade barriers imposed so as to protect a specific industry. By effectively shutting out competitors, the protected industry may be able to make super-normal profits at the expense of society as a whole. Similarly large firms may make use of their market power to establish effective monopolies, again allowing the accrual of super-normal profits.

In *Wealth of Nations*, Smith notes:

> people of the same trade seldom meet together, even for merriment and diversion, but the conversation ends in a conspiracy against the public, or in some contrivance to raise prices. It is impossible indeed to prevent such meetings, by any law which either could be executed, or would be consistent with liberty and justice.
>
> (Smith 1776: I.10.82)

Thus rent-seeking behaviour is generally not illegal; indeed, it could be argued law-makers have a major incentive in not criminalising such behaviour. Those who seek rents generally may be able to influence law-makers to ignore or even to impose such market distortions. A good example of such behaviour is the creation of 'artificial' DVD zones to allow the establishing of higher than market prices in some sub-sections of the market. If the global market were operating efficiently, there would be one world price for legitimate CDs and DVDs, subject to the costs of shipping.

Rent-seekers are aiming to create a market structure that allows them to accumulate wealth created by others. That society is made worse off as a result of rent-seeking behaviour is clear as rent-seekers themselves are producing less than they might (or nothing at all) as they devote resources to their schemes; also the freedom of the market is restricted, meaning the return to those who engage in the market is reduced. Hence fewer trades will take place in line with the Khaldûn/Laffer effect as agents respond to the reduced incentives to work.

The principal–agent situation

It is common to assume economic agents will act in their own best interests, but clearly this can only be done if they possess all relevant information. In practice, complex economies will often generate situations where there is asymmetry of information; that is to say, market participants do not possess all information relevant to their transactions. Indeed, this is virtually certain to arise given specialisation. As participants in an economy become more and more specialised, they will often require others to act on their behalf; the carpenter might be a dab hand at pulling nails, but not so good at pulling teeth.

Where participants hire others to perform a service on their behalf, the one who benefits from the action is described as the 'principal', the one hired to carry out the action, the 'agent'. The reason why the interaction between principal and agent is often described as a problem arises from their potentially competing objectives.

Consider, for example, the case of real estate agents discussed in *Freakonomics* by Levitt and Dubner (2005). They show estate agents are more careful in the sale of their own houses (in other words, when they are both principal and agent) and achieve higher prices, than in the sale of other people's houses. This leads to the conclusion that estate agents may not necessarily always act in their principal's best interests.

Similar issues arise in areas as diverse as company directors' vs shareholders' interests, medicine, law, education and politics; in any situation, in short, where there are asymmetries of information or power.

The asymmetry of objectives and information will tend to reduce economic efficiency; if principals feel they cannot always trust their agents, they may either undertake fewer transactions, reducing gains from trade, or engage in activities for which they are not trained as well as the principal, reducing the gains from specialisation.

Market failure – externalities and public goods

Externalities

Even in the absence of such obvious distortions as the principal–agent problem and rent-seeking behaviour, and even if there were complete information available to all, markets might not operate as efficiently to maximise societal well-being. Such a situation might arise when the costs and benefits of a good or service are not exactly aligned with the purchaser. Consider, for example, a good or service where the cost of purchase falls at least in part on those who do not receive its benefit. A common example is the use of the private motor vehicle. The owner of the car has, let us assume, paid the market price for the vehicle, paid for the servicing, fuel, etc. However, the additional costs of driving, borne by society in general, include: congestion (and thus slower journeys for all); deterioration of road infrastructure; increased risk of accidents; and pollution.

When some or all of the cost of a market transaction is borne by those who do not reap any or all of the benefit, we say the transaction has a negative externality associated with it. Other examples include degradation of the environment, fisheries stocks, etc.

In general, as the full costs of the transaction are not borne by those who trade in the market, more trades will take place than would be the case at the societal optimum. To see why this is so, consider Figure 2.4. Suppose a good or service produces a negative externality as it is consumed. The demand curve of the consumer will be represented by the downward-sloping solid curve, which relates the level demanded to the price paid. Recall the price paid is also the benefit to the consumer of purchasing the marginal unit of the good. The dashed curve represents the same market demand but, in this case, the price is augmented by the notional cost of the externality. Because of the negative externality, the marginal benefit of each unit is reduced (from society's point of view).

In this situation, the consumer will choose to purchase an amount q^* of the good or service, and pay price p^*; however, if the means existed to charge the consumer

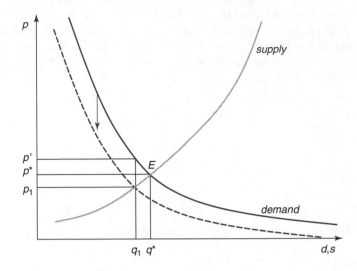

Figure 2.4 A negative consumption externality.

both the cost of production and the cost of the externality visited on society, they would consume less; q_1. They would pay the price p_1 directly to the supplier and an additional amount c (where $c = p' - p_1$) to cover the external cost of consumption. It is clear that the presence of externalities will result in an amount of consumption which is greater than the societal optimum.

Another market may well have a positive externality associated with it. Examples of such include maintenance of attractive (private) gardens, inspiring architecture, vaccinations against disease, public research and development, etc. If, for example, my neighbour is vaccinated against illness, I am less likely to catch it myself. Even if I am not vaccinated, there is one fewer person likely to infect me. Another example of a positive externality is education. As a society becomes educated, increased specialisation is possible in the economy; this will benefit all. Adam Smith contends, 'an instructed and intelligent people . . . are always more decent and orderly than an ignorant and stupid one' (Smith 1776: V.1.189).

We have seen in Figure 2.4 how a negative consumption externality will cause more of a good or service to be consumed than would be chosen in order to maximise societal well-being. In the case of a positive consumption externality, less of a good or service will be consumed than is optimal.

Public goods

A concept related to that of positive externalities is that of public goods. A public good is a commodity where exclusion from use is not possible. If any of a public good is produced, all society will benefit. For example, consider public service television such as the BBC. There is nothing in the market for entertainment services to prevent each agent in Britain enjoying the output of the BBC. The same amount of broadcasting is made available to all, regardless of who has paid and who has not. Similarly, roads, municipal parks, flood control measures, etc., benefit both those who have paid and those who have not.

Because exclusion from use is not possible, there is no market incentive mechanism for anyone to pay for a public good. In a completely free market, the level of production of public goods is likely to be zero as the rational individual decision is not to pay for something which one might enjoy without paying.

Let us develop somewhat the specific public good 'law and order' which might seem at first sight not a good at all. It is not a good paid for in money, it is paid for with forgone utility by those who could have benefited from disregarding law and order – and in doing so would have impeded the smooth running of the market – but who choose not to. For example, a trader might choose not to engage in insider dealing, an agent might choose not to put their own interests before that of their principal, etc.

As we have seen, Adam Smith argued that the pursuit of individual self-interest will promote the good of all. This is sometimes mistakenly interpreted as justification for the famous phrase from the movie *Wall Street* 'Greed is Good'. However, specialisation in and of itself cannot promote the good of society or individuals. Agents' well-being relies crucially on their being able to trade at agreed prices for the things they themselves do not produce. Hence more stable economies might be expected to be more prosperous than less stable economies.

Instability will impact negatively on society in (at least) two ways: if there is less opportunity for trade (because, for example, to travel is dangerous) agents will specialise less. Pin makers, for example, must clearly have access to a large pool of people who want pins if such a specialism is to feed them and their family. Second, an increase in instability will reduce the incentive to work. Farmers, for example, are likely to work less hard than they might if they fear a passing group of barbarians will take the harvest. At the least, a farmer might choose to invest some time in learning to fight or building a defence – time that otherwise could have been spent on farming. As instability increases, the overall level of income will decline. Also, of course, the barbarians themselves are spending their resources (i.e. devoting their time) on plundering. Such resources would have been better spent (from a societal point of view) on their producing their own food.

Clearly stability is a public good in the sense that, for example, a thief will benefit from an overall low level of theft in the economy. In the same way a drunk-driver will benefit if every other driver on the road is sober. A person who refrains from behaviour which would benefit themselves but impede the market has paid an opportunity cost; however, the benefit of the individual's orderly behaviour will also accrue to those who are disorderly. Economics predicts that, left to its own devices, the 'market' for, for want of a better phrase, 'law and order' will produce far less stability (if any) than is socially optimal.

The limits of the market

It is clear then that economic theory cannot be taken to imply 'Greed is Good'. Economists have long understood that self-interest must be linked to self-control. Consider Marshall (1890: I.II.1) who argues 'Everyone who is worth anything carries his higher nature with him into business; and, there as elsewhere, he is influenced by his personal affections, by his conceptions of duty and his reverence for high ideals.' More recently Ratzinger (1985) argues 'It is becoming an increasingly obvious fact of economic history that the development of economic systems which concentrate on the common good depends on a determinate ethical system'. Reflecting in the *Los Angeles Times* on the recent global economic crisis Pagliarini (2010) writes:

> But not all greed is created equal. The greed that nearly brought the world economy to a screeching halt in 2008 is disgusting. The greed that led to millions of hardworking people around the world losing their jobs is not 'good greed.' You can (and must!) be greedy without exploiting others.[8]

Game Theory and the prisoners' dilemma

We have discussed how the market, for all its efficiency, cannot necessary produce what is best for society as a whole. By pursuing their own goals, agents may occasionally work against the well-being of society. Without any ethical construct, rationality (i.e. doing the best for oneself regardless of the effect on others) will lead to a socially sub-optimal solution. This can easily be shown using a branch of economics called 'Game Theory'. As a simplification, consider a situation in which each of two agents' decision affects only the other. There is a standard application used here, the so-called 'prisoners' dilemma'.

Consider two criminals, for the sake of convenience denoted Larry and Rudy, brought in by the police under suspicion of a bank robbery. Let us suppose they are guilty; however, there is no direct evidence upon which to charge them for robbery. On the other hand, there is clear evidence they broke the speed limit and drove dangerously during the escape. The police offer Larry amnesty from prosecution from both dangerous driving and robbery if he will testify against Rudy. If he does not testify, he will be charged with the driving offence and spend a nominal year in jail. If Larry testifies, Rudy will go to jail for 10 years. Rudy is made a similar offer. If both testify against the other, they will each get six years for the robbery and driving offence. The game may be analysed by considering the pay-off to Larry and Rudy with each of their options and resulting pay-offs represented in Figure 2.5: Larry's pay-off is on the left of each co-ordinate pair, and Rudy's on the right.

It is clear the best pay-off from the point of view of their 'society' is that neither should testify. The total cost is two in this case. However, consider Larry's choice: If he knows Rudy will choose *not* to testify, Larry's best outcome will be received if he *does* testify. He can move from the top-left pay-off (1,1) to the bottom-left (0,10). Remember, both players are trying to minimise their *individual* pay-out.

		Rudy's choice	
		Don't testify	Testify
Larry's choice	Don't testify	(1, 1)	(10, 0)
	Testify	(0, 10)	(6, 6)

Figure 2.5 The prisoners' dilemma.

If Rudy testifies, Larry is better off also to testify, as he will move from (10,0) to (6,6). Thus Larry will choose to testify regardless of Rudy's decision. Rudy faces an equivalent choice and so he too will testify. The only sustainable outcome is where both testify. This leads to a total cost of 12. From the point of view of their 'society' this is actually the worst outcome.

The prisoners' dilemma situation is played out in real life whenever there is a good or service which provides an externality, or whenever a public good is required to be provided. Although society as a whole will be better off if everyone cooperates to achieve the greatest good for all, in practice, it is in each individual's interests to default and the negative externality will persist or the public good will not be provided.

It might be argued it is cynical to suppose no-one will choose to cooperate to provide the public good; in any economy there will be those who contribute in the interests of society. However, at best there will be more negative externalities and less positive externalities, and less public goods produced than society needs at the optimum.

Economists would argue the easiest way out of this dilemma of mutual non-cooperation is to change the incentive structure. Suppose Larry and Rudy come under oversight of a 'Godfather' figure, one who will punish them if either breaks the rules. Just for the sake of argument, let us suppose this punishment will entail a cost of the defaulter of five, as shown in Figure 2.6.

We see in Figure 2.6 that the imposition of a penalty from outside the system can move the game to a societal optimum where neither player will default. Whether Larry testifies or not, Rudy is better off not to cooperate. Notice that the penalty will not actually have to be paid, so long as it is sufficiently great to move the game to a point where both players cooperate. Such a role in the market – a role which involves manipulating the incentive structure so as to ensure a socially efficient outcome – may be played by the State, which is to say the institution which is comprised of, and governs, society.

		Rudy's choice	
		Don't testify	Testify
Larry's choice	Don't testify	(1, 1)	(10, 5)
	Testify	(5, 10)	(11, 11)

Figure 2.6 The prisoners' dilemma, with penalties.

Inequalities of income and wealth

Before drawing this chapter to a close it is worth considering one further challenge to the market. Even in a perfectly free market with perfect information, no rent-seeking behaviour principal–agent problem or externalities, equilibrium might well not lead to the greatest good for the greatest number of people for the simple reason that the ability to pay is not equal.

To see why the overall good of society is maximised when income/wealth is equally distributed, consider the following thought experiment: suppose you and another 99 survivors of a shipwreck are marooned on a desert island. Rescue is on the way and will arrive in less than one day. No one is going to die of hunger in a single day and, by way of rations to tide you over, an aeroplane has parachuted down a crate containing 100 tins of baked beans. However, you have the only tin-opener. Clearly, because of the power asymmetry, you might enjoy all the beans. However, because of satiation, you will enjoy eating the second tin of beans less than the first; and the third tin even less. Assuming all cast-aways are equally fond of beans, the greatest satisfaction will come from each person eating one tin, i.e. equal consumption.[9]

Practically, inequality reduces well-being because the simple market model (which supposedly guarantees efficient allocation of resources) assumes agents can pay the cost of their valuation of a good or service. Consider the example of eyesight (which we may reasonably assume is equally valued throughout the world). A cataract operation costing less than this book is beyond the reach of many in the developing world. Arguably, the resources which have gone into pro-ducing this work could have increased well-being on a global scale by more if devoted to some other cause.

However, before you begin to feel too guilty about buying this book,[10] consider that it has been reported (Tozer, writing in the *Daily Mail*: 3 July 2008) that, in the UK, highly paid professional footballers who might earn upwards of £50,000 a week openly flout parking laws because £70 fines are 'too easy to pay'. Com-pare the years of satisfaction this book purchase will give with the transitory convenience of not having to walk too far to a nightclub. Indeed, for the cost of a parking ticket, you may have three paperback copies of this volume. Spread the news!

Income distribution

Considering only the UK, it is clear incomes are not evenly distributed, and therefore the allocation of resources is not at its most efficient. If your own experience isn't enough to convince you of this, consider the distribution of weekly household income for the year 2006/7 in Figure 2.7. The vertical axis represents the number of households in each income class.

The different shades represent 'deciles', which is to say, the bottom 10 per cent is represented in light grey, the next 10 per cent of households represented in dark grey, and so on. It can be seen the distribution of income is skewed, with most households clustered in the left hand side of the distribution.

In 2006/7, the average weekly income was £463 and approximately 66 per cent of households earned less than this. Indeed, the income of the average household was only £377 per week. It may seem counterintuitive that the average household earns so much less than the average income; however, as average income is simply the total income divided by the number of households, it would remain unchanged if one household had an income of £27,538,975,164 and the rest had no income at all.

The skewed nature of the income distribution may be summarised in the so-called GINI coefficient; the interpretation of which is easiest to show graphically. Figure 2.8 represents the same data as Figure 2.7, except we have summed the number of households and incomes and expressed them as a percentage.

If income were exactly evenly distributed, the least affluent 20 per cent of the population would earn 20 per cent of the income, and so on. Perfectly even distribution is represented by the light grey line in Figure 2.8. The actual proportion of

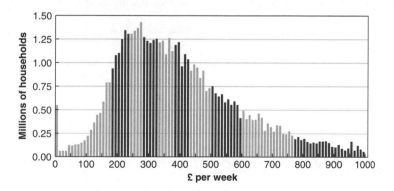

Figure 2.7 Distribution of weekly household income.

Source: Office for National Statistics (2009).

Note: Individuals with incomes greater than £1,000 per week are excluded. There were 2.7 million such in 2006/7. If these individuals were not excluded, the scale of the graph would be so great it would require all the data shown here to be compressed into a 'spike' on the extreme left-hand edge.

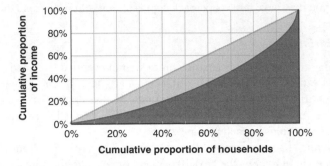

Figure 2.8 Cumulative distribution of weekly household income.

income earned by the least affluent 20 per cent of the population is 7.11 per cent; this is one point on the dark grey curve which describes the actual income share of each proportion of households sorted in order of growing affluence. The further the curve from the line, the greater the income inequality. To put it another way, the greater the light shaded area, the greater the income inequality.

The GINI coefficient, generally represented as a percentage, is easily calculated as the ratio of the light shaded area in Figure 2.8 to the sum of the areas of the light and dark shapes. It ranges from 0 per cent (perfect income equality) to 100 per cent (perfect income inequality). The GINI coefficient for the UK economy was 35.1 per cent in 2006. This number in isolation may not tell us much; however, by considering the value of the GINI coefficient over time (see Figure 2.9) we may see whether inequality is increasing.

Over the last half century, income inequality in the UK has generally increased, especially once the rise in housing costs is taken into account. Thus it may be assumed the allocation of resources is becoming less efficient over time.

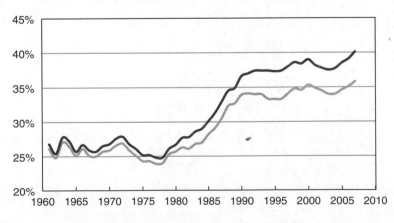

Figure 2.9 UK GINI coefficients before housing costs (light grey) and after housing costs (dark grey).

Source: Institute for Fiscal Studies Commentary (2010).

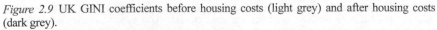

Conclusion: what can economics contribute to the study of crime and the criminal justice system?

In summary, we have seen stable and well-ordered societies are likely to be those in which societal good is maximised. Agents who do not trust each other are less likely to trade and are therefore less likely to specialise. If an agent turns from a productive job to (for example) fraud, society is less well off because that agent's output has been lost, and because potential victims will produce less if the return for their labour is more likely to go to someone else.

Consider again the Laffer curve (Figure 2.2), which suggests that reducing the incentives to work through tax will reduce the amount produced. A similar argument can, of course, be made about the level of instability in any society. If (a proportion of) the benefits of a producer's trade accrue to someone else – whether through theft, market inefficiencies or so-called rent-seeking behaviour – the producer will work less and spend their time in leisure or in seeking redress.

As lawlessness increases it will choke off the very markets on which it feeds; as Ratzinger (1985) puts it (referring to ethical behaviour) 'the decline of such discipline can actually cause the laws of the market to collapse'. Similarly Wilber (2004: 27) argues, 'Self interest leads to the common good if there is sufficient competition *and* if most people in society have internalized a general moral law as a guide for their behaviour' (emphasis his).

Thus economics predicts that the well-being of society will be at its greatest where the pursuit of self-interest is constrained by ethical judgements. Economics does not define a moral code – this is beyond the scope of the discipline. However, economic arguments may be applied after the moral code has been agreed in order to apply the code with the most efficiency. We shall see that the market itself may be utilised or manipulated in an attempt to bring about socially efficient results.

This has important implications for the role of the State. We have seen in the cases of externalities and the provision of public goods, it is clear the societal optimum levels of production and consumption will not result from a purely market-led approach to the economy. Indeed, a market-led approach is not even possible without provision of a legal framework, itself a public good.

In Figure 2.10 we summarise the areas of individual choice where the state may choose to become involved. The vertical axis represents the good to the individual; generally higher is better, below the origin (where the axes cross) the individual is made worse off by their actions. The horizontal axis represents the good to society as a whole. The further to the right the better. To the left of the origin, society is made worse off by the individual's actions.

Society may choose to become involved, whether informally and/or (if it is more efficient) through government, in influencing preferences away from the upper left corner and (where appropriate) towards the lower right corner – that is to say to promote actions which will benefit society as a whole, at the cost to the individual, or to discourage actions which will benefit the individual, but impose a cost on society. An example of the former is taxes which provide transport infrastructure, education (primary and/or higher) and other public goods; examples of

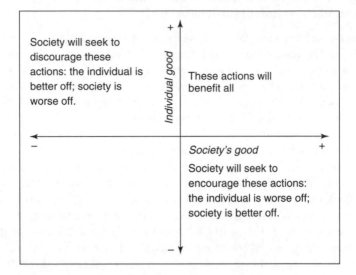

Figure 2.10 The impact of individual choice on society.

the latter range from littering to homicide. The degree of encouragement or coercion depends on the form of the society.

Such encouragement, or coercion, need not necessarily involve a criminal justice framework. For example, to promote pro-social behaviour, society may run an education campaign, whether in families, schools or through advertising.

Education is obviously effective, but has its drawbacks; it works at a level beyond rationality and the market. It may be difficult to convince individuals they should consider society's good as well as their own. Also, of course, it requires near universal coverage. Consider the public good, 'politeness'. Regardless of what our parents told us about politeness, if no-one else is polite, eventually we too will cease to be polite. Similarly if everyone else were to drop litter, we might reason our own contribution might not be noticed. In short it is unlikely an individual will accept education to consider the good of society above their own good if no-one else in society has taken such a stance.

Society may also seek to promote behaviour from which it benefits through religious belief. This has several advantages over education. It can appeal to individual self-interest with a promise of a certain reward for pro-social behaviour or a certain punishment for anti-social behaviour. Further, coverage need not be universal. Even if everyone else in the world were impolite, we might persevere, secure in the knowledge of our ultimate reward; we might refrain from dropping litter for fear of certain eternal punishment.

Notwithstanding, both education and traditional religion have their drawbacks; for example, a form of the principal–agent problem. It may be that education, and/or religion, is promoted in a way that benefits the good of those in charge of education and religion rather than society as a whole. The political economist Karl Marx's contention was that the promise of an ultimate reward might lead oppressed man to forgo improving his lot, but to accept injustice with stoicism. He wrote that 'Religion is the sigh of the oppressed creature, the heart of a heartless world, and the soul of soulless conditions. It is the opium of the people. The abolition of religion as the illusory happiness of the people is the demand for their real happiness' (Marx 1844: 1).

Marx's main complaint was not, of course, against religion but against the market system promoted in capitalist economies. He felt a system of pure communism, where decisions were made perfectly democratically, would be preferable to a market system with the inherent problems discussed above. Sadly, however, understanding the complexities of a modern economy is beyond the reach of even the most intelligent central planner. In seeking to remove the market and its associated societal inefficiencies 'command' economies created even greater principal–agent problems. Thus 'economic life and social conditions and social relations under Communist rule merely worsened the condition of the masses of people' (Boettke 1990: 130).

Of course, the principal–agent problem exists wherever there are those who exercise political and legal power, i.e. government, whether in democratic or non-democratic states. To mitigate this, economists are generally agreed, the role of the state should be curtailed to those areas where it is strictly necessary. Abraham Lincoln summarised it thus: 'The legitimate object of government is to do for the people what needs to be done, but which they can not, by individual effort, do at all, or do so well, for themselves' (Shaw 1950: 136).

Ideally then, from the point of view of society, government should reflect the moral and ethical stance of the community it serves. It should seek, through the most efficient means possible, to establish customs, laws and incentives which will allow both the flexibility of the market system, and the ethical and legal framework which will allow it to work to produce the best overall good. It is by no means a straightforward balancing act: 'what men need most is good government, with freedom and order. But order puts fetters on freedom and freedom rebels against order' (Sayers 1945: 58). As Plato put it:

> if a city were composed entirely of good men, to avoid office would be as much an object of contention as to obtain office is at present. . . . The true ruler is not meant . . . to regard his own interest, but that of his subjects.
>
> (Plato – *The Republic*: Book 1)

3 Modelling criminal behaviour

It has been shown that the happiness of the individuals, of whom a community is composed, . . . is the end and the sole end which the legislator ought to have in view.

(Bentham 1789: Ch. III: I)

Introduction

We have seen in Chapter Two how it is that the market will not provide the complete solution to harmful behaviour (i.e. behaviour which reduces societal utility), even though it might be presumed that this is behaviour of which society disapproves. Two of the suggested ways society might seek to address these market-based problems involve preference modification: education (in the general sense); and religion. However, as we discussed in Chapter Two neither of these is likely to be entirely satisfactory. The third possibility involves the creation of a system of incentives and disincentives so as to encourage selfless behaviour on the part of economic agents and discourage behaviour which society finds costly. It is this third category, the criminal justice system, that is the focus of this chapter.

We begin by considering the seminal work of Becker (1968), on which all subsequent analysis is based, and show how, through the use of complex mathematics, economists can 'prove' the intuitively appealing proposition that, starting from a basis of individual and societal preference, both offenders and society act rationally in their actions. As will be seen later in the chapter, the importance of Becker's work is not in proving that offenders and society act rationally, rather it is in providing a set of 'economic building blocks' that have helped other economists go on to develop a range of theories and specify research projects that have provided further insight into the nature of offending and different interventions that might reduce it. Becker's original paper makes extensive use of complex mathematics; however, we will not reproduce the mathematics here. Instead we provide a narrative of the key elements of Becker's arguments; Becker's mathematical formulation will be represented using diagrams.

The Becker model

Becker, and those who build on his work, consider the market for 'crimes of commission' – where an agent chooses to undertake actions which impose a cost on society (for example, littering or theft). Becker doesn't consider 'crimes of omission' – where an agent will choose *not* to undertake actions which benefit society (for example, paying their TV licence). However, the basic analysis is generalisable to both. What follows will not be a precise presentation of the model, for which readers are referred to the original paper, but a discussion of the assumptions and general import of the approach. As with the discussion of the market in Chapter Two, the illustrations used do not represent data, they represent the basic concepts and workings of the economy.

The harm resulting from activity O

Consider a particular activity which society wishes to discourage. For the sake of simplicity of expression, and following Becker, we denote this activity O. It stands to reason some agents must benefit from undertaking this activity – else the level of O would equal zero. Given that these offending agents must also be a part of society, there may be a level of O which society is prepared to accept. Consider, for example, the production of a good which might involve carbon dioxide emissions. Although society in general would prefer less carbon dioxide, in the interests of, for example, electricity generation, food production or transport, some level of carbon dioxide will be accepted. Other activities will be so harmful (for example, murder or theft), that society will prefer an activity level of zero.

As we may wish to permit some of activity O, but not too much, we represent the relationship between the level of O and the harm it does to society in Figure 3.1. It will be noted that, for very low levels of activity, less than O^*, the harm to society is below the horizontal axis, i.e. society may benefit from a small amount of this activity. However, as the level of activity increases above O^*, not only does the level of harm increase, but the relationship becomes steeper – as the level of activity increases, the damage caused by any further increase is greater. It need hardly be stated that for many activities, the socially desirable level of O is zero.

The cost of justice: detection, apprehension and conviction, and punishment

Now, society will wish increasingly to discourage agents from activity O. It is assumed such discouragement will come at a cost. If this were not the case, i.e. if there were no cost in creating a disincentive structure, society would eliminate the activity altogether, or at least limit it to O^*. The costs are realised in two distinct contexts: the cost of detection, apprehension and conviction (we will simply refer to this as the cost of conviction); and the costs of the punishment itself. The costs of conviction arise as it seems reasonable to assume that the perpetrators of activity O will not necessarily voluntarily attend prison to 'pay their debt to society'. Thus society has to bear not only the harm caused by the activity, but also the cost of attempting to find out 'whodunit' (and subsequently proving this in a court of

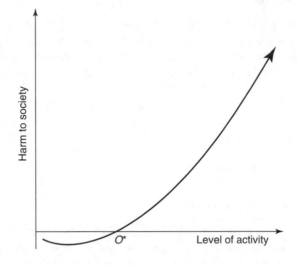

Figure 3.1 The harm done by activity *O*.

law). Not all occurrences of activity *O* will result in a conviction; the proportion which does we may term the 'clear-up' rate. The cost of punishment will include the cost of prisons, probation, etc., but may also include other, non-monetised, costs. For example, in the case where a capital punishment is imposed, the value of life, and the value to society of killing or not killing, must be considered.

Both these costs, the cost of finding out (a proportion of those) 'whodunit' and the cost of punishing them, will increase as more of the activity is committed. By way of illustration, suppose the amount of theft in society were to double; if society wished the clear-up rate to remain the same, the increase in theft would lead to a greater demand for conviction and punishment. Hence justice costs will increase as the level of theft increases. Similarly, the costs of justice will increase as the clear-up rate increases, both because detection is expensive, and also because more prisons may need to be built as more perpetrators are convicted. Finally, the costs of punishment will increase as the level of punishment increases. Bear in mind the perpetrator is a member of society and if, for example, they were punished by a custodial sentence, society as a whole becomes less well off.[1] In addition, if the level of theft were to double, there might be a call for longer or harsher sentences, which will mean still more prison places must be provided, and these use resources that might otherwise be used to pursue other social goods, such as providing more hospital beds.

Agents' response to 'justice' services

We consider now the supply of offences. Because of the different preference sets and attributes of members of society, some agents will be discouraged from

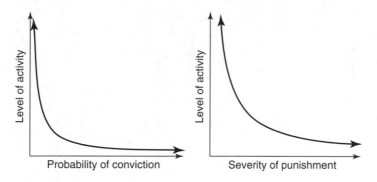

Figure 3.2 The disincentive effect of justice on activity *O*.

activity *O* relatively easily; others may take more persuading. In general, it is not unreasonable to assume that agents will become increasingly discouraged with activity *O*, as: it becomes more likely they will be caught and convicted; and/or punishment becomes more severe. These relationships are represented in Figure 3.2.

Becker argues the greater the level of justice (i.e. the greater the probability of conviction and the severity of punishment), the less effective is a further increase.[2] This is shown by the relationships becoming flatter as the probability and severity of punishment increase. Becker also states, if there is a societal optimum, it will be at a level of punishment where (on average) 'crime does not pay'. In other words, those who continue to commit crime are not risk-averse, but indeed prefer risk. It follows that this implies that a 1 per cent increase in the probability of conviction will reduce the level of activity *O* by more than a 1 per cent increase in punishment severity.[3]

The most efficient level of 'justice' services

It can be seen from the above discussion that society can influence the level of activity *O* by varying the probability of conviction and/or the severity of punishment. However, increasing either or both of these will increase justice costs. Also, as has been noted, the effectiveness of increases in either of these will decline the greater is their current level. Thus it is appropriate to consider which is the most efficient combination of these policy tools. In order to examine this issue, Becker defines the total cost of crime in society to be the sum of the actual harm done by the activity, the cost of apprehension and conviction and the cost of the punishment. First, let us consider the effect of sentence severity on these.

As we have seen, the more severe the sentence imposed, the less will be the supply of activity *O*. As the level of the activity declines, so will the harm it causes society and, similarly, the fewer the agents who engage in this activity, the less it will cost to convict them. The relationship between these costs and the severity of the sentence is represented in Figure 3.3. It will be noted that the (sum of the)

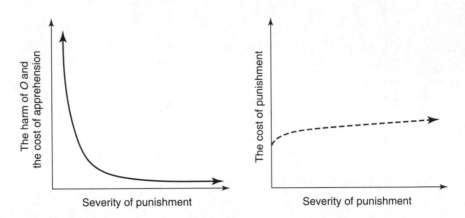

Figure 3.3 The effect of sentence severity on costs.

harm of the activity and the costs of conviction will decline as the severity of punishment increases, and the costs of punishment will increase as the severity of punishment increases.

The two components are reproduced in grey in Figure 3.4. The total cost of activity O to society is simply the sum of these two components. The total cost is indicated by the black curve. It will be noted this total cost reaches a minimum point below which it cannot be reduced. The reason for this is that, although increasing from zero the severity of punishment will cause a great decline in the level of O, the severity of punishment becomes less and less of a deterrent as it increases, while the cost of punishing will continue to increase.

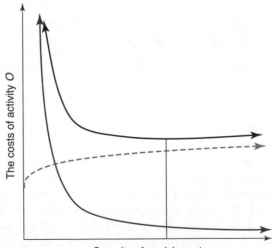

Figure 3.4 The effect of sentence severity on total costs.

The level of severity which minimises total costs – that is to say the sum of: the harm done by *O*; the cost of conviction of (a proportion of) those who carry out the activity; and the cost of punishing them – is indicated by the vertical line. If the level of severity is set either to the left or the right of the vertical line, punishment is not at its most efficient level. To the left of the efficient level, not enough of the activity is being deterred; to the right, the costs of punishment are too great.

We may similarly analyse the most efficient clear-up rate (shown in Figure 3.5). In comparison to Figure 3.4, we see the costs of conviction begin to increase as the clear-up rate increases. These are included (along with the harm from *O*) in the light grey solid curve. Although the level of activity *O* will decline as the clear-up rate increases, the actual cost of conviction will increase because more resources will be required to detect more occurrences of *O*, and to convict the culprits. Also, of course, if the clear-up rate increases, the costs of punishment, indicated by the dashed curve, must also rise – more convictions means more punishment costs. Again, the most socially efficient level of the policy variable is indicated by the vertical line.

If the clear-up rate is to the left of the vertical line, society is not convicting enough culprits, and too high a level of activity *O* is being tolerated. On the other hand, if the clear-up rate is to the right of the vertical line, society is putting too much resource into conviction and punishment.

We have presented Becker's model here without his mathematical notation for the sake of simplicity. This has the advantage (we hope) of allowing the easy understanding of the concepts, but it has the disadvantage of making proof of Becker's results implicit rather than explicit. The interested reader is referred to the original paper should the intuitive analysis carried out below not satisfy their curiosity about the results.

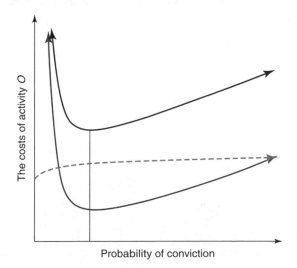

Figure 3.5 The effect of the probability of conviction on total costs.

Interpretation of the Becker model

Becker's (1968) analysis was controversial when it was first published and, indeed, arguably is still controversial today, in that it clearly implies there is such a thing as a society too rigidly controlled for its own good; a society with too high a level of punishment. Another clear implication is that it is quite simply not possible fully to stamp out an undesirable activity (or at least, not through a criminal justice system). However, are these observations really so controversial? Many sociologists and criminologists have reached similar conclusions. For example, Durkheim argues that crime is a normal feature of a society with high levels of 'mechanical solidarity', where punishment is a mechanism that helps reinforce moral consensus (see Hopkins-Burke 2005). Conversely Merton sees crime as one form of 'innovation' by individuals who use illegitimate means to achieve socially acceptable ends. In some cases these 'innovations' will over time lead to the development of new, legitimate social practices (ibid.).

It will be noted from the above that the analysis does not predict how the most efficient levels of punishment and the clear-up rate are to be determined. The figures above do not represent data, they represent postulated relationships. We cannot simply read off the socially efficient level of anything. However, the strength of Becker's analysis comes from what economists call 'comparative statics', which is to say, changing one aspect of the model and comparing the result to that which was obtained before the change.

A change in the harm of the activity

For example, consider the effect of an increase in the harm done to society by activity *O*. This is shown in Figure 3.6. The lighter curves represent the original situation, the heavier curves the situation which will apply as a result of the change in the parameter.

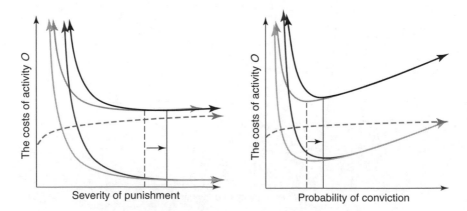

Figure 3.6 An increase in the harm of activity *O*.

We see, as the harm of the activity increases (or, to put it another way, as we compare two activities, one of which does more harm than the other), more harm will attract a higher optimal penalty and society will choose a higher clear-up rate – a fairly straightforward, one might even say obvious policy implication. Thus we see it is entirely rational that the detection rate for the crime of homicide – 90 per cent in England and Wales in 2008/9 – is greater than the detection rate for the crime of assault without injury (other than on a police constable) – 36 per cent in England and Wales in 2008/9 (Home Office 2009).

Similarly, the comparative cost to a rational society of different kinds of activity is explicitly allowed for in sentencing. In the UK 'Parliament attaches to each criminal offence a maximum sentence that gives a broad indication of offence seriousness' (Sentencing Advisory Panel 2010a: 5). Murder, for example (where there are no aggravating or mitigating factors), has a minimum term of 14 years, while the *maximum* custodial sentence for burglary (adult offender; minimal loss and damage and no raised culpability and/or harm) is 12 weeks. Likewise, the United States Sentencing Commission (2009) attempts to summarise sentencing custom and practice based on an analysis of over 40,000 convictions. Sentence length for the 'charge' offence is determined based on the severity of the activity (the cost to society) and the number of previous offences committed by the individual. For example: 'First Degree Murder' is judged to have a base offence level of 43 (implying a sentence of 'life' even on a first offence); 'Possessing Dangerous Weapons or Materials While Boarding or Aboard an Aircraft' a base offence level of 9; and 'Minor Assault' a base offence level of 7 (4 if no dangerous weapon or physical contact was involved). In general, the higher the offence level, and the more previous convictions, the longer the length of the indicated custodial sentence. The reason why previous convictions are important, as we shall see, is society may wish to punish more harshly those who have indicated they are relatively inured to penalties imposed.

A change in the ease of detection

It will, of course, also be the case that some crimes are easier to detect than others. We have seen the detection rate for the crime of assault without injury (other than on a police constable) was 36 per cent. It is not unreasonable to suppose the police will be able to 'detect' an assault perpetrated against a constable more easily than an assault perpetrated on a member of the public. It is entirely rational then that the clear-up rate for the crime of assault without injury on a constable (England and Wales) was much greater, to be precise 92 per cent over the 2008/9 period (Home Office 2009). Using a similar approach to that described above, Becker shows that the optimal clear-up rates of crimes which are easy to detect is greater than the optimal clear-up rate of crimes of equal severity where detection is more difficult. However, as crimes become easier to detect, the optimal level of punishment imposed declines. As Becker's model suggests, agents respond more readily to detection than punishment and the optimal level of such crime falls. Conversely, society will respond to an increase in the difficulty of clearing up certain kinds of crime by tolerating more of that activity and punishing much more harshly those few who are caught; in effect, 'making an example of them'.

In reviewing clear-up rates statistics, it should be borne in mind that some crimes will only come to the attention of police through detection. For example, the (so-called) clear-up rate of 'possession of controlled drugs (cannabis)' was 95 per cent in England and Wales in 2008/9 (Home Office 2009). This is not because it is easier to detect than murder, or that society considers it more serious than murder, it is merely a reflection that, *of those people known to have possession of cannabis*, 95 per cent of them were successfully 'detected' (we may speculate how the other 5 per cent of those known to have possessed cannabis managed to escape detection).

A change in the effectiveness of punishment

Becker also briefly comments on the effect of changes in (potential) criminals' behaviour as they, for example, become 'hardened' (inured to punishment). Society's rational response in this case is to reduce the level of punishment of a convicted offender, but to increase the probability of conviction. Note that Becker does not seek to explain why such an effect might occur, merely how society might rationally respond to it. In practice, however, society is not in a position to detect more carefully those crimes committed by persistent offenders. Indeed, it is likely to be the case that the background of the offender will only become known after the crime has been cleared up. Thus although a rational society with perfect information might choose to increase the clear-up rate for such offenders, in practice, as we have seen, persistent offenders attract heavier, not lighter, sentences.

A change in the cost of punishment

An interesting further insight is what will happen if the costs of punishment are increasingly borne by society. Society at large may begin to feel, for example, its use of capital punishment is imposing increased non-monetised costs or perhaps the cost of incapacitation may increase due to successful campaigns to improve the conditions for prisoners; such campaigns themselves arise out of a desire to reduce society's non-monetised costs of punishment. We illustrate this in Figure 3.7.

As society pays increasingly more to punish convicted criminals, so there is a decrease in the severity of punishments handed down on conviction. This is in part offset by an increase in the rate of conviction; however, overall the level of the activity will increase. We see that, in Becker's model, if society wishes to reduce the cost of punishment the trade-off is increased crime. As the level of punishment is related, not only to the length of the sentence, but to prison conditions, any improvement in prisoners' conditions, unless compensated by increased sentence length, is 'paid for' by an increase in the cost of crime. Also it will generally take additional resources to improve prisoners' conditions. This is not to say, of course, that a humane society might not choose such a trade-off, merely that the trade-off exists.

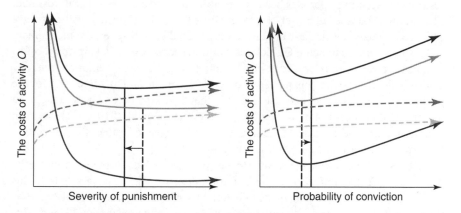

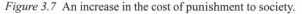

Figure 3.7 An increase in the cost of punishment to society.

Fines and compensation

Becker concludes by demonstrating the most efficient form of punishment which society may adopt in seeking to discourage activities of which it disapproves; the use of fines. Becker's use of the term 'fine' encompasses any compensation payment made to the victim of crime, as well as further payments required of the offender by way of deterrence and vengeance. Becker (1968) states fines are the predominant form of punishment in most countries, arguing that this is because of optimality conditions. The argument for fines is the converse of the one made regarding the effect of an increase in societal costs of punishment. In the case of fines, part of the cost of punishment is borne by the perpetrator of the activity. Therefore the cost to society as a whole is reduced. As the cost to society of punishment declines, punishments will increase in severity, the probability of conviction will decline and the level of the activity will fall. By setting the level of the fine equal to the harm society suffers from the activity (including the cost of detection and punishment) the optimal level of any activity can be achieved.

Becker notes, however, that in criminal law, 'fines' may reflect the three goals of deterrence, compensation and vengeance. In practice, compensation is often specified separately from a fine. Consider the crime of corporate manslaughter, for example, a crime generally punished by a fine given the difficulty of incarcerating a corporation. In England and Wales sentencing guidelines state 'Fines cannot and do not attempt to value a human life in money. Civil compensation will be payable separately' (Sentencing Guidelines Council 2010: 7).[4] The guidelines suggest that the fine should be set at such a level so as to remove from the firm the 'profit' of their illegal activity (the illegal activity in this case being the gross negligence or infringement of Health and Safety regulations which led to death, not the actual death itself) with 'an appropriate additional penalty' (Sentencing Guidelines Council 2010: 7). The appropriate additional penalty would, in a rational society, reflect the fact that some (perhaps many) instances of negligence do not result in prosecution – perhaps because (fortuitously) no death or other ill resulted. The rational fine should be set at a level so as to set the *expected* profit to zero. This is obviously not straightforward to operationalise. However, the mechanism suggested by the Sentencing Guidelines Council seems somewhat arbitrary, referring as it does to: turnover; profit before tax; assets; directors' remuneration, etc. The guidelines state the 'means of any defendant are relevant to a fine', not for the purposes of efficiency but because it is 'just that a wealthy defendant should pay a larger fine than a poor one' (Sentencing Guidelines Council 2010: 5). This would tend to indicate the purpose of the fine is one of vengeance, rather than of setting the expected return of the activity to zero.

Perhaps writing with some irony, Becker points out that, although former prisoners may face discrimination in the labour market, former fine payers do not. This may well be a function of the types of offences which are currently punishable by fines of course. However, if we are to take his point, it implies there will be no further penalties levied by society (whether unwittingly or otherwise) on the offender once he or she has paid their 'debt to society'. Becker implies that this is a further factor which indicates fines are to be preferred to a custodial sentence.[5] Notwithstanding Becker acknowledges there are some activities (for example murder) which are too heinous to be punished with a mere fine, no matter at what level. Also, the imposition of a fine will work only in the case where the perpetrator has the means to pay. Even where the offender has the means to pay, the trade-off with the time spent in prison disadvantages the less well-off. Consider the maximum penalty in England and Wales for domestic burglary (adult offenders) when tried summarily: a level 5 fine (at the time of writing, £5,000) and/or 6 months imprisonment (Sentencing Advisory Panel 2010b). If the alternative to imprisonment is working at the minimum wage, this seems a fair trade-off. An employee on the minimum wage will earn £5,800 (net) in a six-month period. If the perpetrator is earning more than the minimum wage the trade-off seems less attractive.

How might rational outcomes be determined?

Becker establishes that there will be a rational level of detection and punishment of crime in order to minimise society's (expected) cost from crime. However, the issue of how to translate this into criminal justice policy is an open one. We outline briefly here some of the implications of the model and highlight how governments have sought to address these. Many of these themes will be developed further in later chapters.

A tale of two externalities

It is worth noting that generally the 'costs' of criminal activity fall on an individual, or a small group of individuals, rather than on society at large. Thus it is not unreasonable to expect the victim to feel the need for compensation, detection and vengeance. However, the cost of this vengeance is largely borne by society. Thus we have an externality problem. The transaction 'vengeance' for 'closure'[6] is made between the victim and the offender with society's facilitation; however, the criminal justice costs are borne by society. Economic theory tells us in such circumstances a greater than optimal number of transactions will take place under these circumstances.[7] In other words, where compensation is paid by society, theory would seem to indicate victims will demand a greater than optimal level of criminal justice services. The implication of this is that it is entirely rational for society as a whole to agree to fail to satisfy the entirely rational requests for 'justice services' from victims. Note that this argument does not apply in the case of fines and compensation payments.

One further cost which does fall on society in general is the 'fear' of crime. This may be thought of as a further externality of criminal activity. Most criminals do not directly benefit from the generation of society-wide fear and, indeed, might prefer their actions not to become known. However, it would seem perverse to blame the innocent in society for wanting to know the nature of the risk they face. A case might be made that the media exaggerate – or at least emphasise – the risk of being a victim of crime (for example, Cohen 1972 and Browne 1992; see also Reiner 2001, who argues the UK media has increasingly focused on violent crime). However, as Ditton *et al.* (2004: 608) contend, 'a connection between media consumption and the fear of crime . . . cannot convincingly be made'. Johnston (2003: 6) sums it up, 'Cut the crime and the fear will diminish, whatever the tabloids say'.

Irrational democracy

It cannot be taken for granted, however, that society will necessarily choose an efficient or rational approach to setting the clear-up rate. Indeed, the Chief Inspector of Constabulary in England and Wales, Denis O'Connor, has gone on record as stating government targets have distorted local police priorities (*The Daily Telegraph*, 26 November 2009). For example, *Guardian* columnist Peter Walker (*The Guardian*, 16 April 2010), in answer to his own question 'Why do police target cyclists who jump red lights? Why not devote the resources to real traffic dangers like light-jumping cars and trucks?', finds the answer is 'Police forces are now obliged by central government to tackle issues flagged up by local communities. In the City, this tends to bring complaints about rough sleepers and law-flouting cyclists' (ibid.).[8] Although it is certainly not true the police are unconcerned with traffic-light-jumping cars and trucks, the plain fact is, there are far fewer of them than cyclists who do the like. By choosing a metric – in this case number of complaints – which does not reflect the seriousness of the offence,[9] police are misallocating resources in responding to the volume of public concern.[10] Denis O'Connor is of the opinion 'There are just so many people, with so many different interests in play . . . I think the whole thing needs rationalising significantly' (*The Daily Telegraph* 2009).

Whither rehabilitation?

In his analysis Becker considers the deterrence, compensation and vengeance effect of punishment, but not the ability of society to utilise the punishment to rehabilitate an offender (i.e. the modification of an offender's preference set). Recall, Becker considers the supply of offences function to be given – this assumption is relaxed by Ehrlich (1973) amongst others, as we discuss in the next section. Practically, a rational society may take the opportunity, once an offender is identified, of attempting to reduce the probability of future offending through (in economic terms) re-parameterisation of the individual's offence supply function. This distinction, between deterrence and rehabilitation, is clear to policy-makers notwithstanding it is not straightforward to measure the relative impact of these effects.[11] For example, in England and Wales, it is suggested fines are appropriate where 'punishment is the sole or primary purpose of sentencing' (Sentencing Advisory Panel 2010a: 52); however, 'rehabilitation of the offender is considered to be an important aim of the sentence, a community sentence . . . is likely to be more appropriate' (ibid.).

Modelling criminal choice

In his seminal article, Becker (1968) acknowledges criminals have differing preferences and proclivities, but does not seek to model these explicitly. His analysis deals with the socially optimal choice of detection and punishment. Becker's supply of offences function recognises the cost to potential criminals of punishment, but not the opportunity cost of illegal activity; to wit, the resources devoted to illegal activity might have been devoted to legal activity. We shall see that adding such costs to the model allows a greater depth to the analysis.

Such opportunity costs are specifically addressed in the model of Ehrlich (1973). Potential criminals are assumed to be able to make use of their financial resources, human capital (i.e. their abilities) and temporal resources (i.e. available time) to engage in both legal and illegal activities depending on which is expected to give the greater return to the agent. In Ehrlich's model, agents do not choose whether to specialise in criminal activities or not, but rather to determine how much time should be devoted to each. Ehrlich's so called 'One-Period Uncertainty Model' is designed to allow us to 'eavesdrop' as it were on the potential criminal as they decide how to occupy their time in this 'one-period'.

The potential criminal (for the sake of argument, let's refer to him or her as 'Moriarty') has the choice whether to engage in a legal activity – with a particular return and risk – or an illegal activity with its own return and risk. If Moriarty engages in the latter, there is also the possibility of apprehension and punishment. Moriarty need not specialise, he may split his time between the two activities. In making the decision which proportion of these two activities will occupy his resources, Moriarty seeks to maximise his expected return, net of the costs of the activity.

The costs of each activity must be incurred whether or not apprehension and punishment follow. For example, he may have to purchase equipment, expend time and/or effort on the activities, hire accomplices, etc. In addition, there may also be a preference set involving: levels of distaste for illegality; attitudes to risk (it might be assumed, following Becker (1968), that all potential criminals prefer risk; however, Ehrlich considers also the risk-averse and risk-neutral); akrasia (aka weakness-of-will); personality; personal attributes, etc. As an example of the levels of distaste for illegality, it might be that Moriarty will impose the psychological cost 'guilt' on himself if he succeeds in his illegal activity.

Ehrlich notes that his model allows the agent to specialise more in illegal activity as: the acquisition of a criminal record reduces their opportunity for legitimate gains; the agent (through experience) gains skills which reduces the cost of such activity; and/or their preference for crime increases. Of course, the converse, specialising in legal activity, is also possible.

To operationalise the model, Ehrlich assumes that the return on each activity is known with certainty, i.e. that the only risk involved is that of detection and punishment.[12] However, if Moriarty chooses legal activity, there is a possibility of not finding any – of being, in other words, unemployed for that period. The problem faced by Moriarty is to maximise the expected return from the one-period of activity through the choice of the level of the legal and the illegal activity.

Ehrlich notes the agent will engage in illegal activities if the marginal gain from illegality exceeds the marginal gain from legal activities. Thus, if the net return from legal activities declines, or the net return to illegal activities increases, more time is expected to be devoted to criminality. By net return, Ehrlich means the return after costs are taken into account. For example, if Moriarty finds henchmen more expensive to employ and/or targets become more costly to find or access, less time will be devoted to illegal activities.

The effect of punishment varies depending on whether Moriarty is risk-averse, risk-neutral or prefers risk. While it follows that an increase in the likelihood of being caught and punished will result in less time being spent in illegal activities, the effect of the severity of the punishment is unclear. In general, the more risk-averse Moriarty is, the less he will engage in criminal activity as the punishment increases. In the case where Moriarty is not risk-averse, but rather is a risk-seeker, the apparently paradoxical conclusion is reached that an increase in the severity of the punishment may (in some cases) lead to more time being devoted to illegal activities.[13] It should be noted that this conclusion is reached without consideration of the incapacitative effect of the punishment. That is to say, we might conclude less time is available for criminal activity if an increasing proportion of it is spent in prison.

The effect of unemployment

It hardly needs noting that, in general, as the unemployment rate increases, the opportunity cost of crime falls. This result is suggested from consideration of the two labour market effects distinguished by economic theory: voluntary unemployment and involuntary unemployment.

Economic models which emphasise voluntary unemployment tend to focus on labour market conditions to explain it. Recall the supply–demand model of Chapter Two. In essence, those who supply labour services wish for the maximum return on their time. Voluntary unemployment occurs where suppliers of labour leave a particular job to devote their efforts to searching for another with an increased expected return for given input (for example, a higher salary). Voluntary unemployment is a necessary part of the smooth running of the labour market.

Involuntary unemployment results where workers are forced into a search for employment against their will and are unable to find work at the prevailing wage (i.e. the wage paid to other similarly qualified workers who *are* employed). One solution to this problem is to reduce wages. As we have seen, as the price demanded for any good or service declines, demand for that good or service increases. Consider the labour market represented in Figure 3.8, where p represents the price of labour (the real wage). Suppose that the prevailing price of labour is p_1. The difference between the amount of labour supplied at this price, q_s, and the level of demand, q_d, is the level of involuntary unemployment.

The solution suggested by classical economics is for wages – the price of labour – to fall until the market comes to equilibrium at the point E. Thus involuntary unemployment may be eliminated (in theory) by a reduction in the real wage. However, the demand and supply of labour may not necessarily behave in the same way as the demand and supply of goods and services in general. In practice those still in employment are loath to see their conditions eroded (and indeed, given that the cost of living is to some extent fixed, may not be able to afford such erosion). Thus real wages do not adjust completely.

If real wages fall, the return on legitimate employment falls and therefore illegitimate employment will become relatively more attractive. However, given that wages may not necessarily fall to the market clearing level, involuntary unemployment persists. In this case Moriarty's trade-off between devoting temporal resources to illegal activities rather than legal activities changes. If there is a reduced likelihood of finding legitimate employment, its expected return falls. Thus Moriarty is more likely to choose illegal activities.

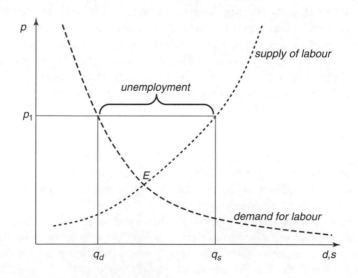

Figure 3.8 Supply and demand for labour.

Of course, not all crime will be a substitute for (legal) income generation. The effect is most likely to be observed in property crime. We consider the empirical evidence on this issue in greater detail in Chapter Five.

Impact on the model of individuals' attributes

Risk aversion

Given the above comparative static results, it is reasonable to consider the attribute sets of distinct groups of individuals in the economy. The most straightforward of these is the attitude of Moriarty to risk. We have discussed, given the set-up of the model, the more Moriarty comes to accept or prefer risks, the more likely he is to engage in illicit behaviour. Looking at this in another way, it follows if there are two groups of individuals the same in every way, except for their attitude to risk, that group which is less risk-averse is the more likely to become involved in illegal activities. Practically, consider it is generally held that younger people are less risk-averse than adults (see, for example, Galvan *et al.* 2007, and Steinberg *et al.* 2009) and, indeed, that men generally may be more inclined towards risk than women (Slovic 1966). Therefore, Ehrlich's model implies, other parameters being equal, a higher rate of deterrence is required to discourage young men from criminal activity, relative to young women or older men. Alternatively, we might state that, for a given level of deterrence, young men are more likely to commit crime than other demographic groups.

The effects of both age and gender on criminal behaviour are well known. For the purposes of our discussion here, however, it is worth noting that the relative proclivity of young men to illegal activities does not prove Ehrlich's model is valid, merely that the data do not contradict the implications of the model. Indeed so well accepted is the age profile of crime that it has been argued by Hirschi and Gottfredson (1983) that it has very little predictive power and should not serve as the basis for targeting criminal justice interventions. As they put it (p. 582), 'the causes of crime are likely to be the same at any age'.

Education

As well as influencing Moriarty's rational choice over whether to commit crime through deterrence, society might seek to encourage him away from crime by increasing his prospects for legitimate employment, thereby increasing the opportunity costs of crime. One way of doing this would be by increasing his educational attainment.

It seems intuitively obvious increasing education will increase access, through the labour market, to a greater variety of legal employment opportunities, thereby increasing the opportunity costs of illegal activities and thus shifting the balance of incentives away from crime. Increasing the level of educational attainment may also have other benefits: for example, educated individuals have successfully completed a programme of study requiring their work in the present for a future goal (end of year exams, assignments, etc.). Such individuals may have succeeded, partly because they are prepared to defer rewards and satisfaction. In economic terms, this is known as the time rate of preference. The reason why the time rate of preference matters is because it is not unreasonable to suppose the reward from illicit activity is a more or less immediate gratification, whereas the punishment which might arise is at some future time. Thus, the more emphasis is placed on the present at the expense of the future, the more crimes will be committed. Conversely, the more emphasis is placed on the future compared to the present, the fewer crimes will be committed (Groot and van den Brink 2007).

Also, the successful completion of a course of study involves the student receiving legitimate rewards earned through 'diligence, performance, conformity, cooperation and competition' (Groot and van den Brink 2007 quoting Arrow 1997). If we accept this, sadly we must accept the converse argument. Those who, for no fault of their own, are ill-equipped to cope with education will find that legitimate rewards do not necessarily arise from diligence, etc. This is likely to increase their proclivity to crime.

Before moving on from education, it is worth noting that there is some evidence of up-skilling in the economy, which is to say that employers are asking for greater levels of education from potential employees (see Cappelli 1993 for example). This would tend to indicate that, for a given level of education, the range of employment opportunities is diminishing.

In the UK, Barrett (2010) notes that, in 1995, the employment rate for people with low or no qualifications[14] stood at 60.1 per cent, which was 17.0 percentage points lower than the rate for people with higher qualifications.[15] This discrepancy was relatively stable, increasing slowly until the start of the 2008/09 recession when it began to increase more rapidly and (at the end of 2009) stood at 21.6 per cent. Over the same period the proportion of people in this group fell by more than one third. In short, a greater proportion of the workforce with qualifications appears to be associated with an increasing difficulty in finding work for those who have no qualifications. Thus, other things being equal, the opportunity cost of illicit 'employment' is decreasing for those less academically able. Over time, the less academically able will have fewer opportunities for legitimate employment *even if the overall unemployment level remains unchanged*. This implies that they will require increased deterrence from illegal activities.

Labour market conditions

It will be noted, in Ehrlich's (1973) model, the individual, our so-called Moriarty, must choose how to allocate his time between legal and illegal activities. We have discussed already how Moriarty's opportunity cost in engaging in illegal activity will decrease as the opportunities for legitimate employment decrease. Other things being equal, as we have seen, an increase in Moriarty's education will allow greater access to the labour market and thus increase the opportunity cost of illegal activities. If, however, the level of employment in the economy

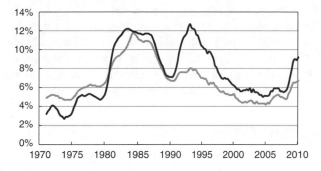

Figure 3.9 UK unemployment rates: male (black) and female (grey).
Source: Office for National Statistics (2010).
Note: Male: 16+ years, Female: 16+.

were to decline, Moriarty will conclude the opportunity cost of illegal activity
has decreased.

Over the last 40 years we may observe the change in the level of unemployment
in the UK economy, which, according to Ehrlich's (1973) model we might suppose
will be inversely related to the opportunity cost of crime (Figure 3.9). The link
between the state of the economy, unemployment and crime will be considered
analytically in Chapter Five. However, it is worth noting the male unemployment
rate is generally higher than that of females, and, at times of increasing unemployment, generally the rate of male unemployment increases by more than the rate of
female unemployment.[16] It has been suggested (see De Boer and Seeborg 1984)
that this change results from the move from a manufacturing oriented economy to
one that is increasingly based on the services sector.

Social and cultural background

We have thus far considered Moriarty's decision whether or not to commit a crime
in isolation. In practice, there are interactions between Moriarty and his peers and
social network. There will be some activities in which he cannot engage if he is
on his own: burglars need their fence; drug users often fund their habits through
further illegal activities; Robin Hood needed his 'Merry Men' and of course drug
runners in general will require a dedicated organisation (see Chapters Ten and
Eleven) and so on. Such interactions tend to de-stabilise crime trends.

Peer groups and families

The evidence suggests strongly that presence of others tends to impact on individual decisions, for better or for worse. Self-made millionaire Jim Rhon, the 'farm
boy who made it to Beverly Hills' summarised it, 'You are the average of the five
people you spend the most time with'. Longitudinal studies of criminal careers
have regularly shown the importance of delinquent parents, siblings and peers

as factors that increase an individual's propensity to offend (see for instance Farrington 2007 and Smith 2007). In the context of our current discussion, associating with people who engage in illegal behaviour might mean Moriarty is exposed to activities he did not previously consider. Through a process of imitation and learning, facilitation and peer pressure, Moriarty may find his preference set is becoming more attuned to such activities.

Interacting agents: fads and stigma

A slightly different effect is considered by Sah (1991) and Glaeser *et al.* (1996), among others: the so-called Interacting Agents theory. In attempting to understand why the variability of crime rates is so high across 'time and space', Glaeser *et al.* postulate that one agent's decision to enter a life of crime will influence another. In one sense this adds to the evidence on 'peer pressure'; however, it goes beyond this in that the agents need not necessarily even meet. Our friend Moriarty takes his cue on which behaviours are acceptable or fashionable from the general environment in which he finds himself. Examples of crimes which are reinforced by 'community mores', however loosely defined, include: the understanding many road users have that they flash headlights at an oncoming car to warn of a police speed trap (*Washington Post* 2009); the 'fad' of happy slapping (*The Guardian* 2005) (assaulting people at random with a view to filming their discomfort); or football violence. It has been suggested that in England such violence may be linked to the (one would have thought) innocuous decision to televise live matches (Marsh *et al.* 1996).

The Interacting Agents theory also goes some way to explain why it is that the rational behaviour of a group of people, a *mob*, cannot necessarily be forecast from the rational decisions of each individual. We have seen how Becker's (1968) analysis would suggest an increase in the likelihood of arrest and punishment ought to deter individuals from crime. However, in some situations a group of people may face *increased* incentives to illegal activity as the level of punishment increases because of positive feedback through the *mob*. Thus we may have some rational support for the apparently irrational claim that football violence is made more likely through 'heavy-handed policing' (JournalLive 2008). Similarly positive and negative dynamic feedback loops can mean a very small change in deterrence, or indeed in societal perceptions, may have a major impact on how much crime is committed by making it fashionable and cool or, conversely, unfashionable. For example, Superman's famous real-life victory over the Ku Klux Klan in 1940s USA (Mental Floss 2009) was possible because he stripped the mystique from the organisation and made it a thing of ridicule. The crusade of an entirely fictional character would have been unlikely to change Klan members' choice of activity without interacting agents.

Similarly, as particular criminal acts become more fashionable or widespread, there is a reduction for the criminal in the cost of crime arising from stigma, society's valuation of an individual on the basis of disapproved actions. According to Rasmussen (1996) stigma may be of two kinds, both arising from the general knowledge someone has committed a criminal act: economic (for example, difficulty finding work); and social. Stigma is a cheap (from society's point of view) and powerful tool in reducing crime and may be likened to an informal fine which society levies on the wrong-doer.

Stigma may also be seen as a means of imparting information so that market decisions will become increasingly efficient. If it is brought to the attention of society in general that 'Moriarty Mechanics' is notoriously unreliable or overcharges, this information may then be taken into account by customers and, through supply and demand, eventually be reflected in a modified price or performance. It has been argued (see Bowles and Gintis 2002) that smaller communities are more efficient than large societies in the dissemination of such information. Hence, insofar as we see local communities weaken and stigma become more difficult to apply, we might expect to see an increase in anti-social behaviour. However, the power of the internet to promote transmission of such information is likely to become increasingly important with sites such as eBay and Amazon offering to allow users to rate each others' honesty, and in the UK, Which-Local allowing the rating of tradesmen and market participants in general.

Notwithstanding, as a particular crime becomes increasingly carried out by the population at large, the costs arising from such stigma will fall and hence more people will commit the act. In effect, the wrong-doer becomes a normal member of society. In a perverse turn-around, it may be that those who refrain from the illegal act are themselves stigmatised (Glaeser *et al.* 1996) as being 'up-tight' or 'puritanical'. Thus Dalrymple (2008: xi) comments 'A cultural gestalt[17]-switch has taken place in the meantime: old virtues such as fortitude were now considered vices, or at least self-betrayal, and self-control a form of emotional blockage'.

Offenders therefore have an incentive to reduce the stigma attached to their activities. According to the *New York Times* (2009) the phrase 'everyone does it' has recently become the favoured defence of 'lenders, borrowers, brokers, investors, credit agencies, government regulators and elected officials alike'. While such a rationale might lessen the social approbation that might be expected by such, as a legal plea, its use is limited.[18] In any event, consideration of such a plea in the light of Becker's (1968) model implies a rational society will apply a high level of punishment to such crimes. It is not unreasonable to assume a crime which 'everybody does' is one where the likelihood of conviction of any one individual is relatively small – a society in which 'everyone' is punished is a society in which no-one is punished. As we have seen, Becker's analysis suggests society would be wise to increase the penalties paid by those who commit offences for which the clear-up rate is relatively low.

Of course, there are indeed activities which become normalised. As society becomes prepared to tolerate those with no punishment or stigma imposed, they become, in effect, legal. In the area of corruption, for example (a topic we develop more in Chapter Ten), it has been argued (de Sardan 1999) the activity is much more difficult to control because of the absence of effective sanctions leading to corruption's routine nature and perpetrators' perception of its legitimacy.

Thus there is an increased cost which society must pay from widespread anti-social activity. Not only will society lose directly from the presence of the activity, as it becomes increasingly normalised the effect of stigma is reduced and more of the activity will take place. Society's rational response to the plea 'everybody does it' is 'yes, that's part of the problem'.

The increasing observance of an activity may necessitate further legislation to curtail it when previously it might have been kept in check by community stigma. An example of this is the institution of building regulations in London (1189). It might reasonably be assumed that those who purchased accommodation before 1189 were no more keen to live in an unfit dwelling than those who purchased or built houses after. However, as villages grow to towns and cities, the information required to determine which builders and house types are suitable, and which are not, becomes increasingly difficult to access. Thus formal sanctions became required.

Societal mores

It is clear different cultures and nations (and indeed times) have different ideas on what is and is not acceptable on the basis of their own societal objectives. A rational society will be at pains to publicise clearly what it is and is not prepared to accept. As an example of practical law, it is clear society will wish to publish on which side of the road we may drive. If Moriarty were to take a holiday in the USA he would be wise to adopt the norms of the locals rather than to persist in applying his own standards about on which side of the road he drives. Similarly Moriarty would be wise to familiarise himself with the local norms of any society in which he finds himself – societies' view of such behaviours as, for example, what may be worn in public, the level of tipping, what may legally be drunk and at what age and so on.

Moriarty may, however, choose not to adopt the local norms, but rather to stick to those of his home culture – in which case frictions between him and the society in which he finds himself are likely to arise. This question of whether individuals from different cultural backgrounds adapt to local mores has been considered by Fisman and Miguel (2008) in the context of analysing the parking violations identified to have been committed by UN delegates. In the period prior to November 2002, the application of diplomatic immunity to parking violations allowed delegates to escape local (New York City) sanctions for illegal activity.

Fisman and Miguel suggest, other than their cultural background, diplomats are a relatively homogeneous group, being well educated and articulate. Also delegates from all nations are accorded the same privilege in not having to pay fines for traffic violations. Thus we might expect the same rate of violation for all. However, there is observed to be a significant difference between the rate of violations committed by diplomats from different cultural backgrounds. Fisman and Miguel interpret differences in offending rates as evidence of differences in the 'underlying propensity to break rules for private gain when enforcement is not a consideration' (ibid.: 1021). Results indicate corruption norms of the diplomats' home countries are an important predictor of whether they engage in corruption of this form in New York. In other words they neglect, or refuse, to adapt to local societal norms. Moreover, frequency of violations increases with the length of time delegates have spent in New York, indicating increasing rejection of local mores. That this is true of delegates from all cultural backgrounds tends to indicate the adoption of the mores of a diplomatic sub-culture, at least in so far as traffic violations are concerned. That society can indeed force adoption of local norms is shown by the 98 per cent reduction in parking violations which followed the confiscation by New York City of diplomatic plates from vehicles which had three or more unpaid fines associated with them.

Conclusion

Following Becker's work, we have seen how society can structure the market so as to dissuade agents from behaviour of which society disapproves, and how agents of differing backgrounds respond. Therefore the 'theory of deterrence thus obtained is regarded as nothing but a special case of the general theory of rational behaviour under uncertainty' (Eide 1999: 345).

The preceding discussion assumes that potential offenders are everyday rational agents. For a given level of sanctions, agents' social conditions, family background, personal inclination, etc., will influence their decisions on whether or not to commit an illegal or anti-social act. Such conditions act on agents' choices through the formation of their set of preferences.

We have not discussed the *formation* of such preference sets here, any more than we have discussed the formation of agents' human capital – attributes such as: health; intelligence; strength; and manual dexterity. Preferences and abilities alike are taken as a given set which each agent brings to the market. However, the *rational effect* of differing preference sets and human capital has been discussed. Nevertheless, it is clear that the human capital and preference set of agents is an important determinant in their rational choices. In the next chapter we broaden our discussion of rationality, looking in detail at how the concept of rationality has influenced sociological and criminological theories. We end that chapter with a discussion of the formation of agents' preferences.

4   Rational Choice theory in criminology

Evidence shows that we do much less thinking than we believe we do – except, of course, when we think about it.

(Nassim Nicholas Taleb[1])

Introduction

Most criminological textbooks start their discussion of criminological theory with the ideas of classical thinkers such as Beccaria and Bentham. Beccaria believed that 'pleasure and pain are the motives for action among sentient beings' (Beccaria 1764: 15). This is an early elaboration of what, in modern times, we refer to as Rational Choice theory. Beccaria was a strong supporter of 'social contract' theory and free will and Enlightenment ideas associated with classical thinkers who developed theories of political economy. He argued that:

> Laws are the conditions by which independent and isolated men, tired of living in a constant state of war and enjoying a freedom made useless by the uncertainty of keeping it, unite in society. They sacrifice a portion of this liberty in order to enjoy the remainder in security and tranquillity.
>
> (Beccaria 1764: 7)

His ideas were developed by the utilitarian Bentham best known for stating the principle of 'the greatest happiness for the greatest number'. Bentham is familiar both to students of economics and criminology (as well as other related disciplines such as sociology).

To some extent, then, criminology and economics have a common heritage. However, during the late nineteenth and for much of the twentieth century the two disciplines went in different directions. Most criminological textbooks, having considered the classical thinkers, go on to examine the rise of the 'positivist' paradigm and the strong influence this has had on a range of theories about crime, before moving on to 'interpretive' theories which rose to prominence in the middle of the twentieth century. If we were to continue towards the end of our standard criminology textbook's discussion of criminological theories we would find that, in the last quarter of the twentieth century, criminology and economics started to converge again. Becker's (1968) article applied the Rational Choice theory of economics to an analysis of crime and criminologists subsequently developed a distinct criminological version of Rational Choice theory.

In this chapter our primary interest is how Rational Choice theory has developed as a distinct theory within criminology. Before we look specifically at criminology, it is useful first of all to describe in general terms the attraction of Rational Choice theory to social scientists and second to explain briefly how the theory has developed more generally within the social sciences. As we will go on to discuss, a distinct, criminological variant of Rational Choice theory has developed as a means of explaining crime. We consider how Rational Choice theory is also central to a related group of theories sometimes referred to as 'the criminologies of everyday life'. Rational Choice theory, however, is not without critics and we examine key criticisms before finishing with a brief discussion of how Rational Choice theory has influenced policy and practice in the crime and criminal justice sector.

The attraction of Rational Choice theory to social scientists

In understanding the rise of Rational Choice theory as an important theoretical paradigm in modern criminology, it is useful to compare it briefly to alternative theoretical paradigms. Although it is beyond the scope of this book to provide a detailed account of such alternative paradigms, we provide a very general critique of 'positivist' and 'interpretive' approaches to social science in an effort to show the attraction of Rational Choice theory.

Positivism

During the late nineteenth and early twentieth centuries, theorising about crime was dominated by positivist approaches which Hopkins Burke (2005) categorises as biological, psychological and sociological variants of positivism, ranging from the early biological positivism of Lombroso to the work of Durkheim. Positivism[2] is based on a belief in a unified scientific method that can explain both the natural and social worlds. In other words, it is assumed that man is a part of nature, albeit a particularly complex part. Hence the same form of scientific method can be used to explain man as well as everything else in the natural world. Human behaviour is assumed to be determined in the sense that it always has a causal explanation (Hollis 1977). Thus, for the positivist operating within the social sciences, the key to discovering 'statements of a law-like character' is the measurement and quantification of human behaviour. The scientific method advocated by positivism is based on the empiricists' conviction that all true knowledge is grounded in empirical observation of the external world. The social scientist's suggested 'law' or initial hypothesis emerges from empirical observations and it is then verified by the empirical testing of the accuracy of its predictions against empirical experience. As hypotheses are validated, a theory emerges. Thus, positivism provides a scientific method which allows for the objective and neutral validation of theories.[3] Empirical observation is therefore the ultimate and objective arbitrator of the validity of a theory (Hollis 1977).

The key to the positivist claim to be able to produce objective, scientific knowledge is that hypotheses – and hence theories – are based upon objective, empirical observations rather than the scientist's particular views and prejudices. However, this approach has been criticised as not so objective as is supposed. For instance, Popper (1972) argues that:

> The belief that we can start with pure observations alone, without anything in the nature of a theory, is absurd . . . Observation is always selective. It needs a chosen object, a definite task, an interest, a point of view, a problem. And its description presupposes a descriptive language, with property words; it presupposes similarity and classification, which in turn presupposes interests, points of view and problems.
>
> (Popper 1972: 46–7)

If, however, we accept that observation is never theory-neutral and that any examination of the social world involves interpretation, this undermines the positivist claim to be able to validate theories objectively. Once it is recognised that there is more than one possible interpretation of the social world, then it also has to be recognised that the social researcher's choice of which interpretation to adopt must be based on their particular *values*. Hence, while positivism might claim the knowledge it produces is 'objective' and 'scientific', in actual fact this knowledge is based upon a whole series of pre-existing value judgements. These value judgements concern the nature of the social world and the best way to carry out social research.[4] As Bacon notes:

> it is the peculiar and perpetual error of the human intellect to be more moved and excited by affirmatives than by negatives; whereas it ought properly to hold itself indifferently disposed toward both alike. Indeed, in the establishment of any true axiom, the negative instance is the more forcible of the two.
>
> (Bacon 1620: XLVI)

Interpretivism

In the middle of the twentieth century, an awareness of the limitations of the positivist paradigm gave rise to alternative paradigms grounded in concepts and insights such as interactionism, phenomenology and ethnomethodology (Hopkins Burke 2005). The essence of interpretation is to accept that the social world must be understood from within (Hollis 1994). From the perspective of this paradigm it is accepted that all observations are in some sense an interpretation and that we can never directly experience the external 'objective' world in the way that empiricism maintains we can. This leads to a fundamental problem in the pursuit of knowledge about the world: if we cannot experience raw data directly, we cannot rely on it to provide an objective validation of theory (Hollis 1994). When we come to make enquiries about the social world the problem becomes even more acute. Not only must we recognise the limitation of our own minds, but we must also try to understand the actions of other minds.[5] Thus, the interpretive social scientist recognises the plurality of possible descriptions in any one instance. An objective and final description is an impossibility because every sociologist's interpretation of their subject's point of view will be different. There is always room for a new interpretation and there is no way of adjudicating between existing interpretations (Bauman 1992). The implication of this view of the limits of knowledge is relativism, where objectivity is an impossibility and the possibility of more than one valid point of view is welcomed as an accurate reflection of the idea that knowledge is shaped by human interests (Bauman 1992; Doyal and Gough 1991; Toddington 1993).

Rational Choice theory to the rescue

While the objective truths promised by positivism are attractive – both to social scientists who want to explain the causes of crime, and to policy-makers who would like clear guidance on what works in reducing crime – the edifice of objectivity is hard to maintain in the world of social research. But, if the only alternative is relativism, the ambitions of social scientists must remain modest and the guidance that they can give to policy-makers will be limited. This is where Rational Choice theory makes a contribution to the philosophical debate about the nature of knowledge and social enquiry. Rational Choice theory appears to provide an approach which combines objectivism and interpretation. Hollis neatly sums up the advantages of using rationality as a way of preserving objectivism in theorising, while recognising the need for an interpretive (or hermeneutic) approach:

> The hermeneutic imperative is to understand action from within. How do we know when we have succeeded? How can we tell a better interpretation from a worse one? The answer cannot be meekly to accept the actor's own verdict. For, firstly, there is a notorious Other Minds problem in understanding the actor's own understanding, and it is further complicated if the actors are to be the judges of its solution. Secondly, more goes on in the social world than actors, singly or collectively notice and understand. . . . So we need a vantage point for assessing insider accounts . . . We need a category which lets the enquirer know when he has identified what actors are doing and when he has understood why they are doing it. That sets a riddle: 'When is a science not a science?' The best answer in the hermeneutic vein seems to me: 'When it studies rational action'. . . . *The category which lets us make the most objective yet interpretive sense of social life is Rationality.*
> (Hollis 1987: 7, emphasis added)

To put it simply, the only way we can make sense of other people's actions, while remaining trapped in our heads and unable to get inside theirs, is to assume that they are acting rationally and that they place the same meaning on their actions as a rational person would.

Rational Choice theory in the social sciences

Here we look at how Rational Choice theory has developed in the social sciences. We also look at some critiques of the theory, which, as we shall see later in the chapter, have to some extent been addressed in the development of a distinctly criminological version of Rational Choice theory.

A basic model of Rational Choice theory

Rational Choice theory depicts the world as being made up of instrumentally rational individuals (Hargreaves Heap *et al.* 1992; Hollis 1987, 1994). Hargreaves Heap *et al.* (1992) define instrumental rationality as 'the choice of actions which best satisfy a person's objectives'. They go on to say that Rational Choice theory 'identifies the individual with a set of objectives, and treats an action as rational because it is the one most likely to satisfy those objectives' (Hargreaves Heap *et al.* 1992: 4).

The theory has at its heart a single, ideally rational individual who has a set of fully ordered preferences, complete information and a perfect internal computer to allow them to calculate correctly which action will be most instrumental in satisfying their preferences (Hollis 1994). Rational Choice theory thus assumes that the individual has a complete ranking of all possible outcomes, regardless of their probability, and that this information is complete so that they know how likely is each outcome. The individual is thus in a position to calculate the expected utility of each course of action, compare it with each other possible course of action, and choose the action with the greatest expected utility.

Rational Choice theory allows the social scientist to assess whether an individual has chosen the most rational means of achieving a *given* end. No judgement is made about whether the individual's preferences are 'good' or 'bad'. Individuals can pursue whichever set of preferences they choose. Rational Choice theory simply assumes that the self-interested individual will pursue them to the exclusion of all other preferences (Hollis 1994).

> It does not matter whether people prefer oranges to apples, guns to butter or virtue to vice. Rational agents can have any (consistent) preferences, and are rational if and only if their choices maximise their expected utility accordingly. There is no further question of the rationality of their ends.
>
> (Hollis 1994: 118)

To make judgements about the ends which an individual chooses is to consider the morality of an individual's actions and this is beyond the scope of Rational Choice theory. This should not be taken as suggesting, of course, that society has no interest in whether an individual chooses 'virtue' over 'vice'. Clearly, as we have discussed in earlier chapters, society will rationally prefer some of the individual's choices over others.

An individual might be motivated by egoism or by altruism, but, irrespective of his particular preferences, Rational Choice theory assumes self-interest will lead the individual to pursue them consistently. Hollis says of the altruist and the egoist that:

> Both are moved to seek whatever rewards are important to them. If the martyr's faith is important enough to him, he will go to the stake for it; and the theory of rational choice is set no problem in assigning his utilities accordingly.
>
> (Hollis 1994: 62)

The point then is that although different individuals have different preferences they all have the same underlying disposition which is to pursue these according to their self-interest.

> In this sense saints are as self-interested as sinners and the theory of Rational Choice is not committed to any view about how saintly or sinful we are.
>
> (Hollis 1994: 118)

Conflicts between rationality at the individual and group level

At the heart of Rational Choice theory is the instrumentally rational individual who pursues their own self-interest. If Rational Choice theory is to form the basis of a successful social theory, its claim that everything in the social world can be explained as the sum of instrumentally rational action must be justified. However, when we consider complex social institutions this claim starts to look vulnerable.

If we assume that individuals have a mutual interest in coordinating their rational choices so as to avoid conflict Game Theory suggests a consensual social contract can explain the existence of social institutions.

> Since there is no conflict of interest, it would be odd if rational agents failed to find mutually beneficial solutions, . . . Superficially at any rate, this thought offers a simple key to the existence of a society where 'every agent is actuated solely by self-interest'. Provided that individual interests are mutually served, it is not surprising that individuals form associations. There is no puzzle about the emergence of a society which improves on the state of nature for everyone. Furthermore, conventions which benefit everyone need no enforcing among rational agents.
>
> (Hollis 1994: 123)

The situation just described mirrors Rousseau's (1968) consensual social contract. However, interests often conflict. Where there is a pure conflict of interest then there may be no solution; but what happens where interests overlap?

Hobbes (1943) suggested that each individual tries to advance their own interests at the expense of everyone else's. But, if everyone does this, a perpetual state of war is the result and man's life is 'solitary, poor, nasty, brutish and short'. Hobbes (1943) introduced the social contract to remedy this situation. Individuals place themselves voluntarily under an all-powerful, self-perpetuating sovereign: the Leviathan. This, then, is a social contract premised on conflict. However, this view of the world doesn't seem to fit particularly well with our experience of society. Do we really only cooperate out of fear of reprisal from the Leviathan? The solution to such conflicts is to be found in the social institutions, norms and moral obligations which individuals are unable to establish due to their lack of cooperation. It seems that cooperation sometimes requires the prior existence of social norms or moral obligations, but the traditional model of Rational Choice theory is unable to show why such norms and obligations would exist in the first place (Hollis 1994). This echoes the finding of Arrow (1951) whose 'Impossibility Theorem' shows there is no method for constructing societal preferences out of arbitrary individual preferences. Thus social norms are required to be imposed from outside of the market.

Conflicts between rationality over different time horizons

There is a further tension between rationality of choice and outcome; that which arises from the reconciliation of the pursuit of preferences on long-term or overall scale (i.e. the outcome of a series of decisions), or on a short-term marginal scale. We have seen in Chapter Two, economists prefer to see all decisions as being taken 'at the margin' – which is to say, each decision is approached as follows: the decision-maker in essence asks him/herself, 'Given the situation I am currently in, with the knowledge currently available, will I choose "A" or "B"?' This might make sense when considering whether to expand or contract production; it makes less sense when applied universally.

Consider, as an example, the decision whether or not to go to the gym, which, let us suppose, our friend Moriarty is making. Although it is generally regarded as beneficial to exercise from three to five times a week (see Haskell *et al.* 2007), by its very nature the advice implies Moriarty need not go today. The benefit gained by one single trip to the gym is negligible and accrues in the future; the cost is immediate and must be accrued in the present. Therefore there is no compelling reason to go today. Conversely, suppose Moriarty enjoys a smoke now and then; the damage done by one single cigarette is very low – the costs of smoking are borne in the future, the enjoyment arises now. Moriarty might as well leave the gym for today, have a smoke and kick-back.

However, every day Moriarty is faced with the same marginal decision and, looked at from a marginal point of view, he will always reach the same conclusion. In effect, Moriarty will never go to the gym; rather, he will smoke himself to death. Moriarty might not be happy with that overall decision, he might not even realise he has made that decision; a decision about his lifetime pattern of behaviour has been taken all unawares.

Public goods and meta-preferences

One way to address the two problems we have identified with Rational Choice is through the construction of meta-preferences.

The traditional version of Rational Choice theory is contested by Sen (1977) in 'Rational Fools: A Critique of the Behavioral Foundations of Economic Theory'. Sen caricatures the rational choices made by the un-constrained utility maximiser thus:

> The purely economic man is indeed close to being a social moron. Economic theory has been much preoccupied with this rational fool decked in the glory of his one all-purpose preference ordering. To make room for the different concepts related to his behavior we need a more elaborate structure.
>
> (Sen 1977: 336)

Sen argues that, while the traditional model of Rational Choice theory works fairly well when analysing consumer behaviour where consumption is confined to private goods that only one person can consume, the theory starts to break down when we consider public goods (for example, roads or parks) which more than one person can enjoy. The issue is that the traditional Rational Choice model struggles to explain how a society of 'egotistic' individuals would successfully come together to create and maintain public goods. Sen illustrates this with an imagined conversation between two people who always seek to maximise their gain in every decision they make. Cooperation soon breaks down and both individuals are the worse off:

> 'Where is the railway station?' he asks me. 'There', I say, pointing at the post office, 'and would you please post this letter for me on the way?' 'Yes,' he says, determined to open the envelope and check whether it contains something valuable . . .
>
> (Sen 1977: 329)

As discussed above, it seems that for public goods to be created and maintained we need something more than individuals who maximise their personal gains in every decision; we need norms and rules. This suggests that individuals may make decisions which go against their short-term interests. In other words, agents voluntarily limit their range of actions. The drawback of the traditional version of Rational Choice described above is that it precludes the concept that an individual might wish to improve their preference set. Under the simple rationality approach the (commonly heard around New Year) statement 'I wish I didn't smoke so much' has no meaning; such individuals have indicated there are activities or actions they would prefer not to prefer. Such a concept is essentially nonsense in the simple rationality framework.

Building on Harsanyi's (1955) discussion of 'ethical preferences' and 'subjective preferences', Sen distinguishes between what a rational individual would prefer to prefer, and what they do prefer. Sen frames such a seeming paradox as follows: in any given situation individuals rationally choose what is best for them on the basis of ranking all possible actions by their expected return. However, Sen suggests individuals go beyond this and rank all their possible rankings. This ranking of preference sets is made on the basis of what Sen calls a meta-preference. So, let us return to our friend Moriarty who has yet to go to the gym. In order to make a fully rational decision, Moriarty might form what Sen (1977) would term a 'commitment' to being a particular kind of person – a person who goes to the gym. Suppose he decides he will commit to being such a person; he then makes the constrained rational decision, 'Given that I am going to go to the gym, when is the best day/time?'

Once it is recognised that rational individuals may order their preference sets rationally, a statement such as, 'I wish I could give up cigarettes altogether, but, given that I am a smoker, I prefer Brand X', does not indicate an irrational individual. Just because an individual would prefer a certain set of tastes, it does not mean they have those tastes.

Sen discusses the conflict between the desired meta-preference ranking and the actual preference adopted in the context of akrasia, aka weakness of will. If an individual, despite their meta-preference ranking, acts (rationally) according a sub-optimal set of preferences, that does not make them irrational, it merely means they lacked the means or power to move to the preferred set. This is no more an action of irrationality than stating 'I would prefer to choose from the menu at a restaurant than from what is in the fridge. However, given my finances, I will choose from what is available in the fridge'. However, the individual may take steps to modify their preference set to fit in with their meta-preferences (for example, those who wish they were not smokers at all may address their akrasia through, let's say, nicotine patches, while I might save sufficient cash to go out to the restaurant). It should be noted the theory of meta-preferences does not necessarily mean everyone will choose the same 'commitment'.

The limits of meta-preferences

As discussed above economists prefer to see all decisions as being taken 'at the margin'. A second reason why marginal decision theory might undermine rationality is because however rational is the meta-ranking, the fact that it is required at all, means it is at odds (to some extent) with marginal preference rankings. For example, having decided at the start of the week he is indeed going to go to the gym three times – and decided that, conditional on going three times a week, Tuesday, Thursday and Saturday are the best days – Moriarty must abide by this latter decision. Notwithstanding when it is time to go to the gym on Tuesday, it still makes sense at the marginal level not to go.

Thus a decision, once rationally taken, becomes re-opened to negotiation, *even if the surrounding circumstances remain unchanged and are exactly as expected*. If Moriarty decides to overturn his earlier decision, i.e. decides that, after all, he will *not* go to the gym on Tuesday despite the fact that he knows he is being irrational at a meta-ranking level, he might reproach himself for weakness of will.

Just as different agents have different preferences and meta-preferences, so we might assume they will exhibit different levels of akrasia as part of their human capital. The combination of these three makes the theory of revealed preferences impossible to realise.

Suppose we observe that Moriarty does not go to the gym, the following are observationally equivalent: Moriarty has rationally decided (at a meta-preference level) he is not the kind of person to go to the gym; Moriarty would like to be the kind of person who goes to the gym, but lacks the will-power to realise that decision; Moriarty does not even realise it is possible to make a decision over what kind of person he is (gym-goer or not), and every day decides not to go on a marginal basis. Although the outcome is the same in each case, the underlying preference sets differ.

In order fully to be rational, Moriarty must recognise that a meta-ranking of preferences is required (a decision which type of individual he wishes to be), and have enough will-power to over-ride short-run marginal preferences when they are counter to his overall meta-preference ranking. There are some important implications here for criminal behaviour.

In the context of criminological behaviour, the apparently 'irrational' nature of prisoners has been well documented. For example, Marris (2000: 26), writing of convicted and imprisoned criminals, notes:

> There was a strong impression that they themselves felt their own behaviour was, in the long run, 'irrational', and conflicted with their own interests. Rather the problem seemed to be that like an addict, they suffered inability to resist short-run temptation.
>
> (Marris 2000: 26)

It is, however, not just the inability to overcome short-term temptation which leads to rationally inexplicable decisions, it is the fact that often important decisions are made without individuals being aware of them, merely resulting from ill-thought-out short-term reasoning. Prison psychologist Theodore Dalrymple (writing in irony) wonders at the lack of responsibility accepted by some of his patients. Dalrymple (1994) captures the absence of rationality, or at least caricatures it, thus:

> The knife went in – unguided by human hand, apparently. That the long-hated victims were sought out, and the knives carried to the scene of the crimes, was as nothing compared with the willpower possessed by the inanimate knives themselves, which determined the unfortunate outcome.[6]

Thaler and Shefrin (1981) model this paradox as a conflict situation between two 'selfs': one a myopic 'doer', the other a 'planner'. Each wants to maximise their respective utilities; however, the 'doer' is the self who chooses the actions ultimately carried out. This idea was suggested by Adam Smith (see Ashraf *et al.* 2005) who discusses the rivalry between the 'passions' and the 'impartial spectator'.

According to Thaler and Shefrin, one way to resolve this conflict of interests is through the application of principal–agent considerations. In this framework, the agent is the doer, and the principal is the planner. For example, the planner may schedule tight deadlines to motivate the doer to work, or the planner might directly alter the doer's preference set, perhaps by scheduling gym sessions with a colleague. Also, the planner may keep track of the doer by (for example) creating a checklist of tasks which must be accomplished. Thus, although there is a seeming conflict between the two levels of rationality, there are rational approaches which might resolve this. In sum, Thaler and Shefrin argue it is entirely rational for an individual to place constraints on their own behaviour.

Satisficing vs optimising

The fully rational individual, it is postulated, makes use of all available information in reaching the decision which will optimise their objective. However, in practice, this behaviour is not observed. Often not all information is available, which does not in itself pose a problem to strict rationality. What is more difficult is that some information may be available, and be known to be available, but be too costly (in time or resources) to acquire. In the interests of efficiency, for example, we do not research the relative benefits of types of chocolate bars so assiduously as we do the relative merits of cars or mortgages. The reason is because the savings to be made from accessing more information are less than the costs of acquiring the information. Applying the marginal theory much-loved of economists (see Chapter Two), we see extra information will be sought if the expected benefits of the information outweigh the costs of its access. Thus individuals do not fully maximise their behaviour, they choose actions that 'satisfice' (see Simon 1956). Satisficing offers a solution to the problem of imperfect information because whereas a maximiser only succeeds if he arrives at the correct solution, a 'satisficer' is content with a good enough one (Hollis 1987).

This, of course, leads to the further question, as noted by Hargreaves Heap *et al.* (1992). If the individual will acquire information up to the point at which the marginal benefit of additional information (in terms of additional utility) exactly matches the marginal cost of acquiring the information (in terms of utility forgone in other activities which might have been pursued), how is the individual to know what marginal benefits are to be had without knowing all the information? 'Satisficing' allows the individual to overcome this problem by using rules of thumb to guide their action. If the concept of instrumental rationality is to be preserved, such procedures must amount to nothing more than short-cut devices for decision-making which economise on the use of the brain's limited computational capacity. Individuals will still be motivated by the desire to satisfy their objectives but their rationality has become 'bounded' because they are not fully informed (Hargreaves Heap *et al.* 1992: 17–18). If it is conceived too broadly, bounded (or procedural) rationality can undermine the individualism inherent in Rational Choice theory by suggesting that that action is ultimately rule bound and inextricably linked to its social context. This would undermine the fundamental individualism of Rational Choice theory (ibid.: 18).

Rational Choice theory in criminology

At the heart of the criminological variant of Rational Choice theory is the image of the reasoning offender. The perspective is premised upon the assumption that offenders seek to benefit themselves by their behaviour and that this involves making decisions and choices. These thought processes will exhibit a degree of rationality. The claim is that there is a rational component present in all offences. Therefore, Rational Choice theory emphasises the importance of opportunity (Gilling 1997). Potential offenders make a rational choice whether or not to offend. This decision is made by weighing up the relative costs and benefits of a whole range of situational factors including the presence or absence of surveillance and physical security. The notion of a 'reasoning' offender implies that the offender is essentially non-pathological and commonplace and that actions that are criminal are, in essence, no different from any other, non-criminal acts (Cornish and Clarke 1986a).

Criminology's response to Becker (1968)

Becker (1968) and Ehrlich (1973) apply the Rational Choice theory beloved of economists to crime. Thus, they propose the potential offender calculates the legitimate opportunities of earning income with illegitimate opportunities and chooses the activity that offers the best return. However, while Becker's thesis has been influential in criminology, from a criminological perspective:

> these early [economic] theories have been accused of implying too high a degree of rationality by comparing criminal choices too closely with marketplace decisions.
>
> (Hopkins Burke 2005: 44)

Although the version of Rational Choice theory outlined by Cornish and Clarke is based on economic theories of crime, Clarke makes it clear, that as criminological Rational Choice theory has developed, it has sought to avoid criticisms made of those theories which he identifies as follows:

> (i) that under economic models the rewards of crime are treated mainly in material terms . . . while mostly ignoring rewards that cannot easily be translated into cash equivalents; (ii) that economists have not been sensitive to the great variety of behaviours falling under the general label of crime, with their variety of costs and benefits, and instead have tended to lump them together as a single variable in their equations; (iii) that the formal mathematical modelling of criminal choices by economists (sic) often demands data that

are unavailable or can only be pressed into service by making unrealistic assumptions about what they represent; and, finally, (iv) that the economist's image of the self-maximising decision maker, carefully calculating his or her advantage, does not fit the opportunistic and reckless nature of much crime.

(Clarke 1995: 97–8)

In an attempt to address these criticisms, Cornish and Clarke (1986a and b; Clarke 1995) have outlined a version of Rational Choice theory which they argue is more attuned to criminological usage and, in particular, explaining crime control. This version of the theory emphasises the importance of complex or 'fluid' decision-making (Crawford 1998: 73), of separating criminal involvement from criminal events, of limited rationality and of different decision processes for different events. We discuss each of these issues in more detail below.

Complex decision-making

In criminological Rational Choice theory, relationships between concepts are expressed, not in mathematical terms, but through the use of 'decision diagrams' (Clarke 1995: 98). Thus, Cornish and Clarke (1986b) outline a series of decision diagrams to show an 'initial involvement model', an 'event model', a 'continuing involvement model' and a 'desistance model' (Cornish and Clarke 1986b: 10–14). The emphasis in these models is on showing the complexity of the decisions offenders make, as well as the extended and repeated nature of these decisions. This is an important distinction from Rational Choice theory in economics, which generally (but not always, see discussion below) considers individuals' decisions to be taken at the marginal (i.e. next event) level. Thus the decision of whether to become involved in crime at all is not one generally addressable through standard utility modelling.

For Cornish and Clarke (1986b: 9) the decision to become initially involved is broken down into 'two important decision points': 'readiness' and the decision actually to commit the crime. At each of these decision points the offender (in Cornish and Clarke's (1986b) example, a domestic burglar) contemplates crime as a solution to their needs, having evaluated other ways of satisfying these and under the influence of a range of variables including their previous learning experience, psychological, familial and socio-demographic background factors, and chance events (Cornish and Clarke 1986b). In other words, the individual first considers rationally whether burglary is a possibility in the abstract; and, having decided it is, proceeds to consider rationally which particular crimes to commit.

The choice of criminal involvement

The decision diagrams perspective seeks to make a distinction between criminal involvement (criminality), the criminal event and desistance (Cornish and Clarke 1986b).

Criminal involvement refers to the processes through which individuals choose to become initially involved in particular forms of crime, to continue, and to desist. The decision processes at each of these stages are influenced by a different set of factors and need to be separately modelled.

(Clarke 1995: 98)

Thus, Rational Choice theory sets out to explain both involvement and the event and thus to explain both crime and criminality (or disposition) (Gilling 1997: 60), both of which are modelled in terms of the rational decisions involved. This accords with Sen's (1977) discussion of preferences and meta-preferences (see above). In Sen's terms, the individual has made a 'commitment' to criminality, or chosen at a meta-preference level it will be the preference structure of the criminal which will be used for subsequent rational decisions.

When explaining criminal involvement (criminality), Rational Choice theory emphasises the importance of choice (Gilling 1997). The claim is that rationality can explain the processes through which individuals choose to become initially involved in particular forms of crime. According to Rational Choice theory these decision processes tend to be multistage and extend over substantial periods of time, drawing upon a wide range of information, not all of which is directly related to the crime eventually committed (Cornish and Clarke 1986a). Clarke distinguishes involvement decisions from event decisions thus:

Involvement decisions are characteristically multistage and extend over substantial periods of time. Event decisions, by contrast, are frequently shorter processes, using more circumscribed information largely relating to immediate circumstances and situations.

(Clarke 1995: 98)

The claim to be able to explain criminality in terms of rationality is supported by empirical evidence from investigations into criminal careers. For instance, Bennett's (1986) article 'A Decision-Making Approach to Opioid Addiction' argues that the concept of an individual criminal career explained in terms of the individual's rational choices can be applied to heroin addiction. This emphasis on choice draws attention to the strongly individualistic nature of Rational Choice theory.

Cornish and Clarke's extension of criminological Rational Choice theory to a consideration of criminality as well as crime events does not suggest that the basic model of instrumental rationality underpinning the theory is in need of revision. It simply suggests that the process of mapping out rational choices in order to understand criminal events is a more complex business than the earlier versions of Rational Choice theory suggested. Consider, for example, Cornish and Clarke's description of 'readiness', one of the decision points in the offender's initial involvement in residential burglary:

'Readiness' . . . implies that the individual has actually contemplated this form of crime as a solution to his needs, and has decided that under the right

circumstances he would commit the offence in question. In reaching this decision, he will have evaluated other ways of satisfying his needs and this evaluation will naturally be influenced by his previous learning experience – his
moral code, his view of the kind of person he is, his personal and vicarious
experience of crime, and the degree to which he can plan and exercise fore-
sight. These variables are in turn related to various historical and contemporaneous background factors – psychological, familial and socio-demographic
. . . In a decision-making context, however, these background influences are
less directly criminogenic; instead they have an orienting function – exposing
people to particular problems and particular opportunities and leading them
to perceive and evaluate these in particular (criminal) ways.

(Cornish and Clarke 1986b: 9)

In this passage the emphasis is on the individual reaching a *solution* based on an
evaluation of a range of factors. The individual is portrayed as being involved in
a *decision-making* process. Although some concessions are made to the bounded
nature of rationality and the importance of the individual's perception in evaluating the costs and benefits, the emphasis is still very much on an instrumentally
rational individual pursuing their chosen ends (i.e. satisfying their needs) using the
most rational means available to them.

Different decision processes for different offences

Having decided to become involved in crime, the individual must consider, on a
marginal basis, which particular activities will lead to the greatest expected return.
This modified version of Rational Choice theory has a 'crime-specific' focus.
Clarke notes that:

the decision processes involved in the commission of a particular crime
(i.e., the criminal event) are dependent on their own special categories of
information.

(Clarke 1995: 98)

This aspect of the theory's development is partly a response to empirical information showing that offenders' decision-making processes are markedly different for
different types of crime (Clarke 1995). Some crimes, for example drug running,
require careful planning; others, for example shop-lifting, may require limited
planning or may be spontaneous actions taken in response to circumstantial factors. Thus, different crimes meet different needs and take place in different contexts, meaning that the offender's decision-making process will vary from offence
to offence. However, although distinctions must be made between the decision-
making process in different types of offence, it is not being suggested the decisions
made are anything other than the instrumentally rational decisions of individuals.
In other words, the emphasis on crime-specific explanations is designed to show
the adaptability of Rational Choice theory to a range of different events, not to
challenge the applicability of the theory to certain types of crime.

Limited rationality

In the version of Rational Choice theory which is influential in criminology, the 'limited' nature of the rationality in decision-making is recognised (Clarke 1995: 98). Clarke (1995) and Cornish and Clarke (1986b) note two particular criticisms of economic versions of Rational Choice theory are: the economist's image of the self-maximising decision-maker does not fit the opportunistic and reckless nature of much crime; and the formal mathematical model makes unrealistic demands on the data available for making decisions.[7] To counter these criticisms, advocates of criminological Rational Choice theory point to the 'limited' nature of rational thought processes whereby decisions and choices are constrained by 'limits of time and ability and the availability of relevant information' (Clarke 1995). This view of 'limited' rationality is analogous to mainstream Rational Choice theory's reliance on satisficing[8] as opposed to maximising.

Advocates of the theory have also suggested that another means of overcoming the problem of imperfect information is to explain some choices as arising from a 'standing decision' (Gilling 1997: 63). When making a 'standing decision' the individual does not rationally calculate the expected utility of each course of action but instead simply follows a 'rule of thumb'. This is a rule which is followed in certain situations to avoid the costs of acquiring all the information that would enable the calculation of the optimal course of action to be made (Hargreaves Heap *et al.* 1992). For example, a burglar might make a standing decision not to attempt to force entry into houses which have alarm boxes on display. From a rational point, it is acknowledged that some of the boxes may be dummies; however, to acquire the extra information to determine which are dummy alarm boxes and which are not might prove costly and hence the decision is taken simply to avoid all houses with alarm boxes.

Criticisms of criminological Rational Choice theory

Many key criticisms of criminological Rational Choice theory are the same as those of the wider sociological variant of the theory. Throughout their explanation of Rational Choice theory and its applications to criminology and in particular crime control, Cornish and Clarke emphasise the need for a theory that 'gives a central role to the rational and evaluative components of offender behaviour' (Cornish and Clarke 1986b: 5). However, the question is whether the criminological version of Rational Choice theory can overcome successfully the criticisms which have been made of Rational Choice theory in general. As we have seen, these include the difficulty that the theory has in explaining the development and maintenance of social structures and of reconciling shorter- and longer-term rationality. Crawford concludes his assessment of this criminological version of Rational Choice theory (referred to as the 'limited rationality' model) thus:

> This model of 'limited rationality' offers a more complex, sophisticated and specific means of analysing measures to address proximal circumstances.

> *However, its fundamental organising framework remains trapped in the ana-*
> *lytic embrace of the abstract rational choice actor*, regardless of how limited
> or fluid this should be interpreted.
>
> (Crawford 1998: 74, emphasis added)

The new criminologies of everyday life

Rational Choice theory, with its focus on the rational decisions of the individual,
works principally at the micro-level and yet it also claims to be able to explain
both crime and criminality. This has led to criticism of the theory:

> Given its explanatory ambition to unite crime and criminality, event and
> involvement, or situation and disposition, it is not surprising that rational
> choice theory has come under attack from a number of sources, and the sense
> of much of the criticism is that the focus on both areas means that neither is
> covered entirely adequately.
>
> (Gilling 1997: 64)

Proponents of the Rational Choice theory have answered this type of criticism
in two ways. First they have emphasised the importance of explaining criminal
involvement, the nature of limited rationality and the importance of distinguishing
between different decision processes for different offences. These arguments have
been explained in the section above. Second, they have attempted to synthesise
Rational Choice theory with elements of environmental criminology, Lifestyle
theory, and in particular with Routine Activity theory. Collectively these have
been referred to by Garland (1996 and 2001) as the new criminologies of everyday life.

Routine Activity theory

One of the chief proponents of Routine Activity theory is Felson who says of
Routine Activity theorists that they:

> focus on crime incidents rather than on offenders themselves, examining how
> these incidents originate in the routine activities of everyday life. One of the
> most important features of such activities is their contribution to informal
> social control, a quiet and natural method by which people prevent crime in
> the course of daily life.
>
> (Felson 1994: xii)

Routine Activity theory starts with the observation that the crime rate has
increased alongside improvements in social and economic conditions. This is a
somewhat paradoxical result, as it is generally thought criminality may be encour-
aged by poverty and social strain (see Chapter Five). Routine Activity theory
explains the sharp rises in crime by arguing that routine activities have changed

along with social and economic conditions. These changes in routine activities have affected the relationship between the three necessary conditions of crime: a suitable target; a motivated offender; and the absence of a capable guardian. For instance, an increasing proportion of women have joined the workforce and leisure activities are more likely to take place outside the home. These two effects reduce the supply of capable guardians. At the same time increasing consumerism has led to a rise in suitable targets in the form of cars and electronic goods – the latter becoming progressively smaller, and more easily portable, and with a higher value to weight ratio (Felson 1994; Gilling 1997).

Routine Activity theory concentrates principally on the criminal event rather than the offender, although in later elaborations Felson has placed more emphasis on the offender and relied on Control Theory to explain the offender's disposition (Felson 1994; Gilling 1997). Thus, he has added the concept of the 'handler' to the three necessary conditions of crime (Felson 1986). A handler is someone capable of exercising informal social control in the sense of Hirschi (1969).

Lifestyle theory

Lifestyle theory is closely related to Routine Activity theory. It suggests that the differential risks of victimisation are partly a function of differential exposure to motivated offenders. One of its main proponents is Hindelang who has undertaken both empirical and theoretical work to demonstrate the importance of victim lifestyle on offending (Hindelang *et al.* 1978). Clarke makes the point that:

> This exposure varies not only with the sociodemographic characteristics of the victim (age, race, place of residence, etc.) but also with the victim's lifestyle. A person's work and leisure activities that increase exposure to potential offenders (such as alcohol consumption in public places or late-night use of public transport) increase the risks of victimisation.
>
> (Clarke 1995: 100–1)

The implication of this insight is that, by modifying patterns of activity, risks of victimisation might be modified (Clarke 1995).

Pease (1994) compares Lifestyle theory with Rational Choice and notes that Lifestyle theory highlights the importance of role expectations and structural constraints and thus incorporates routine daily activities by emphasising that personal victimisation is influenced by the individuals with whom the victim comes into contact (Pease 1994). He goes on to argue that 'Lifestyle theory differs from routine activities theory more in emphasis than in substance' (ibid.: 664). In support of this assertion he argues that, though the concept of the capable guardian is more prominent in Rational Choice theory – and Lifestyle theory has tended to be tested using cross-sectional data while Routine Activity theory is tested using longitudinal data – 'the theories are not clearly distinguishable in the predictions which they make' (ibid.). He is not alone in taking this view and attempts have been made to synthesise Rational Choice theory, Routine Activity theory and Lifestyle theory.

Rational Choice theory, policy and practice

Traditionally, criminological and sociological theorising about crime has had relatively little impact on criminal justice policy and practice. Downes and Rock (1995) suggest a number of reasons for a division of labour between criminologists and sociologists on the one hand and crime prevention practitioners on the other. These include the role of academics in which teaching and research take priority, problems with translating social theories into social policy and, most importantly, the salience of a theory for policy-makers. By 'salience' they mean the factors important to policy-makers such as: the scope of the proposals for action; the resources required; the extent to which significant interests are engaged; the likely ratio of cost–benefits; and the correspondence between the theory and policy-makers' timetables and rhetoric.

However, Rational Choice theory and related theories have arguably been more influential than many other criminological theories. In this section we consider two manifestations of the influence of Rational Choice theory: within situational crime prevention and within the 'culture of control'.

Situational crime prevention

Situational crime prevention draws its theoretical justification from Rational Choice theory which emphasises the importance of choice in criminal involvement or criminality. However, according to this theory, opportunity is central to understanding the potential criminal's decision-making process at each specific criminal event. Situational crime prevention therefore focuses on the reduction of opportunities to commit crime. Clarke (2005) outlines a number of opportunity-reduction techniques that have been used in situational prevention. The techniques are divided into five groups: increasing effort; increasing the risks; reducing the rewards; reducing provocations; and removing excuses.

Situational crime prevention, utilising one of these five preventative strategies, has become an influential component of local and national strategies for reducing crime on both sides of the Atlantic. We discuss such approaches in more detail in Chapter Eight on 'Crime reduction'.

The culture of control

In an influential series of papers and books Garland (see for instance Garland 1996 and 2001) outlines the effect of what he refers to as 'the new criminologies of everyday life' upon the delivery of crime control activities.[9] The new criminologies of everyday life consist of Rational Choice theory, the associated Routine Activity theory, crime as opportunity and situational crime prevention. Garland notes the extent to which these theories have been taken up by policy makers to reorient government action and create new techniques for acting upon the problem of crime. However, not only have they led to new types of strategies for managing crime, they have also influenced the way in which crime management strategies are delivered. Garland argues that:

> In particular, it is significant that many programmes of practical action which flow from these theories are addressed not to state agencies such as the police, the courts and the prisons, but beyond the state apparatus, to the organizations, institutions and individuals of society. The theories take it for granted that the state has limited capacity, and they look to the everyday world to bring about change.
>
> (Garland 1996: 451)

This move from state responsibility for crime towards individual and private sector responsibility would seem to be logical, following the adoption of Rational Choice theory with its strongly individualistic, market-oriented flavour. Thus, while potential offenders calculate the costs and benefits of committing crime, weighing up the situational factors and assessing the opportunities, so potential victims may affect those cost–benefit calculations by altering situations and changing their routine activities, etc. Crime prevention becomes the responsibility of individual victims, rather than the responsibility of the collective state (Crawford 1997; Garland 1996).

Garland refers to this new mode of thinking in crime management as the 'responsibilization strategy':

> [The responsibilization strategy] involves central government seeking to activate action on the part of non-state agencies and organizations. This is the essence of the new crime prevention approach developed by the UK government in the last 10 years. . . . Its primary concern is to devolve responsibility for crime prevention on to agencies, organizations and individuals which are quite outside the state and to persuade them to act appropriately.
>
> (Garland 1996: 452)

The logic of a strongly individualistic, market-oriented theory such as Rational Choice theory is to stress the role of the individual and the private sector in managing crime. However, it is too simplistic to suggest that the 'responsibilization strategy' has led to a simple off-loading of state functions (Garland 1996). Nor has it amounted simply to the privatisation or 'hiving-off' of crime control:

> The state does not diminish or become a nightwatchman. On the contrary, it retains all its traditional functions – the state agencies have actually increased their size and output during the same period – and, in addition, takes on a new set of co-ordinating and activating roles, which, in time, develop into new structures of support, funding, information exchange or co-operation. Where it works . . . the responsibilization strategy leaves the centralized state

machine more powerful than before, with an extended capacity for action and influence. At the same time, however, this strategy serves to erode the notion of the state as the public's representative and primary protector.

(Garland 1996: 454)

How can the seeming contradiction between the strong individualism implied by Rational Choice theory and found in the 'responsibilization strategy' be reconciled with the simultaneous centralisation of state functions that has occurred in practice? The best answer seems to be that the shift in responsibility that has been witnessed is only partially driven by the application of 'the new criminologies of everyday life'. Other factors have also been important. First, it has been suggested that a free-market economy requires a powerful state to maintain law and order (King 1992). Second, the dominant political ideology of recent decades – 'Thatcherism' – sought to blend New Right neo-liberalist thinking with a strong moral agenda more reminiscent of traditional Conservatism and a political instinct for maintaining a strong centralised state (Giddens 1998). Arguably this trend has been continued by New Labour. Third, there is some evidence that, over recent decades, central government has only limited trust in local government. Commenting on the Conservative administration of the 1980s and 1990s Gilling (1997) detects a contradiction in government policy with regard to the role of local government within the multi-agency approach. It could be argued that local government should play a major role in multi-agency partnerships and yet this has not been the case.

The emphasis has been upon soliciting greater responsibility for, and interest in, crime prevention, while simultaneously seeking to control the terms of this. This is because while local authorities are accepted as necessary, the Home Office's various promotional activities demonstrate, they are not well trusted.

(Gilling 1997: 133)

Beyond Rational Choice theory: behavioural economics

We have discussed the situation where the application of rationality is not as straightforward as it would at first appear. However, perhaps the application of rationality itself is limited. Certainly there is evidence (see Plous 1993 and references therein) that many individuals' life decisions are made on a basis of a mix of heuristics, rational and psychological factors, rather than a background of pure rationality.

Emotions

Consider, for example, the ways agents react to transitory factors, e.g. emotion, *even when it is known that they are transitory*. Like Mr Spock, rationalists have a problem with understanding the basic human experience of emotion. Some emotions are more rational than others it would seem and Loewenstein (2000) argues economists prefer to consider anticipated emotions, that is, emotions not experienced at the time of making the decision but which are expected to result from it: satisfaction, disappointment, regret, enjoyment. Conversely, psychologists consider more immediate emotions, so-called 'visceral factors'. Loewenstein groups these into: negative emotions (e.g., anger, fear); drive states (e.g., hunger, thirst, sexual desire); and feeling states (e.g., pain), and argues that these tend to influence decisions away from what might be expected from the rational calculation of long-term costs and benefits.[10] This is a problem related to, but distinct from, the conflict between short-term and long-term preferences discussed above. Visceral factors may lead to an individual decision which is irrational on all levels. Loewenstein contends such factors are 'excessively' effectual and operate with no, or virtually no, higher level cognition.

As visceral factors are transitory, they may vary (for example) according to whether the decision-maker has a cold, whether they had a good sleep last night or were up all night at a party or whether their football team has won recently. The random nature of visceral factors is such that even rational individuals find it difficult to condition on these. Notwithstanding, life-changing decisions are made on the basis of these transitory emotions. Loewenstein suggests the difference in individuals' attitudes to risk, depending on whether they stand to gain or lose, arises from just such visceral factors, as does their attitude to bargaining and intertemporal choices. For example, an angry negotiator may become so intent on causing pain to the other party, they may undermine their own long-term preferences.

However, rationalists need not turn off the lights on the way out. While we may not be able fully to account for such factors, we may observe how their strength is accentuated or diminished as a result of circumstantial and rational factors. Loewenstein argues 'Visceral factors depend in predictable ways on the situations that people get into, and consciousness allows people to anticipate these effects and exploit them strategically'. Whether or not individuals indeed have this 'consciousness' is an open question; those who do, Loewenstein argues, 'avoid temptations that could lead to shortsighted behaviour'.[11,12] In practice, however, agents are more likely to do such if they have formed a rational expectation of the strength of such temptations. Sadly, as Loewenstein concedes, there is evidence humans tend to underestimate the degree to which they are susceptible to such transitory factors (see, for example, Loewenstein 1996). As Bacon (1620: xlix) notes 'Numberless, in short, are the ways, and sometimes imperceptible, in which the affections color and infect the understanding.'

One of the implications of Loewenstein's argument is that it is visceral factors which explain the well-known observation that individuals may be both risk-takers and risk-averse depending on whether they stand to gain or lose. We may be risk-averse when it comes to potential losses (thus we insure our homes and contents) and risk-takers when it comes to potential gain (thus we buy lottery tickets). According to Adam Smith (as quoted in Ashraf *et al.* 2005), 'the chance of gain is by every man more or less over-valued, and the chance of loss is by most men under-valued, and by scarce any man, who is in tolerable health and spirits, valued more than it is worth'. Such seemingly irrational biases in expectations may give rise to seeming irrational choices.

Consider the following example of Tversky and Kahneman (1981):

Imagine that the USA is preparing for the outbreak of an unusual Asian disease, which is expected to kill 600 people. Two alternative programmes to combat the disease have been proposed. Assume that the exact scientific estimate of the consequences of the programmes are as follows:
- If **Programme A** is adopted, 200 people will be saved.
- If **Programme B** is adopted, there is ⅓ probability that 600 people will be saved, and ⅔ probability that no people will be saved.

Which of the two programmes would you favour?

When this was asked of 152 respondents, 72 per cent chose Programme A. Tversky and Kahneman note that this result is indicative of risk-averse behaviour. Although the expected number of people saved is the same for both programmes, the risk-averse will prefer to save some with certainty.

A second group of 155 respondents was given the same situation and the following choice:
- If **Programme C** is adopted, 400 people will die.
- If **Programme D** is adopted, there is ⅓ probability that nobody will die, and ⅔ probability that 600 people will die.

Which of the two programmes would you favour?

When the questions were phrased in this way, 78 per cent chose Programme D. Tversky and Kahneman note that this result is indicative of risk-taking behaviour. Although the expected number of people saved is the same for both programmes, it seems respondents shy away from condemning 400 to certain death when all might be saved.

All well and good, except (as you will have spotted) actually Programme A is equivalent to Programme C, and B is equivalent to D. Thus the decision is reversed depending on the way the choice is framed. This is a major challenge to rationality. Similar challenges to rationality arise from the 'standing decision' approach to rationality (see above). Because of the way in which such a default position operates – it exists so as to cut down on the number of fully rational decisions which must be taken – there is a tendency in individuals to bias their short-run decision-making towards the default.

Nudge

Sunstein and Thaler (2003) argue:

in many domains, people lack clear, stable, or well ordered preferences. What they choose is strongly influenced by details of the context in which they make their choice, for example default rules, framing effects (that is, the wording of possible options), and starting points. These contextual influences render the very meaning of the term 'preferences' unclear.

(Sunstein and Thaler 2003: 1161)

This approach, further developed in their book *Nudge: Improving Decisions about Health, Wealth, and Happiness* (Thaler and Sunstein 2008), argues human beings don't really like decisions (hardly surprising when even the simplest decisions may require extensive information gathering to ensure rationality). The essence of 'nudge' is that, although from the strictly rational point of view, it makes little difference whether individuals have to 'opt-in' or 'opt-out' of (let's say) a savings scheme, generally people are more likely to 'choose' whatever is offered as the default position, whether because of 'standing decisions' or social inertia. Thus, through adroit use of the way choices are framed, policy-makers can achieve their ends while still respecting the autonomy of the individual.

Consider, for example, the ongoing debate about organ donation.[13] From a purely rational point of view, there is no difference between: (i) assuming all a nation's citizens do not wish to donate their organs in the event of their death, but offering the choice to 'opt-in'; (ii) assuming all citizens would wish to donate organs after their death, but giving the opportunity to 'opt-out'; (iii) assuming neither, but forcing people to choose either to 'opt-in' or 'opt-out'. In his recent article in the *New York Times*, Richard Thaler (2009: unnumbered) notes 'In Germany, which uses an opt-in system, only 12 percent give their consent; in Austria, which uses opt-out, nearly everyone (99 percent) does.' The basic logic behind the principle of 'nudging' is that, wherever a choice is offered, the default should be that option which is likely to benefit society (or the individual) the most.[14] Whether the strength of a nudge has much to say on criminality, however, is an ongoing debate. According to *The Sunday Times* (2010) at least, 'against shamelessness and greed, nudge seems powerless'.[15]

Even the very information base of individuals – that which they might use to form their rational decisions – seems to be formed from subjective, potentially irrational preferences. It is a well-established fact of human nature that we believe we see objectively, but in fact what we understand is filtered through our perceptions (Bacon 1620; Rowe 2007). Thus no two human beings experience the world in the same way. Plous (1993: 18) suggests 'perception is affected not only by what people *expect* to see; it is also coloured by what they *want* to see' (emphasis added). As an example of this, Plous discusses the findings of Vallone *et al.* (1985) who consider the effect of background on students' perceptions of the media. Amongst other events, Vallone *et al.* consider the differences in attitudes of three self-categorised groups of students: 'pro-Israeli', 'pro-Arab' and 'neutral' to reports on the so-called Beirut Massacre of 1982.[16] Each group of students were shown the same series of news reports. In sum they found each of the pro-Israeli and pro-Arab groups felt the reports were generally biased against their point of view; the effect was stronger amongst those who felt themselves the more knowledgeable on the subject. The perceptions of the neutral group (unsurprisingly) were somewhere about the middle. In a related study Lord *et al*. (1979) consider whether students' pre-conceptions influence their view on how reliable is objective evidence on the efficacy of the death penalty. Students were self-selected on whether they supported or did not support capital punishment and asked to review a number of research papers. In general, students felt those papers which supported their own beliefs were the most robust. Indeed, Lord *et al*. note 'strongly entrenched beliefs can . . . survive the addition of nonsupportive evidence'.[17] This conclusion, to some extent, supports the 'standing decision' hypothesis, though a rationalist would argue that standing decisions may be modified in the presence of appropriate counter-information. In practice, Lord *et al*. (1984) suggest a strategy based on conscious consideration of the 'opposite' may reduce biases in decision-making.

Conclusion

We have looked at the attraction to social scientists of Rational Choice theory with its promise of making objective yet interpretive sense of human behaviour. In criminology a distinctive version of Rational Choice theory has been developed and this has become both an influential criminological theory as well as a factor in shaping recent criminal justice policy and practice.

However, we have also discussed some serious challenges to the theory. We have asked whether Rational Choice theory can really explain how social norms and institutions emerge; why instrumentally rational individuals would ever come together to create and sustain public goods. We have also seen how the concept of making decisions based on complete information is impossible to realise. Thus a simplistic view of rationality may not necessarily be observed in individuals' actions. Concepts such as meta-preferences and satisficing offer at least partial solutions to these challenges to the theory.

The distinctly criminological version of Rational Choice theory faces the same challenges and the sometimes chaotic nature of offenders' lives, their substance misuse and their focus on the here-and-now serve only to emphasise how difficult it is to develop a concept of rationality that is equally applicable to all forms of human behaviour. The solutions developed in criminology mirror, to some extent, the broader discussion of the limits of Rational Choice theory in the social sciences.

Thinking specifically about criminal behaviour we can also draw some useful conclusions for policy and practice. As we saw in earlier chapters, when thinking about crime, economists have tended to concentrate mainly on deterrence as a mechanism for changing offenders' behaviour. Deterrence is a long-term strategy, yet there is evidence from our analysis of rationality that short-term planning may be weak in potential criminals and established offenders. What are the most effective ways to make offenders and potential offenders aware that a meta-ranking of preferences is required (a decision about which type of individual the offender wishes to be), and ensure that they have enough will-power to over-ride short-run marginal preferences when they run counter to the offender's overall meta-preference ranking? Thaler and Shefrin's discussion of the principal–agent framework provides one useful set of ideas. In a criminal justice context a Planner might be a probation officer or perhaps a mentor or coach. Behavioural economics and the concept of 'nudge' provide other potential mechanisms whereby rationality is, at first sight, undermined as a model of human behaviour.

Should we therefore give up on Rational Choice theory? On balance, we think not. In each of the cases considered, the apparent lack of rationality has its root in the restricted model of rationality adopted. In most cases, the solution is to impose more rational analysis on the problem, not necessarily fully to grasp it, but at the least be sure our actions at the margin are likely to move us towards, not away from, the societal optimum.

5 The labour market, poverty and crime

Introduction

Drawing on rationality in complex decisions theory (see Chapter Four, in particular the discussion of Cornish and Clarke's (1986a) model of complex decision), we assume that individuals make choices over standing decisions, or commitment to a criminal lifestyle (Gilling 1997; Hargreaves Heap *et al.* 1992; Sen 1977). Conditional on this 'meta-preference', the individual goes on to consider particular actions on a rational basis. In this chapter we discuss the impact of poverty and labour market conditions on this constrained choice. Specifically, we consider the impact of the labour market and poverty on crime through an examination of two self-reinforcing individual choices: the decision to enter the market (i.e. the decision to engage in crime); and the decision over which particular crimes are most likely to improve personal utility.

The chapter starts by looking at how some of the more influential criminological theories have explained the relationship between the labour market, poverty and crime. Using these theories we discuss how prevailing economic conditions may lead an individual to choose a criminal lifestyle.

Having established the theoretical underpinnings of the relationship between the state of the economy and crime, we go on to consider whether there is statistical evidence to support the theory, and (if there is such evidence) to measure the strength of the influence. However, before doing so we look in detail at the concepts of 'employment' and 'unemployment'.

Poverty, economy and the decision to commit criminal acts

Most criminological theories have something to say either explicitly or implicitly about the relationship between the decision to engage in crime and economic factors such as poverty and unemployment. In this section we review some of the more influential criminological theories which have suggested such a relationship might exist between crime and economic conditions. A good overview is provided by Hale (2009), who, in turn, summarises and develops the work of Box (1987). Hale's overview forms the basis of this section in which we discuss the implications for the relationship between crime and economic conditions for some of the more influential criminological theories.

Anomie – the breakdown of social norms and values

There is a strong tradition within criminology which argues people would con-
form to prevailing norms and laws but for the stresses and contradictions in their
lives: so-called Strain Theory (Hale 2009). That is to say, the individual's initial
'standing decision' is to abide by the social contract but, for reasons beyond their
control, they are unable, or feel unable, to do so.

Durkheim

Durkheim's (1893) concept of anomie[1] – literally a state of normlessness –
describes a situation in society where rules are breaking down or are confused
and, as a result, people do not know what to expect of each other (Hale 2009). For
Durkheim, writing at the end of the nineteenth century, anomie arose during periods of rapid social change. In particular he describes the development of industrialised society where a high level of 'mechanical' solidarity that characterises
pre-industrial societies is superseded by 'organic' solidarity (although as Hopkins
Burke (2005) notes, no society is entirely mechanical or organic). Societies with
high levels of mechanical solidarity are characterised by group conformity and
individuals have common attitudes and beliefs. In industrial societies there is a
more developed division of labour and solidarity relies less on the maintenance of
uniformity between individuals and more on the management of diverse functions
of different social groups (Hopkins Burke 2005).

Crime can rise in modern industrial societies either because excessive individualism undermines social solidarity or because the likelihood of inefficient
regulation is greater during times of rapid modernisation (Hopkins Burke 2005).
However, Durkheim is not suggesting that change from an agrarian economy to
an industrial one leads to an inevitable breakdown of morality and rising crime.
As Hopkins Burke argues:

> For Durkheim, the division of labour is a progressive phenomenon; its appear-
> ance signals not the inevitable collapse of morality, but the emergence of a
> new content for the collective conscience. In societies dominated by mechan-
> ical solidarity the emphasis is on the obligation of the individual to society;
> with organic formations, the focus is increasingly on the obligation of society
> to the individual person. Now to give the maximum possible encouragement
> to individual rights does not mean that altruism . . . will disappear; on the con-
> trary, moral individualism is not unregulated self-interest by the imposition of
> a set of reciprocal obligations that binds together individuals . . .
>
> (Hopkins Burke 2005: 94)

This is a theory that does not just help us explain historical rises in crime. As Hale
(2009) notes, the decline in manufacturing industries and the rise in the service
sector which we have witnessed in industrialised countries at the end of the twentieth century has arguably produced similar effects.

Merton

Merton (1938), writing in the USA in the late 1930s after the Great Depression, adapted anomie as the basis of Strain Theory. According to Reiner (2007: 349) 'Merton's anomie theory is the most influential and cogent formulation of a political economy of crime outside the Marxist tradition.'

For Merton, strain is produced when there are unequal opportunities available for achieving the cultural goals through institutionalised means defined by the dominant culture (Hopkins Burke 2005). Cultural goals might include: material possessions; and symbols of status, accomplishment and esteem which established norms and values promote. The institutionalised means are the distribution of opportunities to achieve these goals in ways which are allowed under the social contract (Hopkins Burke 2005). Merton outlines five possible responses to strain, one of which (termed by Merton as an innovative response) might be crime. 'Innovators' (in Merton's sense) relatively overemphasise the goals of achievement over means (Hopkins Burke 2005). During an economic recession, when unemployment rises and inequality widens, more people are likely to experience the strain of lacking the opportunities to achieve culturally prescribed goals of success (Hale 2009). According to this argument, crime is likely to be a predominantly lower class phenomenon, since working class people will be most likely to lack the means of achieving cultural goals (ibid.).

However, Reiner (2007) emphasises that Merton's analysis of anomie is not a straightforward 'strain' theory because his analysis is only partly directed at explaining individual or sub-cultural deviance within a society. The theory also explains differences between societies and is 'a paradigm for a political economy of crime, suggesting links between a materialistic culture and overall problems of moral regulation' (Reiner 2007: 350).

Thus, Merton writing in the USA of the 1930s argues:

> A high frequency of deviate behaviour is not generated simply by 'lack of opportunity' or by this exaggerated pecuniary emphasis. A comparatively rigidified class structure, a feudalistic or caste order, may limit such opportunities far beyond the point which obtains in our society today. It is only when a system of cultural values extols, virtually above all else, certain common symbols of success for the population at large while its social structure rigorously restricts or completely eliminates access to approved modes of acquiring these symbols for a considerable part of the same population, that antisocial behaviour ensues on a considerable scale.
>
> (Merton 1938: 680)

For Merton, anomie is not just a product of strain between culturally prescribed goals and structurally limited legitimate means to achieve them, but is a consequence of the nature of the goals (Reiner 2007). A highly materialistic culture such as the USA, which places 'cultural emphasis on monetary accumulation as a symbol of success' (Merton 1938: 681), is prone to anomie and hence crime at all levels of society, not just among the relatively deprived (Reiner 2007). Merton (1938) argues that this has important implications for the relationship between poverty and crime:

> Poverty as such, and consequent limitation of opportunity, are not sufficient to induce a conspicuously high rate of criminal behaviour. . . . Only insofar as poverty and associated disadvantages in competition for the culture values approved for all members of the society is linked with the assimilation of a cultural emphasis on monetary accumulation as a symbol of success is antisocial conduct a 'normal' outcome.
>
> (Merton 1938: 681)

The effect of the great depression on US crime rates is discussed by Sellin (1942) who notes property crime rates in particular increased rapidly in the early 1930s and declined as swiftly from 1933/34. Burglary, for example, increased by 21 per cent from 1931 to 1933 and robbery by 29 per cent. In England and Wales too, burglary increased by 18 per cent in the period 1931 to 1933 and 'Total theft and handling stolen goods' increased by 57 per cent over the same period.[2] Notwithstanding, it should be noted that in England and Wales neither burglary nor theft rates reduced substantially after the Depression and indeed continued to rise until after the war (and generally since then also), indicating there might be other factors to be considered. Indeed Halpern (2001) suggests it is an increase in 'self-interested values' which might explain this discrepancy.

Challenges to the concept of anomie

A challenge to the general theory of anomie as a general explanation of crime is made by Marris (2000). Referring to Farrington (1997) who finds only 6 per cent of families account for 50 per cent of convictions, Marris suggests the problem might not be individuals without norms but rather a group of individuals with the 'wrong' norms – that is, 'anti-society' collective codes. Marris also points to the rise in crime during the three decades following the Second World War. During this time unemployment was low and employees in the so-called 'first world' shared the benefits of rising productivity with capitalists. That the theory of anomie cannot explain this rise in crime does not mean it cannot explain subsequent increases of course. As Marris (2000: 21) notes of the period of economic adjustment beginning in the mid 1980s, 'overnight, it seemed, the golden age had gone'.

Relative deprivation

A concept related to 'strain' is relative deprivation. Strain might occur not because the individual lacks the means to meet their own legitimate needs, but because some other has even more. This effect may arise from two contributing factors: clearly the more some people have, the more another may take from them, legitimately or otherwise. In addition, it is argued, although the UK and the USA are richer societies than 100 years ago, it is possible to be well off and yet still feel relatively deprived (Hale 2009). James (1997) argues the increasing envy with which individuals regard others is one of the root causes of increasing alienation. He is of the opinion 'the media have overheated our aspirations' and 'advanced capitalism makes money out of the depression and rage that are engendered by unrealistic aspirations' (James 1997: unnumbered). Individual adherence to the implicit social contract can only be undermined as individual life experiences fall short of what the media tell us is our 'right'. A related concept is that of 'identification/alienation' discussed by Duclos *et al.* (2004). They suggest income inequality 'fuels' polarisation of society. Polarisation is caused by alienation/identification, where individuals identify with those similar to themselves and are alienated from those from whom they differ. Obviously there are several ways in which individuals feel they may differ, relative income is merely one such.

Relative inequality may also indicate absolute decreases in the quality of life for certain sectors of society. For example, Burtless (1999) has argued the least well-off American households have seen their real income eroded in the period 1979 to 1996. Some of the decline in household income has been offset by the increase in the proportion of double-income households. However, in their study of marriage in the USA, Edin and Reed find that, while in the 1960s marriage rates were similar across income groups, in 2005, 'poor men and women are only about half as likely to be married as those with incomes at three or more times the poverty level' (Edin and Reed 2005: 118). This is despite the fact that marital expectations are high amongst Americans of all social classes. Hence, as Burtless (1999) notes, the increasing inequality has been particular pronounced for men in the lowest income groups who have seen, not only their real income decline, but their relative likelihood of finding a life-partner (and thus their chance of actually being in a double-income household) reduce. Such mutually reinforcing effects are likely to add further to the general alienation from society. As Laub *et al.* (1998) show, the forming of 'quality marital bonds' has been shown to provide a significant level of informal social control which contributes to crime desistence – and as it is shown that children living with both parents (which it is reasonable to suppose is likely to follow the forming of 'quality marital bonds') are least likely to offend in later life (Marris 2000) – the disappointment of marital expectations of those in the lowest income group is likely to have a long-lasting impact on rates of crime.

The effects of relative inequality are likely to be confounded with the effects of unemployment and other labour market effects as such inequality rises from the increasing hostile labour market faced by American males with relatively low human capital (Karoly and Burtless 1995). In the UK also, although the early twenty-first century saw the level of absolute poverty decline, real incomes of the least well off have fallen in recent years (Brewer *et al.* 2007).

Social disorganisation theory

A similar concept to that of alienation/identification is that of social organisation. In general, it is posited that stronger community ties will tend to lessen criminality. The Chicago School established links between environmental factors and crime (Shaw and McKay 1942, 1969). One element of this work was to characterise a zone of transition within cities that was characterised by poor quality housing, high levels of residential mobility, high levels of poverty and poor levels of health. This zone was typically the first home for newly arrived immigrants who, once economically established, would move out to more prosperous neighbourhoods, making way for the next immigrant group. The zone of transition was an area of social disorganisation and Shaw and McKay's (1942, 1969) empirical work found that it was the area of a Chicago associated with the highest delinquency rates. Generalising, Hale (2009) suggests that it is logical to posit that in times and neighbourhoods where unemployment is high or economic prospects are poor 'it will be difficult to muster the necessary resources to combat social disorganisation and maintain informal social control' (Hale 2009: 368).

Control theory

Control theory considers not social structures but the individual in explaining crime. Specifically, it examines why people do *not* commit crime, the underlying assumption being, in line with earlier theorists such as Hobbes (1943) and Locke (1689), that offending is part of human nature. Hirschi's (1969) social bond theory is one version of control theory. Hirschi argues that social bonds to social institutions such as family and work insulate people against deviant behaviour and that crime occurs when these social bonds are weakened. As Rock (2007) notes, this is an explanation of crime which is close to theories based on the concept of anomie (see above) in its focus on the regulation of potentially unbridled appetites through the individual's attachment to social structures. Those who are high in attachment have a strong commitment to the future, in that they believe conventional behaviour will lead to long-term rewards and are involved in conventional activities. They hold beliefs which coincide with conventional rules and norms and are less likely to be involved in deviant or unlawful behaviour. Conversely, there may be a sense the social contract has been broken if individual effort in persevering at education and hard work is not recognised or rewarded. This seeming breach of the implicit contract goes some way towards absolving the individual of their duty to society.

Summarising and building on the work of Box (1987), Hale (2009) argues economic recession and unemployment might be expected to weaken social bonds and hence lead to increased levels of crime. Hale notes:

> Unemployment and increasing inequality are not likely to improve family relationships. Rather they will produce increased tension, anger and sullenness against society that may be transferred onto the family leading to its breakdown.
>
> (Hale 2009: 369)

Unemployment will 'cast a long shadow' over institutions which are supposed to prepare people for employment and this will undermine individual commitment to the future (Hale 2009, referencing Box 1987). Individual beliefs in the legitimacy of conformity will be weakened as recession undermines families and schools (ibid.). More unemployment, shorter working hours and more part-time work will reduce people's involvement in conventional activity (ibid.).

It may be the case, however, that a standing decision to undertake criminal acts is not made at a conscious level. This certainly is the implication of Gottfredson and Hirschi's (1990) analysis. They reject social bond theory to develop a version of control theory with more emphasis on individual self-control and impulsivity rather than structural explanations of crime. In their *General Theory of Crime* Gottfredson and Hirschi (1990) argue crime is a result of low self-control and provides gratification to those who cannot (or will not) postpone pleasure (Rock 2007). It is likely to be committed by those who are impulsive, insensitive, physical, risk-taking, short-sighted and non-verbal (Gottfredson and Hirschi 1990). For Gottfredson and Hirschi (1990) self-control is a permanent internal state that depends on the quality of parenting in the early years (Hale 2009). Research by Wilson (1980) shows the close relationship between this theory and economic factors such as unemployment and recession (Hale 2009; Rock 2007). Wilson's research on socially deprived families in Birmingham, England, concludes that what most sharply differentiates families of delinquent children from those with non-delinquent children is the exercise of 'chaperonage'. Wilson (1980) notes lax parenting is often linked to chronic stress resulting from factors such as long periods of unemployment, poor physical and mental health and poverty. It should be borne in mind that it may be that the children of those suffering periods of long unemployment may draw their own unconscious conclusions about adherence to the social contract, particularly if their parents have adhered to its constraints. The role model status of parents cannot but be eroded by periods of adversity, regardless of their skills at 'parenting'.

If this version of control theory is correct then an important implication for attempts to test it empirically would be that 'Parenting might be expected to deteriorate in times of recession. However, the effect on crime would not be immediate. Rather it would impact in perhaps eight to ten years time' (Hale 2009: 370).

An appropriate way therefore to determine the validity of this version of control theory is through the use of longitudinal data sets to study the life-course of offenders. Sampson and Laub (1993) and Laub and Sampson (2003) look at the development of and desistance from crime in men over long periods of time. In particular they consider how social bonds such as family, friends and employment work as controls that filter influences emanating from the wider social structure (Rock 2007). The life-course perspective of Sampson and Laub is underpinned by the concept of a trajectory, which is a pathway or line of development over the life span. The trajectory is a long-term pattern of behaviour marked by a sequence of transitions. Transitions are marked by life events such as marriage or a first job. Trajectories and transitions interlock to generate turning points or changes in the life course (Sampson and Laub 1993). As Rock explains:

> Laub and Sampson portray the process not as a grim and ineluctable progression into criminality, but as a sequence of events and actions which is

influenced always by the capacity of people to interpret and choose how they will respond. The part played by human agency and contingency is repeatedly underscored, leading them to observe how impossible it is to predict future criminality from present circumstances.

(Rock 2007: 16)

In this perspective, where agency and social structures interact, the potential effects of structural economic conditions such as recession and high rates of unemployment are similarly clear.

Routine Activity theory

Once an individual has decided to 'join the market' for criminal acts, they subsequently must rationally evaluate opportunities which come their way to decide where their greatest expected return lies. As we saw in Chapter Four Rational Choice theory is primarily an economic theory of human behaviour that has been applied to the study of crime by both economists and criminologists. The model of offending developed by Becker (1968) and refined by Ehrlich (1973) makes assumptions about the impact of unemployment rates on crime. Thus, Ehrlich (1973) argues the potential offender calculates the legitimate opportunities for earning income, the rewards these offer, the amounts offered by illegal opportunities, the probability of arrest and the likelihood of punishment. The individual will choose the activity – legal or illegal – which offers the best return on investment.

As noted in Chapter Three, Ehrlich's (1973) model posits individuals will engage in illegal activities if the marginal gain from illegality exceeds the marginal gain from legal activities. Thus, if the net return from legal activities declines, or the net return to illegal activities increases, more time is expected to be devoted to criminality. In general, as the unemployment rate increases, the opportunity cost of crime falls and more crime is predicted.

Paradoxically, however, it may be the case improvements in economic conditions may lead to increases in crime. This is one of the implications of Routine Activity theory (Felson 1994, 1995). This starts with the observation that as social and economic conditions have improved in the post-war years the crime rate has also increased. It explains the sharp rises in crime by arguing that, as social and economic conditions change, so do routine activities. These changes in routine activities affect the relationship between the three necessary conditions of crime, namely a suitable target, a motivated offender and the absence of a capable guardian. So, for instance, more women now work and more leisure activities now take place outside of the home, reducing the supply of capable guardians. At the same time increasing consumerism has led to a rise in suitable targets in the form of cars and electronic goods, the latter becoming progressively smaller, and more easily portable, and with a higher value to weight ratio (Felson 1994; Gilling 1997).

The effect of this, as Cantor and Land (1985) suggest, is that rising unemployment will have two offsetting implications: first increasing the level of motivated offenders – Cantor and Land consider this effect will happen with a one period lag. That is to say, last year's unemployment increase leads to this year's property crime; and second the level of guardianship – which Cantor and Land consider will be a contemporaneous effect. That is to say, this year's unemployment will increase this year's guardianship and hence reduce this year's crime. Levels of guardianship increase because rising unemployment means that more individuals remain at home, both reducing opportunities for burglary and increasing informal social control. Hence, unemployment has two opposite effects on crime: on the one hand increasing numbers of motivated offenders will cause crime to rise; on the other hand increased levels of guardianship will cause crime to fall.

Cook and Zarkin (1985) suggest the relationship may be further developed. Along with Cantor and Land, they note it is easier for individuals to find work in a strongly growing economy, which will reduce crime. However Routine Activity theory and the accumulation of goods implies there are also more opportunities for property crime (as noted above). They further consider the uses to which increased prosperity may be put. For example, as consumption rises generally, purchase of drugs, alcohol and guns becomes easier, which might lead to increased risk of crime; private and public spending on deterrence and criminal justice might also increase, thus leading to a reduction in the crime rate.

Reverse causality

As has been noted by Levitt (2001) and Raphael and Winter-Ebmer (2001) the link between unemployment and crime is not necessarily one where the former causes the latter. It may be that causality works in both directions. For example, it may well be the case that individuals with a criminal record find it more difficult to get employment. However true this might be on an individual basis, in studies which consider the macro-economic effect of unemployment, it is unlikely to be observed. In general in the UK and the USA there has been sufficient labour market flexibility, particularly in the unskilled area of the economy, that firms have been able to fill vacancies even if they do screen out individuals with criminal records. Thus, the unemployment *rate* might not reflect whether some applicants have criminal records, so long as sufficient applicants without criminal records exist to fill available positions.

It has also been suggested by Levitt (2001) that an increase in crime makes it more difficult for legitimate business to survive, both because of predation by criminals, but also because criminal justice costs are borne by taxpayers. As legitimate businesses close or relocate, employment becomes more difficult to find. On a micro-level we might observe regions where there is very little employment, as a result of a vicious circle between crime and an increasingly hostile business environment. Levitt also suggests there may well be a third factor causing both. For example, an increase in society's preference for alcohol may lead to both an increase in crime through, for example, visceral factors (see Loewenstein 2000) and, potentially, difficulty in finding work.

Summary

The implicit social contract which allows an individual to identify with their neighbour, and thus to one extent or another identify with the good of society, is a fragile construct. At times of economic or social strain, such as recession and depression or as a result of the increasing poverty (relative or absolute) of a socio-economic class, we might expect increasing polarisation, increasing alienation, and the weakening of this link. As a consequence, we might postulate, individuals will become rationally more disposed towards the standing decision to engage in illicit activities – not only for private gain but also, through 'vindictiveness' (Young 2003), to crimes against the person (see also Blau and Blau 1982, and Green *et al.* 1998, who suggest the link from economic conditions to hate crime depends on whether and how political leaders frame and mobilise grievances). Once an individual is predisposed to criminal activity, it follows that increasing levels of unemployment are likely to lead to an increase in that activity, for the reasons that the relative gain from illicit activities increases. The relationship will, however, not necessarily be straightforward to capture because of reverse causality and offsetting effects. Hence empirical specifications must be carefully considered.

Employment and unemployment

Before we go on to consider the empirical evidence for a link between economic conditions and crime, it will be helpful to look in a little bit more detail at the concept of 'employment' and 'unemployment'. Not all the theories we have looked at, nor all of the empirical evidence we review in the next section, concentrate solely on the relationship between unemployment and crime. However, in most of them, the concept of employment and/or unemployment is mentioned. In this section, we look at how economists understand employment and unemployment.

Voluntary and involuntary unemployment

Although we have discussed above the breakdown in social norms and the resulting anomie which might arise from unemployment, this is not to say that any level of unemployment is undesirable. In theory economists recognise the best-run society will have a 'non-zero level' of unemployment; even at 'full employment', there will still be some level of unemployment in the economy. To see why this is so, it is useful to distinguish between 'voluntary' and 'involuntary' employment. From an economic point of view, full employment is generally taken to mean that all unemployment is voluntary; those individuals not working have rationally decided to adopt such a state. This does not mean they have left the labour market. The unemployed are those who wish to work but do not have legitimate employment in the current time period. Individuals who have chosen not to work at all are not regarded as being unemployed.

Economic models which use the concept of unemployment tend to focus on labour market conditions to explain it. Recall the supply–demand model discussed in Chapter Two (Figure 2.1). In the labour market, 'suppliers' are those who supply labour services (i.e. employees) and 'consumers' are employers. In general employees wish for the maximum return on their time, while employers wish to pay as little as possible. Voluntary unemployment occurs where suppliers of labour finish education and search for work or leave a particular job to devote their efforts to searching for another with an increased expected return for given input (for example, a higher salary).[3] Therefore, such voluntary unemployment (if it exists) is a result of negotiations in the labour market and is unlikely to result in a breakdown of societal norms. According to neo-classical and monetarist labour market models, in any well-ordered economy a natural rate of unemployment will be observed (Friedman 1968). Notwithstanding, Davidson and Davidson (1996: 48) claim economic policy has interfered in the labour market to 'pursue a natural rate of unemployment'. In which case, it must be concluded the rate observed is in fact not natural.

Conversely, involuntary unemployment results where workers are forced into a search for employment against their will and are unable to find work at the prevailing wage (i.e. the wage paid to other similarly qualified workers who *are* employed). Classical market analysis would suggest the solution to this is simply to lower wages. As we have seen, as the price asked for any good or service is reduced, demand for that good or service is increased. Consider the labour market represented in Figure 5.1, where p represents the price of labour (the real wage[4]). Suppose that the prevailing price of labour is p_1. The difference between the amount of labour supplied at this price, q_s, and the level of demand, q_d, is the level of involuntary unemployment.

The solution suggested by classical economics is for real wages – the price of labour – to fall until the market comes to equilibrium at the point E. Thus involuntary unemployment may be eliminated (in theory) by a reduction in the real wage. However, the demand and supply of labour may not necessarily behave in the

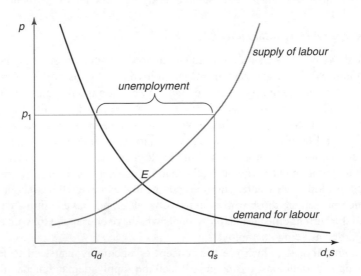

Figure 5.1 Supply and demand for labour.

same way as the demand and supply of goods and services in general. In practice those still in employment are loath to see their conditions eroded (and indeed, given that the cost of living is to some extent fixed, may not be able to afford such erosion). Thus real wages may not adjust completely.

There is the further problem that, if individuals in the labour market take too long to find employment, they find it increasingly hard to get work. This may result from one or more of: the unemployed experience a loss of skills needed in the labour market; those still employed effectively shut out competition from the unemployed through unionisation, for example; or the preference set of the unemployed might adjust as they become unused to a work routine. It is suggested therefore that increases in unemployment may happen relatively quickly at times of economic stress, while reductions in unemployment are relatively slow. Indeed, it may be that recessions cause a permanent increase in the natural rate of unemployment. This effect is known as 'hysteresis' (see Blanchard and Summers 1987). Whether such increases are indeed permanent (particularly in the case of the USA) is challenged by Song and Wu (1998). Notwithstanding, it is clear unemployment is faster to rise than to fall.

Unemployment has two effects on the work–crime trade-off. If real wages fall, the return on legitimate employment falls and therefore illegitimate employment will become relatively more attractive. In the situation where wages do not fall to the market clearing level, involuntary unemployment persists. In this case an unemployed individual's trade-off between devoting temporal resources to illegal activities rather than legal activities changes. If there is a reduced likelihood of finding legitimate employment, the expected return of continuing to search for work declines. Thus an individual not actually in full-time work is relatively more likely to choose illegal activities. In a situation where the real wages fall so low it is no longer possible for a worker to maintain their standard of living, or if the search for employment over a protracted period is fruitless, the result is relative depravation, social disorganisation, anomie, etc.

Full-time and part-time unemployment

The role of unemployment is further clouded by the relationship between full-time and part-time employment. Clearly an individual in a full-time job not only has less economic incentive to search for illegal activity, but also less temporal flexibility. Ehrlich's (1973) model assumes individuals have a free choice about how much time to devote to legal vs illegal activities. This will not necessarily be true for those in full-time employment, but it will be more likely to be the case for those in part-time jobs, those with short-term contracts or the self-employed. Such jobs are relatively more prevalent in the UK.

Hale (1998, 2009) notes changes in the UK economy, leading to shifts in the structure of the labour market. In particular, over the last 30 years, there has been: an increasing shift in emphasis from manufacturing to the service sector; an increase in part-time and temporary unemployment; and a shift in patterns of employment from men to women (Hale 2009). A dual labour market has developed with a primary or core sector of skilled workers usually working full-time for large organisations with good employment and benefit rights, and a secondary sector where people have low skills, low wages, few benefits with regard to sick pay, holidays or pensions and a high propensity to unemployment. There is high turnover in this secondary sector. Davidson and Davidson (1996: 49) suggest 'often it requires two members of the household to work merely to keep up the standard that was obtainable with only one worker . . . in previous years'. Note, however, a shift from full-time to part-time employment will not be recorded in unemployment statistics; neither will an erosion in non-monetised conditions of employment. This change in employment conditions is, therefore, somewhat difficult to quantify and will be captured indirectly through inequality measures. This is not to say full-time jobs no longer exist, of course, merely that they form a lesser proportion of the labour market (Leppel and Clain 1988; Euwals and Hogerbrugge 2004).

Now, it is generally the case that people who participate in legitimate full-time employment may not choose so easily how to allocate their time – they are either employed full-time or not employed at all. Where an individual might choose to be self-employed or to work part-time, he has increasing opportunities to mix legal with illegal activities. The reasons for this are straightforward: if he is working full-time, he generally will have few temporal resources free (i.e. not much time left after work). Thus the decision to become involved in crime becomes to a great extent *either/or*. As the economy moves to a greater proportion of part-time jobs, the extra flexibility will allow workers with such jobs to enjoy a greater mix of activities of all kinds: a second part-time job, leisure or illegal activities.

Wage inequality

It should also be noted that, for men at any rate, part-time employment generally pays less than full-time employment; for women there is little strong evidence of an earnings gap (Hirsch 2005). Moreover, there is some evidence that, where workers leave or lose a full-time job and take part-time work in a different industry or occupation, there is a substantial reduction in income both for men and women (ibid.). In such a case, individuals might well feel some financial pressure arising from the lack of full-time posts for which they might apply.

Hale (2009) argues that wage inequality is an important factor in the relationship between crime and the economy. Thinking about economic models of offending such as those developed by Becker and Ehrlich, he argues:

> The economic model of crime argues that individuals will choose between legal and illegal work on the basis of their relative rewards. Many individuals find that, whilst in work, their jobs are insecure, low-paid, and low-skilled. Often they are in part-time or temporary work and they are on the economic and social margins. Many of the theoretical arguments presented above for why unemployment and crime might be related apply equally well to that between low wage, low-skill employment.
>
> (Hale 2009: 375)

Empirical evidence

In the following we discuss the recent literature on the link between labour market conditions and the level of crime. When discussing recent research we therefore focus on those results most related to this link. The reader should bear in mind that, as with all the determinants of crime, there are many related factors. It will be obvious that at a micro-economic level, poorer educational outcomes are related to labour market satisfaction. However, so far as is possible, we factor out such effects, and consider them elsewhere.

The rise of crime

Hale (2009) provides a useful summary of empirical work on the potential links between crime and the economy and his work forms the basis for the structure of this section.

Hale (building on earlier work by Radzinowicz 1939) starts with a useful observation about economic development:

> [T]he more multi-faceted the economic structure of society becomes, the harder it is to measure cycles of depression and prosperity. While relatively straightforward in a simple agricultural community, in a complex industrial society measuring change is more complicated and relating these changes to trends in crime a more demanding task. Hence it will be necessary to use multiple economic indices rather than relying on single measures such as unemployment.
>
> (Hale 2009: 371)

Indeed, the empirical evidence of macro-economic impacts is framed in such a way as to specify, for example, unemployment rates, as merely one of a range of factors contributing to levels of crime. In addition, it should be borne in mind that the impact of poverty and unemployment might well vary with the type of crime being considered. Ehrlich (1973), for example, in the empirical analysis of his theoretical model, considers crimes against the person – murder, rape, assault – separately from crimes against property – robbery, burglary, larceny, auto-theft.[5] Ehrlich's analysis deals with a consideration of the crime rates for the years 1940, 1950 and 1960 measured over a cross-section of states in the USA and seeks to explain whether these are dependent on a range of social and economic variables: crime rate in previous year; probability of apprehension; average length of sentence; and spending on police; the income of the average family; the proportion of the population earning less than half the income of the average family; the proportion of males and non-whites in each state; the degree of urbanisation; the average level of education and (crucially for our concern here) the level of unemployment.

Ehrlich's results generally support the Rational Agents hypothesis, in that crimes against the person and property crimes vary with the probability of apprehension and length of punishment and other socio-demographic factors (age, ethnic background, etc.). Crimes against the person do not vary with poverty measures; property crimes, however, do. States with above-average family income are more likely to suffer above-average property crime – possibly because there is more to steal in relatively affluent states – while those states with a higher proportion of families living in relative poverty (below half average family income) also have, on average, a greater rate of property crime. There is, however, no consistent significant variation of property crime with unemployment rates.

As Hale (2009) notes, this lack of evidence of a consistent relationship between unemployment and crime rates is, well, consistent. Hale identifies two major surveys of early statistical work on the relationship between unemployment and crime: Chiricos (1987) and Box (1987). Both concluded that, while the evidence is 'slightly in favour' (Hale 2009: 371) of there being a positive relationship between the two – as unemployment goes up, crime goes up – there is no consistent finding. For instance, Box (1987) reviewed 50 studies (a mixture of longitudinal and cross-sectional) and found that 32 supported a link between higher unemployment and more crime. However, as Reiner (2007) points out, the studies reviewed by Box were all carried out before the mid-1980s in decades of virtually full employment; that is to say unemployment would be mainly transitional and voluntary.

The oil-shocks of the 1970s and 1980s, and the advent of monetarism,[6] neo-classical economic policies and labour market reforms, resulted in long-term unemployment for growing numbers of young men. This permanent shift in the market for labour was especially pronounced for males with a relatively low skill-base, resulting in a significant erosion of income even for those who were employed. Although arguably based on sound economic policy, such reforms – generally emphasising the pursuit of individual self-interest – had negative consequences for the UK society:

> The social impact and meaning of this, especially in an increasingly consumerist culture, is quite different from what unemployment represented in earlier decades. It signified a fatal combination of enhanced anomie and an erosion of controls represented by legitimate work, and indeed marriage and family responsibilities.
>
> (Reiner 2007: 360)

Similarly, considering the performance of the US economy, Davidson and Davidson note:

> In the last quarter century, however, there has been a slow erosion of the civilised economic base and a slippage towards the barbaric laissez-faire[7] system that required a significant number of people to be relegated to a perpetual underclass to maintain an inflation free environment.
>
> (Davidson and Davidson 1996: 212)

This point of view is generally, but not universally, held. For example Allen (1996) argues that decreases in poverty and income inequality are associated with *increases* in criminal activity. Considering annual USA data from 1959 to 1992, Allen discusses the factors which affect the rates of burglary, vehicle theft and robbery. His list of possible causes is comprised of: the rate of poverty; GINI coefficient; the unemployment rate; price inflation rate and a range of socio-economic and criminal justice factors. Allen concludes as poverty declines there is a significant increase in burglary and vehicle theft. This, he suggests, is because the benefits of poverty reduction programmes go to 'women with children and the elderly' (Allen 1996: 302), while those most likely to commit crime, young unskilled and semi-skilled males, have seen their relative economic standing decline. Allen finds the effect of unemployment is mixed, with increases in current unemployment associated with increasing burglary and robbery in the short term and reducing vehicle crime in both the short and long term (possibly because there will be fewer new cars to steal during times of recession). Allen concludes:

> These findings indicate that macroeconomic stability (especially anti-inflation) policies are the only macro-policies consistent with both economic and crime abating objectives.
>
> (Allen 1996: 302)

Whether keeping price inflation under control really is sufficient to reduce crime is debatable as Allen's results indicate price inflation is significantly related only to burglary rates.

It matters what is missing – trends and underspecification

This seeming contradiction might be resolved by considering that empirical results depend not only on which explanatory factors are considered, but also which are not! The properties of estimates vary with which data have been left out of the model. As researchers may have different model specifications, inconsistent results are to be expected. A further problem with early empirical studies is that some do not adequately allow for non-stationarity, i.e. 'trends' in the data. When considering data series which exhibit trends, care must be taken to avoid the problem of spurious correlations. Simple statistical analysis often indicates significant relationships between totally independent series if they both happen to be increasing (or decreasing) over time (see Chapter Six for a more detailed discussion of this problem). For example, Allen (1996) while recognising his crime rate data are non-stationary does not seem to have allowed for this in his model.

Both these issues are addressed by Field (1990), one of the more influential of recent studies in England and Wales. Field includes a wide range of explanatory factors and *changes* in unemployment and crime rather than the actual rates. Field, in his introduction, notes:

> The analysis of trends in crime, as with any similar series of data, is a com-plex technical and theoretical task. To demonstrate a statistical relationship,

it is not enough to show that two factors show trends in the same direction; this could easily be pure coincidence. Instead the revelation of a more subtle interconnection of patterns over time is required.

(Field 1990: 1)

Field also considers that there may be a distinction between short-term effects and long-term effects of macro-economic variables.

Compared to Ehrlich's analysis, Field's is relatively atheoretic. That is, he does not attempt to justify the variables he uses to explain the crime rate using a rational actors model; rather he selects a list of explanatory factors from earlier studies. Field further acknowledges his analysis deals with the rate at which crimes are reported to the police, which may differ significantly from the rate at which crimes are committed: for example, he notes that only 10 per cent of vandalism offences are recorded by the police. However, as he considers the growth rate of crime – which, he argues, is reasonably proxied by the growth rate of recorded crime – this should not affect the import of the analysis.[8]

Field considers growth rates in a range of crimes: residential and non-residential burglary; theft from a person or shop; theft of a vehicle; other theft; robbery; violence against the person; sexual offences; and fraud. Bearing in mind that statistical results differ depending on what is *not* included in the analysis, Field considers growth rates in a variety of potential explanatory factors: consumption (with consumption of alcoholic beverages specified separately); demographics (including the proportion of young men and the number of live births); unemployment; and spending on criminal justice and the police. Field also considers potential interaction between criminal activities and allows for the changing definitions of some types of crime by including dummy (qualitative) variables.

Somewhat surprisingly, Field shows that, in England and Wales, the level of unemployment does not significantly affect property crime, though there is a relationship between unemployment and crimes against the person. The main explanatory influence he identifies is a link between levels of consumption and crime. Field distinguishes between a short-term and a long-term effect of consumption growth on property crime and crime against the person. Increases in consumption reduce property crime in the short-run; however, in the long-run rate of growth of property crime increases with consumption. He suggests the short-term effect of affluence is both an increase in consumption, and less incentive to commit property crime. However, as high levels of consumption persist, indicating the economy is continuing to grow, there will be more goods and money available to steal (Hale 2009). Sexual offences and violence against the person increase rapidly at times of growing affluence and growing consumption.[9] Field argues that Routine Activity theory might account for this rise. Increases in affluence might be associated with increases in time outside the home where, he suggests, individuals are more at risk of crimes against the person.

Field suggests the reason earlier studies might have demonstrated a link between unemployment and growth in property crime is because the effect of consumption has not been considered. It should be borne in mind, during periods of relative economic prosperity, unemployment is likely to fall, and consumption is likely to rise. Thus there is, to some extent, a relationship between the two:

> The strength of the analysis conducted here is that it demonstrates an extremely strong relationship between crime and the business cycle, and demonstrates unemployment adds nothing to this pattern once consumption growth – the key factor – is taken into account.
>
> (Field 1990: 7)

Field thus implies that results from studies such as those of Reilly and Witt (1992) and Carmichael and Ward (2000, 2001), who find the rate of unemployment is related to crime, are subject to specification bias as they do not consider consumption.

Pyle and Deadman (1994) argue that unemployment may not be the best indicator of the state of the economy because unemployment and its official measurement underwent numerous revisions during the 1980s. Also it is argued unemployment lags behind the business cycle by between 6 and 12 months (Hale 2009). Thus an economic recession will affect the labour market first through reduced overtime, more part-time work, and falling real wages with unemployment rising only after the recession has been underway for some time. Echoing Field, Pyle and Deadman suggest Gross Domestic Product (GDP) or Consumers' Expenditure might better approximate the business cycle.

In the light of reductions in the crime rate observed towards the end of the last century and improvements in econometric techniques, Field (1999)[10] reappraises his earlier work on property crime. More advanced techniques notwithstanding, he comes to the same broad conclusions as he had reached in his earlier work, that property crime decreases with consumption in the short-term, and increases with consumption in the long-term. Field (1999) speculates that there is an equilibrium rate of crime and the reduction in crime rates seen towards the end of the 1990s will lead to 'upward pressure on the recorded crime figures in the coming years'.

Explaining the 'drop'

To see whether Field's prediction about upward pressure on crime is correct we consider recorded crime in England and Wales for the period 1960 to 2008 (the most recent data at the time of writing). There was indeed a short-run increase in recorded crime in the first few years of the twenty-first century; a return of crime rates to a 'natural' level has so far not been observed (see Figure 5.2).

Data on the rates of a number of crimes are considered: homicide; violence; sexual offences; robbery; burglary; theft and handling; fraud and forgery; criminal damage; miscellaneous; and all offences. All these data show an absolute decline in crime rates in the early years of the twenty-first century. Each crime rate is compared to data on other crime rates to capture association effects and: the proportion of young males in the economy; unemployment rates (male and female); the GINI coefficient; real[11] income and consumption per capita; per capita consumption of alcohol (beer; spirits; wine; cider; total); and the incarceration rate. Following

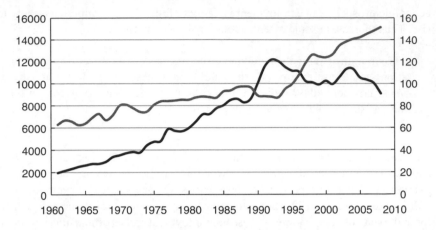

Figure 5.2 All offences per 100,000 (black on left axis) and prison population per 100,000 (grey on right axis) (England and Wales).

Source: authors' analysis based on data provided by the Home Office.

Field (1990, 1999) we use reported crime rates and allow for changes in definition, etc., through the use of qualitative variables.

The difficulty of establishing exact relationships between the data may be illustrated by considering the rate of reported crime and the prison population shown in Figure 5.2. Over the period 1960 to 1988 an increase in the crime rate is associated with an increase in the prison population. This does not mean, of course, that putting people in prison causes crime, merely that as crime rates rose the rate of incarceration also rose. It will be noted, from 1988 to 1992 crime rates increased markedly, and this was associated with a decline in the incarceration rate. However, as the UK economy was in recession at this time (coinciding with a brief encounter with the European Exchange Rate Mechanism, ERM), it might be suggested criminals were responding to declining economic prospects rather than the reduced likelihood of punishment. Following the UK's leaving the ERM in September 1992, the economy experienced a period of sustained growth, allowing the government to commit more resources to criminal justice. Whether it is this, or the improvement in economic prospects, or some other factor, which led to the decrease in crime is an empirical matter.

Following Field, we adopt an atheoretical approach and consider simply whether changes in one data series can be used to forecast changes in another; that is, we test for Granger Causality (see Chapter Six). In sum, we find few causal relationships between the data. It would appear real consumption is a Granger-Causal factor only in the rate of sexual offences. The only other crime rate where Granger-Causal factors are identified is criminal damage, which is related to: inequality (as measured by the GINI coefficient); burglary; theft and handling; and the incarceration rate. We are not aware of other studies which consider the impact of the economy on criminal damage (technically a non-property crime, in that it does not involve the illegal acquisition of another's resources) and its relationship with inequality supports theories of anomie, alienation and social disorganisation. Notwithstanding, there is evidence the link between consumption and property crime is not as strong as Field suggests. In the early years of the twenty-first century, increasing consumption has been observed at the same time as declining crime rates.

The UK is not the only nation to have experienced declines in crime rates in recent years – crime has also been in decline in the USA since the early 1990s – and Field's (1999) analysis is not the only one to have missed the turning point. Economists were unanimous in the 1990s in their consideration that crime rates would continue to increase.

Rethinking the business cycle

It should be borne in mind, Field's work is relatively atheoretical. Which is to say, the link between consumption and crime is justified by the data rather than drawing on models of human behaviour. The power of consumption as an explanatory factor may be justified (as in Pyle and Deadman 1994) by considering it as a proxy for the state of the business cycle. However, the link between the business cycle and crime is by no means straightforward. As we have noted above, Cantor and Land (1985) and Cook and Zarkin (1985) suggest the various effects of the business cycle should be considered separately. Cantor and Land suggest an increase in unemployment reduces criminal opportunities in the short-run, as there are fewer available targets. In the long-run, persistent higher levels of unemployment create a motivation effect which may increase crime. Using annual USA data from 1946 to 1982 they consider each effect separately, and find strong evidence of a short-term reduction in crime as a result of increases in unemployment. Thus there is evidence the opportunity effect operates across both personal and property crime. Moreover, in the case of property crime, there is evidence of a longer-term (lagged) motivational effect which tends to increase crime.

Cantor and Land's study, amongst others (Britt 1994, 1997; Devine *et al.* 1988; Smith *et al.* 1992), is criticised by Greenberg (2001) who considers, in general, they are mis-specified,[12] failing to take account, for example, of the changing nature of the US economy and the changing nature of statistical analysis – particularly the way non-stationary data is treated. Tongue in cheek, Greenberg points out that the US divorce rate and homicide rate are 'related', in that they have a common trend. He speculates those couples who divorce do not necessarily then engage in homicide,[13] but that both data series are in fact responding to a third, the 'strain' placed on the nuclear family. Greenberg concludes:

> Recent advances in the econometric analysis of nonstationary time series suggest that many – perhaps most – sociological analyses of crime rate time series (and, very likely, other kinds of rates as well) suffer from serious methodological deficiencies.[14]

(Greenberg 2001: 323)

That the link between unemployment and crime is a subtle one is also emphasised by Levitt (2001) who considers national[15] level crime series data are not the ideal tool to use to estimate the strength of the unemployment–crime nexus. Using panel data (that is to say, data with a time dimension: 1950 to 1999, and a cross-section: states of the USA), Levitt considers the relationship between rates of property crime and violent crime and a set of factors comprised of: current and last year's unemployment (cf. Cantor and Land 1985); the rates of imprisonment and executions; real per capita income; and a series of socio-demographic variables (though not, curiously given his comment on Greenberg (2001), poverty measures).

Levitt finds a 1 per cent increase in unemployment is associated with a 1.4 per cent to 2.7 per cent increase in property crime – the effect on violent crime is not statistically significant. The previous year's unemployment rate does not significantly explain either crime rate, casting doubt, as Levitt notes, on both Cantor and Land (1985) and Greenberg (2001).

In a similar vein, Raphael and Winter-Ebmer (2001)[16] consider earlier analyses suffer from omitted variable bias in not considering, for example, alcohol and drug use and access to firearms, which increase with prosperity. Raphael and Winter-Ebmer (2001) summarise Cook and Zarkin's (1985) four categories of factors that may create linkages between the business cycle and crime: (1) variation in legitimate employment opportunities; (2) variation in criminal opportunities; (3) consumption of criminogenic commodities (alcohol, drugs, guns); and (4) temporal variation in the response of the criminal justice system. The impact of these effects is estimated using a panel of data.

One of the difficulties found in the estimation of the effects of unemployment on crime is that, in general, unemployment varies with the business cycle and, for reasons given above, so does crime. Hence the direct relationship is confounded with other effects. Noting that military contract awards fluctuate independently of the business cycle, and are correlated with unemployment, allows Raphael and Winter-Ebmer to estimate the size of this direct relationship.

The variables of interest to Raphael and Winter-Ebmer are the rates of: murder; forcible rape; robbery; aggravated assault; burglary; larceny-theft; and motor vehicle theft. Their explanatory factors include: the unemployment rate; state populations and age structure; poverty and urbanisation rates; and state annual per capita consumption of each of beer, wine and spirits. Their initial model specification does not include the effects of alcohol consumption and Raphael and Winter-Ebmer find unemployment is a determinant of property crime but not violent crime. However, when alcohol consumption is included, and when appropriate allowance is made for simultaneity (through the use of military contract award data) it is found that the level of unemployment is strongly related to burglary and auto-theft – a 1 per cent increase in unemployment is estimated to be associated with an approximately 4.5 per cent increase in the burglary rate and a 7 per cent increase in the rate of auto-theft. In contrast to their earlier results (where alcohol effects are not considered), Raphael and Winter-Ebmer's final specification indicates significant relationships exist between the unemployment rate and robbery, rape and assault – a 1 per cent increase in unemployment rates is estimated to be associated with 6 to 7 per cent increase in the rates of these specific violent crimes, particularly robbery (which is also associated with acquisitive crime).

Levitt (2001) is somewhat sceptical of these results, partly because of the strength of the effect found, and partly because he is concerned the military contracts data is not in fact independent of the business cycle.

A similar type of panel study is carried out for the 16 German Laender (states) by Entorf and Spengler (2000). The time dimension of the panel is from 1975 to 1996. Their basic 'criminometric' model is based on that of Ehrlich (1973) and suggests crime rates are related to deterrence, income and other factors comprised of: absolute and relative income; unemployment; and socio-demographic factors. In general Entorf and Spengler's results echo those of other studies. There is a positive relation between income[17] and all crime rates (except 'rape' and 'murder'), and a negative relationship between relative income and all crime rates (again, except 'rape' and 'murder'), which is to say, as relative incomes fall, the rate of crime increases. The effect of unemployment is mixed and generally insignificant. However, Entorf and Spengler note that the relative income variable, measuring as it does the average state income compared to the national average, may be picking up relative differences in the labour market – with relatively affluent states enjoying buoyant labour markets.

Relative poverty and the changing nature of employment

As has been noted already (Davidson and Davidson 1996; Reiner 2007) the nature of employment in the USA and UK has changed significantly over the last 20 years. This has arguably placed social fabric and the 'nuclear family' under increasing strain. Hale (2009) identifies several studies from around the world that link the shift from manufacturing to service industry jobs with increases in crime through increased female employment rates. According to Witt and Witte (2000) this is likely to increase crime rates as women in traditional, domestic roles guard their homes and those of neighbours, as well as supervising children who would otherwise be more likely to become both victims and offenders (see, for instance, the earlier discussion of social control theory, and Wilson's 1980 empirical study on the importance of 'chaperonage'). On the other hand (Triggs 1997 as summarised by Hale 2009) women in the labour force have more opportunity to commit crime, although, conversely their motivation might decrease. They might also be more prone to victimisation if they are out more or if their work leads to increased domestic tension. Conversely domestic tensions might decrease if female employment leads to an improvement in the household economic situation.

To determine the magnitude of these effects, Witt and Witte (2000) use data from 1960 to 1997, and estimate the effect of female participation in the labour force on the FBI's Uniform Crime Reports (UCR) Crime Index. They also allow for the prison population and the level of durable goods per capita (to proxy the availability of targets). They find the labour participation effect has a greater effect on crime than does imprisonment. Somewhat cautiously, Witt and Witte suggest the participation rate may be acting as a proxy for other social factors which have occurred in the USA over the same period (the rise of single-parent families, for example); however, they do not mention the impact of this change in the supply of labour on income and relative poverty and through relative poverty to crime rates.

In a study using data on female labour participation, wages and property crime for 41 police force areas over 24 years during the 1970s, 80s and 90s, Hansen (2003) examines the effect of increasing female employment on male crime in England and Wales. Her particular focus is the impact the increase in the labour supply has had on wages in the (previously male-dominated) labour market, particularly at the lower end of the distribution where men are particularly vulnerable and may already be on the margins of crime (Hansen 2003). Her findings:

> support the view that the substitution of women into the low wage male labour market is a mechanism through which increasing female employment is associated with male crime. But, while a positive relationship between the female share of employment and crime has been shown, . . . [t]he results suggest that the real issue may be where females entering the labour market are substituting for low skilled males.

> (Hansen 2003: 19)

It is worth noting that Hansen does not consider the increase in the labour force resulting from immigration over the period. Between 1979 and 1998, net migration to the UK increased from approximately zero to the order of 100,000 per year. In 1998, 7.92 per cent of those in work in the UK were born outside the UK. This expansion in the labour force will also have placed downwards pressure on wages.[18] Whether or not females entering the labour market are bidding down wages for low-skilled workers, there is clear evidence from the USA that low-skilled young male workers found the labour market increasingly hostile in the 1980s. This is the demographic group which is likely to have the least opportunity cost arising from the decision to engage in crime (see Chapter Three). Compared to the mid-1970s real wages paid in this labour market declined by 23 per cent. Over the same time period, criminality in this group (as proxied by arrest rates) increased by 18 per cent (Grogger 1998).

Gould *et al.* (2002) extend this analysis and consider the relative improvement in the USA labour market in the 1990s.[19] Using a panel data set which covers 705 counties over the period 1979 to 1997, Gould *et al.* seek to explain variations in: auto-theft; burglary; larceny; aggravated assault; murder; robbery; and rape. Their explanatory factors include the wage and unemployment rates in the unskilled male labour market and the state income per capita. Deterrent effects, county arrest rate and police employment and expenditure are separately specified; other socio-demographic factors are controlled for using prior-regression. With the exception of the crimes of 'larceny' and 'rape', the change in the wage rate significantly explained changes in the crime rate – the lower the wage rate, the more arrests were made (and therefore, by proxy, the more crime was committed). The effect of unemployment was significant (and positive) only in the cases of 'burglary' and overall 'property crime' (which includes burglary). Overall, they estimate 60 per cent of the standardised growth in property crime in the 1980s and 1990s may be attributed to the declining real wage of young unskilled males (see also Machin and Meghir (2004) who reach similar conclusions when considering crime in England and Wales).

Introducing the minimum wage in the UK

If a decline in wages paid to the least well off leads to an increase in crime, it seems reasonable to suppose an increase in their wages will lead to a reduction in crime. In the UK the government recently legislated to bring about such an increase by imposing a national minimum wage. A priori, the impact of a minimum wage on unemployment (and crime) cannot be forecast. While clearly benefiting those who have low-paid work, monetarist and neo-classical economists would argue such political tampering in the labour market will lead to wages above the level required for labour demand and supply to match. Thus, neo-classical economic thought would suggest the minimum wage will lead to involuntary unemployment of those workers with the lowest skill-base (as discussed above). However, Keynesian macro-economists would argue this effect (if it exists) would be offset to some extent (or completely) by the increased spending of those who see their wages increase. Hence opportunities for employment will be created, the demand for labour will increase (thus bidding up the equilibrium price of labour) and the market will naturally adjust to clear at the new wage rate. In any event, perhaps because the minimum wage was introduced in 1999 at a time of strong economic growth in the UK, its introduction did not lead to a significant break in trend of unemployment (Stewart 2004).

The effect of this legislation on crime in England and Wales is considered by Hansen and Machin (2002). Specifically, they consider rates of four different crimes: total notified offences; property crime; vehicle crime; and violence against the person. Hansen and Machin collect data for 41 police force areas in England and Wales, controlling for demographic factors, changes in the crime clear-up rate and changes in the unemployment rate. Comparing crime rates before and after the minimum wage legislation, they find crime rates increased in those areas with the least proportion of low-paid workers. Crime rates increased by less as the proportion of low-paid workers increased. The greatest relative reductions[20] in crime rates following the introduction of the minimum wage are in those regions which have a relatively greater proportion of lower paid workers (i.e. those areas which saw greatest reductions in relative poverty).

These findings accord with those of Gould *et al.* (2002) and Machin and Meghir (2004) in supporting the hypothesis that incentive structures, in this case wages paid to the most vulnerable, have an important effect in altering the balance between legal and illegal activities (as per Ehrlich 1973). However, although the introduction of the National Minimum Wage went some (small) way towards reducing inequality in the short term, as shown by Dickens and Manning (2004), these effects are not permanent as the minimum wage has not been increased in line with average earnings in the economy. As Dahlberg and Gustavsson (2008) observe, it is permanent increases in income which are likely to lead to the most substantial reductions in crime.

Conclusion

Different theories suggest that different economic factors are important in explaining crime. Broadly speaking these can be divided into time allocation models and opportunity models (Narayan and Smyth 2004). The first approach is typified in the theoretical work of Becker (1968) and subsequent empirical research of Ehrlich (1973). Here unemployment is an indicator of the expected returns of legitimate earning activities (Narayan and Smyth 2004). From this perspective, when an individual is unemployed or employed part-time the marginal returns from legitimate earning activities are lower, reducing the opportunity cost of crime. Also he or she will have more time available to commit crime (Narayan and Smyth 2004). Thus the unemployment rate should have a positive effect on the crime rate (Narayan and Smyth 2004).

The second approach typified by Routine Activity theory and the work of Cantor and Land (1985) suggests crime is a function of the supply of suitable targets for victimisation. This perspective suggests that crime rates will fall during times of high unemployment because the circulation of people and the level of spending on new consumption items is reduced (Narayan and Smyth 2004: 2080) and thus fewer targets will be available. Similarly, as the unemployed spend more time at home, their property is better guarded and (arguably) they provide a greater level of supervision and social control over children.

There is wide variation in the way that different studies operationalise key economic concepts. While existing studies provide broad support for a link between economic factors and crime, the available studies use a number of different economic factors including employment rates, income, and various measures of wage inequality. Different studies also consider different non-economic factors, including demographics, alcohol consumption and various measures of criminal justice activity (incarceration rates, police numbers, etc.). When studies are taken chronologically, the independent variables used in different studies do not always seem consistently chosen. Independent variables that seem to have explanatory power in one study are not then taken into account in subsequent studies. Different studies assume different time-lags between changes in the economy and changes in crime rates.

There is no overall consensus on the broad relationship between unemployment and crime; however, the link between relative poverty and crime is supported by studies in which it is considered (Entorf and Spengler 2000; Gould *et al*. 2002; Hansen and Machin 2002; Machin and Meghir 2004). Simple poverty reduction programmes in which transfers are made to sectors of the community may be associated with *increases* in crime (Allen 1996) as they fail to affect labour market conditions, but increase the availability of targets.

We have seen that for the least well off the opportunity cost of crime (i.e. income) has been declining in the USA and the UK since the 1980s. This will affect crime in a number of ways, through the opportunity cost effect, but (more subtly) through anomie, alienation and the impact on the family, with the least well off finding it more difficult to achieve lifetime aspirations to maintain stable life-partnerships. This latter effect impacts both on the individuals' propensity to commit crime, and that of their children. It seems reasonable to suggest the most effective way of reducing poverty, alienation and their effect on crime is to provide meaningful reasonably paid work to those at the lower end of the income scale. However, the broad thrust of the last three decades of economic policy has arguably been orientated to the opposite effect (Davidson and Davidson 1996).

6 Economic tools

Estimating the bottom line of criminal justice interventions

> Men are greedy to publish the successes of [their] efforts, but meanly shy as to publishing the failures of men. Men are ruined by this one sided practice of concealment of blunders and failures.
>
> (Lincoln quoted in Burlingame 2008)

Introduction: a range of economic methods

We have seen in the preceding chapters there is no shortage of theories proposed to describe how criminals and society at large respond to incentive structures. However, as Becker (1968) (see Chapter Three) makes clear, all criminal justice systems have a trade-off to make between the cost of an intervention (for example, imprisonment) and the benefits to be realised. In order to apply these theories in practice, economists use a range of methods to evaluate the efficiency of different approaches to tackling crime. In this chapter we focus on two broad approaches: economic evaluation and econometrics.

Economic evaluation

When evaluating any criminal justice policy, analysts may consider:

- What was the true cost of an intervention?
- Did the outcome(s) achieved justify the investment of resources?
- Was this the most efficient way of realising the desired outcome(s) or could the same outcome(s) have been achieved at a lower cost through an alternate course of action?
- How should additional resources be spent?

(Dhiri and Brand 1999: 11)

In general, attempts to address these issues fall into one of four forms:

- *Cost analysis*: this is a partial form of economic evaluation that deals only with the costs of an intervention (Drummond *et al.* 2005).
- *Cost-effectiveness analysis*: a form of evaluation where the consequences of an intervention are measured in the most appropriate natural effects or

physical units (Drummond *et al*. 2005), such as burglaries avoided or drug-free years resulting. The consequences are not valued and the results are expressed as a cost-effectiveness ratio such as £1,000 per burglary avoided.
* *Cost–benefit analysis*: a form of evaluation where the consequences are valued in monetary terms (Drummond *et al*. 2005). Potentially this makes it the broadest form of economic evaluation method; however, as we will discuss later, difficulties in capturing and measuring wider consequences of an intervention mean that, in reality, its scope can be limited (Roman 2004).

Sometimes it is not possible to undertake the empirical work necessary to complete a cost-effectiveness or cost–benefit analysis. This might be because the programme has yet to be implemented, because the programme has already been completed or because resources for evaluation are limited. A method that is sometimes used involves drawing data from a number of different sources and developing a decision-analytic model.

Econometrics

As we have seen in previous chapters (see, in particular, Chapter Five) economists are interested in explaining what causes crime and looking at the relationship between interventions designed to reduce crime and levels of crime. While economists will often draw on various types of research study to do these things,[1] a particular type of study with which they are often associated is the econometric study. Econometrics literally means the measuring of economics, and in essence it is a tool kit of analytical and statistical methods designed to quantify the parameters of economic relationships. Consider, for example, the model of Becker (1968) discussed in Chapter Three; one of the parameters of the model is the response of potential criminals to the (perception of the) probability of punishment, severity of punishment, etc. However, simply because we know such a parameter exists does not mean we know its value.

The analysis of economic relationships is complicated by the fact that many factors are changing simultaneously. Suppose, for example, a government comes to power which pursues a whole range of economic and social policies, and generally achieves (or fails to achieve) its objectives. How can we know whether an individual policy was effective or ineffective if several were implemented simultaneously? For example, the economic policies of Margaret Thatcher and John Major, prime ministers from 1979 to 1990 and 1990 to 1997 respectively, coincided with peak production of UK North Sea oil. Was it their economic policies or the exploitation of valuable fossil fuels; both; neither; or some other factor altogether which allowed the UK to experience (in general) three decades of strong economic growth?

Thus economics as a science suffers a severe disadvantage compared to laboratory-based sciences where it is possible to exercise greater control and vary one input at a time. In addition, few would criticise a chemist, biologist or physicist for carrying out laboratory-based experiments. Also, of course, such experiments may be replicated and results checked. However, the testing ground of economic experiments is the economy. It is generally considered not 'the done thing' to experiment with the economy. Where experiments (or government policy) are carried out it is clearly not possible to repeat these. In general econometricians are faced with the task of getting as much information as possible out of very limited data sets; this has led to the establishing of a number of complicated statistical techniques.

Organisation of this chapter

This is not primarily a book about economic research methods and so our coverage of different approaches to economic research is selective and has been shaped by the types of studies we refer to in this book. We do not assume that the reader has any prior knowledge of research methods or statistics. Neither do we go into these in great detail; rather we outline what are the problems faced when estimating relationships, and give an intuitive discussion of possible solutions. For each of these approaches we use practical examples to illustrate the concepts being used.

The remainder of the chapter is organised as follows: we begin by looking at cost analysis. A cost analysis will be of use as a 'stand-alone' exercise, but it also forms the basis for cost-effectiveness analysis, cost–benefit analysis and, sometimes, a modelling exercise. As the tools used to evaluate cost-effectiveness are a sub-set of those used in cost–benefit analysis, we do not include a separate section on cost-effectiveness analyses. The discussion of cost–benefit analysis is followed by consideration of economic and behavioural modelling and a discussion on econometrics and associated problems.

Cost analysis

Viewpoint

The starting point for a cost analysis is to establish the viewpoint for analysis (Drummond *et al*. 2005), in other words, 'who pays?'; the viewpoint taken could have a radical effect on the analysis undertaken. For example, consider a drug arrest referral project operating in police stations with a primary aim to identify offenders who may have substance misuse problems and refer them to appropriate drug treatment services operated by the UK National Health Service (NHS). There are several ways of considering the costs of this intervention. If we consider only the costs to the criminal justice system, the intervention costs will be the project costs together with costs incurred by the police in facilitating the delivery of the service. However, if the point of view of the public sector is considered, we must in addition consider the costs incurred by the NHS in providing services to those offenders referred by the intervention. As the criminal justice budget is distinct from the NHS budget, considering only the former implies NHS services are (so far as the intervention is concerned) a 'free good' and thus a greater than optimal number of offenders is likely to be referred.

Different viewpoints commonly used in economic evaluation relating to crime include a criminal justice perspective, public-sector (government) perspective and a societal perspective. In the latter, costs incurred by individual victims and/or offenders will be included, whereas in the first two perspectives only costs incurred by the criminal justice system or the wider public sector will be included.

Different types of cost

As Roman (2004) notes, criminal justice programme costs are generally divided into four areas. The first is direct project expenditure. Often, in crime reduction and criminal justice interventions, a substantial proportion of the direct project expenditure goes on staff (salaries and employer contributions such as – in the UK – National Insurance and pensions). The second area consists of estimates of the value of public resources used by the intervention (ibid.). These might include costs resulting from a referral to another agency, made as part of the intervention. For example, a project working with young people at risk of offending might make a referral to a social service provider. The third area consists of estimates of the costs of services or facilities used by the intervention which are 'free'[2] or discounted (ibid.). An example of this would be the use of (unpaid) volunteers' time or where an intervention makes use of (formerly surplus) office space provided *gratis*.

The fourth cost category is more subtle. Evaluators must also identify to where resources have been diverted as a result of the intervention. Resources which would have been mobilised anyway, in the absence of the intervention, are generally excluded from cost analyses (Dhiri and Brand 1999). These make up a fourth category of costs, those relating to:

> changes in the use of program resources by program participants as compared with the counterfactual (comparison) condition.
>
> (Roman 2004: 258)

This is the concept of 'additionality of costs' (Dhiri and Brand 1999). To illustrate the concept of additionality, Dhiri and Brand (1999) take the example of a change of approach to policing that could involve: (a) hiring additional police officers; (b) reallocating officers from one activity to another; or (c) a more effective approach to existing tasks. They suggest that while (a) involves a clear additional resource requirement and therefore should be included as a cost of the intervention, (b) and (c) may well not constitute additionality; there are no additional costs incurred. In other words, replacing one intervention with another or working more efficiently (through the already planned upgrading of existing technology, for example) requires no additional resource. Roman (2004) considers such costs should be considered, however he notes when discussing cost–benefit analysis (CBA) 'few CBAs explicitly study this fourth cost category' (Roman 2004: 259).

In the short-run, economists generally break the costs of any good or service into two, so-called 'fixed' costs and 'marginal' costs. Consider, by way of illustration, the decision whether or not to drive to work today. In the context of the commuting decision, the fixed cost would be the purchase, insuring and taxing of a motor vehicle. This cost is fixed in the short-run, no matter how many times you choose to drive to work. However, the cost of each additional journey, the cost of fuel and wear-and-tear are marginal costs. These costs vary with the number of trips. A further concept is that of average cost. In this context, the average cost of travel would be the total cost of the motor vehicle (fixed and marginal cost) divided by the number of miles travelled. Because the fixed costs are, well, fixed, the further you drive, the lower is the fixed cost per mile, thus the average cost of motoring is likely to decrease as you drive further.

In the context of a criminal justice intervention, the fixed costs are those which do not vary with the number of participants on a programme or intervention, whereas costs that vary are incremental or marginal costs (Cohen 2000). Thus the concept of additionality makes a distinction between incremental or marginal costs on the one hand and fixed costs on the other. As Cohen notes:

> Conceptually, all costs of a crime prevention program should be included in a cost analysis *if* those costs would not otherwise be incurred. . . . There is a fundamental economic principle at work here: only the costs (and benefits) that vary with the decision should be considered.
>
> (Cohen 2000: 278, original emphasis)

A complicating factor is that a cost which is incremental for one decision might be fixed for another (Cohen 2000). Cohen (2000) illustrates this using a decision about whether or not to increase the average sentence for violent offenders. If there is spare prison capacity then the incremental costs associated with this decision will primarily be the cost of food, medical care, etc., for additional prisoners. However, if the policy decision requires additional prison capacity to be built, the annualised cost of prison cells becomes an incremental cost to include in the analysis. In the longer run, economists tend to argue that all costs are incremental. Thus, while a maintaining a prison which already purchased is a fixed cost, over a long enough time horizon, extra capacity might be built, or indeed, existing facilities might be moth-balled or sold off. It may be the case, of course, that in the short-run the 'cost' of incarcerating violent prisoners for a longer period is a greater number of non-violent offenders for whom space cannot be found.

Therefore, although in principle, including 'only the costs (and benefits) that vary with the decision' (Cohen 2000) is an uncontentious rule, to implement this rule is often less than straightforward. Careful analysis is required of which costs and benefits vary with a decision.

Gathering data on inputs

There are different ways of gathering data on inputs, which is to say, the resources used by a programme or intervention. For the first three categories of cost described above, estimates are often developed through: a review of financial reports; invoices and progress reports to funders; and interviews with key staff (Roman 2004). In some cases these might be supplemented by surveys, activity diaries or activity sampling exercises (Dhiri and Brand 1999).

For the fourth category of costs a counterfactual is required to estimate the difference between the costs incurred by the intervention and costs which would have been incurred anyway. The counterfactual might take the form of comparing current budgets to the baseline (pre-intervention) level of resources (Dhiri and Brand 1999) or the cost of the next best approach to delivering the desired outcome.

If an intervention allows for variation in the way a service is delivered it will be important to consider the distribution of costs. For example, an intervention with the aim of offender rehabilitation[3] might allow for variation in the intensity of service delivered to offenders with different needs or levels of risk. Alternatively, the costs incurred by other parts of the public sector may vary according to the types of support given to different groups of offenders. The needs of some might be addressed primarily by the new programme or intervention while others might be referred to different parts of the public sector. In both of these circumstances the distribution of costs will vary between different groups of offenders and between different parts of the public sector. Analysis of this distribution might provide insights as to the relative efficiency of working with different groups of offenders or working with offenders in different ways.

It is common practice to identify both set-up and ongoing costs of an intervention. Take the example of a three-year youth outreach project, the annual costs for which are the salaries of two part-time youth outreach workers (say £25,000) and rent for some office space at a local community centre (say £5,000). The annual cost of the project would therefore be £30,000. Suppose, however, that at the start of the first year of the project a minibus costing £15,000 is bought. This is a start-up cost of the project. It is a one-off cost which will not be repeated again during the project's three-year lifespan. It is important this one-off cost is taken into account because it will raise the overall cost of the three-year project and, depending how it is handled, is likely also to affect the estimate of the annual cost for project delivery (see below for a discussion on handling capital costs).

It is also important to consider the time period over which costs will be tracked (Drummond *et al.* 2005). One risk is that if costs are based on a short time period they will be influenced by unusual events or circumstances. Another risk is that, if the costing period is early in the implementation phase of an intervention, resource use may be relatively inefficient. Those implementing the intervention may have to learn how to do so most efficiently. A third risk is that, if a unit of treatment takes a long time to deliver (compare the length of time taken to deliver a heroin substitution intervention with the time taken to target-harden a residential property), a short time period during which costs are captured might not take account of the full cost of implementation.

For many interventions studied, the costs involved are extremely complex. Therefore when gathering costs data there will normally be a trade-off made between the time and effort required to gather data and the magnitude of the costs involved in data collection.[4] As Drummond *et al.* note:

It is not worth investing a great deal of time and effort considering costs that, because they are small, are unlikely to make any difference to the study result.

(Drummond *et al*. 2005: 57)

Valuing inputs

Once relevant costs have been identified, individual items must be measured and valued (Drummond *et al*. 2005). A general principle is that the economic cost of an input should be estimated. The economic cost of using a resource is the value of its next most valuable alternative use (Dhiri and Brand 1999). The economic cost of an input may differ from its financial cost (ibid.); however, generally, the market value of a resource is assumed to reflect its opportunity cost (ibid.).

While it may be relatively straightforward to estimate the market value of office space utilised in the delivery of an intervention where it has not been the subject of a cash transaction, making such an estimation for some non-market items will be more difficult. For example, a mentoring project for young offenders where the mentoring is provided by volunteers may have a relatively small budget but, through the time of volunteers, might be deploying a substantial (if non-monetised) resource. The value given to this time will depend in part on the view-point adopted (see above). For example, if this is a project being run by the local authority then, from a local authority viewpoint, the cost of volunteers' time may be zero. But from a societal perspective, there is a value to this time – volunteers might use their time for other voluntary activities or paid employment. Different approaches to valuing volunteer time will be used in different studies and might be based on the cost of paying the market rate to a professional mentor or (in the UK) the minimum wage. In addition to the choice of viewpoint, the choice of estimate will be based in part on the type of person who volunteers and whether the time volunteered is time which would otherwise be used for paid work or leisure.

Capital costs are the costs to purchase major assets required to deliver an intervention; generally equipment, buildings and land (Drummond *et al*. 2005). They represent an investment at a single point in time, often during the set-up phase of a project (see above). The benefit of the investment is realised over time. Drummond *et al*. (2005) identify two components of a capital cost. First there is the opportunity cost of tying up in a capital asset funds which cannot then be invested in some other way and second there is the depreciation over time of the asset itself. Drummond *et al*. (2005) suggest that the best method of measuring and valuing capital costs in an economic evaluation is to annuitise (that is, to distribute) the initial capital outlay over the useful life of the asset. They argue that this approach incorporates both the depreciation aspect and the opportunity cost aspect of the capital cost.

Discounting future benefits and costs

In an economic analysis, costs (and benefits) are generally paid or received at different points in time. In general, changes in price alter the value, i.e. buying power, of a sum of money over time. To illustrate this, suppose you are considering putting £100 in the bank for one year, and the rate of interest is 5 per cent. After one year, the £100 you invested today will be worth £105. Or, to put it the other way about, £105 in one year's time is worth £100 today. If you leave your money in the bank for a further year, it will be worth £110.25 and so on.[5] Thus £110.25 in two years' time is worth £100 today. The process of reducing a nominal future value to today's value (that is to say, the Present Value) is known as discounting. Thus, £105 in one year's time is discounted to £100 today (implying a discount rate of 5 per cent).[6] Although the formulae used to discount may become somewhat complicated once (for example) discounting by parts of years or at different rates are included, in principle the concept is the same.[7] However, discounting is not simply a response to price change. It extends beyond money transactions to goods and services (Drummond *et al.* 2005) and it recognises a more fundamental aspect of human nature: that people generally prefer to receive a benefit today rather than tomorrow. To put it another way, individuals require a greater benefit tomorrow to create an incentive to forgo consumption today.

Suppose, for example, a farmer has three bushels of grain and is thinking of sowing a field with this. If he knows planting the three bushels will only give a yield of three bushels, there will be no incentive to sow; he gets back just what he planted but had to expend effort to carry out the work. However, if the return from planting is greater than the cost of the seed, he may sow the grain in the expectation of getting a greater amount back come harvest time. The same basic philosophy applies to whether or not we should invest our money in the bank (or in business). When we invest, we must expect to receive more back in the future, or we will not invest.

Discounting is used so that the Net Present Value of costs and benefits can be calculated. Net Present Value (NPV) is defined by the UK government in the Treasury Green Book as 'The discounted value of a stream of either future costs or benefits' (HM Treasury undated: 103). The 'Net' in the 'Net Present Value' implies that all costs have been factored out of the resulting total.

How might a cost analysis be used?

A piece of cost analysis is likely to present the average cost of the intervention being examined. The average cost provides a measure of the overall return to an intervention (Dhiri and Brand 1999). This is useful information on its own. It also forms one of the key building blocks for a cost-effectiveness or cost–benefit analysis.

The calculation of the average cost allows the evaluator to answer the question 'What is the relative value for money of the intervention(s)?' (Dhiri and Brand 1999). However, another important question to answer is 'What level of investment in an intervention yields the highest net benefit?' (Dhiri and Brand 1999). To answer this second question the evaluator must calculate the marginal cost of the intervention. Marginal cost can be defined as the cost of producing one extra unit of output. As discussed above, when calculating the marginal cost, only those inputs which are required to achieve the extra unit of output are included. Fixed costs such as premises or staff are excluded unless they are required to achieve this extra unit (Dhiri and Brand 1999).

Fixed costs may be included, however, in the calculation of the average cost of the intervention. Drummond *et al.* suggest two reasons for the significance of the average cost/marginal cost distinction:

> First, when making a comparison of two or more programmes it is worth asking independently of each, 'What would be the costs (and consequences) of having a little more or a little less?' . . . Second, when examining the effects on (cost) of small changes in output, it is likely that these will differ from average costs.
>
> (Drummond *et al.* 2005: 65–6)

To give an example, the marginal cost of keeping a prisoner in custody for one additional day might be less than the average daily cost of their whole stay in prison, because the average of their total stay includes the fixed cost of their incarceration in the first place. Similarly, the marginal cost of fitting one extra CCTV camera in a town centre might be less than the average cost per camera of the whole CCTV installation.

Of course, sometimes the marginal cost might be higher than the average cost. For example if a prison is at full capacity, taking one additional prisoner might necessitate building a further prison wing and recruiting more staff, in which case the marginal cost of accommodating that one extra prisoner will be far higher than the average cost per prisoner.

Cost analysis example: Dedicated Drug Courts

An evaluation of Dedicated Drug Courts, undertaken by The Matrix Knowledge Group (2008), included an economic analysis, the first stage of which was a cost analysis. Dedicated Drug Courts are specialist courts which exclusively handle cases relating to drug-misusing offenders from conviction through sentence to completion (or breach) of a community order. Offenders are sentenced to a Drug Rehabilitation Requirement (DRR) which is then supervised by the court. This includes regular drug testing, probation supervision and the offender returning to court regularly to report on their progress. The evaluation looked at two magistrates' courts that had been piloting the Dedicated Drug Courts, one in Leeds and one in West London (Matrix 2008).

Data for the cost analysis was gathered via interviews with practitioners, other key stakeholders and a review of relevant documentation. The analysis of costs identified the extra resources when compared with what would have happened in the absence of the Dedicated Drug Court. This counter-factual was defined as delivery of a DDR in courts that comply with the minimum National Standards relating to a DRR but that do not operate the DDC model.

The cost analysis distinguished between the costs of setting up drug courts (for example, the costs of training magistrates) and ongoing running costs (for example, the costs of maintaining a steering group). The costs analysis also identified direct and indirect costs. Direct costs included the steering group, training and judiciary rota administration. Indirect costs included the cost to the probation service of undertaking additional drug tests and writing and presenting additional reviews for the courts. By looking at the number of offenders processed by the Dedicated Drug Court a unit cost (the cost per offender) was also calculated. These costs are set out in Table 6.1.

Table 6.1 Cost analysis of the Dedicated Drug Court pilots

		Leeds	West London
Set up costs	Systems design	£22,013	£22,013
	Training	£3,744	£971
	Total first year set-up cost	**£25,757**	**£22,984**
Running costs	Steering group	£3,233	£2,567
	Magistrates meetings	£3,518	—
	Communication	£4,564	—
	Rota administration	£852	—
	Total first year running cost	**£12,167**	**£2,567**
Total cost		**£37,924**	**£25,551**
Number of offenders per annum		276	60
Cost per new offender		**£137**	**£426**

Source: The Matrix Knowledge Group (2008: Table 3.1).

Cost–benefit analysis

Cost–benefit analysis is the pre-eminent form of economic analysis for assessing the efficiency of interventions and as such we will examine its use in the field of crime reduction and criminal justice in detail.

Cost–benefit analysis is concerned with both measuring the effectiveness of an intervention and whether an intervention is efficient in that the benefits of the intervention are greater than the costs (Dhiri and Brand 1999; Welsh and Farrington 2001a). In a cost–benefit analysis, the effects – the outcomes of an intervention – are valued in standardised monetary units, such as dollars or pounds, and compared with the costs of the interventions inputs. This approach creates a standardised measure which, in principle, allows for a direct comparison of two or more interventions even if those interventions vary in their goals and objectives and target heterogeneous populations and outcomes.[8] However, it must also be recognised that 'Benefit-cost analysis is an art that is built on many important assumptions' (Cohen 2000: 266). Some of these assumptions, such as the perspective taken, have already been discussed in this chapter. Others will be discussed below.

A cost-effectiveness analysis is essentially a partial cost–benefit analysis and so, while there is no separate section in this chapter examining cost-effectiveness analysis, some key issues in relation to cost-effectiveness analysis can be imputed from this section.

Before we continue, a word on terminology. It is common in conversation for people to use the term cost–benefit analysis to refer, generally, to economic evaluation (Drummond *et al.* 2005). However, for economists cost–benefit analysis has a specific meaning and is clearly distinguishable from other approaches to economic evaluation such as cost analysis or cost-effectiveness analysis. When we use the term cost–benefit analysis we are referring to its more technical meaning.

Stages in a cost–benefit analysis

There are a number of stages in a cost–benefit analysis (Welsh and Farrington 2001a):

1. *Define the scope of the analysis*: key issues to decide at this stage include: the perspective to take in the analysis (for example, will the perspective be that of the state, the criminal justice system or the whole of society); what outcomes are to be measured; and the alternatives to be compared (for example, participation in a programme versus non-participation) (Welsh and Farrington 2001a).
2. *Obtain estimates of programme effects*: there are different ways to measure programme effects, but most economists favour an outcome evaluation in which an experimental or quasi-experimental design has been used. This is a complex issue and we return to it below.
3. *Estimate the monetary value of costs and benefits*: we have already discussed how the monetary value of costs is estimated in the section on cost analysis. The defining feature of a cost–benefit analysis is that the effects of the intervention – the outcomes – are valued in standardised monetary units. Thus the benefit of the intervention, expressed in monetary terms, can be compared directly with the costs of the intervention, also expressed in the same monetary terms.
4. *Calculate present value and assess efficiency*: as we discussed when looking at cost analysis (see above) if the monetary expressions of the costs and

benefits of an intervention are to be compared directly then it is important we recognise not all of these costs and benefits accrue at the same point in time. Unless all of the costs and benefits accrue within the same year, it is important to account both for the effect of inflation and for the fact that people generally prefer to receive a benefit today rather than tomorrow (Dhiri and Brand 1999; Welsh and Farrington 2001a). Therefore a process of discounting is used to calculate the Net Present Value of all costs (see above for a more detailed discussion). Once the Net Present Value of costs and benefits has been calculated then the intervention's efficiency can be calculated in the form of a benefit/cost ratio (benefits divided by costs) or net value (benefits minus costs) (Welsh and Farrington 2001a).

5. *Describe the distribution of costs and benefits*: describing the distribution of programme costs and benefits involves identifying who gained and who lost from the intervention (Welsh and Farrington 2001a). For example, in a cost–benefit analysis of a criminal justice intervention it is common to find an analysis of efficiency from the perspective of the state rather than from the perspective of wider society.

6. *Conduct sensitivity analysis*: once the intervention's efficiency has been calculated it is important to check how sensitive the resulting figure is to variations in the estimates that have been used in the cost–benefit analysis. One approach to sensitivity analysis is the calculation of switching values in which analysis is undertaken to ascertain by how much a variable would have to fall (if it is a benefit) or rise (if it is a cost) to switch the calculation of efficiency from positive to negative or vice versa (HM Treasury undated).

All of these stages are required for a cost–benefit analysis. For a cost-effectiveness analysis the third and fifth steps are omitted (Welsh and Farrington 2001a). Two aspects of a cost–benefit analysis are particularly challenging. Estimating the monetary value of costs and benefits is one. In the field of crime reduction and criminal justice the benefits are often, but not always, a reduction in crime. Therefore a key issue for cost–benefit analysis in this field is how to place a value on different types of crime. Crimes give rise to tangible costs, such as repairing a car that has been broken into or replacing stolen property, but they also give rise to intangible costs such as the physical and psychological harm done to victims. This is a complex area which merits its own chapter, which follows this one. A second challenge is obtaining estimates of programme effects. Most economists favour an outcome evaluation in which an experimental or quasi-experimental design has been used. This is critical to the success of a cost–benefit analysis and also much contested within social science and so the following section looks at this issue in more detail.

Estimating programme effects

An important element of the cost–benefit analysis process is estimating the programme or intervention effects. There are different ways to measure these, but most economists favour an outcome evaluation in which a social experimental or quasi-experimental design has been used.

Social experiments test whether a programme or policy has led to change in the outcomes the programme or policy was designed to influence, over and above that which would have occurred in the absence of the programme or policy (Government Social Research Unit 2007). Central to a social experiment is the concept of random allocation, alternatively referred to as random assignment or randomisation (Government Social Research Unit 2007), and this is illustrated in Figure 6.1.

The units in a social experiment can be individuals, institutions or areas and the control group is the 'counterfactual' (Government Social Research Unit 2007). This group represents what would have happened in the absence of the new intervention and as such normally receives either the next best treatment or treatment as usual (Government Social Research Unit 2007). Welsh and Farrington (2001a) note that a social experiment is only a convincing method of evaluation if a sufficiently large number of units is randomly assigned to ensure that the programme group is equivalent to the control group on all possible extraneous variables. As a rule of thumb they suggest that at least 50 units in each category are needed.

Social experiments are preferred by economists because they can deliver potentially unbiased estimates of the programme or policy being evaluated (Government Social Research Unit 2007). This is because, if implemented properly, they have the highest possible level of internal validity. Internal validity refers to 'the correctness of the key question about whether the intervention really did cause a change in the outcome' (Farrington 2003: 52). The main threats as set out by Shadish, Cook and Campbell (2002: 55) and reproduced in Farrington (2003: 53) are:

1. *Selection*: the effect reflects preexisting differences between experimental and control conditions. In other words, the allocation to the experimental and control groups is not random.
2. *History*: the effect is caused by some other event occurring at the same time as the intervention. A suitably specified control group should allow the researcher to determine whether this is indeed the case.
3. *Maturation*: the effect reflects a continuation of pre-existing trends in normal human development. It is known, for example, that a proportion of offenders naturally desist from criminal activity as they mature. Thus any intervention

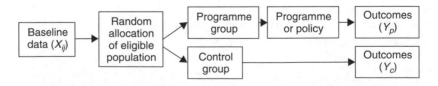

Figure 6.1 Design for a social experiment.

Source: Government Social Research Unit (2007: Figure 7.2).

running over a period of years might be expected to show some (natural) desistence in the intervention group. Again, examination of the outcomes of the control group should allow the researcher to allow for such effects.

4. *Instrumentation*: the (observed) effect is caused by a change in the method of measuring the outcome.
5. *Testing*: the pre-test measurement causes a change in the post-test measure.
6. *Regression to the mean*: where an intervention is implemented on units with unusually high scores (e.g., areas with high crime rates), natural fluctuation will cause a decrease in these scores on the post-test. This may be mistakenly interpreted as an effect of the intervention. The opposite (an increase) happens when interventions are applied to low-crime areas or low-scoring people. To illustrate, consider a simple experiment where 60 students roll a regular die: all those who roll a 'six' are regarded as being at high risk of crime. So these are selected for an intervention – let's suppose the intervention is standing on one leg when the die is re-rolled. Standing on one leg then, only the group of students who scored a 'six' on the previous round re-roll the dice. It is likely most of them will not roll another 'six'. Proof positive that standing on one leg reduces the probability of rolling a 'six'?[9]
7. *Differential attrition*: the effect is caused by differential loss of units (e.g. people) from experimental compared to control conditions.
8. *Causal order*: it is unclear whether the intervention preceded the outcome.

It is not always possible or desirable to implement a social experiment (for a brief discussion of some of main critiques of social experiments see below) and this is why economists often favour the use of a robust quasi-experiment. These are:

> experiments that have treatments, outcome measures, and experimental units, but do not use random assignment to create the comparisons from which treatment-caused change is inferred. Instead, the comparisons depend on non-equivalent groups that differ from each other in many ways other than the presence of the treatment whose effects are being tested.
>
> (Cook and Campbell 1979: 6)

In essence, as the design moves further away from the 'gold standard' of a social experiment, the less strong the internal validity assured by the design. As part of an extensive review of what works in crime prevention, Sherman *et al.* (1998a) developed the Maryland Scale of Scientific Methods that sets out a ranking of study designs with Level 1 being the weakest and Level 5 the strongest (see Figure 6.2). Level 5 describes a social experiment. Levels 3 and 4 describe robust quasi-experiments that economists would be likely to favour when evaluating the impact of a programme or policy.

The use of social experiments is contested within the social sciences and many of these criticisms are also applicable to quasi-experiments. Methodological criticisms include that social experiments do not collect or do not look for unintended consequences of a policy or programme and that in providing average impact estimates

---

The Maryland Scale of Scientific Methods

Level 1: Correlation between a crime prevention programme and a measure of crime or crime risk factors at a single point in time.

Level 2: Temporal sequence between the programme and the crime or risk outcome clearly observed, or the presence of a comparison group without demonstrated comparability to the treatment group.

Level 3: A comparison between two or more comparable units of analysis, one with and one without the programme.

Level 4: Comparison between multiple units with and without the programme, controlling for other factors, or using comparison units that evidence only minor differences.

Level 5: Random assignment and analysis of comparable units to the programme and comparison groups.

Figure 6.2 The Maryland Scale.

Source: Sherman *et al.* (1998a).

significant variation in outcomes may be hidden (Government Social Research Unit 2007). Ethical concerns include the argument that individuals allocated to the control group are discriminated against because they are not receiving an intervention given to the treatment group, although a counter argument is that until a social experiment is completed we do not know that intervention is beneficial (Government Social Research Unit 2007). More fundamentally, social scientists and evaluators arguing from different paradigms question philosophical assumptions upon which social experiments are based. One of the most widely discussed critiques of recent years has come from Pawson and Tilley (1997) who argue that:

> For us, the experimental paradigm constitutes a heroic failure, promising so much and yet ending up in ironic anticlimax. The underlying logic . . . seems meticulous, clear-headed and militarily precise, and yet findings seem to emerge in a typically non-cumulative, low impact, prone-to-equivocation sort of way.
>
> (Pawson and Tilley 1997: 8)

They put forward an alternative approach to evaluation, which they place within a 'scientific realist' paradigm of social enquiry. Pawson and Tilly argue that, instead of undertaking experiments and quasi-experiments, researchers should investigate context–mechanism–outcome configurations:

> Programs work (have successful outcomes) only in so far as they introduce the appropriate ideas and opportunities (mechanisms) to groups in the appropriate social and cultural conditions (contexts).
>
> (Pawson and Tilley 1997: 57)

The pros and cons of cost–benefit analysis

As Marsh, Fox and Hedderman (2009) note, economists make a number of arguments in favour of analysing the costs and benefits of criminal justice interventions.

First, even though an intervention may yield positive outcomes (such as desistance from crime and increases in pro-social behaviour such as getting a job) the cost of the intervention may outweigh the intervention's benefits; and an alternative intervention may achieve the same outcomes for a lower cost. Marsh *et al.* (2008) have illustrated the importance of cost–benefit analysis to decision-making in criminal justice. They demonstrate that the effect of a criminal justice intervention at reducing offending is only weakly related to net benefits in terms of savings to the Exchequer and/or wider society and that, in about one quarter of cases, considering both costs and benefits would produce different policy recommendations to just analysing changes in offending rates.

Second, whereas observational studies examine outcomes one at a time, cost–benefit analysis considers all outcomes jointly, using the standardised (monetised) estimates of costs and benefits as weights that generate a single measure of intervention effectiveness.

Third, cost–benefit analysis allows for the valuation of hard to observe outcomes, such as fear, pain and suffering.

Fourth, cost–benefit analysis has the potential to account for externalities – outcomes for individuals not directly involved in the intervention, but who are nevertheless impacted by its results. Finally, since public resources are scarce, it is incumbent upon policy-makers to choose the most efficient intervention, the scheme where costs are minimised and/or benefits are maximised (Cohen 2000).

There are also criticisms of the use of cost–benefit analysis in the fields of crime reduction and criminal justice. Some of these focus on the challenges of valuing cost and, particularly, benefits (see for instance Zedlewski 2009) and are considered in more detail in Chapter Seven. Others focus on the relationship between evaluation and valuation. As we have seen, cost–benefit analysis relies heavily on the results of a robust outcome evaluation and these suffer from numerous threats to validity (Farrington 2003; Roman 2004). However, Roman (2004) suggests, by taking the results of an outcome evaluation and translating these programme effects into monetary values, the cost–benefit analysis introduces additional threats to validity which are not present in an outcome evaluation. The problem is that a traditional cost–benefit analysis cannot identify 'externalities', whether positive or negative. These are transactions where part of the costs or benefits of the transaction are borne by individuals not party to the transaction (Roman 2004). So, for example, if a prison stay is averted because of a successful programme intervention, the outcome evaluation will capture data to show that, compared to the control group, a victimisation and a prison stay have both been averted and a traditional cost–benefit analysis will place a value on these outcomes. But in doing so most traditional cost–benefit analyses implicitly assume that the prison bed will go unused. However it may be taken up by another offender and further victimisation might be averted due to that offender being incapacitated (Roman 2004). These externalities are not easily captured in a traditional cost–benefit analysis. Thus, Roman (2004) argues that a traditional cost–benefit analysis introduces two biases. First, it overestimates programme benefits by assuming that the prison bed remains empty and second it underestimates programme benefits when incarceration of a different offender prevents other victimisation. Considering the utility of cost–benefit analysis to policy-makers and the policy-making process leads Roman to argue that:

> A CBA that does not accurately describe the beneficiaries and the benefactors of programming will not assist in this policy-making process. CBAs that report benefits to administrators who cannot observe those differences will not benefit anyone.
>
> (Roman 2004: 270)

Roman (2004) suggests that, while one response to this issue would be to tailor the cost–benefit analysis to meet the practical constraints of crime research, a better option is to choose policy questions more appropriately answered in an economic analysis:

> Generally, CBA researchers will test whether the program results in a change in net benefits from the programs, which implicitly focuses the research on individual participant outcomes. Instead, researchers could test a hypothesis about whether the intervention results in economic welfare changes (positive or negative) within the community it serves.
>
> (Roman 2004: 271)

Roman's suggestion is that one successful programme completion that diverts an offender from custody will simply make room for a further offender to enter prison (the benefits of whose incarceration are not included in the CBA). The point may, however, be made that, if an intervention succeeds in reducing the prison population by a large number, future (planned) capital investment might not be required. Thus there is, what economists would call, a non-linearity – the cost–benefit associated with 1,000 successful completions (for example) is not simply 10 times as great as the saving made from 100 completions. This point is often overlooked in traditional CBA. Roman suggests that a range of studies be carried out for different effect sizes and different programme sizes to determine the trade-off.

Cost–benefit analysis example: High/Scope Perry Preschool Program

One of the most often quoted cost–benefit analyses in the field of crime reduction is the High/Scope Perry Preschool Program. The results of this 40-year follow-up study have been reported in a number of publications over the years. This account draws principally on Belfield *et al.* (2006) who report analysis of data on individuals aged 40.

The programme involved an intensive pre-school intervention delivered to at-risk children in Michigan in the 1960s. The provision was composed of three parts: first a centre-based programme for two and half hours per day for each weekday, with a child-to-teacher ratio of 5:1; second, home visiting for one and a half hours per weekday; and third group-meetings of parents (Belfield *et al.* 2006). The programme effect was evaluated using a social experiment. Of the sample of 123 children, 58 were randomly assigned to receive the programme and 65 to be in a control group. The children have been surveyed periodically since the programme.

Costs information was taken from school district budgets and the programme administration unit. Costs identified included both operating costs (instructional staff, administrative and support staff, overhead, supplies, and developmental screening) and capital costs (for classrooms and facilities). Using both individual-level data on participants and the control group of non-participants and national data sets, the advantages from programme participation are calculated in dollar amounts up to age 40 and projected forward to age 65. Belfield *et al.* (2006) report that these advantages are primarily gains in earnings, reductions in crime, and changes in welfare receipt, but there also are differences in schooling and adult-education costs. Benefits accrue to the individual, the general public, and to society and so a number of separate cost–benefit analyses are necessary to cover each perspective (Belfield *et al.* 2006).

Programme costs are compared against treatment impacts on educational resources, earnings, criminal activity and welfare receipts. Net present values were calculated for participants, the general public, and society. Sensitivity analysis was also undertaken. The treatment group obtains significantly higher earnings. For the general public, higher tax revenues, lower criminal justice system expenditures, and lower welfare payments easily outweigh programme costs: they repay $12.90 for every $1 invested. However, programme gains come mainly from reduced crime by males (Belfield *et al.* 2006) as illustrated in Figure 6.3.

Modelling studies

It will be noted, from the cost–benefit analysis discussed above, that the savings to society from the High/Scope Perry Preschool Program fall into two broad categories: costs and benefits which are realised now, the values of which we may reasonably estimate from social service and education budgets; and costs and benefits which are speculative in nature, arising at a point in time after the study/ intervention concludes. A large proportion of the savings identified from the High/

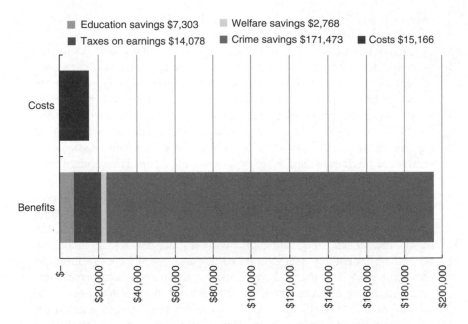

Figure 6.3 High/Scope Perry Preschool Program public costs and benefits using data from the age-40 follow-up.

Source: taken from Schweinhart (undated: Table 3.1).

Note: figures are per participant in 2000 constant dollars discounted at 3 per cent annually.

Scope Perry Preschool study result from 'crimes which did not occur' amongst the intervention cohort compared to the control cohort. How can we know the savings arising from 'crimes which did not occur'? In the High/Scope Perry Preschool the researchers were able to answer this question by undertaking an empirical study in which individuals were followed up for several decades and data on key outcomes collected. In many studies, however, there is no matched cohort or we have no information stretching out forward into the future regarding costs which did not arise. How then can we address issues such as determining the saving from crimes which did not arise? Such questions are crucial in valuing criminal justice interventions.

Take, for example, the relatively simple choice: whether to send an offender to prison or not. Currently in England and Wales it costs society around £40,000 per prisoner per year of incarceration. Logically, society should only be prepared to bear such a cost if the benefits from the sentence (revenge, incapacitation, deterrence, rehabilitation) outweigh the costs.[10] Focusing on incapacitation; the reduction in crime which comes from incapacitating an individual for, say, one year comes from the calculation of how much crime that offender *would have committed* had they not been in prison. Similarly, the effect of deterrence comes from determining the amount of crime which *would have been* committed if prospective criminals knew for a fact that they would not be punished – or if the punishment had been less severe. Again, the benefit of a rehabilitation programme comes from determining how much crime an individual *would commit* if they undergo rehabilitation compared to the amount they *will commit* if they do not engage with rehabilitation. The value of all of these is, as economists would say, an empirical matter – which is to say that they must be measured. However, the measuring process is by no means straightforward. Given the practical challenges and huge resource commitments to undertake long-term follow-up studies involving intervention and control groups, to say nothing of the long period of time that policymakers will have to wait before they receive an answer, it is not surprising that economists often build models to capture these long-term effects.

The principles of modelling

The principles of modelling do not differ much in economics from the sciences (what economists would call the 'other' sciences), but may consider different effects. In essence a model provides a reasonable and workable approximation to reality which will allow forecasts to be made about the results or outcomes of certain actions or changes in policy structures.

By way of illustration, let's use a modelling example from the world of sport. Suppose we wish to throw a dart at a dart board – let's say we are aiming at the bull's-eye. In general our brain considers this task on a subconscious level. We do not actually calculate mathematically how much force to apply to the dart, indeed, we wouldn't be able to state with any certainty how much force in Newtons we will apply, but (through observations of the results of previous throws of the dart and memory of the technique used, the force applied and other associated variables) our brain works out how much force to apply, the trajectory and the likely outcome.

Now, enter a physicist armed with: $e = mc^2$; weights and measures; the force of gravity; data on the cross wind; diagrams of human musculature; etc. It is, in theory, possible to represent perfectly accurately the flight of the dart from hand to board.[11] Technically the flight of a dart can be described as a parabola, a mathematical equation which describes how a number of variables interact: the position of the dart, the force with which it was thrown, the time since it left our hand, etc. This mathematical equation is what is known as the model. For a given level of the initial variables, a mathematical model exists to predict with a great deal of precision where the dart will hit the board. However this model relies on very precise measurement of input factors.

Finally a social scientist enters the room. The model they suggest will deal more with the human aspect of playing darts. A social scientist will not seek to address specifically the precise relationship between the forces of gravity, the spin of the earth, the force applied to the dart and so on, but will rather ask: how long has the individual been playing darts; how old are they; what is their blood alcohol level; is the game of darts common in their cultural background; etc., and (if the social scientist is an economist) how much money depends on the accuracy of the throw?

Clearly then social science models will be far less precise than physical models. Two individuals with the same level of experience will throw differently because of, for example, innate skill. However, we may be reasonably sure than any individual, regardless of their innate skill, will throw more accurately as they practise more. Thus the social scientist might not necessarily predict exactly where on the board the dart will hit, but might predict, where two people are playing darts, who is the more likely to win having considered all relevant factors such as which person practises the more, who has had the less alcohol to drink, etc. Such models deal with overall tendencies, rather than the specific outcomes of individuals.[12]

To build our economic model, in this admittedly trivial case, we must consider: first the main factors which go into the accuracy of the darts player – the input (or explanatory) variables; second how they relate to each other and whatever objective is considered; and ultimately seek to measure somehow how important each factor is, and the result of varying these inputs on the objective. For the sake of practicality or through issues of measurement, some degree of discernment or theory must be employed to select appropriate inputs. The input variables are combined using a set of weights which represent their relative importance to give an overall estimate of the outcome measure (for example accuracy at darts). The weights applied to the input variables are called 'parameters'. Such variables and parameters are often represented by letters in mathematical formulae.

An example: models of criminal justice and the decision to commit crime

We have already come across several of the mathematical models economists use to forecast or illustrate the interactions between incentives and human behaviour; for example, the simple supply–demand framework we discuss in Chapter Two is based on a mathematical model. We illustrate the model using a simple diagram; however, the underlying theory has a mathematical representation. Similarly Becker (1968), Ehrlich (1973) and the majority of economic representations of the incentive structures which influence an individual's propensity to criminal activities are expressed mathematically. In the context of the determination evaluating criminal justice interventions, a useful illustration of the strength of the approach is shown in the calculation of the costs of a criminal career, as discussed in the Appraisal of Prisoner Resettlement Projects for Short-sentence Prisoners of the United Kingdom (Ministry of Justice 2008). This insightful model has been used in a number of break-even analyses: internally at the Ministry; and externally (Fox *et al*. 2010).

The model of costs of future criminal career seeks to estimate the cost to society of an offender *after they have paid their debt to society for previous crimes*, and represents the average of lifetime crimes they are expected to commit weighted by the probability of their occurring. A feature of all such mathematical models is that they seek to simplify, through reasonable assumptions, the number of parameters. Following MacLeod in Home Office (2003a) let us write the probability of reconviction in the first year after release from prison using the symbol p. MacLeod assumes this same probability applies irrespective of the number of previous convictions. In practice, this *probability* will be measured using the *proportion* of offenders who re-offend after their release. This follows because a proportion in the population with a particular attribute is equivalent to a probability of any one individual chosen at random having that attribute. If, for example, it is known that 10 per cent of the population are left-handed, the probability that any one individual is left-handed is 10 per cent (if they are chosen at random).

Clearly, when a cohort of prisoners is released from prison, a proportion, p, will be re-convicted in their first year after release, while the remainder will not. Of those who are not re-convicted in the first year, a lesser proportion, modelled by Ministry of Justice (2008) as p^2, will be re-convicted in the second year after release. Of those who do not re-offend in the first two years, a lesser proportion, p^3, will be re-convicted in the third year after release and so on. Note that, following MacLeod, where an offender is re-convicted, their probability of being convicted of future offences is 'reset' to p on their release.

The Home Office (2003a) model of future criminal career on release from custody is represented in Figure 6.4 where the height of the walking person represents the size of the cohort (for example, a person of half size represents 50 per cent of the cohort have made it to that stage), the width of horizontal arrows represents the proportion which 'goes straight' (i.e. not being re-convicted in that year), while the width of downwards pointing arrows represents the proportion which is re-convicted. We see clearly the proportion which continues without re-conviction is less and less as time goes on until, after three years (though mathematically the model continues indefinitely), the majority have been re-convicted – as shown by the relative heights of the walking persons on the right hand margin.[13]

It should be noted however, in all years but the first, ex-offenders are more likely *not* to be re-convicted than to be re-convicted – this is demonstrated by the

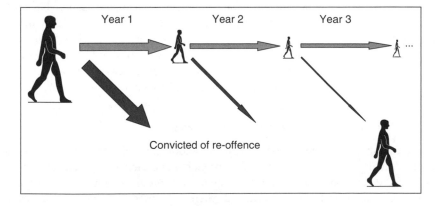

Figure 6.4 Representation of re-conviction over time.

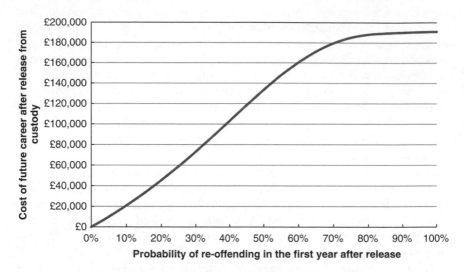

Figure 6.5 The relationship between future career costs and the probability of a re-offence
in the first year after release from custody.

horizontal arrow being of greater width than the downwards arrow in any year
after year 1. The parameter p is determined by considering the re-conviction rate
of cohorts of offenders in the first year after their release from prison.

Having thus determined the probability of re-conviction, the Ministry of Justice (2008) use the costs of crime, as calculated by the Home Office (2005) and
Brand and Price (2000) (see Chapter Seven for more discussion on these), together
with the observed proportions of crimes leading to re-conviction, to determine
the expected cost to society of the future criminal career of an offence leading to
re-conviction.[14]

Fox *et al.* (2010) wish to determine the cost of the future criminal career, as a
function of the probability of re-offending, in order to monetise the benefits of
interventions which reduce this probability. The function appears somewhat complicated in its mathematical form and is represented graphically in Figure 6.5. It
is clear the costs of the future career increase approximately linearly with p, for p
ranging from 60 per cent to 0 per cent. Each 1 per cent point reduction in p saves
society approximately £3,000 at 2010 prices. For p in excess of 70 per cent, we
require a much greater reduction in p to save an equivalent amount.

Estimating the known unknowns – econometrics

In the example from the Ministry of Justice (2008) discussed above, the parameters of the model, the probability of re-offending and the cost of each offence are
estimated directly by considering the outcomes of previous cohorts of prisoners.
This straightforward technique is useful where outcomes or data occur independently but is less useful when factors may be interrelated, and where effects cannot

be taken as independent. In such situations, a more powerful technique, for example regression analysis, may be applied.

By way of illustration, consider the simple data set which is represented in Figure 6.6. The two factors or variables which are being considered here are simply labelled *y* and *x*, and it is clear that, as *x* increases, on average *y* will also increase.

It will be seen the data do not all line up – it is not possible to draw a straight line which 'joins the dots'. The aim of regression analysis is to determine the straight line which is 'closest'[15] overall to the set of data points. We have added such a line in Figure 6.7.

All well and good, it would seem. However, it should be borne in mind that we have not necessarily captured the true relationship, merely described the data we have. This is a subtle, but important, distinction. To see why this is so, consider: in this case the data represent a somewhat artificial experiment – *x* is the numbers of coins tossed by the authors in a simple experiment, while *y* represents the number of heads which were observed (for example, when 35 coins were tossed, 24 heads were observed, etc.).

It is clear the 'line of best fit' is rather closer to the data set than the true relationship (see Figure 6.8) and this will always be the case in regression analysis for a simple – and tautological – reason: the 'line of best fit' lives up to its name. Further, it is clear that, although we have presented a legitimate data set in Figures 6.6, 6.7 and 6.8, the same data-generating process (i.e. tossing coins) may be repeated, and will give rise to a different set of data, and thus a different line of best fit. Hence the results of a regression estimation process do not give actual parameter values, but merely estimates; and those estimates are subject to statistical variation.

When the techniques of regression analysis are applied to economic data, the resulting estimation procedure is called 'econometrics', that is to say, 'measuring economics'. In the case just discussed, it is, of course, possible to generate as many data sets as we wish and therefore we may describe, not only a whole series of lines of best fit (one for each data set) but also how they vary with different data

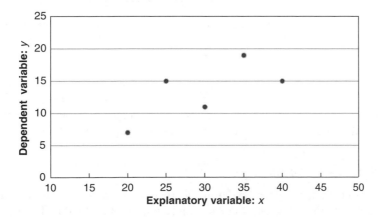

Figure 6.6 Linear regression, an example showing a data set.

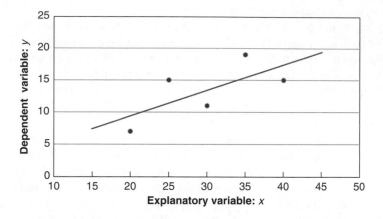

Figure 6.7 Linear regression, an example showing a data set and line of best fit.

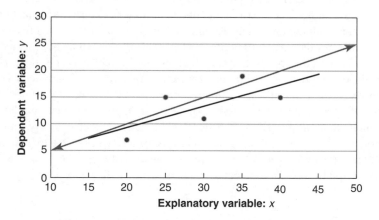

Figure 6.8 Linear regression, an example showing a data set, line of best fit and true (average) relationship.

sets. In economics, however, we generally cannot generate new data – the data set we have is generally all there is. This, as we shall see, poses an additional set of problems. In sum, the regression line fits the data set the best, but it does not necessarily fit the true and underlying (but generally unknown) relationship the best.

The significance of insignificance

Given that the estimates we have from any regression equation arise from random processes – in that they are calculated based on one of any infinitely large set of random data, and thus are not necessarily equal to the true parameter values – it is reasonable to carry out some further analysis to determine what they do – and do not – tell us about the true parameter values. For example, in the data set presented above in Figures 6.6, 6.7 and 6.8, we can say with 95 per cent confidence, 10 extra coins tossed will lead to, on average, between 3.2 *fewer* heads and 12.05 *more* heads observed. The explanatory power of this perfectly legitimate and correctly analysed[16] data set is so weak, we cannot even be sure that increasing the value of the explanatory variable, x, will lead to an increase in y – it might lead to a decrease.

In this case we know the true data-generating process and, if we toss a further 10 coins, we would expect to observe five more heads. However, because of the random process by which the data was generated, predictions based on the observed variables are not as accurate as predictions based on the true model. In econometrics, of course, the true model is not known; we have only predictions based on the observed variables, the data set.

When regression models are estimated by an econometrician, the question is generally considered: 'Can we be confident the dependent variable y is related to the explanatory variable x in a significant way?' By chance, in the case of the data set we are considering here, we have seen an increase in x could be associated with either a decrease or an increase in y. This leads to the conclusion – based on this data – there is insignificant evidence y is likely to change systematically with x. Now clearly, y, the number of heads observed, is indeed related to x, the number of coins in the true model. Hence it is clear, *lack of evidence of a relationship is not to be confused with lack of a relationship*. The problem here is simply that we do not have enough data to be sure the variation in y has a systematic pattern.

Statistical inference of this sort may be thought of as a court case under English or American law; the conclusion the defendant is 'guilty' or 'not guilty' depends on the explanatory power of the data – the evidence. In the absence of strong evidence, the defendant is found 'not guilty'. This is not the same as finding them innocent, they may indeed be guilty, but it has not been proven beyond reasonable doubt. To a statistician, 'beyond reasonable doubt' generally means with 95 per cent confidence. If we may not have 95 per cent confidence in the statement 'y varies systematically with x', the effect is said to be insignificant at the 95 per cent level.[17]

In sum, regardless of how well analysed and appropriately analysed is a representative data set, we cannot be sure, a priori, it will have sufficient explanatory power to allow us to draw correct conclusions.

The impact of unknown unknowns – pre-testing

In the previous section, the authors were somewhat perturbed at being unable to prove that the number of heads observed varies with the number of coins so, to check their results, they generated a further set of data, presented in Figure 6.9.

The reader will be relieved to hear that, in this second set of data, we may be 95 per cent confident that the number of heads observed does vary systematically with the number of coins tossed. Indeed, we may be 99 per cent confident in

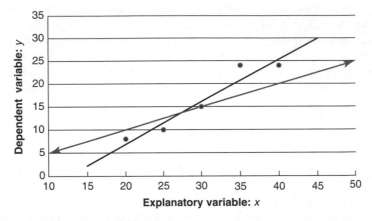

Figure 6.9 Linear regression, a further example showing data set, line of best fit and true (average) relationship.

making this statement – given this second set of data. However, we have now created a further problem; that of pre-testing. In essence, by continuing to generate data until we find a set of variables which demonstrate the result we hope to find, then stopping, we make it much more likely that we will eventually get the result for which we were looking. Returning to our court case analogy, in Magna Carta, the barons insisted King John not continually re-try criminal cases until the result is observed for which John was presumably hoping. Once a defendant is found 'not guilty', if they are re-tried on the same offence the result will be biased.[18] Thus, when reading econometric investigations, it should be borne in mind the power of our estimation and inference depends, in part, on the known (the data which is being reported) and also on the unknowns (all the work the researcher did in advance without reporting it).

Sadly researchers may not disclose how many experiments were carried out before the reported results were 'discovered'. Consider the suspicious case of the supposedly biased Belgian Euro coin described in *The Guardian* newspaper (2002). Two Polish mathematicians are reported to have spun a Belgian one-euro coin 250 times and observed 140 heads. The observation of more than 139 heads on 250 spins of a coin is a very unusual event, occurring with probability only 3.33 per cent. Thus, *if this were the only experiment carried out*, we would say we may be more than 95 per cent sure the coins were biased.[19] Hang on a minute though, were the researchers only looking for an excess of heads (and, if so, why)? Perhaps they were looking for an excess of either heads or tails but the reporter just forgot to mention that in the article. If this is so, the observation of more than 139 heads or more than 139 tails will occur with probability 6.66 per cent. OK, so now we cannot be 95% confident the coins are biased – but we might still be 90 per cent confident.

But, just another minute, was the one-euro coin the only one they tried? The article states they also tried a one-cent coin (although the results of this are not given). They may also have tried a two-euro coin and all the other coins too and not mentioned it. Given the nature of the results reported, one-euro and one-cent, it is not unreasonable to suppose they did indeed try the one-cent, two-cent, five-cent, 10-cent, 20-cent, 50-cent, one-euro and two-euro coins. The probability of getting at least 139 heads or at least 139 tails on at least two of the eight coins is 5.44 per cent. So again, we may not be 95 per cent sure it is not all just a coincidence, though we may be 90 per cent sure.

But did they restrict themselves to Belgian coins and if so why? Suppose they had tried the same experiment with coins of all the 12 eurozone nations, which (as the statisticians were not themselves Belgian) seems a reasonable supposition. If all the coins of all the nations were tested in this way, the likelihood that, in at least one set of national coins, at least two coins would come up with at least 139 heads or at least 139 tails is roughly speaking 50/50. So, is the Belgian one-euro coin biased? Well, we can't answer the question because we don't know the results which were not reported or if there were such results. Perhaps all coins were tried, but only the highest scoring ones were reported.

The reader may reflect that this is a somewhat whimsical argument; however, misreporting by omission of negative results is common in journalism and the scientific and business literature. Suppose an individual has written a book on how a particular strategy made £10,000,000 on the stock market – we'd rush out to buy the book, certain we would also make money. However, the information is worthless unless we also know how many others tried the same strategy and did *not* make money. However, generally people who do not make money do not write books. The information in an investor's guide might be worthwhile, but it might have the same value as a lottery winner publishing the self-help book 'How I won first prize on the national lottery'.[20]

In sum, what we don't know about what we don't know makes a big difference when it comes to interpreting statistical results. It is for this reason econometricians carry out what is called meta-analysis; considering, not only the results which are reported in earlier studies, but also the process which went into carrying out the estimation.

Spurious relationships

As if we didn't already have enough difficulties with regression modelling, we must also bear in mind the problem of spurious results. Consider the set of data in Figure 6.10 which represents a pair of potentially correlated time series. It would appear that when the 'explanatory' variable (the series shown in black) increases, the incarceration rate increases. Indeed, if we carry out standard regression modelling and statistical inference we find we may be nearly 100 per cent confident[21] the series are related. However, they are in fact independent. The so-called explanatory factor is in fact the life expectancy at birth of inhabitants of French Polynesia (Catalog Source: World Development Indicators).

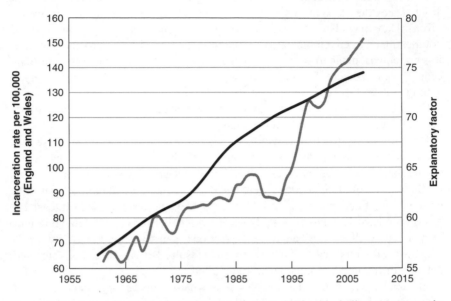

Figure 6.10 An explanation of the incarceration rate? The black line represents the 'explanatory' variable, and the grey line represents the incarceration rate.

The reason why standard statistical procedures fail here is that both series exhibit a trend. In general, where two series – both with a trend – are analysed together, they will appear to be related whether or not they are indeed related. This is because they are both changing consistently over time – increasing or decreasing. In this case the 'observed' relationship between the series is said to be spurious. In the case of the two series listed, there is clearly no relationship on an intuitive level. However, consider Figure 6.11, which seems at first sight to present a plausible relationship. Can we be sure the consumption of wine leads to homicide?[22] It seems plausible – well, more plausible than that the life expectancy in French Polynesia causes the England and Wales incarceration rate. However, we will require somewhat more sophisticated analysis to answer this question. We might analyse, for example, the changes in the series rather than the original data (see, for example, Field 1990[23] amongst many others). Alternatively where two sets of data are trended, we might consider whether there is a single trend which describes them both (so-called cointegration analysis), whether the underlying trends are independent, or whether there is yet another factor which might explain both series.

Causality – the turkeys are causing Christmas

Let us suppose two data series are analysed and it is found there *is* a significant relationship between them; for example, the two series unemployment and burglary. We have seen in Chapter Five, the discussion on causation is ongoing with

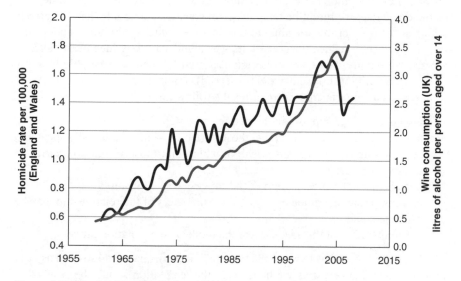

Figure 6.11 England and Wales homicide rate per 100,000 (black) and UK consumption of wine (litres of alcohol per person aged over 14, grey).

Source: Home Office (2010, 2011) and Institute of Alcohol Studies (2010).

Levitt (2001) and Raphael and Winter-Ebmer (2001) amongst others postulating that increased crime rates might lead to increases in unemployment, as well as vice versa. The direction of causation is, so it is said, an empirical matter, in other words we need to consider data to be able to answer this; however, the question, to economists, is framed in a particular way.

So as to avoid ambiguity, causality in econometric studies (or more precisely, Granger Causality; Granger 1980) is defined in the following way: effect 'A' Granger-Causes effect 'B' if taking 'A' into account improves our forecast of 'B', and the reverse is not true. In other words, changes in 'A' occur before changes in 'B', but not vice versa. It will be noted that this definition of causality, while unambiguous, differs from the general English usage. According to this definition, going to see a doctor 'causes' the trip to the pharmacy and turkeys (or geese, if you are a traditionalist) growing fat cause Christmas. This somewhat simplified example illustrates one of the weaknesses in the Granger Causality approach – if an event is easily forecast, or expected, we may take steps to prepare for it before the event occurs. Thus it may appear our pre-emptive measures are a Granger-Cause, not a response to the actual event.

Another issue with Granger Causality is empirical (i.e. data related): there will obviously be situations where one effect does indeed precede the other; however, the data is not collected with enough frequency for us to determine which comes first. In quarterly data, for example, an increase in crime which is followed very quickly by an increase in the number of arrests will appear to be two simultaneous events. If the data indicate that the number of arrests increases at the same time as the crime rate, we might be tempted, erroneously, to conclude that it is arrests which are causing crime – leading to the (incorrect, one would hope) conclusion that, if we wish to reduce the crime rate, we should start to reduce the number of arrests. We require data to be collected at a high frequency to be able to apply Granger Causality testing and avoid (observed) simultaneity.

In sum, econometric analysis requires the following:

- a set of variables supposedly related in some way;
- a partition of the variable set into those variables which are, broadly speaking, reactive, the *caused* or *dependent* variables, and those which are *causes* or *explanatory* variables;
- a mathematical representation of the suggested relationship;
- an appropriate technique by which the parameters of the relationship may be estimated; and
- a determination of the adequacy of the model and estimation process.

The last step may lead us to conclude the model is inadequate, and so send us back to square one. However, as we have seen, the temptation should be resisted to carry on estimating different data sets until we have found the results we want (at which point we report only those results).

An example: Levitt's (2002) study on police numbers and crime

The issue of simultaneity in the data is addressed in a clever and insightful way by Levitt (2002). Levitt begins by pointing out 'The challenge in estimating a causal impact of police on crime is to overcome simultaneity bias' (p. 1244). Levitt (2002) considers three studies have taken simultaneity bias seriously: Levitt (1997), Marvell and Moody (1996) and Corman and Mocan (2000). The later two studies use monthly data in an attempt to eliminate simultaneity, arguing it takes authorities more than one month to increase the size of the police force in response to increases in crime. Levitt (2002) suggests that this approach depends crucially on policy-makers being unable to forecast changes in the crime rate. If they are aware that crime rates may increase and increase police numbers as a precaution, the direction of causality will be confused.

To counter this problem, Levitt (2002) suggests using the budget for fire-fighters as an instrument to capture the way police budgets may be affected by issues other than the crime rate. Although police and fire-service budgets within USA cities are correlated with, for example, the electoral cycle, Levitt suggests the fire-service budget will not be directly related to crime. Thus we can determine the effect of a change in budgets unprompted by crime rates (technically, an exogenous change).[24]

In the case of property crime, Levitt's results where simultaneity issues are ignored are represented in Figure 6.12. The magnitude and significance of the effects estimated are represented in these graphs in the following way: along the horizontal axis are the suggested explanatory variables; the size of the estimated

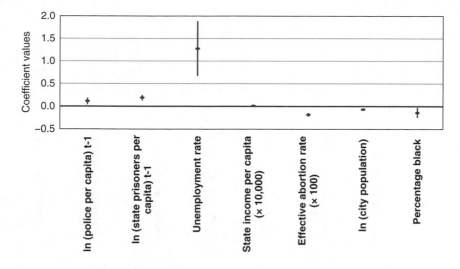

Figure 6.12   Property crime coefficient estimates (OLS – city-fixed effects) and 95 per cent confidence intervals.

Source: Levitt (2002).

effect is show on the vertical axis. Simple estimates of the effects are shown by dots or points, while the level of uncertainty is shown by vertical lines in each case.[25] If a point is greater than zero it implies the expected impact of the variable is positive. If, however, the uncertainty bars cross the zero line, it implies that we cannot be sure the effect does indeed differ from zero. See above for the discussion of significance and insignificance. For example, consider the coefficient on the unemployment rate – the point estimate is 1.283, shown by the point at the centre of the vertical line which represents the range of uncertainty. The fact that the vertical line representing uncertainty does not cross the zero axis implies we may be 95 per cent sure there is a positive impact of unemployment on the dependent variable – property crime.

It will be noted that the level of crime *increases* as the size of the police force and the incarceration rate increase. However, these results are spurious because of simultaneity bias.

The same model, re-estimated in an appropriate way, gives more credible coefficient estimates as shown in Figure 6.13. The earlier conclusions are now reversed and we see that the size of the police force and the incarceration rate now have a negative impact on property crime rates. That these are significant effects is shown by the fact that the 95 per cent confidence interval does not cross the zero-line (horizontal axis). By contrast, the income per capita and percentage black are not significant effects.

The effect of the size of the police force on violent crime is less significant[26] as shown in Figure 6.14.

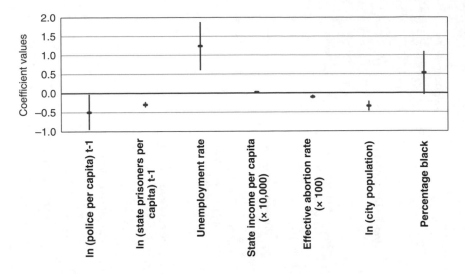

Figure 6.13 Property crime coefficient estimates (IV – city-fixed effects and year dummies included) and 95 per cent confidence intervals.

Source: Levitt (2002).

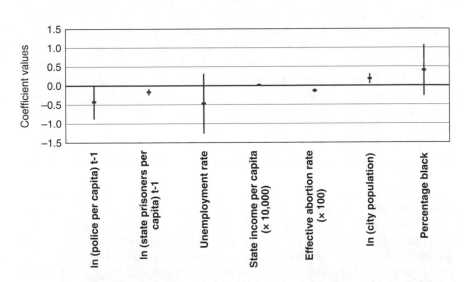

Figure 6.14 Violent crime coefficient estimates (IV – city-fixed effects and year dummies included) and 95 per cent confidence intervals.

Source: Levitt (2002).

Conclusion

The use of economic methods in criminal justice policy is relatively new, particularly in the UK. Its advent has by no means met with universal approval; indeed a number of criticisms have been made of the approach. Cohen (2000) summarises a number of criticisms of cost–benefit analysis, but several of the points also have some application to elements of the econometric approach that we have also discussed in this chapter.

First, it is argued on ethical or philosophical grounds, some things, such as safety, cannot or should not be valued. A related issue is that cost–benefit analysis assumes economic efficiency is the goal, at the expense of other socially desirable goals such as equity or fairness (Cohen 2000). Answering criticisms of this type, Cohen argues that:

> This is not a criticism of the methodology – only of those who want to impose benefit-cost analysis as the sole criteria for public decision making. Instead, when viewed as one policy tool available to policymakers, benefit-cost analysis has many benefits and only limited costs. Indeed, most texts on benefit-cost analysis include an analysis of the 'incidence' of costs and benefits – i.e., who bears the costs and who reaps the benefits – as an integral part of benefit-cost analysis.
>
> (Cohen 2000: 280)

A second concern is that cost–benefit analysis presents 'an aura of precision and objectivity that might not be justified' (Cohen 2000: 303). Consumers of cost–benefit analysis (policy-makers) often have little understanding of the methodology and of the assumptions underlying the analysis and therefore are ill-equipped to make appropriate use of the results from such tools. Cohen argues:

> Like any statistical tool, benefit-cost analysis is vulnerable to misapplication through carelessness, inexperience, or deception . . . The results can be no more precise than the assumptions and valuations that are employed.
>
> (Cohen 2000: 303)

A third criticism is that cost–benefit analysis and more straightforward valuation exercises incorporate inequities in society. This is not to say that economic tools discriminate on the basis of socio-economic status because, as Cohen (2000: 305) notes: 'A $1,000 medical cost is valued at $1,000, regardless of whether the injured person is rich or poor. Thus, the tool is politically neutral and can (and will) be overridden when other policy goals come into conflict'. The concern is a more subtle one (Cohen 2000): the fact that the methodology itself may incorporate inequities in society, as Cohen (2000) demonstrates using the example of measuring wages lost by victims of crime. If those victims tend to be in the lower income quartiles, the benefits of a crime prevention programme will be skewed downwards (Cohen 2000). A similar outcome might result from a contingent valuation survey of potential victims to determine their willingness-to-pay for crime reduction programmes with the value likely to be highly dependent on their relative wealth or ability to pay. Cohen therefore concludes:

> [F]rom a public policy standpoint, benefit-cost analysis does indeed discriminate against society's less wealthy. If society deems this to be unfair, the analyst needs to make adjustments in the estimated costs and benefits to 'neutralize' the effect of wealth on the estimated costs and benefits.
>
> (Cohen 2000: 305)

A fourth issue (revisited in the next chapter) is that the public's perception of the risk of crime may not be the same as the actual risk (Cohen 2000). The challenge for economists working in this field is that asking the public about their willingness-to-pay for reduced crime might be influenced by the public being misinformed about the risk and severity of crime (Cohen 2000).

For Cohen (2000), who is primarily interested in CBA, the key issue is therefore that the analyst is careful to set out assumptions that have informed the analysis, projected benefits, how those benefits are valued and how alternative assumptions might affect results (sensitivity analysis). However, the same points could, in broad terms, be applied to all of the economic analysis considered in this chapter. When used in this way, one of the great strengths of economic analysis is that it forces analysts to be explicit about their assumptions and thus encourages 'an open process where the issues can be debated on an informed basis' (Cohen 2000: 303).

7   The costs of crime

Introduction

Understanding the costs of crime allows us to compare the costs of different types of crime and to assess how much we, as a society, should invest in different types of crime reduction. However, understanding the costs of crime is not purely an economic issue. We also need to draw on the latest thinking about estimating the extent of crime and understanding the physical and psychological impacts of crime.

While attempts to estimate the costs of crime started over 75 years ago in the USA with the congressionally mandated Wickersham Commission in 1931 (Cohen 2007) these early estimates focused on public sector costs such as police, courts, and prisons. Attempts to capture less tangible costs such as those incurred by victims started relatively recently (ibid.). The first attempt to incorporate intangible costs arguably dates back to 1978 (ibid.) where a study in the USA looked at the effect of crime rates on housing prices. In the UK a key study that attempted to capture both public sector costs of crime and less tangible costs incurred by victims was published in 2000 (Brand and Price 2000). Therefore this is very much a developing area of research and further methodological development is likely over the coming years.

Why measure the costs of crime?

There are at least three, inter-related reasons why a study of the costs of crime is important:

1. Crime imposes a substantial cost on society. As we shall see, in 2000 the UK Home Office (Brand and Price 2000) estimated that crime cost England and Wales around £60 billion per year.[1] Understanding the cost of crime therefore helps governments and individual citizens to better understand the burden of crime on society, leading, potentially, to more informed debates about how to respond to crime and how to view crime in the context of other public policy priorities.
2. Different crimes vary widely in the impacts that they have on individuals and wider society. For example, an incident of criminal damage to a car might

result in the owner of the car incurring a financial cost in repairing the car. Perhaps the damage to the car might also make them late for work. By contrast the victim of a rape might experience a range of serious physical and psychological injuries including cuts and bruises, contracting sexually transmitted diseases and post-traumatic stress disorder. If a way can be found to place an economic value on these very different impacts it will be possible to use this 'common currency' to compare the relative impacts of different types of crime and the relative burden different types of crime place on society.

3.   Unsurprisingly, the research on the costs of crime shows that the costs of different types of crime vary widely. Information on the costs of different types of crime is combined with data on the total numbers of those crimes to calculate the total burden of different crimes. When this information is set against the costs of different responses to crime we can make better-informed decisions about which policy measures are most effective in reducing costs.

However, using estimates of the costs of crime can also present challenges. Consider for instance the first rationale for estimating the cost of crime described above. Cohen (2000) identifies two potential difficulties. First, even if measured in comparable ways one cannot simply compare aggregate cost estimates of crime with estimates of the cost of other social ills to arrive at policy recommendations for future public spending priorities. The more relevant question is, how much additional reduction would we observe if we spent more on crime prevention as compared to a similarly measured return on investment related to another social ill. Second, the true cost of crime is likely to be more than the sum total of its parts.

> If there were no more robbers or rapists, hitchhiking probably would be a way of life for a huge portion of the population. If violence was eliminated from society, organised crime might evaporate (as it depends on the threat of violence for its survival), and the standard of living for many inner-city residents would increase as businesses returned to previously abandoned storefronts. These massive changes in social structure could come about only with equally impressive changes in social behavior. Thus, any aggregate estimates of the cost of crime would need to account for these factors.
>
> (Cohen 2000: 270)

Measuring the tangible costs of crime

Some of the costs of crime are more amenable to measurement than others. Those more amenable to measurement are referred to as tangible costs, those less amenable as intangible costs.

Tangible costs of crime can be broken down into realised costs and anticipatory costs (Dolan *et al.* 2005). Realised costs are those incurred as a result of a crime happening. Anticipatory costs are those associated with reducing the chances of a crime occurring (ibid.).

Realised costs

In order to illustrate the nature of tangible, realised costs we'll use the example of the owner of a car whose vehicle is criminally damaged. The owner of the car experiences both direct and indirect costs. Direct costs are those diverted from other uses as a result of the crime occurring (Dolan *et al.* 2005). In our example, the repair of the car is a direct cost and it is straightforward for us to measure it because it has a market value – the charge that a garage makes for carrying out the repair.

Indirect costs are the loss of earnings and productivity that result from a crime. In our case, the owner of the car was late for work as a result of the offence. Again this loss in productivity is relatively easy to measure because it has a market value – the cost of employing someone else to cover the hours the car owner misses from work. This type of cost is known as an 'opportunity cost'. The opportunity cost is a central concept in economics and is defined as 'the value of the resource in its most valuable alternative use' (HM Treasury 1997 as quoted in Brand and Price 2000: 17). The concept of opportunity cost provides a way of valuing human, physical and financial resources that are 'freed up' for potential alternatives when a crime is prevented (Brand and Price 2000).

Anticipatory costs

Anticipatory costs relate to those resources spent attempting to reduce the chances of a crime occurring (Dolan *et al.* 2005). Sticking with the example of our motorist, one anticipatory cost that she might have taken prior to her car being criminally damaged might have been the installation of a car alarm. This cost can be estimated based on its market value.

Our motorist might also have insured her car. From an economic perspective, insurance involves a transfer of resources and is therefore not a cost. This is because potential victims who take out insurance in anticipation of crime pay premiums to an insurance company and then the insurance company *transfers* those resources to actual victims of crime. The only resource involved in insurance that represents a cost of crime (as opposed to a transfer) are the resources used in insurance administration. Insurance companies have staff, premises and equipment and the use of these resources represent an opportunity cost (Brand and Price 2000).

Where do the costs fall?

In the discussion of the motorist whose car was criminally damaged we focused on costs which were incurred directly by the motorist or, in the case of the indirect cost, their employer. However, the costs of crime will not always fall only on individual crime victims or potential victims.

Brand and Price (2000) draw on earlier research to categorise the costs of crime according to costs in anticipation of crime, costs as a consequence of crime and costs in response to crime.

Costs in anticipation

Costs in anticipation of crime fall mainly on the potential victim of the crime. They might include expenditure on security incurred by the individual (for example, the installation of a burglar alarm) or by the wider community (for example, the installation of a CCTV system). Brand and Price (2000) outline a number of difficulties in estimating costs in anticipation of crime including the following:

• Often, both the costs incurred by individual victims and by communities will not be incurred just to reduce the risk of victimisation. For example, an individual may drive their child to school partly because of a perceived risk that their child may become a victim of crime and partly because they believe that it is more convenient than walking or using public transport. Similarly a local government organisation may install street lighting partly to reduce the risk of street robbery and partly to reduce the risk of pedestrians tripping on the paving stones at night. When estimating the cost of crime it will be necessary to estimate the proportion of this expenditure that is incurred in anticipation of crime (ibid.).
• The security choices of fellow potential victims will affect expenditure by others (ibid.). The concept of 'displacement' and 'diffusion' are well researched in criminology. There are numerous examples of crime reduction measures displacing the crime to other areas or other groups of victims or leading to offending behaviour being displaced to different types of offending activity. Similarly, there are examples of the benefits of a crime reduction measure being diffused to adjacent areas and groups.
• Many security features (for example, engine immobilisers in cars) come as standard without the potential victim making a conscious choice to incur costs in anticipation of crime. It is therefore necessary to include the design and manufacturing costs of features built into products as part of an estimate of the costs in anticipation of crime.

Costs as a consequence

Costs incurred as a consequence of crime fall mainly on victims and include the cost of loss or damage to property as well as the physical and mental injuries to victims (this latter group are intangible costs and are discussed in more detail below). From the perspective of an economist, stolen property not subsequently recovered by the victim is a benefit to the offender. Therefore, strictly speaking, the value is transferred, not lost (ibid.). However, because such transfers are outlawed by society, in practice such a valuation would make little sense and stolen property is treated as a loss (ibid.).

Costs incurred as a consequence of crime also fall on the agencies that deal with the immediate aftermath of crime such as health services and victim support services (ibid.).

Costs in response

Costs incurred in response to crime fall mainly on the criminal justice system. These costs will include police activity, the work of the courts, the cost of carrying out sentences of the court such as imprisonment or community sentences and the cost to the offender and his/her family resulting from such sentences. An example of losses to an offender might be the loss of earnings resulting either directly, due to the imposition of a prison sentence, or indirectly, for example, an accountant convicted of embezzlement being unable to gain employment as an accountant in the future (ibid.).

Emotional and physical costs of crime

Emotional and physical costs of crime are intangible costs that occur as a *consequence* of crime. As we shall see, it is widely accepted that current estimates are subject to various limitations. Nevertheless, the Home Office estimates that emotional and physical harm accounted for 50 per cent of the total cost of crime against individuals and households in 2003/04 (see Figure 7.1).

Dolan *et al.* (2005) suggest that there are three general approaches that might be used to value the intangible victim costs of crime. We might:

- estimate the costs directly on the basis of people's revealed or stated preferences.
- identify analogous values used in other parts of the UK public sector.

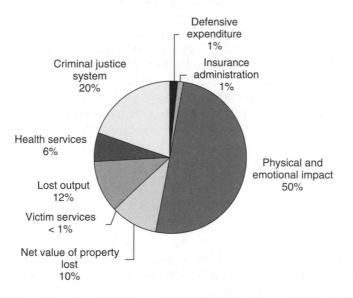

Figure 7.1 Estimated total cost of crime against individuals and households in 2003/04 by cost category.

Source: Home Office (2005: Chart 4.2).

- identify the nature and extent of the physical and psychological outcomes of offences and use an approach from health economics in which different outcomes are converted into comparable, numerical values using a quality of life index. These values are converted into monetary values.

It is the third approach that has increasingly been adopted by criminologists and economists in the UK. However, all three approaches will be briefly discussed below.

Stated or revealed preferences

The first approach is to use values from revealed or stated preference studies. Economists often seek to identify people's preferences for acquiring benefits or averting losses. There are two ways of doing this. The first is to identify people's 'revealed' preferences. The second is to ask for their 'stated' preferences.

Revealed preferences

People's preferences are 'revealed' by analysing their behaviour. A decision to take a taxi at night to avoid walking through a particular area might reveal how much an individual is prepared to pay to reduce their risk of being a victim of a mugging (street robbery). Similarly a decision to park their car in a well-lit and supervised car park as opposed to on the street might indicate how much a potential victim is prepared to pay to avoid the risk of their car being broken into or stolen. However, in practice it will be extremely difficult to identify all the different factors in play when such decisions are made and to hence calculate the proportion attributable to avoiding a crime. For example, the decision to take a taxi might also have made the journey quicker and the car park might have been more convenient for the supermarket. Cohen (2000) describes how a study in the USA sought to infer property owners' willingness-to-pay for a safer neighbourhood through higher property prices, but he also identifies limitations to this study. In particular data limitations have prevented such property value studies from isolating the cost of any individual crime type and instead have estimated the cost of an aggregate measure of crime. For reasons such as these there is relatively little data on the value of crime, generated from revealed preference studies.

Stated preferences

Stated preferences can be derived by either asking the public directly about how much they are (or would be) willing to pay to avoid an injury or asking them how much they would be willing to accept to compensate them for the same injury.

In the USA the only direct source of victim costs of crime is the ongoing National Crime Victimisation Survey (NCVS) which interviews households and elicits information from those who have experienced a recent incident of criminal victimisation (Cohen 2000). However, while the survey asks crime victims several questions about their out-of-pocket losses – including an estimate of the dollar cost of medical care, lost wages, and property loss – these estimates are an underestimate of costs for several reasons (ibid.). As Cohen (2000) explains, a key limitation is that the reference period for NCVS is crimes committed during the previous six months and, because the average crime will have occurred about three months prior to being reported, any medical costs are necessarily limited to those short-term costs. In the UK the British Crime Survey asks victims of violent crime about injuries they have experienced (see for example Table 3.06 in Walker *et al.* 2009) but does not ask victims to value these losses.

Willingness-to-pay studies

Willingness-to-pay or avoid studies, and specifically contingent valuation studies, where potential victims are questioned, provide another strategy for ascertaining people's stated preferences. As Cohen (2000) notes, contingent valuation is a well-developed methodology in fields such as environmental economics where it is used to place values on non-market goods, such as improvements in air quality or endangered species. However, it is relatively new in the field of criminal justice studies.

Atkinson *et al.* (2005) cite a number of willingness-to-pay studies have been undertaken in the USA by Cook and Ludwig (2000) and Ludwig and Cook (2001). Based on non-fatal, gun-related violence they asked respondents whether they would vote for a specified tax increase in return for a 30 per cent reduction in gun injuries. Another US study by Cohen *et al.* (2004) asked respondents to place a value on the benefits of public programmes to reduce different types of crime such as burglary and violent crime.

To date there have been few willingness-to-pay studies in the UK. Atkinson *et al.* (2005) is the first stated preference study of crime risks in the UK. The study used a contingent valuation approach to elicit respondents' willingness-to-pay for reductions in the incidence of various types of physical assault. In their study they administer a questionnaire to 807 respondents. The questionnaire describes different categories of physical assault such as 'common assault', 'serious wounding' and 'other wounding'. These categories of crime are taken from the British Crime Survey. It is important for the success of the study that respondents understand easily the physical and psychological symptoms likely to be suffered if they are a victim of the crime and the ways in which these symptoms would affect their life and well-being. As discussed above, some information of this type is collected as part of the British Crime Survey and Atkinson *et al.* use this information as the starting point for developing descriptions of the effects of different types of crime. Respondents are asked to indicate the amount they would be willing to pay to reduce the risk of suffering from one or other of these crimes, based on their assessment of the intangible effects of the crimes. Specifically, respondents are told the probability of being a victim of one of the specific offences before and after a particular policy intervention. They are asked to express their willingness-to-pay to reduce their chance of being a victim of the offence by 50 per cent over the next 12 months. On the assumption respondents would be prepared to pay twice as much to reduce the chance of their being a victim by 100 per cent, the amount that the individual stated they would be willing to pay to completely avoid the incident is calculated by multiplying the respondent's original answer by two. This figure is the estimate of the intangible costs of a particular type of crime.

Willingness-to-pay studies are subject to a number of challenges. The Atkinson *et al.* (2005) study which is discussed above is illustrative of many of these. First, of the 807 respondents in the study, 279 gave a zero valuation (i.e. they weren't prepared to pay anything to reduce the risk). Atkinson *et al.* (2005) define these as 'protests' to the contingent market and exclude their data from their analysis having demonstrated that doing so did not bias the sample. A second challenge is that the amounts respondents were willing to pay to reduce the chance of victimisation vary widely. Although the vast majority of respondents are prepared to pay amounts between 50 pence and 150 pounds a small number were prepared to pay much higher amounts with at least one person being willing to pay 1,500 pounds or more for each type of violent crime included in the study (ibid.). These outliers mean the average amount respondents are prepared to pay varies widely depending upon whether the mean or median average is used. A third challenge (Atkinson *et al.* 2001, unpublished, summarised in Dolan 2005) is that, when respondents were asked alternative questions such as how much they would be willing to pay to avoid an attack that would otherwise occur with certainty and how much they would be willing to pay for an instant cure to physical harm sustained in the attack, the resulting values were less than the values inferred from the risk reduction questions by a factor of between 40 and 150.

There are two related problems here. First, surveys ask respondents to rank the seriousness of various crimes. While these result in relatively consistent rankings over time and across populations, they are based on subjective public perceptions concerning the severity of crime and may be based on misperceptions about the frequency of injuries resulting from different criminal events (Cohen 2000). Cohen (2000) summarising his work on this issue argues that public perception surveys tend to underestimate the harm associated with violent crimes relative to property crimes. They are also generally unable to distinguish between the generic harm associated with an injury and the actual consequences of any particular victimisation – an issue of importance if one is interested in the extent to which the consequences of victimisation vary across different segments of the population. For example, the subjective consequences of an assault may be different for an elderly woman as opposed to a young man. A second problem suggested by Atkinson *et al.* (2005) and, confirmed in other studies, is an insensitivity amongst respondents to different sizes of risk reduction. It is widely recognised that people find it difficult consistently to assess and quantify risk. Economists have noted, when trying to make sense of the data derived from willingness-to-pay studies, the amounts people are apparently willing to pay to avoid a negative outcome are lower than the amounts people state they are willing-to-accept to compensate them for the same negative outcome (Dolan *et al.* 2005).

Victim compensation

An alternative approach to ascertaining the public's preferences is to look for instances where society has explicitly stated how much it would be willing to pay to avoid or to be compensated for an injury. Examples include jury awards made in civil cases in the USA and Criminal Injury Compensation awards made in the UK. Cohen (2000) summarises his earlier work which made use of jury award data to estimate the monetary value of pain, suffering, and lost quality of life for *nonfatal* injuries. Cohen's work used jury awards in civil cases where injuries were the result of accidents and matched the type and severity of injury with crime victim data in NCVS. However, as Cohen (2000) notes, such an approach is controversial because jury awards are unpredictable. While Criminal Injury Compensation awards made in the UK are predictable, the amounts awarded are set by Parliament and it is not clear that they accurately reflect social preferences (Dolan *et al.* 2005: 961).

Using values from other contexts

A second strategy identified by Dolan *et al.* (2005) to cost intangible victim costs is to take willingness-to-pay values to avoid death or injury from other, non-criminal contexts and apply them to the criminal context. They identify a number of potential sources of such values. As with studies undertaken directly on crime victimisation (described above) there are both revealed and stated preference studies we can draw on. Dolan *et al.* (2005) note one source of data is revealed preference studies in the field of occupational risk. Studies have sought to estimate the wage premium associated with job fatality risks and from these the value of preventing a fatality can be estimated. These values might be used as the basis for assigning values to homicides.

Stated preference studies have been undertaken in the field of health and safety. Although they suffer from similar limitations to the stated preference study undertaken by Atkinson *et al.* (2005) described above, the values they generate have been used in other areas of UK public policy. Dolan *et al.* (2005) note that the UK Department of Transport has used values generated from such studies undertaken in relation to road traffic accidents for over a decade. They suggest studies undertaken in the health and safety field have gained a collective authority because a number of them have produced values which lie in broadly the same range (ibid.).

The limitations of relying on accident data to ascertain the cost of injuries sustained during a criminal offence are illustrated by Shepherd *et al.* (1990). They compare assault and accident victims who sustain similar jaw injuries. While both groups suffer from similar levels of depression and anxiety a week after sustaining the injury, after three months psychological symptoms are more severe in victims whose injury was sustained during an assault.

Calculating and valuing QALYs

The approach which Dolan *et al.* (2005) favour, and which has subsequently been incorporated in the Home Office's (2005) estimates of the costs of crime, involves three stages. The first is to identify the nature and extent of physical and psychological outcomes of offences. These are converted into a single index so that different outcomes resulting from different offences can be compared on the same index. The index favoured by Dolan *et al.* is one that estimates losses in terms of so-called Quality-Adjusted Life Years (QALYs) (see box on p. 155). The third stage is to convert the QALYs into monetary estimates.

Each of these stages presents challenges. First, to identify the nature and extent of physical and psychological injuries, empirical data, representative of victims' experiences, are required. In the UK the best source of this data is currently the British Crime Survey. This is a survey of approximately 45,000 victims per year who are selected at random and interviewed face-to-face. Respondents who have been victimised are asked about the physical injuries they have sustained. It is possible to cross-tabulate the frequencies of different physical injuries by categories of offences (Simmons 2002: Table 6.07 as quoted in Dolan *et al.* 2005). The two main limitations with the British Crime Survey data are that victims are not asked about psychological trauma (Dolan *et al.* 2005); and that the study is cross-sectional. It is not possible to identify how the effects of victimisation change over the time period following the crime. Second, these injuries need to be converted into QALYs. Dolan *et al.* (2005) do this by matching injuries identified in the British Crime Survey as closely as possible with ones listed in health studies which include comparable injuries for which disability weights and durations have been calculated.

The third stage is to convert the QALY losses resulting from different types of crime into monetary amounts. Dolan *et al.* (2005) suggest two ways of doing this. One is to use a value that has already been assigned to a QALY for its use in the evaluation of health-care interventions. The National Institute for Clinical Excellence (NICE) uses the concept of the QALY when making decisions about which health-care interventions should be funded by the National Health Service. NICE has not made public the value it assigns to a QALY but commentators who have examined the decisions NICE has made suggest the figure must be in the region of £30,000. This means that a health intervention which costs less than £30,000 for each QALY delivered is likely to be approved and those which cost more than £30,000 are likely to be rejected (ibid.). Using this approach (and ignoring discounting), if an incident of crime victimisation left a victim in a health state valued at 0.5 for half a year (a loss of 0.25 QALYs) the value of this loss would be £7,500 (a quarter of the value of a QALY). As Dolan *et al.* (2005) note, the limitation of this approach is that the value assigned to a QALY is one derived by experts and therefore reflects their judgements rather than the rates at which the public would be willing to pay to trade off their wealth against health. The alternative is to look at a monetary value which has been elicited from the public for their willingness-to-pay to avoid an injury equivalent to one QALY.

Dolan *et al.* (2005) identify a study in which the public were asked about their willingness-to-pay to avoid an injury resulting from road accidents and tie this to an equivalent injury resulting from crime for which they are able to calculate the QALY value using the process described above. This eventually leads them to a QALY value of £81,000 – a figure substantially higher than the one assumed to be used by NICE.

Quality-adjusted life years (QALYs)

QALYs are used in the health sector to aid decision-making about alternative treatment options by analysing the number of additional years patients may be expected to live, and their expected quality of life in each of those years (Brand and Price 2000). Using a QALY, any profile of health can be represented by assessing quality of life on a scale between 0 and 1 where 0 represents death and 1 represents full health, and multiplying this by the duration of the health state. A simplified example (in which discounting is ignored) set out by Dolan *et al.* (2005) is as follows:

A 10-year profile where 7 years are spent in a health state valued at 0.75 and 3 years in a health state valued at 0.4 would have a score of 6.45 QALYs. This figure is reached by multiplying the health state 0.75 by 7, multiplying the health state of 0.4 by 3, and summing the two results. An alternative way of viewing this health profile is as a loss of 3.55 QALYs, compared with 10 years of full health.

By placing different health states on the same index, the QALY thus allows us to compare different health states resulting from different types of crime. Because we are using an index it does not matter whether or not people are in full health prior to criminal victimisation. This is because the loss in quality of life is measured in absolute decreases – as opposed to proportional losses – thus the baseline quality of life does not affect the results (Dolan *et al.* 2005). While this is true of all non-fatal injuries, the exception is homicide where the loss of life in terms of QALYs depends on the remaining life expectancy and expected quality of life of the victim (ibid.).

Quality of life

We can identify two aspects of quality of life which will also give rise to further intangible costs of crime. First, there is the impact of crime on *potential* victims which will manifest itself as fear of crime. Fear of crime may be experienced both by recent victims fearful of future victimisation and those who have not been victimised recently but, nevertheless, are concerned about future victimisation. We discuss a recent UK project on the fear of crime below. Second, there is the broader impact of crime on quality of life in particular communities. The aggregate impact of crime may be greater than the sum of fear of individual crime experience. For instance, the cost of installing a burglar alarm is a cost in anticipation of crime incurred by an individual. A similar cost incurred by a local agency with responsibility for crime reduction in an area might be the cost of installing CCTV. However, the growth in the use of burglar alarms and CCTV in an area might change the perception of crime perhaps discouraging people from purchasing houses in there or setting up new businesses. These costs will not be captured in an approach to costing crime that focuses on the costs of criminal justice agencies such as the police, courts and prisons and the physical and emotional costs of individual victims. Thus, Cohen argues, when valuing crime control benefits (a key usage for cost of crime estimates), 'a holistic approach should consider the impact of crime on the "quality of life" in a neighborhood or city' (Cohen 2007: 1).

The costs of fear of crime

Fear of crime and changes in behaviour potential victims make to avoid becoming a victim are intangible costs in *anticipation* of crime. These are costs which capture the reduced quality of life of potential victims and are challenging to estimate. As Brand and Price note:

> The reduced quality of life of potential victims is perhaps the most nebulous cost of crime. What is quality of life? How can it be measured? How can we measure how much quality of life is reduced from what it would be without crime? And how can we measure the effects of a reduction in the level of crime on quality of life?
>
> (Brand and Price 2000: 23)

Dolan and Peasgood (2007), setting out boldly to go where Brand and Price (2000) do not, address the issue of costs which arise from changes in behaviour in response to crime. These may range from, for example: individuals' choice of mode of transport; to lifestyle choices, such as a reduction in physical activity; and mental distress caused by anticipation of crime. The term 'fear of crime' itself is subject to different interpretations. Dolan and Peasgood (2007: 123) conceptualise it as the 'tangible and intangible costs in anticipation of victimisation'.

Some tangible costs of the fear of crime have been described above, for example, direct security expenditures and insurance. Over and above these, there is likely to be a general loss in society's productivity resulting from an increase in the fear of crime. The impact of crime is likely to skew the incentive structure of society away from productivity for the same reason taxation does (see Laffer 2004). Clearly, the more people expect the benefit of their labour to be taken from them by force, the less incentive there is to supply labour. In addition, as the societal costs of crime (detection, judgement and justice) increase, the greater the tax levied on those who remain honest. These two effects taken together imply honest labour will increasingly be discouraged as the crime rate increases.

Although these effects are extremely difficult to estimate, it should be borne in mind that their exclusion from analyses implies that official figures very much under-estimate societal costs of crime.

The changes in behaviour people make to reduce the likelihood of being a victim involve both intangible costs and anticipatory costs of crime, both of these extremely difficult to measure. Indeed, people's fear of becoming a victim might well be out of proportion to the actual level of crime in the community. Dolan and Peasgood, in discussing Cohen *et al.* (2004) who apply stated preference studies in the USA, note people respond to their own understanding of crime, rather than the actual risk of victimisation. For this reason, and because of the general problems with stated preference studies, Dolan and Peasgood follow Dolan *et al.* (2005) in basing their estimates on the QALY index.

Dolan and Peasgood begin with the survey data of Farrall and Gadd (2004), which measures the extent of respondents' fear of crime. It is possible to assign these levels of fear to loss of health data using the 'tariff' developed by Dolan *et al.* (2005), and so to calculate the QALYs lost through general fear of crime.

If the NICE (assumed) valuation of £30,000 per QALY is used, the monetary cost of the fear of crime may be shown to be £19.00 per person per year – an aggregate cost in England and Wales of £776 million per year. Conversely, if the QALY is valued at £81,000, as suggested by stated preference studies, the aggregate intangible cost of the fear of crime is £2,098 million.

Costing specific types of crime

We have discussed in detail approaches that have been adopted to cost crime. However, so far we have treated crime as a single phenomenon for which a universally applicable method can be developed. In this section we consider some specific manifestations of crime that pose particular challenges when developing cost elements.

The costs of domestic violence

Attempts to put a cost on domestic violence involve all of the issues that have been documented above, particularly in relation to valuing intangible harm to victims. However, because domestic violence tends to be less visible than some other forms of violent crime and because of its distinct patterns of occurrence, additional challenges are faced when estimating costs. Some of these challenges are captured by Walby (2004) who draws heavily on the methodology developed by Brand and Price (2000), together with additional data on the nature and prevalence of domestic violence gathered from the British Crime Survey.

An initial challenge in this area is defining what is domestic violence. There is no single, universally agreed definition. For Walby (2004), domestic violence includes: physical violence; sexual assaults; and stalking perpetrated by intimates (or former intimates). Intimates are defined as spouses, partners or girl/boyfriends. Walby (2004) notes that this is a narrower definition than that used by the police in England and Wales which also includes other family members.

In broad terms, Walby extends the methodology developed by Brand and Price (2000) in two ways. First, domestic violence brings with it implications for service provision not incurred by other forms of crime. Walby identifies costs in response to domestic violence incurred by:

- social services, particularly children's services involvement where there is a risk of co-occurrence of domestic violence and child abuse;
- housing services, particularly expenditure on emergency housing for those made homeless because of domestic violence; and
- civil legal services, particularly legal aid to fund both specialist legal actions such as injunctions to restrain or expel a violent partner, as well as actions consequent on the disentangling of marriages and relationships such as divorce and child custody.

A second extension of the methodology in response to the particular nature of domestic violence is, in some elements of the costing methodology, to treat domestic violence as a course of conduct rather than an isolated incident. The implication of this is that, in some parts of the methodology, costs are calculated per victim rather than per incident. As Walby (2004) explains:

> Domestic violence is often a repeat offence; indeed its nature is often that of a course of conduct, rather than an isolated incident. It is often a pattern of coercive control, and incidents may have a cumulative effect beyond that of individual incidents. Nevertheless, each incident is of consequence. Some of the ways in which costs are identified focus on the number of victims, while others focus on the number of incidents.
>
> (Walby 2004: 27)

The costs of business crime

Attempts to estimate the costs of crime against business, so-called white collar crime, are less developed than those which seek to estimate the costs of crimes against individuals. There are a number of challenges.

First, estimates of the prevalence of crime against business are less reliable. There is not a survey as comprehensive or as regularly undertaken as the British Crime Survey in the UK or the NCVS in the US. Cohen (2000) notes that although various estimates exist in the USA, the sampling methodology and crime definitions are seldom transparent, making comparability across crimes particularly difficult.

Second, there is a conceptual difficulty in estimating the cost of crime against business. As Cohen (2000) explains, if money is taken, the value is straightforward. However, if the loss is merchandise, it is not clear whether the loss should be valued at retail or wholesale. The value depends on the opportunity cost to the business. If the victimised business can easily replenish the product and does not lose retail sales, the loss is the cost to the owner, the wholesale price. However, if the item is scarce and cannot be readily replaced, the value of the loss would be the full retail price. The theft of services involves further complexity. Cohen (2000) explains that some white-collar crimes involve theft of services which involve essentially zero marginal costs to the victim and might not have been purchased at all in the absence of the theft. In this scenario it is hard to ascertain any victim. Examples include schemes which allow people to obtain telecommunications services for which they have not paid and would not purchase. The same issues arise with bootlegged music which users would not otherwise have bought (Cohen 2000).

The costs of drug-related crime

Another area where the costs of crime are distinct is that of drug-related crime. We discuss these costs in Chapter Eleven in the overall context of the market for illegal drugs.

Case study: estimating the costs of crime for England and Wales

In this section we look at how the methodologies described above have been applied to estimate costs of crime for England and Wales.

The most comprehensive and authoritative cost of crime estimates produced in the UK are to be found in two Home Office publications. The first (Brand and Price 2000) titled *The Economic and Social Costs of Crime* provides an estimate of the aggregate (net) cost of crime in England and Wales. The same report also provides estimates of the unit costs of particular types of crime and estimates of how these costs are distributed across anticipatory, consequential and responsive categories. Some of these figures are updated in a subsequent report (Home Office 2005) titled *The Economic and Social Costs of Crime Against Individuals and Households 2003/04.* Elements of the methodology are changed in the second report meaning that, although more accurate estimates are provided for some of the specific costs associated with specific types of crime against individuals and households, an overall estimate of the aggregate cost of all crime was not provided.

The Economic and Social Costs of Crime *(Brand and Price 2000)*

There are two major challenges to overcome in producing aggregate costs of crime. The first challenge is selecting and implementing a methodology to calculate the costs of crime. The second is to identify the number of offences that occur: i.e., *the incidence* of crime.

We have already discussed the methodological challenges in estimating the different costs of crime in detail (see above) and so the methodology used by Brand and Price will only be covered briefly here. For tangible costs Brand and Price (2000) generally opt for national figures. So, for example, the tangible costs in response to crime are predominantly costs of running the criminal justice system. One element of this cost will be policing; Brand and Price (2000) therefore take the national budget for policing as the cost of the police response to crime. Some costs are more complicated to estimate. For example, one of the tangible costs as a consequence of crime is that of victim support services. Brand and Price identify the Home Office budget for these. However, victim services also employ volunteer staff, the full value of whom will not be reflected in the budget taken to run the service. But this does not mean the time provided by volunteers has no economic value. Volunteers could be using their time in other ways: there is an *opportunity cost* for their time. Brand and Price (2000) therefore include an estimate of this opportunity cost when calculating the full economic cost of providing victim services. Brand and Price do not attempt to calculate all intangible costs. For example, they do not attempt to calculate intangible costs in anticipation of crime (one category of which would be fear of crime). Their chosen methodology for calculating the emotional and physical impact of crime (intangible costs as a consequence of crime) is to use values from studies undertaken in another context. Specifically, they use estimates for equivalent road traffic accidents, calculated using stated preference techniques and used by the UK Department of Transport in the cost–benefit analysis of new road schemes.

The second challenge in estimating aggregate costs of crime is to identify the number of offences which occur: the incidence of crime. The primary reason why we need to identify the incidence of crime is illustrated by considering how different costs are calculated. Some costs of crime can be identified at a national level. For example, as previously mentioned, Brand and Price (2000) take the national budget for policing as the cost of the police response to crime. However, other costs are calculated at the level of the individual crime. For example, whichever of the three methods described above is used to calculate the emotional and physical cost of crime, the estimates will be for individual crimes. To generate an aggregate cost it will be necessary to multiply the estimate for an individual crime by the number of crimes which occur. At first glance this seems to be a simple exercise as the Home Office publish data on police recorded notifiable offences. However, there are a number of problems with using this data. First, notifiable offences do not include all types of crime. An obvious group of offences not included are less serious road traffic offences. Second, numerous research studies have shown that not all crime is reported to the police and that not all crime reported to the police is recorded by them. If, when calculating the aggregate cost of emotional and physical impacts of crime, the unit cost of a crime was multiplied only by the number of crimes recorded by the police, then we would underestimate the total cost. Brand and Price therefore take Home Office data on different categories of notifiable offences and apply multipliers to it to arrive at an estimate of the total number of each type of offence. Many of the multipliers are derived from the British Crime Survey and others either from research studies or expert opinion.

On the basis of this approach, Brand and Price (2000) estimate the total cost of crime to England and Wales in 1999/2000 is around £60 billion. However, they state that this figure is 'far from comprehensive' (Brand and Price 2000: vii) as some categories of cost are excluded – one of these being the costs associated with fear of crime. The £60 billion estimate is broken down as follows:

- Approximately £19 billion is the cost of property stolen or damaged.
- Approximately £18 billion is the cost of the emotional and physical impact of crime on victims and of this approximately £14 billion is the result of violent crime.
- Approximately £12 billion is accounted for by the criminal justice system's response to crime.
- Approximately £5 billion is accounted for by costs in anticipation of crime (e.g. security expenditure and insurance administration).

There are also estimates of the average unit costs for different types of crime, which vary widely. For example, the average cost of a homicide is estimated to be £1,100,000 while the cost of an average burglary is estimated to be £2,300. These average costs are also broken down across costs: in anticipation; as a consequence; and in response to crime. Of particular interest to policy-makers and managers working in the fields of community safety and criminal justice is the estimated breakdown of these average unit costs across different agencies. So, for example, the average cost of a sexual offence is estimated at £19,000 and of this £1,200 is the average cost health services incur as a consequence of such a crime. A further £3,900 is the estimated cost of the criminal justice system's response to such a crime. This is further broken down; the average cost of police activity is estimated to be £1,900 and the average Crown Court costs to be £180. If some of these figures seem low it should be remembered they are average costs and therefore reflect the relatively low proportion of sexual offences which are reported to the police and the even lower level of such offences which will result in a Crown Court trial.

The Economic and Social Costs of Crime Against Individuals and Households 2003/04 *(Home Office 2005)*

This study updates Brand and Price's (2000) estimates of crimes against individuals and households. Updates for estimates to the costs of crime against commercial and public sector victims are not included. Because only part of the £60 billion estimate of crime put forward by Brand and Price is revised in the 2005 publication, the more recent publication does not attempt to revise the £60 billion estimate for total crime.

Two updates to the 2005 estimates are a straightforward response to the time elapsed since Brand and Price's 2000 publication. First, in the intervening period since the 2000 publication there is some evidence from sources such as the British Crime Survey that the incidence of many types of crime has dropped. This necessitates updates being made to the multipliers used by Brand and Price to estimate the incidence of crime. Second, annual inflation led to changes in prices used in Brand and Price's publications.

There are also two more fundamental revisions to Brand and Price's (2000) methodology. First, in relation to violent crime, Home Office (2005) uses the methodology developed by Dolan *et al.* (2005) to estimate the emotional and physical costs of violent crime. This leads to substantial changes in some estimates. For example, Brand and Price (2000) estimate the average cost of the physical and emotional impact of a sexual offence to be £13,219. In the more recent publication this is revised to £23,015 (Home Office 2005: 19 Table 2.1). Second, various changes are made to the methodology Brand and Price (2000) develop to estimate criminal justice system costs; in particular police and correctional service costs. Brand and Price have relatively little information available on how to allocate police costs across different types of offences, and rely on an activity sampling exercise undertaken for Humberside Police. By the time of the later publication an activity-based sampling exercise had been undertaken in each of the 43 police forces in England and Wales providing more detailed and more robust estimates (Home Office 2005). Brand and Price (2000) use a Home Office flows-and-costs model to estimate criminal justice costs. However, this model constrains unit costs for specific crimes so that, when applied to the total number of crimes committed in the year in question, the resulting figure would be equal to the criminal justice system budget for that year. Such a model does not account for the fact that some offences result in costs which are spread over more than one year (Home Office 2005). An example would be an offence which resulted in a prison sentence lasting several years. This methodology is revised to take account of the average length of disposal for each crime type.

In 2000 Brand and Price estimate that crime against individuals and households is £32.2 billion. This cost therefore accounts for just over half of the £60 billion estimate for the cost of all crime in England and Wales. The Home Office (2005) estimate that in 2003/04 this cost is £36.2 billion. This is despite using lower estimates of the incidence of crime. The apparent increase is due to a combination of changes to the methodology and inflation. When the estimate for 2000 is re-run using the revised methodology – and with figures upgraded to take account of inflation so that the two figures are directly comparable – the estimate for the cost of crime against individuals and households in 2000 rises from £32.2 billion to £39.9 billion (Home Office 2005: Table 4.2).

The costs of specific types of crime, broken down between costs: in anticipation; as a consequence; and in response to crime, is reproduced in Table 7.1. Note the estimates for average costs of different type vary widely. Sexual offences (£31,438) and violence against the person (£10,407) are the most costly types of offences. Property crimes are generally less costly. The most costly property crime is theft of a vehicle (£4,138).

Conclusion

Work on the costs of crime has advanced enormously in recent years. However, there is still much work to do. Cohen, after a thorough review of existing attempts to cost crime, concludes:

> There appears to be a general consensus among criminologists and economists who are interested in conducting social cost-benefit analyses of crime control programs that 'cost of crime' estimates need to go beyond earlier

Table 7.1 Estimated average costs of crimes against individuals and households in 2003/04 by crime type and cost category

Offence category	Costs in anticipation of crime (£)		Costs as a consequence of crime (£)							Costs in response to crime (£)	2003 prices
	Defensive expenditure	Insurance administration	Physical and emotional impact on direct victims	Value of property stolen	Property damaged/ destroyed	Property recovered	Victim services	Lost output	Health services	Criminal justice system	Average cost (£)
Violence against the person	1	1	5,472	—	—	—	9	1,648	1,347	1,928	10,407
Homicide	145	229	860,380	—	—	—	2,102	451,110	770	144,239	1,458,975
Wounding	1	1	4,554	—	—	—	7	1,166	1,348	1,775	8,852
Serious wounding	1	1	4,554	—	—	—	7	1,166	1,348	14,345	21,422
Other wounding	1	1	4,554	—	—	—	7	1,166	1,348	978	8,056
Sexual offences	3	5	22,754	—	—	—	32	4,430	916	3,298	31,438
Common assault	0	0	788	—	—	—	6	269	123	255	1,440
Robbery	0	21	3,048	109	12	-19	16	1,011	483	2,601	7,282
Burglary in a dwelling	221	177	646	846	187	-22	11	64	—	1,137	3,268
Theft	59	52	192	281	69	-36	1	10	—	217	844
Theft – not vehicle	—	33	118	175	17	-13	1	3	—	301	634
Theft of vehicle	546	370	800	2,367	349	-542	1	47	—	199	4,138
Theft from vehicle	116	50	266	240	126	-11	1	20	—	50	858
Attempted vehicle theft	65	21	194	—	154	—	1	11	—	65	510
Criminal damage	13	36	472	—	212	—	2	6	—	126	866

Source: Home Office (2005: Table 2.1).

estimates of the cost to victims and the taxpayer – and begin to incorporate nonvictim and community costs.

(Cohen 2007: 47)

To do this Cohen (2007) favours the further development and wider use of the willingness-to-pay survey – also referred to as a contingent valuation survey.

While this is a method used extensively in fields such as environmental policy, there have only been a handful of contingent valuation crime studies to date and only one in the UK (Atkinson *et al.* 2005 – discussed above). Cohen (2007) therefore sets out a future research programme which includes: replicating existing contingent valuation studies to see how robust the findings are; expanding the number of crimes captured in such studies; including crimes such as drug abuse, prostitution, illegal gambling, fraud and other forms of white-collar crime. He also discusses a range of methodological concerns including: how questions are phrased; how they are presented to respondents; and the sequencing of questions and types of choices respondents are given. These issues have not yet been fully explored in the limited number of studies undertaken to date.

Thus, a substantial and important programme remains: important not just for academic reasons but because use of cost of crime estimates is becoming common in assessments of the impact and value of policy options.

8   Crime reduction

Introduction

There are many different ways to conceptualise crime reduction. Indeed, crime prevention is sometimes classified according to the population it is targeted upon. For example, Brantingham and Faust (1976) use a medical analogy to distinguish between primary, secondary and tertiary crime prevention. Primary prevention focuses on society as a whole and seeks to reduce the opportunities for crime without referring to any particular group; secondary prevention focuses on those deemed to be at high risk or embarking upon a criminal career; and tertiary prevention focuses on those who have already offended. Van Dijk (1991) expands upon this classification and retains the primary, secondary and tertiary division while also distinguishing between victim, offender and situation-oriented initiatives to create a nine-fold classification. Drawing on some ideas from Routine Activity theory (see Chapter Four) Ekblom's (2000) 'Conjunction of Criminal Opportunity Model' recognises crime has both remote and immediate causes. The more remote causes are all channelled through a common set of immediate precursors which combine to generate the criminal or disorderly event. Here, an offender encounters, seeks out or engineers a crime situation comprising a suitable target of crime in a favourable environment and in the absence of capable preventers (or guardians). Ekblom (2000) identifies 11 causes of crime (each with more remote and more immediate elements. Accompanying these are 11 broad crime reduction interventions.

For our purposes a less technical division of crime reduction is appropriate. Accordingly, this chapter divides crime reduction into the following broad areas, selected because each is based on a distinct research and evaluation tradition and raises distinct issues for a study of the economics of crime prevention:

- policing;
- situational crime reduction; and
- developmental crime reduction.

Our focus is on the economics of crime reduction. However, to facilitate this we start each section with a short explanation of what, in broad terms, these different approaches to crime reduction cover before going on to examine the available economic evidence.

Before looking in detail at different approaches to crime reduction we first discuss the extent of the evidence base.

A limited evidence base

As we saw in Chapter Six economic analysis requires reliable data on the impact of interventions. For example, a cost–benefit analysis takes as its starting point an impact evaluation based either on a randomised control trial or a well-matched comparison group (see Chapter Six for a more detailed discussion of preferable designs for a robust impact evaluation). Economic analysis is still possible if a robust impact evaluation is not available, but the outcomes which might be delivered by an intervention have to be modelled. Thus certainty in the output of the analysis reduces. In the field of crime reduction on both sides of the Atlantic evidence of a move towards more evidence-based policy-making can be seen; however, progress has been slower in the UK.

Evidence in the USA

In the USA much progress has been made and the direction of travel is clear. A key milestone was the publication by Sherman *et al.* (1998a) *Preventing Crime: What Works, What Doesn't, What's Promising.* This extensive, systematic review of the evidence base was commissioned by the US Justice Department. Sherman and colleagues at the University of Maryland reviewed 500 evaluations that reported evidence of a programme's impact upon crime. To assess their methodological rigour they developed a Scientific Methods Scale in which evaluation designs are ranked according to their level of internal validity. Randomised controlled trials are identified as the most rigorous evaluation design and quasi-experiments in which a comparison group is used are established as the 'next best thing'. The full so-called Maryland Scale as described in Sherman *et al.* (1998b: 5–6) is as follows:

- *Level 1*: correlation between a crime prevention programme and a measure of crime or crime risk factors at a single point in time.

- *Level 2*: temporal sequence between the programme and the crime or risk outcome clearly observed, or the presence of a comparison group without demonstrated comparability to the treatment group.

- *Level 3*: a comparison between two or more comparable units of analysis, one with and one without the programme.

- *Level 4*: comparison between multiple units with and without the programme, controlling for other factors, or using comparison units that evidence only minor differences.

- *Level 5*: random assignment and analysis of comparable units to the programme and comparison groups.

For a programme to be classed as 'working' by Sherman and colleagues it has to have at least two Level 3 evaluations and the preponderance of all available evidence showing effectiveness. On the basis of this assessment Sherman *et al.* (1998b) identify 15 programmes which work, 23 that don't and 30 that are promising. A similar approach has been used by the University of Colorado's Centre for the Study and Prevention of Violence, which is funded by the US Health Department. To date[1] more than 800 programmes designed to reduce violence have been assessed. The assessment criteria are more conservative than those adopted by Sherman *et al.* (1998a and b). For inclusion as a 'Blueprint for Violence Prevention', studies must be based on an experimental design; provide evidence of a statistically significant (or marginal) deterrent effect; be replicated at multiple sites with demonstrated effects; and provide evidence that the deterrent effect was sustained for at least one year post treatment. On this basis, 11 programmes have so far been identified which meet these criteria and 19 are designated as promising.

Evidence in the UK

In the UK progress has been slower. Shortly after the Labour government came to office in 1997 the Home Office commissioned a review of evidence on crime reduction. The resulting publication, *Home Office Research Study 187* (Goldblatt and Lewis 1998) is clearly influenced by existing systematic reviews of evidence such as Sherman *et al.* (1998a). However, *Home Office Research Study 187* is not itself a systematic review. Following this report the Treasury and the Home Office invested £250 million in a Crime Reduction Programme in which local Crime and Disorder Reduction Partnerships bid for funding to implement local crime reduction programmes. Sadly, monitoring and evaluation of this initiative and later work of Crime and Disorder Partnerships was fragmented. Chambers *et al.* describe how:

> The task was eventually given to a confusing array of different bodies, including regional crime reduction directors, Crime Concern, Nacro and the Home Office, causing duplication and ineffective monitoring and support. This also exacerbated the difficulties surrounding the crucial issue of evaluation, which was severely hampered by problems of data quality and availability.
>
> (Chambers *et al.* 2009: 22)

By 2005 when Harper and Chitty published *The Impact of Corrections on Re-offending: A Review of 'What Works'*, a systematic review methodology had been adopted and the Scientific Methods Scale developed by Sherman *et al.* (1998a and b) had been adapted for reconviction studies (see Harper and Chitty 2005: Table 1.2). Over recent years government departments have placed increasing emphasis on the importance of designing robust impact studies when evaluating policies and programmes. The Government Social Research Unit

(2007) published extensive guidance in which the advantages of study designs with high levels of internal validity are clear. When commissioning impact evaluations the Home Office and Ministry of Justice increasingly prefer experiments and quasi-experiments with high levels of internal validity. One manifestation of this is the tendency of those departments to commission feasibility studies to explore the possibility of implementing these robust research designs prior to commissioning a full impact study (see for example, Farrington and Jolliffe 2002).

Despite these advances the evidence base upon which it is possible to build robust cost–benefit analyses remains limited and fragmented. Home Office advice and guidance on reducing crime has continued to draw on many examples of 'effective practice' without making clear how robust the evidence to support effectiveness is.[2] Take Closed Circuit Television Cameras (CCTV) as an example. Norris *et al.* (2004) chart the history of CCTV in the UK where, during the 1970s and 1980s, its use gradually expanded in the commercial and transport sectors. Then in 1993 an initial Home Office funding round worth £2 million for CCTV was launched in response, it is suggested, to the killing of Jamie Bulger. 'The fuzzy CCTV images of toddler Jamie Bulger being led away from a Merseyside shopping mall by his two ten-year-old killers placed CCTV in the spotlight' (Norris *et al.* 2004: 111). Over the following 10 years government expenditure (much of it from the Home Office) expanded rapidly; writing in 2004, Norris *et al.* estimate around £250 million of public money has been spent on CCTV in the UK over the last 10 years. However, as they note, this represents 'only a small fraction of total spending' (Norris *et al.* 2004: 112). They quote industry statistics which estimate the UK CCTV market has gone from £100 million annually in the early 1990s to just over £1000 million by 2003. A recent industry report by Market and Business Development (2010) estimated the UK CCTV market in 2009 to be worth £1,181 million. It is interesting to contrast this level of expenditure with that on high quality evaluation of CCTV. We don't have specific figures for expenditure on evaluation of CCTV, but in 2002 Welsh and Farrington undertook a systematic review of the research evidence on the effects of CCTV on crime. They identify only 22 studies of high methodological quality; and only one which included a cost–benefit analysis. Sixteen of the 22 studies were undertaken in the UK.

Making a direct comparison between the development of the evidence base in the UK and the USA, particularly in relation to early interventions for children and young people at risk of offending, Chambers *et al.* conclude that one of the problems with crime reduction in the UK is that:

> There is no effective vehicle for evaluating programmes or establishing an evidence base. In England and Wales, responsibility for interventions lies with many different agencies, programmes are evaluated in different places, with different criteria and different desired outcomes.
>
> (Chambers *et al.* 2009: 7)

Policing

Police spending in the UK

Over recent years spending on the police in England and Wales has increased substantially. Indeed, Mills *et al.* (2010) report police expenditure has nearly doubled over the past decade, from £7.72 billion in 1998/1999 to £14.55 billion in 2008/2009, an increase of 88.5 per cent. Accounting for inflation this is an increase of 48.0 per cent, with an additional £4.72 billion spent on the police during 2008/2009 compared to 1998/1999. In 1999/2000, nearly two-thirds of government expenditure on the criminal justice system (£7.5 billion out of £12.056 billion) was devoted to the police (Mills *et al.* 2010 citing Barclay and Tavares 1999: 70).

There is little evidence to suggest additional resources put into policing are necessarily well spent. Analysis of the headline figures show reductions in crime seen over recent years do not seem to be directly related to such increased expenditure. As Mills *et al.* (2010) note, the issue was considered in 2006/2007 by the Home Affairs Committee which concludes:

> A significant drop in overall crime as measured by the British Crime Survey (BCS) occurred between 1995 and 2001 but the downward trend has levelled off since then. In contrast, the bulk of additional police funding was provided during the second half of the last decade, from 2000–01 to 2004–05. It follows that the significant decrease in overall BCS-measured crime occurred before any significant increase in police funding or police officer numbers. Although it is difficult to draw firm conclusions from high-level data on overall crime and funding levels, the reduction in overall crime levels does not seem to have been directly related to additional resources.
>
> (Home Affairs Committee 2007: 3)

Evaluations of specific policing programmes also provide only limited evidence of police effectiveness. Weisburd and Eck's (2004) extensive review of the evaluation evidence on policing found the strongest evidence of police effectiveness in reducing crime and disorder is found in the case of geographically-focused police practices such as hot-spots policing. Community policing practices are found to reduce fear of crime, but Weisburd and Eck (2004) do not find consistent evidence community policing (when it is implemented without models of problem-oriented policing) affects either crime or disorder. However, a developing body of evidence suggests problem-oriented policing is effective in reducing crime, disorder and fear.

The impact and cost–benefits of policing

While there is some evidence on the economic costs and benefits of policing, the evidence is 'patchy' and, to date, has not been reviewed systematically. For the purposes of this section we make a distinction between evidence on specific functions and procedures associated with policing on the one hand and broader policing strategies on the other.

Specific functions and procedures associated with policing

If we are interested in very specific functions and procedures associated with policing there are several cost-effectiveness and cost–benefit analyses we can draw upon. To provide some examples:

• Roman *et al.* (2009) have undertaken a randomised trial of the cost-effectiveness of using DNA technology to solve property crimes. Roman *et al.* (2009) report that biological evidence was collected at up to 500 crime scenes in five US cities between 2005 and 2007. Cases were randomly assigned to the treatment and control groups in equal numbers and DNA processing added to traditional investigation in the treatment group. It is reported that a suspect was arrested in 22 per cent of treatment cases and 10 per cent of control cases. Across the five sites the cost of these additional arrests, that is, arrests which would not have taken place but for DNA processing, was $14,000. However, in the most cost-effective site the cost of each additional arrest was much less: $4,000.

• Schnelle *et al.* (1978) report on a cost–benefit analysis of a helicopter patrol in a high crime area. They report that the helicopter patrolled one city zone for two 12-day periods. Each 12-day period was separated by a baseline period in which only normal patrol-car levels were maintained. They observed significantly reduced burglary levels during the intervention periods, compared to baseline periods. The cost–benefit analysis showed that 'the marginal costs of the helicopter intervention were exceeded by all estimates of benefits' (Schnelle *et al.* 1978: 1).

• Elvick (2001) describes the application of a cost–benefit analysis to traffic police enforcement. Of particular interest is the examination of the marginal benefit. Elvick (2001) starts from the assumption that increasing traffic police enforcement would be likely to bring benefits in terms of fewer accidents. But the resources allocated to traffic police enforcement could alternatively be used for other road safety measures and it is posited that, beyond a certain point, it is likely that the additional benefits of further increases in enforcement become smaller than the benefits that other road safety measures would give. The first stage of Elvick's work is to review existing effect studies for different types of traffic police enforcement such as the use of speed cameras, enforcement of seat belt laws and penalty point systems. Many of the evaluations reviewed show that different interventions do reduce road traffic accidents. Elvick goes on to examine the relationship between the amount of police enforcement and the size of the effect of enforcement on accidents or the rate of violations. Despite the heterogeneity of the studies reviewed, Elvick is able to draw some broad generalisations: reducing enforcement worsens safety; increasing enforcement improves safety; and the marginal effect of increasing enforcement declines gradually. A cost–benefit analysis shows that 'there is too little enforcement today, and that it would be highly cost-effective to increase enforcement substantially' (Elvick 2001: 73).

These examples have been selected to demonstrate the range of interventions covered by available studies and the range of methodologies they draw on. As is generally the case with economic evaluation and particularly cost–benefit analysis, the availability and robustness of economic analysis will, to some extent, reflect the availability and robustness of effect studies. Weisburd and Eck (2004: 42), in their comprehensive review of the evidence for different approaches to policing, note that:

> [M]any policing practices applied broadly throughout the United States either have not been the subject of systematic research or have been examined in the context of research designs that do not allow practitioners or policy makers to draw very strong conclusions.
>
> (Weisburd and Eck 2004: 42)

Policing strategies

Unsurprisingly, it is difficult to draw conclusions about the economic efficiency of broad policing strategies. While identifying the impact and hence economic efficiency of tightly defined interventions may be relatively straightforward, doing the same for a broader strategy or policy is more challenging. Drawing on a medical analogy, Sherman *et al.* contend:

> The tools of the scientific method are only as useful as the precision of the questions they answer. Medical science, for example, evaluates the effectiveness of specific treatments; it is rarely able to establish the controls needed to evaluate broad categories of funding embracing multiple or varying treatments, such as 'hospitals' or even 'antibiotics.' Variations in treatment place major limitations on the capacity of science to reach valid conclusions about cause and effect. The scientific study of aspirin, for example, assumes that all aspirin has identical chemical components; violating that assumption in any given study clearly weakens the science of aspirin effectiveness. The same is true of crime prevention programs. The more a single program varies in its content, the less power science has to draw any conclusions.
>
> (Sherman *et al.* 1998a: 1/7)

In organising their systematic review of evidence on what works in policing, Weisburd and Eck (2004) develop a typology of broad policing strategies. They represent this in a four cell matrix (see Figure 8.1) in which the vertical axis describes the diversity of approaches and the horizontal axis the level of focus. They argue that 'Innovations in policing over the last decade have moved outward along one or both of these dimensions' (Weisburd and Eck 2004: 45).

We consider briefly each of these four models.

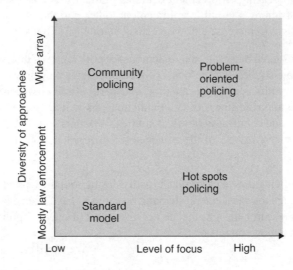

Figure 8.1 Dimensions of policing strategies.

Source: Weisburd and Eck (2004: Figure 1).

Standard policing model

As defined by Weisburd and Eck (2004), the standard mode of policing is a 'one-size-fits-all' application of reactive strategies to suppress crime. As of 2004 it continued to be the dominant form of police practice in the USA and elements of it can still be found in mainstream British policing. This approach is based on the assumption that generic strategies for crime reduction can be applied throughout a jurisdiction regardless of the level of crime, the nature of crime, or other variations. It includes elements such as: random patrol across all parts of the community; rapid response to calls for service; generally applied follow-up investigations; and generally applied intensive enforcement and arrest policies. In their review of evidence Weisburd and Eck (2004) identified five interventions which have been the focus of robust systematic research: increasing the size of police agencies; random patrol across all parts of the community; rapid response to calls for service; generalised investigations of crime; and generally applied intensive enforcement and arrest policies. Their review found relatively little evidence to support the effectiveness of any of these five.

The effect of increasing the size of police agencies merits further discussion. Although Weisburd and Eck (2004) identify relatively little evidence in support of this strategy, they do note that two recent studies using sophisticated statistical designs suggest marginal increases in the number of police are related to decreases in crime rates. These studies (Levitt 1997; Marvell and Moody 1996) have been undertaken by economists using econometric methods (see Chapter Six). Levitt and Miles (2006) divide empirical research on police and crime into two 'generations'. They suggest the first generation of studies, which consisted of cross-sectional designs that compared policing and crime rates across jurisdictions, provided a poor test of the causal effect of police on crime because they failed to correct for the simultaneity problem (see Chapter Six): jurisdictions with higher crime rates often respond by hiring more police, whereas jurisdictions with lower crime rates employ fewer police (Levitt and Miles 2006). However, Levitt and Miles (2006) note a second generation of studies has adopted two methodological innovations to overcome the simultaneity problem. First, they have used larger and richer data sets, for example, using data from a number of years rather than just one. This allows studies to track changes in crime rates over time as well as between jurisdictions. Second, they have used more sophisticated study designs, particularly Granger Causality and natural experiments.

Granger Causality 'refers to a temporal relationship between variables rather than actual causation' (Levitt and Miles 2006: 151). One variable 'Granger Causes' another when changes in the first variable generally precede changes in the second (see Chapter Six for further discussion). Using data from states and cities in the USA over a 20-year period Marvell and Moody (1996) find a 10 per cent increase in police numbers leads to a 3 per cent long-term reduction in crime. A weakness of this study, however, is that it is based on annual crime figures, which might miss short-term fluctuations in crime rates, thus producing an under-estimate of the relationship between police numbers and crime (Levitt and Miles 2006). Corman and Mocan (2000) undertake a similar study using monthly data from New York City. They estimate a 10 per cent increase in police numbers results in a 10 per cent drop in crime rates.

An example of the use of a natural experiment to examine the impact of police numbers on crime is Levitt's (1997) study in which he assumes mayoral and gubernatorial elections are a phenomenon independent of crime rates. He also notes police numbers grow in election years, presumably because increased police numbers give incumbent politicians an advantage at election time (Levitt and Miles 2006). Levitt (1997) therefore assumes the elections are effectively a natural experiment in which an increase in police numbers takes place independently of changes in crime rates. He estimates a 10 per cent increase in police numbers leads to a 3 to 10 per cent reduction in crime (Levitt and Miles 2006). Levitt (1997), using estimates from his study, finds the marginal benefit in reduced crime from employing another city police officer exceeds the costs (Levitt and Miles 2006).

Other than Levitt (1997) we are not aware of economic evaluation of the overall standard policing model or its key elements.

Geographically-focused policing

In contrast to the standard policing model, Weisburd and Eck's (2004) systematic review finds strong empirical support for the effectiveness of the 'hot-spots policing'. They identify a series of experimental evaluations which provide strong support for the effectiveness of such geographically-focused policing. However, we are aware of no economic evaluation of the overall geographically-focused policing model and little relating to its key elements. That is to say, there is evidence it is effective, but its cost-effectiveness remains an empirical matter.

Problem-oriented policing

Problem-oriented policing (POP) was first introduced by Herman Goldstein in 1979. Weisburd *et al.* (2008) describe how Goldstein argues the unit of analysis in policing must become the 'problem' rather than calls or crime incidents as was the case up to then. They describe how POP has had a tremendous impact on American policing; it is now one of the most widely implemented policing strategies in the USA. The same is true in the UK where 'problem-solving' approaches have been widely adopted by the police and Community Safety Partnerships.[3] POP involves the police and other local agencies working closely with communities to identify specific problems and to develop solutions together (Home Office 2006a). A four-stage problem-solving (so-called SARA) model is used widely on both sides of the Atlantic:

- *Scanning*: where problems are identified using local knowledge and data from a wide range of organisations.
- *Analysis*: where the data is used to identify the problems caused.
- *Response*: where solutions are devised to the problem using the situation and social approaches described in the last section.
- *Assessment*: looking back to see if the solution worked and what lessons can be learnt.

(Home Office 2006a)

Weisburd *et al.* (2008), building on the work of Weisburd and Eck (2004), undertake a systematic review of the evidence on the effectiveness of POP. Eligible studies had to use the SARA model, be evaluated using a design including a comparison group and report at least one crime or disorder outcome. Only 10 studies are identified that meet these criteria and a meta-analysis of the data from these studies shows 'overall problem-oriented policing has a modest but statistically significant impact on reducing crime and disorder' (Weisburd *et al.* 2008: 5). Weisburd *et al.* also set out to examine questions of cost-effectiveness but note that only 'one of the studies we examined provided data on cost-effectiveness issues' (Weisburd *et al.* 2008: 10).

Community policing

Weisburd and Eck (2004) note that community policing has become one of the most widely implemented approaches in American policing. Community policing has some similarities to POP but the focus is on the interaction between the police and local communities:

Problem-oriented policing is a method for analyzing and solving crime problems. Community policing, on the other hand, represents a broader organizational philosophy. Community policing includes problem-solving as addressed in problem-oriented policing, but it also includes the development of external partnerships with community members and groups. Additionally, community policing addresses organizational changes that should take place in a police agency . . . to support collaborative problem-solving, community partnerships, and a general proactive orientation to crime and social disorder issues. Community policing is therefore more focused on police-public inter-action than is problem-oriented policing.

(Clarke and Eck 2004: 7)

Only limited evidence is identified by Weisburd and Eck:

[I]n reviewing existing studies, we could find no consistent research agenda that would allow us to assess with strong confidence the effectiveness of commu-nity policing. . . . While the evidence available does not allow for definitive con-clusions . . . we do not find consistent evidence that community policing (when it is implemented without problem-oriented policing) affects either crime or disorder. However, the research available suggests that when the police partner more generally with the public, levels of citizen fear will decline.

(Weisburd and Eck 2004: 59)

We are aware of no economic evaluations of community policing.

In the UK 'neighbourhood policing' has sought to implement a model of polic-ing which includes elements the international research base suggests are effective: a geographical focus; community policing which focuses on problem-solving; and inter-agency working. Evaluations have been undertaken of both the National Reassurance Policing Programme (despite the name, a tightly controlled pilot in 16 neighbourhoods) and the Neighbourhood Policing Programme (the national roll-out). Results from the evaluation of the pilot show: increased public confi-dence in the police; reductions in crime victimisation; reductions in perceptions of crime and anti-social behaviour, as well as improved feelings of safety; bet-ter public perceptions of community engagement; improved police visibility and familiarity with the police (Quinton and Morris 2008). However, evaluation of the Neighbourhood Policing Programme (i.e. the attempt to roll-out the pilot nation-ally) is less conclusive (Quinton and Morris 2008).

Situational crime prevention

A typology of situational crime prevention

Situational crime prevention draws its theoretical justification from Rational Choice theory which depicts the world as being made up of instrumentally rational individuals. We examined Rational Choice theory in detail in Chapter Four, but it is interesting to note here that situational crime prevention is predicated on a micro-economic theory of human behaviour.

Rational Choice theory emphasises the importance of choice to criminal involvement or criminality. According to the theory, *opportunity* is central to understanding the potential criminal's decision-making process at a specific criminal event. Situational crime prevention therefore focuses on the reduction of opportunity. Clarke (2005) outlines a number of opportunity-reduction techniques that have been used in situational prevention. The techniques are divided into five groups: increasing effort; increasing the risks to the offender; reducing the rewards of crime; reducing provocations; and removing excuses (see Table 8.1). Each group is designed to affect one aspect of the potential offender's cost–benefit analysis of the crime opportunity.

Criticisms of situational crime prevention

Various criticisms are levelled against situational crime prevention. One is that, while situational measures may be appropriate in dealing with some categories of crime (e.g. opportunistic, property crimes), they are not appropriate for dealing with more deeply motivated crimes committed by hardened offenders (Clarke 1995). However Clarke (1995) points out that rates of all types of crime are affected by situational contingencies. Whether an assault becomes homicidal, for instance, may depend on the presence of a lethal weapon at the scene; the introduction of baggage screening at airports has virtually eliminated terrorist hijackings (Clarke 1995). A second, related criticism of situational crime prevention is that some types of more serious crime are less common and therefore less likely to cluster in time and space, meaning that they are less amenable to situational controls (Clarke 1995). Clarke answers this criticism by pointing to the control of violence through deflecting offenders (e.g. preventing drunken youths congregating at closing time); the control of crime facilitators such as guns and alcohol; and the reduction of obscene telephone calls by introducing Caller-ID in New Jersey, USA (Clarke 1992, 1995). A third related criticism concerns the phenomenon of displacement. Displacement of crime, following the use of situational crime prevention, has been cited by critics as evidence of the importance of the offender's disposition in explaining and preventing crime. Situational crime prevention focuses on opportunity reduction at specific criminal events. If the crime is displaced rather than prevented then this is evidence of the importance of disposition in explaining crime and shaping crime prevention responses. Clarke tackles the displacement criticism in a number of ways. For instance, he suggests the uncritical acceptance of displacement will lead to increases in crime which might have occurred anyway being attributed to displacement. He also argues in no instance has displacement been complete, suggesting the situational prevention led to at least some benefit. He also points out that sometimes displacement can be 'benign' and sometimes it may be the benefits of the preventative action will be displaced rather than the crime (Clarke 1995): the so-called 'diffusion of benefits' phenomenon.

Cost–benefit analyses of situational crime prevention

Welsh and Farrington (1999, 2001b) undertake a systematic review of economic evaluations of situational crime prevention. Evaluation studies are included in the review if they meet three criteria:

Table 8.1 Twenty-five techniques of situational crime prevention

Increase the effort required	Increase the risks of crime	Reduce the rewards of crime	Reduce provocations to offend	Remove excuses for offending
1. Target harden • Steering column locks and ignition immobilisers • Anti-robbery screens • Tamper-proof packaging	6. Extend guardianship • Go out in group at night • Leave signs of occupancy • Carry cell phone	11. Conceal targets • Off-street parking • Gender-neutral phone directories • Unmarked armoured trucks	16. Reduce frustrations • Efficient lines • Polite service • Expand seating • Soothing music/muted lighting	21. Set rules • Rental agreements • Harassment codes • Hotel registration
2. Control access • Entry phones • Electronic card access	7. Assist natural surveillance • Improved street lighting • Defensible space design • Support whistle blowers	12. Remove targets • Removable car radio • Women's shelters • Pre-paid cards for pay phones	17. Avoid disputes • Separate seating for rival soccer fans • Reduce overcrowding in bars • Fixed cab fares	22. Post instructions • 'No parking' • 'Private property' • 'Extinguish camp fires'
3. Screen exits • Ticket needed for exit • Export documents • Electronic merchandise tags	8. Reduce anonymity • Taxi-driver IDs • 'How's my driving?' deals • School uniforms	13. Identify property • Property marking • Vehicle licensing and parts marking • Cattle branding	18. Reduce temptation • Controls on violent pornography • Enforce good behaviour on soccer field • Prohibit racial slurs	23. Alert conscience • Roadside speed display boards • Signatures for customs declarations • 'Shoplifting is stealing'
4. Deflect offenders • Street closures • Separate facilities for women • Disperse pubs	9. Use place managers • CCTV for double-decker buses • Two clerks for convenience stores • Reward vigilance	14. Disrupt markets • Monitor pawn shops • Controls on classified ads • Licensed street vendors	19. Neutralise peer pressure • 'Idiots drink and drive' • 'It's OK to say no' • Disperse trouble-makers at school	24. Assist compliance • Easy library checkout • Public lavatories • Litter receptacles
5. Control tools/ weapons • 'Smart' guns • Restrict spray-paint sales to juveniles • Toughened beer-bottle glass	10. Strengthen formal surveillance • Red-light cameras • Burglar alarms • Security guards	15. Deny benefits • Ink merchandising tags • Graffiti cleaning • Disabling stolen cell phones	20. Discourage intimidation • Rapid repair of vandalism • V-chips in TVs • Censor details of *modus operandi*	25. Control drugs and alcohol • Breathalysers in bars • Server intervention programmes • Alcohol-free events

Source: based closely on Clarke (2005: Table 3.3).

1. The programme has a measure of the level of personal crime, where the primary victim is a person or household.
2. The outcome evaluation is based on a 'real-life' programme; by this Welsh and Farrington mean the programme outcomes are neither based on statistical modelling techniques or hypothesised from case study data.
3. A benefit/cost analysis is performed that either calculates – or permits the calculation of – a benefit/cost ratio for the purpose of assessing the programme's economic efficiency.

Using these criteria they eventually identify 13 studies. In terms of the interventions covered by the studies, nine focus on residences and four on commercial premises or public facilities (transport systems). Nine interventions involve some form of surveillance: three involve surveillance by employees; three formal surveillance; and three natural surveillance (Welsh and Farrington 2001b).

Welsh and Farrington (2001b) note that the design of the outcome evaluations are generally relatively weak. In particular, they highlight 'almost a complete absence of follow-up of program effects' (Welsh and Farrington 2001b: 104–5) and that few used experimental designs. Nine of thirteen studies report some form of economic analysis, whereas four merely provide cost and benefit data (Welsh and Farrington 2001b). Benefits measured tend to be confined to decreases in direct or tangible costs for crime victims and, to a lesser extent, decreases in criminal justice costs (ibid.). A desirable benefit/cost ratio is calculated in eight of the 13 studies. These show a return on a unit of investment of between 1.31 and 5.04 units (ibid.). Five projects show a poor benefit/cost ratio; the return on a unit of investment ranges from 0.32 to 0.78 units (ibid.).

Developmental crime reduction

Theory and concepts

Developmental crime prevention focuses on the causes of individual criminality from pre-conception through childhood and into early adulthood. This perspective moves us away from the criminal justice system response to crime and from the situations where crimes occur to instead mobilise resources that shape the individual's development. Homel suggests that:

> Developmental prevention involves the organised provision of resources in some fashion to individuals, families, schools or communities to forestall the later development of crime or other problems.
>
> (Homel 2005: 71)

There is a substantial evidence base which underpins much of the thinking around developmental crime prevention. In particular, the approach draws heavily on longitudinal research into risk factors that predict future criminality. In a longitudinal study cohorts of children are tracked over time through adolescence and, in some cases, through much of their adulthood. Data is gathered on a range of factors which might contribute to criminality and statistical analysis is used to identify the factors which are best able to predict future offending. These 'risk factors' are the focus of developmental crime prevention. Chambers *et al.* explain that:

> The predictions of delinquency based on these risk factors are about as accurate as predictions of epidemiologists forecasting who will get lung cancer based on weight, income, or smoking habits.
>
> (Chambers *et al.* 2009: 33)

Chambers *et al.* (2009) provide a useful overview of the most widely accepted risk factors, grouped according to domains such as: 'individual'; 'family'; and 'school' (see Figure 8.2). Research studies consistently show the greater the number of risk factors in a young person's life, the greater the chances they will commit a crime. Similarly, evidence suggests the greater the number of risk factors in a young person's life, the greater the chances of persistent offending. For example, evidence from the Home Office's Youth Lifestyles Survey (Campbell and Harrington 2000), a large cross-sectional self-report survey of young people aged 12 to 30, found that although only 6 per cent of boys under 18 had at least four adverse risk factors, over three-quarters (85 per cent) of them had committed at least one offence at some point in their lives, and more than half (57 per cent) were currently serious or persistent offenders (ibid.). Serious or persistent offenders were defined as those who had committed at least three offences in the last year of any type and/ or one or more serious offence (assault, threatening or hurting someone with a

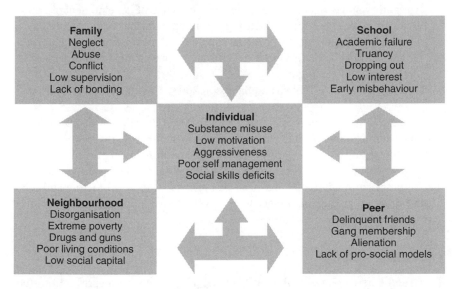

Figure 8.2 Risk factors for future offending.

Source: Chambers *et al.* (2009: Figure 12).

weapon, burglary, car or motorbike theft, pickpocketing or snatch theft). The survey also showed that amongst 18–30-year-old men, only 1 per cent had at least four risk factors, yet all of them had committed an offence at some point in their lives and more than half were serious or persistent offenders (ibid.).

Much of our understanding of risk factors comes from longitudinal studies; this presents challenges to how we interpret our understanding of risk factors and how we 'operationalise' this understanding in crime prevention measures. For example, one methodological limitation of data derived from longitudinal studies is that 'most knowledge about risk factors is mainly based on variation between individuals, whereas prevention requires variation (change) within individuals' (Farrington 2007: 605). Another issue for researchers is establishing which risk factors are causes of future offending and which are merely correlates (Farrington 2007). Ideally, interventions will be focused on causes.

The theory and evidence which underpin developmental crime prevention can be interpreted in different ways. Of particular importance is the debate between researchers who characterise the development of a propensity to commit crime as a 'pathway' and those who characterise it as a 'life-course'. As Laub and Sampson (2003: 33–4) explain:

> Developmental accounts, especially from developmental psychology, focus on regular or lawlike development over the lifespan . . . . The resulting emphasis is on systematic pathways of development (change) over time, with the imagery being one of the execution of a program written at an earlier point in time . . . In contrast, life-course approaches, while incorporating individual differences and notions of lawlike development such as aging, emphasize variability and exogenous influences on the course of development over time that cannot be predicted by focusing solely on enduring individual traits . . . or even past experiences . . . A life-course focus recognizes emergent properties and rejects the metaphor of 'unfolding' that is inextricably part of the developmental paradigm.
>
> (Laub and Sampson 2003: 33–4 quoted in Homel 2005)

This debate is important because, as Homel (2005) explains, if a propensity to commit crime is established in early childhood in such a way that a 'trajectory' is irrevocably set during these early years, then the main focus of prevention should be on these early years. If, however, childhood risk factors have very modest predictive power into adulthood and if human agency, situational factors and other life events are of greater importance then prevention resources should be deployed across the individual's life course (ibid.).

Cost–benefit analyses

Welsh and Farrington (2001b) identify six developmental crime prevention studies meeting the evidential criteria set for their systematic review (the review is described in more detail above). All of these were US studies. Interventions were targeted on people from pre-birth to 18 years old and half of the programmes were pre-school. The six interventions manipulated a range of risk factors, including parenting, education, cognitive development and behavioural problems. The duration of interventions ranged from 10 weeks to four years. Welsh and Farrington (2001b) assess the studies as generally methodologically rigorous. Three were randomised control trials and two had long follow-up periods. One of these was the Perry/Highscope Preschool Project discussed in Chapter Six, the 40-year follow-up of which was presented in Belfield *et al.* (2006).

Five of the six studies yielded a positive benefit to cost ratio. The range of return on a $1 investment ranged from $1.06 to $7.16. Not all of the benefits accrued by these programmes were crime-related. However, for three of the four interventions which began after birth, savings from reduced delinquency and later offending accounted for a substantial proportion of measured benefits (Welsh and Farrington 2001b).

Community-based crime prevention

Community-based crime prevention is the least well-defined approach to crime reduction that we examine in this chapter. Economic evidence on its relative costs and benefits is limited, but there is a literature which discusses its relationship to achieving economic outcomes within communities.

What is community crime prevention?

Hope (1998) defines 'community crime prevention' thus:

> Community crime prevention refers to actions intended to change the social conditions which sustain crime in residential communities. It concentrates on the ability of local social institutions to reduce crime.
>
> (Hope 1998: 51)

Hope (1998: 56–7) classifies a variety of community-focused prevention programmes including:

- *Community-organisation*: programmes which build community-based associations which can provide effective socialisation for young people.
- *Community-defence*: programmes which deter offending by those from outside the community.
- *Order-maintenance*: programmes which seek to control physical disorder and a variety of other types of criminal and sub-criminal behaviour.
- *Risk-based programmes*: programmes which identify risk factors amongst community populations, identify those most at risk and deliver preventive resources specifically for them.
- *Community development*: programmes which seek to rebuild the social, physical and economic fabric of neighbourhoods.

- *Structural change*: programmes which are similar to 'community development' but focus on factors which can be brought about through the operation
  of macro-level socio-economic policies.

As can be seen, these various community crime prevention programmes are
based on different assumptions about the nature of communities and the nature
of the problems they face. Some see crime as integral to community while some
see it as a problem external to the community; some assume the community
has the resources to tackle crime while others concentrate on developing community capacity to tackle crime; and some focus on individuals within the community while others focus on wider socio-economic factors which influence
individuals.

A complicating factor is that definitions of 'community' are contested. Crawford (1998) suggests there is no clear conception of 'community' in 'community safety'. He questions various assumptions which have been made about
community, including its positive and non-criminogenic connotations, its inclu-
sive nature, its spatial location and its capacity for managing crime. It has been
argued communities are often fragmented and diverse. Therefore the type
and extent of resources communities can bring to community safety is highly
variable.

It is often assumed that a low-crime neighbourhood or community is a pre-
requisite for the economic success of the neighbourhood (the possible relationships between the economy and crime are discussed in detail in Chapter Five).
This assumption is clear in several of the conceptions of community crime prevention described by Hope (1998). To some extent, this draws on the literature
around social capital. Social capital describes the pattern and intensity of networks
among people and the shared values which arise from those networks. According to the Office of National Statistics, greater interaction between people generates a greater sense of community spirit.[4] Definitions of social capital vary, but
the main aspects include citizenship, 'neighbourliness', social networks and civic
participation.[5]

High social capital, in the form of social trust and associational networks, is
linked with many desirable outcomes. The Office for National Statistics (2001)
reviews the literature and finds positive correlates which include:

- lower crime rates;
- better health;
- improved longevity;
- better educational achievement;
- greater levels of income equality;
- improved child welfare;
- lower rates of child abuse;
- less corrupt and more effective government; and
- enhanced economic achievement through increased trust and lower transaction costs.

Focusing in particular on the link between social capital and crime, in an important study in Chicago, Sampson, Raudenbush and Earls (1997) find rates of violence are lower in urban neighbourhoods able to activate informal social control; a concept they characterise as 'collective efficacy'. Collective efficacy extends the concept of community cohesion thus:

> Extending the concept of community cohesion, collective efficacy refers to mutual trust among neighbours, combined with willingness to intervene on behalf of the common good, specifically to supervise children and maintain public order.
>
> (Sampson *et al.* 1998: 1)

Their findings are important because they provide evidence that rates of neighbourhood crime are not just a product of factors such as poverty. Sampson, Raudenbush and Earls (1998) find some Chicago neighbourhoods that are poor also have low crime rates. In these neighbourhoods, the researchers conclude collective efficacy is the most powerful factor keeping violent crime rates low.

Cost–benefit analyses

Unfortunately evidence for the effectiveness and cost-effectiveness of community crime prevention is limited.[6] In their extensive systematic review of the evidence for crime prevention, Sherman *et al.* (1998a) find there are no community-based crime prevention programmes proved to be effective, although several are defined in their review as 'promising'. In their systematic review of economic evaluations of crime prevention (see above) Welsh and Farrington (2001b) find only one study of a community crime prevention programme that met their evidential criteria. This is a community-based skill-development programme offered to all children 5–15 years-of-age living in a publicly supported housing complex in Ottawa, Ontario. The evaluation demonstrates clear and statistically significant changes occurred on measures of anti-social behaviour outside home and school. A cost–benefit analysis indicated potential savings, primarily in reduced vandalism but also in reduced police and fire costs, greatly exceeded the cost of delivering the programme.

Conclusion: investment in crime reduction

As we saw in the last chapter the evidence base for the economic benefits of prison is limited. Reviewing the evidence presented in this chapter shows there is relatively little evidence for the effectiveness of mainstream policing strategies and virtually no evidence these strategies are cost beneficial. There is some evidence in support of the effectiveness of both situational crime prevention and developmental crime prevention. However, the number of methodologically robust cost–benefit analyses of both situational and developmental crime prevention interventions is small. That said, the strongest individual cost–benefit analyses are undoubtedly those of the developmental crime prevention measures.

In an interesting exercise in the UK, Chambers *et al.* (2009) analyse government spending on criminal justice and crime prevention. They use Home Office accounts to examine the amount spent on police, courts and prisons compared to that spent on crime prevention. This analysis is summarised in Figure 8.3. As can be clearly seen for every pound spent on crime prevention over recent years, more than £50 (and in some years more than £100) has been spent on police, courts and prisons. This is a fairly crude analysis. For instance, it might be argued that some police expenditure goes directly into crime prevention through, for example, police input into local Community Safety Partnerships. Nevertheless, even if there is some margin for error, the difference in spending is striking. Chambers *et al.* argue that:

> Despite the Government's pledge to be tough on crime and tough on the causes of crime, New Labour has concentrated on law enforcement and the criminal justice system rather than on crime prevention and getting to grips with the underlying causes of criminal behaviour. This has been reflected in the areas to which additional government spending has been directed.
>
> (Chambers *et al.* 2009: 14)

From an economic perspective it is interesting to compare the limited evidence we have about the most cost beneficial means of preventing crime to how we allocate expenditure on crime. Would we be better off investing resources in: preventing individuals from developing a propensity to offend; reducing opportunities to commit crime; or apprehending and reforming offenders once crime is committed? Chambers *et al.* (2009) give us a sense of how resources are currently distributed in the UK, but what would be the most economically advantageous distribution remains an empirical issue.

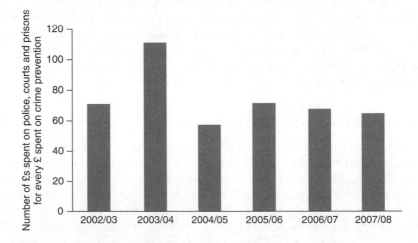

Figure 8.3 Amount spent on enforcement for every £1 spent on prevention.

Source: Chambers *et al.* (2009: Figure 3).

There are two major obstacles to answering this question. The first is that we have a relatively limited body of evidence from which to estimate what programmes are effective. Further, within the available pool of robust impact studies there are variations that make direct comparisons less straightforward. These include variations in the types of outcomes measured, the ways in which outcome measures are defined, and associated data collection and the length of time outcomes are followed-up. However, on the positive side Aos *et al.* (2001a, 2001b) note that the evidence base has improved in recent years. The second major obstacle is that there are few cost–benefit analyses of crime prevention programmes and there is no consistent approach used to undertaking the studies that do exist. This means that, for example, interventions are costed in different ways, and benefits are defined and valued in different ways, making direct comparison between different studies virtually impossible. One solution to this problem is to adopt a common economic approach allowing:

> an 'apples-to-apples' comparison of the economics of programs aimed at very different age groups. This approach is similar to a financial analysis an investment advisor might undertake to study rates of return on mutual funds, bonds, real estate, or other diverse instruments. The focus is on the *comparative* economic bottom line and identifying where an investor – in this case a taxpayer – is likely to get the most bang for his or her buck.
>
> (Aos *et al.* 2001b: 149)

Adopting this approach Aos and his colleagues at the Washington State Institute for Public Policy develop a long-run economic model that provides a direct comparison between a large number of potential crime prevention interventions that between them apply to every stage of the offender criminal career. Development of the model involves five main stages (Aos *et al.* 2001a). First, a systematic review of existing evaluations is undertaken and 'effect sizes' (standardised estimates of a programme's impact) are calculated for each methodologically robust programme evaluation. Second, the long-run effects programmes might be expected to have on future criminality are estimated. Third, Aos *et al.* (2001a) estimate the number of crimes which could be avoided with a programme or policy over a long-run time frame. Fourth, the costs of implementing each programme or policy are estimated. Finally, a set of standard economic statistics are produced to describe the relative costs and benefits of each programme or policy (ibid.). Summarising their results, Aos *et al.* report:

> We found the largest and most consistent economic returns are for certain programs designed for juvenile offenders. Several of these interventions produce benefit-to-cost ratios that exceed twenty dollars of benefits for each dollar of taxpayer cost. That is, a dollar spent on these programs today can be expected to return to taxpayers and crime victims twenty or more dollars in the years ahead. . . . In addition to programs for juvenile offenders, we also found

economically attractive prevention programs for young children and adolescents and, at the other end of the age spectrum, for adult offenders.

(Aos *et al.* 2001a: 5)

They go on to recommend that policy-makers adopt a portfolio of cost beneficial policies and programmes rather than a single intervention. Perhaps this is the key message to take from the review of economic evidence on crime reduction. As Aos *et al.* argue:

> While the research base for 'what works' has improved in recent years, it remains limited . . . . Therefore, we believe it would be a mistake to allocate all prevention and intervention dollars into any one program no matter how attractive the numbers might look; unfortunately, sometimes bad things happen to good programs. Similar to the situation facing any investor, public policy makers should avoid putting all of the prevention and intervention eggs into one basket. Therefore, we recommend that a 'portfolio approach' be developed achieving a reasonable balance between near-term and long-term resources, and between research-proven strategies and those that are promising but in need of research and development. In particular, a portfolio approach should be adopted to reduce the overall risk that some programs, like some stocks in the stock market, may not turn out to be good investments when they are actually purchased and implemented.
>
> (Aos *et al.* 2001a: 7)

9 The economic analysis of prisons and community justice alternatives

Introduction

Two of the state's main approaches to cutting crime are the use of imprisonment and community-based sentences. Prisons in a form which we would recognise today have been in existence since the nineteenth century (see, for instance, Morgan and Liebling 2007) and, despite Dodge's (1979: 243) bold forecast, 'we now have enough evidence to support the assumption that prisons may not be needed in the future', their use is likely to continue.[1] Probation also has a long history in the UK and the USA. In 1952 Grünhut wrote 'Probation is the great contribution of Britain and the USA to the treatment of offenders' (Grünhut 1952: 168 quoted in Raynor 2007). In England and Wales the 'probation order' has been succeeded, first with the 'community rehabilitation order' and latterly with the generic 'community sentence', introduced in the Criminal Justice Act 2003 (Reiner 2007).[2]

Notwithstanding in recent years prison numbers and prison costs on both sides of the Atlantic have risen sharply. Prison numbers have increased absolutely, as a proportion of the total population and relative to the number of crimes committed. An economic analysis would therefore seem to have much to offer. However, this is also an extremely politicised area of public sector policy where an evidence-led debate is often seemingly overtaken by political point scoring and the entrenched views of some sections of the popular press. As Marsh, Fox and Hedderman (2009) note, anyone who argues that money spent on building more prisons is not well spent risks being accused of being soft on crime and uninterested in the consequences for victims. However, it may be that those who make such accusations are the ones failing to account fully for the costs of crime, both past and future. As Marsh, Fox and Hedderman go on to argue, an economic analysis has much to offer because it cannot only take the actual costs of offences to victims into account, but also consider the savings to society which might accrue from favouring one sentencing option over another. Fox and Albertson (2010) point out, in the first decade of this century, there have been several important developments in the application of economic techniques to criminal justice policy including greater interest and investment in evidence-based policy-making and the rise of the Justice Reinvestment movement, particularly in the USA. They also see the economic crisis which is affecting most Western economies at the time of writing as providing further impetus for adopting an approach to criminal justice policy in which economic analysis is central.

In this chapter we consider the economic evidence for the effectiveness of different custodial and community-based sentencing options. After setting the context we consider the theoretical work upon which economists have drawn. We go on to consider whether empirical studies provide support for any of these theories.[3] The concept of Justice Reinvestment, in particular, is examined. This movement, which started in the USA, is now increasingly influential in the UK. At its heart is an economic analysis of different sentencing options and their long-run effects. The contribution of economic analysis to the debate about public versus private prisons is discussed and we conclude by summarising what economists have said about the most efficient ways of delivering sentences.

Context

The demand for prison places

The change in the prison population in England and Wales over the last 40 years is summarised in Figure 9.1. It is clear there has been a substantial increase, particularly since 1997. In 1997 the prison population was 61,114 (Home Office 2003b); as of January 2010 it was 83,378 (HM Prison Service 2010) – a 36.4 per cent increase – yet the Prison Reform Trust (2009) report that the number of people found guilty by the courts has remained largely constant over recent years (Prison Reform Trust 2009).

Indeed, there is widespread agreement that increasing prison numbers have been driven primarily by sentencing policy and the stricter enforcement of community sentences. The Ministry of Justice (2009) report that almost all of the increase in prison numbers over recent years has taken place within two segments of the prison

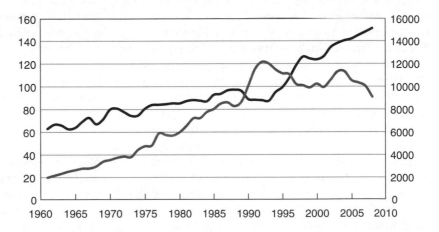

Figure 9.1 Total prison population per 100,000 (black on left axis) and total offences per 100,000 (grey on right axis) (England and Wales).

Source: Home Office.

population: those sentenced to immediate custody (78 per cent of the increase); and those recalled to prison for breaking the conditions of their release (16 per cent of the increase). Increases in custody rates and the increasing length of prison sentences have been responsible for the increase in the numbers of those sentenced to immediate custody (Ministry of Justice 2009).

England and Wales currently have the highest incarceration rate in Western Europe. The Justice Committee (2009) forecasts a potential prison population of 96,000 by 2014, which represents an incarceration rate of 169.1 per 100,000 people in England and Wales. This is supported by the Ministry of Justice (2008) which predicts the demand for prison spaces is likely to increase to between 83,400 and 95,800 by June 2015. The Prison Reform Trust (2009) estimates that the current programme of prison building in England and Wales will take the rate of imprisonment to 178 per 100,000 of the population. This increase will take the UK beyond current rates in Bulgaria (144 per 1,000), Slovakia (151 per 1,000), Romania (126 per 1,000) and Hungary (149 per 1,000) (Prison Reform Trust 2009).

Similarly, prison numbers have been rising in the USA where the adult population in state and federal prisons rose from 585,084 in 1987 to 1,596,127 in 2007. The total adult prison population in the USA (including adults in local jails) at the start of 2008 was 2,319,258 (a rate of approximately 750 per 100,000) and the PEW Center on the States (2008: 5) reports that 'more than 1 in 100 adults is now locked up in America'.

Rising prison costs

As Fox and Albertson (2010) note, the current criminal justice strategy in England and Wales (i.e. planning for increased prison numbers) has serious cost implications. In 2007, the UK Government spent approximately 2.5 per cent of GDP on public order and safety, the highest of all OECD countries (Duffy *et al.* 2007). The Justice Committee (2009) notes that, due to inflation and the rising costs of utilities and food, the costs of custody will keep rising even if numbers stay the same. Alongside increases in the marginal cost of a prison place, the fixed cost has also increased substantially. Between 1998 and 2008, the average capital build cost per prison place, without adjustment for inflation, has approximately tripled to £153,000 (Justice Committee 2009). Over recent years, similar trends have been observed in the USA. In 2008, the USA spent $44 billion on corrections compared to $10.6 billion in 1987 (in 2007, California alone spent $8.8 billion dollars on corrections). Allowing for inflation this was an increase of 127 per cent (PEW Center on the States 2008: 4). One of the biggest drivers of cost increases is medical care for special needs populations, including HIV positive prisoners and geriatric inmates (PEW Center on the States 2008).

Understanding the economics of sentencing

An economic analysis of sentencing begins with consideration of its costs and benefits. Justifications for sentencing take two main forms: retributive and utilitarian.

Retributive justifications look back at the offence and express disapproval for what has happened in the form of punishment. The penalty is usually expected to be proportionate to the offence and the offender's degree of culpability. Utilitarian justifications focus on sentences' expected impact in terms of reducing the chances of such an act being committed again by the same offender, other offenders or both (Hedderman 2008). In the case of imprisonment DiIulio suggests that it:

> offers at least four types of social benefits. The first is retribution: imprisoning Peter punishes him and expresses society's desire to do justice. Second, is deterrence: imprisoning Peter may deter either him or Paul or both from committing crimes in the future. Third is rehabilitation: while behind bars, Peter may participate in drug treatment or other programs that reduce the chances that he will return to crime when free. Fourth is incapacitation: from his cell, Peter can't commit crimes against anyone save other prisoners, staff or visitors.
>
> (DiIulio 1996: 18)

Incapacitation, rehabilitation and specific and general deterrence are all reductivist rationales for sentencing; the underlying justification for all sentences is that they will reduce future crime rates. This can be contrasted with retribution where the rationale is that the sentence is justified as a punishment of past crime. The modern variants of this latter philosophy are based on proportionality and a just punishment. Any individual sentence can of course be imposed with both punishment and crime reduction in mind.

As Marsh, Fox and Hedderman (2009) note, these are not just abstract philosophical discussions. The Criminal Justice Act 2003 sets out the purposes of sentencing (Section 142(1)) and makes clear reference to both reductivist and retributivist rationales. The aims of sentencing are listed as being the:

- punishment of offenders;
- reduction of crime (including its reduction by deterrence);
- reform and rehabilitation of offenders;
- protection of the public; and
- making of reparation by offenders to persons affected by their offence.

Prior to the Criminal Justice Act 2003, the extent to which one or more of these principles was reflected in an individual sentence varied depending, in part, on the implicit or explicit aspirations of the sentence. These might or might not be shared by the offender, the victim, the supervising service or the wider public (Marsh, Fox and Hedderman 2009).

Despite the considerable conceptual differences in retribution, deterrence and incapacitation, interpreting the empirical evidence for and against each of these concepts is not straightforward. In the rest of this section, we look at each in turn, exploring the underlying theory in more detail and reviewing the available empirical evidence.

Deterrence

Economists consider the effect of deterrence using both theoretical models and empirical (mainly econometric) evidence. As we shall see, although in theory it is straightforward to separate the effects of deterrence from those of incapacitation, in practice it is more complicated. Indeed, empirical studies often confound the two effects.

Economic models of deterrence

A good starting point for a theoretical discussion of deterrence from the perspective of an economist is the work of Becker (1968) discussed in Chapter Three. As part of a larger model designed to explore optimal criminal justice policy, Becker develops the supply of offence function. He argues those who offend are rational agents like everyone else, seeking to maximise their expected utility. That is, an individual will commit an offence if the expected utility of doing so is positive and greater than the utility expected of realistic alternatives; otherwise, they will not. Whether the utility gain is positive or negative depends on the relative size of the benefits of committing a crime (the expected income it generates) and the cost of committing a crime (including the expected punishment cost).

The subsequent development of Becker's model is outlined by Eide (1999). The simplest version of the model identified by Eide is that of Ehrlich (1973). In this model the choice to undertake legal or illegal activities is found in the context of 'portfolio choice' models. Individuals are considered to be choosing to 'invest' their time between activities with different risks and rewards. Illegal activities are considered risky because of the uncertainty about punishment. While an increase in the probability of punishment will always deter criminal activity, within this model, the direction and magnitude of the deterrence effect of punishment depends on the attitude of individuals towards risk. Assuming individuals are not risk seekers, increases in the severity of punishment will deter crime; however, if individuals are risk loving, the effect of an increase in the severity of a sanction is uncertain. An increase in severity will reduce the expected gains from crime, which will produce two offsetting effects: a substitution away from crime to legal activities which are now relatively more lucrative; and an increase in criminal activity to maintain 'income' levels now that (expected) returns are lower. The overall effect on crime is indeterminate.

We model the choice to commit a crime as the investment of time, rather than money or wealth, between legal and illegal activities. Within such models individuals choose either to specialise in legal or illegal activities or undertake a mix of the two. The allocation of time between activity types will depend on the monetary and monetised benefits and costs of activities. An increase in the probability or severity of punishment will affect the optimal mix of these activities. The effect of such an increase depends on whether or not leisure time is assumed to be fixed. Assuming leisure time is not fixed, the same results are obtained. However, assuming that leisure time is fixed causes the effect of changes in the severity of sanctions to become inconclusive (Marsh, Fox and Hedderman 2009).

As Marsh, Fox and Hedderman (2009) note a variation of Rational Choice theory is the underpinning of all of these models (see Chapter Four for a full discussion of Rational Choice theory). Understanding deterrence through an application of Rational Choice theory has its attractions. As Becker puts it:

> a useful theory of criminal behavior can dispense with special theories of anomie, psychological inadequacies, or inheritance of special traits and simply extend the economist's usual analysis of choice.
>
> (Becker 1968: 170).

However, whether human behaviour is best described in such terms is an empirical issue.[4] One critique of the Rational Choice model is that it is an inadequate explanation of behaviour if people have insufficient information about the environment and the outcomes of actions to make genuinely rational decisions. As we discussed in more detail in Chapter Four, this criticism has caused economists to suggest the theory of bounded rationality may be a better representation of offenders' behaviour than the Rational Choice theory (see Nagin and Paternoster 1993). Other critiques of Rational Choice theory range from outright rejection in favour of normative explanations of behaviour, to suggestions that Rational Choice theory be augmented by other considerations. For example, it has been suggested people's behaviour is described by procedural rationality – where people follow rules established by history or social relations – or by expressive rationality – where people demonstrate their self-conception and worth by participating in symbolic acts (Eide 1999).

Eide (1999) summarises economic theories assuming preferences to be constant, and individuals choosing between courses of action to satisfy these preferences efficiently given the incentives offered by the environment. Within these theories, there is no discussion of the role of norms in decision-making – preferences are taken as 'given'. In contrast, criminological theories suggest the normative environment is one of the factors which shape people's preferences. Thus, Marsh, Fox and Hedderman (2009) argue while economic theory conceives of the deterrence effect in a narrow sense – the effect of law enforcement on the outcomes of actions – deterrence can be seen from a broader perspective as comprising any factors which exert a preventative force against crime, either by influencing the gains associated with crime or by influencing norms.

In sum, the impact of an increase in the probability of a sanction on the supply of crime is dependent upon the assumptions employed by the models, though reasonable assumptions suggest an increase in the probability of a sanction will reduce the supply of crime. However, the impact of increases in the severity of sanctions on the supply of crime is less clear-cut. Depending on individuals' attitude towards risk, and whether the model employed allows all the costs and benefits of legal and illegal activities to be monetised, an increase in the severity of a sanction could produce either an increase or a decrease in the supply of crime (Marsh, Fox and Hedderman 2009). The implication of the theoretical models developed by economists is that accepting or rejecting the hypothesis: 'the prospect of imprisonment has a deterrent effect' depends on assumptions about the nature of individuals' attitude towards risk. If it is accepted that individuals are risk-averse, and that all social and psychological effects can be monetised, crime is deterred by increases in the probability and severity of punishment. However, if either of these starting points is rejected, then the deterrence effect of prison or any other sanction is indeterminate in some circumstances.

Empirical studies of general deterrence

Even if it is true economic agents are fully rational, and we might determine their degree of risk aversion, theoretical models are generally not capable of measuring the size of deterrent effects; there remain too many unknown factors. Therefore a practical examination of deterrence cannot rely entirely on theoretical models but must also consider the results of empirical studies undertaken both by economists and criminologists. These may be considered to fall in one of two camps: studies of general deterrence, which consider the impact of sentence probability and severity on the crime rate in society; and studies of specific deterrence, which consider the effect of a sentence on the likelihood an offender will commit crime in the future.

Ideally, both individual and general deterrence would be tested using studies of criminal behaviour at the individual rather than the aggregate level. Eide (1999) suggests a number of reasons why this would be preferable. First, from an economic perspective it is 'controversial to posit that behaviour is anything but individual' (Eide 1999: 355); second, the theoretical models being tested are based on individual rational choice; third, studies using aggregate data present problems in establishing the direction of causation (i.e. distinguishing between the two hypotheses: 'the probability of arrest depends on the amount of crime'; and 'the amount of crime depends on the probability of arrest'); and fourth, studies based on aggregate data require 'additional assumptions of questionable validity' (Eide 1999: 355). However, despite these limitations Eide notes empirical tests of general deterrence using individual-level data are few; partly because obtaining suitable data is not straightforward. Much of the available individual level data are statistics on offenders compiled by the criminal justice system. These do not constitute a representative sample of the population (Eide 1999). For this reason, most empirical studies of general deterrence rely on econometric techniques, i.e. they rely on aggregate, observational data and use statistical analysis (models) to draw causal inferences. (Econometrics and the limitations of such approaches are discussed in Chapter Six.)

According to Liedka *et al.* (2006) three of the 'strongest' econometric studies are Marvell and Moody (1994), Witt and Witte (2000) and Levitt (1996). The first of these uses American data from 1973 to 1991 and finds crime rates are negatively correlated with prison populations. The second, using English and Welsh data from 1980 to 1991, finds crime rates are negatively correlated with sentence length. The third examines situations where prison overcrowding litigation in the USA led to changes in the prison population. It also finds crime rates are negatively correlated with prison population. Summarising these findings, Liedka *et al.* (2006) note that collectively the studies suggest that a 10 per cent increase in the prison population led to between a 1.6 per cent and 5 per cent drop in crime rates. For example, Levitt's (1996) analysis suggests incarcerating one additional convicted criminal reduces the number of crimes committed by 15 a year.

These studies are not without critics however. For example, Levitt's (1996) analysis is based on the observation that prison overcrowding lawsuits generated sharp changes in incarceration rates in many US states. Levitt concludes the timing of such lawsuits is plausibly random and unrelated to other determinants of crime levels. Using data on 12 states where the entire prison system eventually came under court order, he attempts to control the direction of causality in his model. However, Von Hirsch *et al.* (1999) argue the study is better able to provide evidence of incapacitation than deterrence. Because the study does not examine the risk profiles of the early-released prisoners, 'any inferences concerning possible incapacitation would not be easily generalisable to other settings' (Von Hirsch *et al.* 1999: 2).

Eide (1999) reviews a large number of similar studies which use econometric analysis of aggregate data sets and concludes they:

> clearly indicate a negative association between crime and the probability and severity of punishment. The result may be regarded as a rather firm corroboration of the deterrence explanation obtained from the theory of rational behaviour: an increase in the probability or severity of punishment will decrease the expected utility of criminal acts, and thereby the level of crime.
>
> (Eide 1999: 360)

However, as we have discussed, while most economic and criminological theorists would probably agree that an increase in the *probability* of sanction will lead to a decrease in crime, the effect of sentence *severity* is more equivocal. Indeed, empirically, Eide (1999) notes, while most criminological studies using a time series design support the hypothesis that the probability of punishment has a preventative effective on crime, results concerning the severity of punishment are less clear cut. Eide concludes that 'in some studies the effect of an increase in the severity of punishment is not statistically different from zero, and a statistically significant positive effect has also occasionally been obtained' (Eide 1999: 360).

Von Hirsch *et al.*'s (1999) survey of the literature on 'marginal deterrence' is similarly equivocal about the effect of increasing the severity of punishment. Marginal deterrence describes the adjustment in agents' behaviour resulting from making a small change to the certainty or severity of punishment. The evidence suggests, while there may be some additional incapacitative or marginal deterrence effect from increasing the rate of imprisonment, increasing the actual and perceived risk of being caught is a more effective, and more cost-effective, way of securing crime reduction (von Hirsch *et al.* 1999). They conclude:

the studies reviewed do not provide a basis for inferring that increasing the severity of sentences generally is capable of enhancing deterrent effects.

(von Hirsch *et al.* 1999: 1)

For Eide (1999) the finding that the effect of increasing the severity of punishment varies between studies is not surprising and can be explained by reference to the theoretical model being tested:

> The theories surveyed . . . tell us that if there is a significant proportion of risk lovers in the population, and/or if the income[5] effect is greater than the substitution[6] effect, and/or the effects of legal activities are risky, and/or household protection expenditures are inversely related to the severity of punishment, an increase in the severity of punishment may well cause crime to increase on the macro level.

(Eide 1999: 359–60)

Von Hirsch *et al.* (1999) note that there is little research on potential offenders' perceptions of sentence severity. Notwithstanding, within the criminological literature there is some empirical evidence to suggest that the general public's knowledge of sanctions tends to be erroneous and underestimates the severity of sanctions (see, for example, Hough and Roberts 1998). As Von Hirsch *et al.* note, if these misconceptions are shared by offenders, more punitive sentences may fail to achieve increased deterrence.

Marsh, Fox and Hedderman (2009) suggest an alternative interpretation of the divergence in findings is that they are the result of a failure in research design; the theoretical model being tested is not always properly operationalised. For example, Mendes and MacDonald (2001) challenge Von Hirsch *et al.*'s (1999) findings and argue they are 'a consequence of theoretical slippage when moving from a verbal theoretical statement to the statistical representation of that statement' (Mendes and MacDonald 2001: 589). In essence they argue deterrence is a theory in which the component parts (certainty of punishment and severity of punishment) are inter-related and inter-dependent. They argue this is how the theory of deterrence was conceptualised by Becker (1968), but not all subsequent research has followed this approach. They review existing empirical studies of deterrence and conclude:

> published empirical studies that fail to find a significant impact of the severity of punishment do not effectively translate the theory.

(Mendes and McDonald 2001: 606)

When the theory is effectively translated as a 'package' composed of three elements – arrest, conviction and punishment – the severity of punishment does represent an important role in implementing the package (Mendes and McDonald 2001).

Even if we accept Mendes and McDonald's argument that a lot of empirical analysis of deterrence effects have used mis-specified models, there remains some ambiguity about the relationship between sentence severity and crime rates. In their review Mendes and McDonald find 16 studies which identify an effect of severity of punishment on offending and seven studies that do not.

Such discrepancy may result from a mis-specification of the functional form of the relationship. Liedka *et al.*'s (2006) econometric analysis explicitly considers the possibility 'that the negative effect of incarceration becomes less as levels of imprisonment increase' (Liedka *et al.* 2006: 260) – the so-called 'less–less' hypothesis. Liedka *et al.*'s acceptance of this hypothesis suggests that US states will observe different results on increasing their incarceration rate, depending on how great is the current size of their prison population. Therefore analysts will estimate different effects of imprisonment, depending on which states they consider. Also, of course, given that prison populations are generally increasing over time, estimates of the efficacy of prison will vary depending on to which time-period the data relate. A further implication of the hypothesis echoes Eide's (1999) conclusion that, in certain circumstances, an increasing prison population can actually lead to an increase in crime (see also Shepherd 2006). However, Liedka *et al.* (2006) are cautious about this interpretation.[7]

In summary, the findings of the empirical literature on general deterrence effect mirrors that of the theoretical literature in that it supports the existence of a relationship between the probability of punishment and offending rates, but suggests an ambiguity about the impact of sentence severity on crime (Marsh, Fox and Hedderman 2009).

Empirical studies of specific deterrence

Studies to identify specific deterrent[8] effects, i.e. the effect of a sentence on the individual's future offending, are more amenable to evaluation using individual level data than studies of general deterrence, and a great number of such exist. These studies use experimental and quasi-experimental methods to look at the relative rates of re-offending of comparable groups of offenders receiving different sentences (we briefly discuss such evaluation methods in Chapter Six). Some studies have compared custodial and non-custodial sentences, others have looked at the differences between specific types of custodial or community-based sentences. However, not all studies are equally robust and a number of systematic reviews have been undertaken to compile relevant analyses, assess their methodological rigour and present their results.

The most recent of these, Villettaz *et al.* (2006), looks in particular at analyses which test the effects on re-offending rates of custodial versus non-custodial sentences. Villettaz *et al.* consider research, published and unpublished, written in any language and prepared between 1961 and 2002. Preliminary searches led to the compilation of a 'rough inventory of more than three thousand studies' (Villettaz *et al.* 2006: 6). Villettaz *et al.* eventually identify only 23 relevant and methodologically robust studies; only five of these are based on a controlled or natural experimental design. They conclude:

Relatively few studies compare recidivism rates for offenders sentenced to jail or prison with those of offenders given some alternative to incarceration (typically probation).

(Villettaz *et al.* 2006: 1)

From the 23 relevant and methodologically robust papers they identify, Villetaz *et al.* (2006) draw 27 comparisons between the comparative effect of custodial and non-custodial sentences. The rate of re-offending after a non-custodial sanction is lower than after a custodial sanction in 11 of these significant comparisons. However in 14 of the comparisons there is no significant difference in re-offending rates between offenders who receive custodial sentences and those who receive non-custodial sentences. Two comparisons are significantly in favour of custody. A meta-analysis of the five most robust studies (controlled or natural experimental designs) found no significant difference between reoffending rates after completion of custodial or non-custodial sentences.

An earlier systematic review by Smith *et al.* (2002) uses a similar methodology, although with a broader remit. Smith *et al.* consider studies which show, not just the relative effects of prison versus a community sentence, but also the effect on recidivism of (a) length of time incarcerated, (b) serving an institutional sentence versus receiving a community-based sanction, or (c) receiving an intermediate sanction. Smith *et al.* identify 117 studies dating from 1958 involving 442,471 offenders which produced 504 correlations between recidivism and the various sentencing options in which they were interested. A meta-analysis shows the type of sanction does not produce decreases in recidivism under any of the three conditions. Second, there are no differential effects of type of sanction on juveniles, females or minority groups. Third, there are tentative indications that increasing lengths of incarceration are associated with slightly greater increases in recidivism (Smith *et al.* 2002).

Taken as a whole, these two extensive systematic reviews suggest: first, there are relatively few studies which have attempted to identify the specific deterrent effects of different sentencing options; and second, on the basis of existing evidence, no consistent difference in effect on recidivism has been identified between different sentencing options, whether custodial or non-custodial.

Cost–benefit analysis of specific deterrence

Even if it is indeed the case there is no significant difference in the deterrent effect of non-custodial sentences, compared to custodial sentences, it is not necessarily the case that they are equally cost-effective. From the point of view of basic economic theory, it is appropriate to ask which of the two provides the more efficient use of resources. This question may be addressed using the approach of cost–benefit analysis, so-called CBA (we discuss cost–benefit analysis in detail in Chapter Six). Despite the advantages of CBA, Marsh, Fox and Hedderman (2009) note there have been few economic evaluations of criminal justice interventions.

This is illustrated by McDougall *et al.*'s (2003) review of the literature. McDougall *et al.* undertake a systematic review of studies carried out between 1980 and 2001 using nine electronic databases, as well as consulting experts in the field. They identify only nine CBAs of sentencing options. The search identifies only two CBAs of imprisonment; both undertaken in the USA. In the first of these, Gray and Olson (1989), assess the cost–benefit of a prison sentence for burglars and include the rehabilitation and deterrence effect of prison in the analysis. The study finds every one dollar spent on prison only produces $0.24 of reduced offending. In contrast, for burglars given a probation sentence, every dollar spent on the sentence produces $1.70 of avoided future offending.

Marsh, Fox and Hedderman (2009) are unconvinced and note, while this result would suggest probation is preferable to prison as a sentence for burglars, there are a number of caveats to drawing this conclusion. First, a before/after study is employed by Gray and Olson to measure the changes in offending resulting from the sentences, meaning any variation in effect may be due to differences in the characteristics of the offenders receiving the interventions. Second, the economic analysis undertaken is judged by McDougall *et al.* to have been incomplete, as it does not include the incapacitation effect of prison. Further, Gray and Olson (1989) do not attempt to capture the intangible victim costs of pain and suffering from future offences.

The second CBA study identified by McDougall *et al.* is that conducted by Piehl and DiIulio (1995). These latter assess the cost–benefit of imposing no sentence compared to giving a prison sentence for different types of offenders, but consider only the incapacitation effect of prison; they do not consider the rehabilitative effect. They find, for persistent offenders – those who commit 12 crimes or more a year – every one dollar spent on prison produces $2.80 of reduced offending. However, taken across all offenders the benefit is substantially lower: $0.36. This would suggest that prison is an efficient sentencing option only for the more serious offenders. Piehl and DiIulio conclude 'prison pays' for most state prisoners who are generally either violent or repeat offenders and/or who present a real danger to the physical safety or property of their community. However, for offenders committing, for example, auto thefts at a rate of three a year, burglaries at a rate of six a year, or petty thefts at a rate of 24 a year, the costs of imprisonment outweigh the social benefits of imprisonment. This is particularly true of those convicted of drug offences. Once again, this conclusion is subject to caveats. While the economic analysis is judged by McDougall *et al.* (2003) to be complete – and the authors attempt to measure the intangible costs of pain and suffering – the analysis only captures incapacitation effects; which is to say, possible rehabilitative/deterrent effects are ignored.

McDougall *et al.*'s (2003) conclusion is that there is a dearth of economic analysis of criminal justice interventions. They conclude their review:

> It is evident that consideration should be given to determining at which point imprisonment ceases (or begins) to be cost-beneficial and a non-custodial alternative may or may not be appropriate. To date there is no spe-

cific research guidance on this, nor evidence on the types of offenders for which a custodial sentence is or is not cost-beneficial. This is an appropriate question for further research.

(McDougall *et al.* 2003: 125).

Incapacitation

Much of the above discussion on deterrence would apply to a range of punishments, both custodial and community-based. However, unlike some other forms of punishment (for example, fines) a complicating factor in an analysis of the efficiency of imprisonment is incapacitation. Indeed, as we have seen, in practical terms, studies of deterrence often fail adequately to factor out the effects of incapacitation. In theory, however, the difference is more clear.

Theorising incapacitation

A key element of the discussion on deterrence is the trade-off between certainty and severity of punishment. However, if, for the sake of argument, the underlying rationale for imprisonment is solely incapacitation this debate is irrelevant. Thus, the theory of incapacitation is relatively clear. If we need not consider the deterrent effect of imprisonment, determining the optimal length of a prison sentence will not depend on the level of certainty of punishment. Rather, the length of a prison sentence will be calculated by considering whether the expected harm from future criminal acts exceeds the cost of incapacitation (Winter 2008). In many cases this purely economic approach may make little practical sense. For instance, in the UK in 2006/07, 68 per cent of female homicide victims and 44 per cent of male victims knew the perpetrator (Coleman *et al.* 2008) and many homicides will occur in domestic settings. The highly context-specific nature of these crimes indicates at least some of these offenders are unlikely to commit a similar crime in the future and therefore considering incapacitation as the sole rationale for imprisonment implies there is little justification for imposing a prison sentence. At the other end of the spectrum, a purely theoretical economic perspective might suggest indeterminate sentences are appropriate for people deemed to be risky who have not yet committed crimes or who have only committed relatively minor crimes. Winter argues that:

> With respect to the incapacitation effect, prison can be best thought of as a place for criminals who are most likely to commit *future* crimes. In theory, this suggests that an individual who has yet to commit a crime may need to be incarcerated if an expected future crime is deemed sufficiently harmful. Of course, this would be an extremely difficult policy to implement. To determine who should be incarcerated it makes sense to identify criminals who have already committed harmful acts. Once these criminals are incarcerated, they should be given life sentences until it is determined that they would impose less harm on society that the cost of incapacitation.
>
> (Winter 2008: 28, emphasis in original)

Empirical studies on incapacitation

As we have seen, much of the empirical work on testing the concept of deterrence is 'econometric'.[9] Such approaches struggle to distinguish deterrence from incapacitation. One potential solution, argue Miles and Ludwig (2007), is to look for situations in which a natural experiment is possible.

A useful example of a natural experiment is considered by Kessler and Levitt (1999) who examine a situation where the Californian State legislature changed the prison sentences for specific types of crime. In 1982 a referendum in California known as Proposition 8 led to enhanced sentences being given for various violent and serious crimes. The sentence enhancements were large in magnitude, leading to substantial increases in the lengths of prison sentences. However, even before Proposition 8, the affected offences were serious crimes for which a conviction almost always resulted in a prison term.

Because a convicted criminal would have been sentenced to prison even without the law change, there was no additional incapacitation effect from the sentence enhancement in the short-run. Therefore, any immediate decrease in crime rates would be due to a general deterrent effect. If the passing of Proposition 8 led to an incapacitation effect, the impact of this on crime rates would not be observed until offenders were starting to serve the additional time in prison, i.e. over and above that which they would have received prior to the change in legislation. Analysis of the data showed that Proposition 8 appears to reduce eligible crimes by 4 per cent in the year following its passage and 8 per cent three years after passage. The immediate effects are consistent with deterrence.[10] However, the impact of the law continued to increase five to seven years after its passage, which allows the estimation of the size of the incapacitation effect (Kessler and Levitt 1999).

The evidence from the UK is more equivocal. During the first decade of the twenty-first century crime rates have generally been falling; however, prison numbers have been rising. While a cursory inspection of the data suggests there might be some degree of correlation between these two trends, there is no evidence to suggest the rise in prison numbers has caused a *substantial* part of the fall in the crime rate. Based on unpublished research, Carter (2003) claims the 22 per cent increase in the prison population between 1997 and 2003 led to a 5 per cent decrease in crime; however, as Hedderman (2008) notes, absolutely no evidence is presented to support this claim. An earlier British study (Tarling 1993) is less optimistic about the scale of incarceration effects. Taking account of crime and imprisonment rates at that time, Tarling calculates a 1 per cent reduction in crime would require a 25 per cent increase in the prison population.

It might seem counter-intuitive to postulate there is little effect of incapacitation on the crime rate. However, as Shepherd (2006) and Liedka *et al.* (2006) note, more recent studies in the USA have failed to find such a relationship and have even found some evidence that imprisoning people might increase crime. Shepherd suggests the seemingly contradictory findings can be reconciled and puts forward the theory that earlier studies examined periods when prison populations tended to grow by adding additional violent and property offenders, whereas later studies examine a period when prison population growth occurred as a result of increased incarceration of drug offenders and increasing sentence lengths for low-level offenders (Shepherd 2006).

Focusing just on the discussion of low-level offenders (which is of more relevance to a UK audience) Shepherd puts forward a number of arguments why longer prison sentences for low-level offenders may not reduce crime; several of these illustrate the difficulties inherent in conceptualising and measuring the concept of incapacitation. For example, Shepherd argues lengthening incarceration periods may have little impact because research on the relationship between age and crime (the age–crime curve) tells us most offenders will stop committing crime as they mature:

> Increasing an offender's sentence from 10–12 years will not reduce crime through incapacitation if he would have stopped committing crime after 10 years anyway.
>
> (Shepherd 2006: 290)

She also points to empirical evidence which suggests longer sentences lead to offenders experiencing more alienation from society, greater deterioration of family relations, and further removal from the prospect of regular employment. All of these factors will increase the likelihood of re-offending.

To conclude, incapacitation is a more complex issue to theorise than it might at first appear. The empirical evidence suggests, while an incapacitation effect might exist, the effect is likely to be strongest for more serious prolific offenders.

Retribution

While there is limited and equivocal evidence on the deterrence and incapacitation effects, the economic evidence on retribution is even more limited. Indeed, Marsh, Fox and Hedderman (2009) identify only one economic study which addresses this question: Nagin *et al.* (2006). Nagin *et al.* consider people's willingness-to-pay for two alternative policy interventions for drug-using offenders. It was explained to those participating in the study the effect of each of the interventions would be to reduce youth crime by 30 per cent and youths in the programmes will be more likely to graduate from school and get jobs. The study took place in Pennsylvania and respondents were randomly assigned to one of two groups, each of which asked to give their willingness-to-pay for one or other of the two interventions. Specifically, the two policy options involved: adding a rehabilitative component (drug treatment) to a one-year prison sentence; or increasing the period of incarceration from one year to two year. Other than the differences in the length of sentence and the availability of treatment, the description of the interventions in the study was identical.

Based on approximately 4.8 million Pennsylvanian households, the authors estimate total willingness-to-pay to be between $387 million and $468 million for a 30 per cent reduction in youth crime. Although Nagin *et al.* do not translate the public's willingness-to-pay into a cost per crime, Cohen (2007) attempts this calculation. He estimates a willingness-to-pay value for one avoided serious crime to be $100,000 in the case of the extended period of incarceration and $125,000 in the case of the rehabilitative intervention.

Marsh, Fox and Hedderman (2009) suggest that, given that the interventions were presented as having the same crime control benefit (that is, the interventions were said to have the same incapacitation, rehabilitation and deterrence effects), this experiment might be interpreted as estimating the value that the public places on the retributive effect of incarceration. More precisely, the fact that respondents were willing to pay more for the less retributive intervention would suggest that retribution is not valued very highly.

However, Marsh, Fox and Hedderman (2009) also note that Cohen (2007) points to a number of caveats to drawing this conclusion. For instance, while the two interventions were presented as being the same in their crime control benefits and their impacts on future educational attainment and employment rates, it might be possible the responses elicited are still picking up people's *expectation* that rehabilitative interventions produce better outcomes than incarceration. It is also important to recognise that there are various biases inherent in willingness-to-pay studies that may undermine this result. For instance, critics of willingness-to-pay studies point out that participants respond differently to the hypothetical scenarios proposed in the studies than they would if faced with the same problem in real life.[11] They also point to the existence of sequencing effects, where the values elicited from willingness-to-pay studies depend on the order in which questions are asked. As noted in Cohen (2007), further details of the challenges associated with such studies is available in Carson (2007).

Justice Reinvestment

We have considered so far the deterrence effect of sentences imposed after an offence has occurred; the threat of punishment. Of course, deterrence might also take place to reduce the likelihood of crimes being committed in the first place through changes to the incentive structure of those at risk of falling into such a way of life. It is from such considerations Justice Reinvestment starts. Justice Reinvestment (JR) begins with the universal criminological truth, people in prison are not drawn in equal numbers from all neighbourhoods (Allen 2007). Justice Reinvestment seeks to move funds spent on punishment of offenders to programmes designed to tackle the underlying problems which gave rise to the criminal behaviour (ibid.). That is to say, the opportunity cost of incarceration may be forgone investment in reducing the occurrence of crime at a local level. Allen suggests JR has two key elements: first, it seeks to develop measures and policies to 'improve the prospects not just of individual cases but of particular places' (Allen 2007: 5). Second, it adopts a strategic approach to the prevention of offending and re-offending by collecting and analysing data to inform commissioning decisions (Allen 2007).

The USA experience

The Justice Reinvestment movement originated in the USA and was, in part, a response to rising prison numbers and costs. For example, the PEW Center on the States reported that

> Three decades of growth in America's prison population has quietly nudged the nation across a sobering threshold: for the first time, more than one in every 100 adults is now confined in an American jail or prison.
>
> (PEW Center on the States 2008: 3)

Alongside this increase in numbers, prison costs were reported to have 'exploded' from \$10.6 billion in 1987 to \$44 billion in 2007; a 315 per cent jump (ibid.).

The Council of State Governments (undated) reports on a number of apparently successful JR projects. For example, the prison population in Texas was projected to grow by more than 14,000 over the period 2007 to 2012. Analyses identified reasons for this trend and a set of suggested policy options, allowing state policy-makers to enact a policy package to avert the anticipated growth and save \$443 million. The package includes: reinvestment of \$241 million to expand the capacity of substance abuse and mental health treatment and diversion programmes; and to ensure the release of low-risk individuals is not delayed due to lack of in-prison and community-based treatment programmes (ibid.). It is reported that, since the enactment of these new policies: the number of people on probation and parole who have been returned to prison has decreased significantly; the prison population has stabilised and is not been projected to grow; Texas has cancelled plans to build any additional prisons for the foreseeable future; and budgetary savings of \$210.5 million were made in 2008–2009, with additional savings of \$233 million achieved by avoiding prison construction (ibid.).

Of particular interest from an economic perspective is the work of the Washington State Institute for Public Policy (WSIPP). Their sophisticated economic modelling project combining analysis of the offending population in Washington State with a wide-ranging systematic review of the evidence base on what is effective in preventing offending and reducing re-offending is reported in Aos *et al.* (2006). This project has allowed WSIPP to develop a number of long-run economic models for different justice reinvestment strategies characterised according to how 'aggressive' is investment in diversionary measures. This analysis is an integral component of a long-term and ongoing project made possible, in part, because WSIPP was established and is directed by the Washington State Legislature to support the implementation of evidence-based policy.

An example of the work of WSIPP is in the area of cost–benefit analysis. As discussed above, relatively few cost–benefit analyses of different sentencing options have been undertaken and those that have been are subject to some important limitations. As Marsh, Fox and Hedderman (2009) note, the main limitation with the CBAs identified by McDougall *et al.* (2003) is that the follow-up periods for measuring recidivism were relatively short. A second limitation of studies of this type is that the study design for measuring effects is often not particularly robust (Marsh,

Fox and Hedderman 2009). For example, in Piehl and DiIulio (1995), changes in offending were assessed by comparing post and pre-release rates of self-reported offending and there was no comparison with other comparable offenders given non-custodial disposals. This approach is not generally considered reliable as it depends on the assumption that offenders would continue to offend at the same rate if they were not incarcerated. This ignores 'maturation, spontaneous remission or regression to the mean'[12] (Hedderman and Hough 2005: 60).

The WSIPP propose a solution to these limitations. They use a different approach to estimate the efficiency of sentencing options – building economic models onto reviews of effect studies. Aos *et al.* (2006) start by conducting a review of research to identify what works to reduce crime. The estimates of short-term changes in offending rates identified in their review are extrapolated over time using data on the relationship between age and crime. These long-term changes in offending are valued, taking account of both the cost to the public sector and to victims. Finally these estimates of the value of sentencing options are compared to the costs of the sentencing options to determine whether they represent an efficient use of public money (Marsh, Fox and Hedderman 2009).

One of the interventions considered by Aos *et al.* (2001a, 2006) is prison. Evidence from six methodologically rigorous effectiveness studies suggests juvenile offenders commit as many crimes following intensive probation as they would if they had received a custodial sentence. However, as intensive probation costs on average $18,854 less than incarceration, they conclude probation is a more efficient use of public resources. Similarly evidence from three well designed and conducted studies of effectiveness for adult offenders finds adults commit as many crimes after intensive supervision as they would after receiving a custodial sentence. However, as intensive supervision costs on average $5,925 less than incarceration, it is concluded supervision is a more efficient use of public resources.

Justice Reinvestment in the UK

As Fox and Albertson (2010) describe, there is considerable interest in the work of WSIPP in the UK. The Matrix Knowledge Group (Marsh and Fox 2008; Marsh *et al.* 2009) has conducted the first stage of such research in the UK, focusing on the effectiveness of prison compared to its alternatives. However, this has not yet been tied to a broader evaluation of the most efficient use of correctional services resources (Justice Committee 2009). Marsh and Fox (2008) estimate the costs and benefits of different sentence structures in England and Wales. Their model estimates the net benefit of non-custodial sentences for adult and juvenile offenders compared to custodial sentences and captures the incapacitation, rehabilitation and specific deterrence effects. For those sentences for which statistically significant differences in post-sentence offending are identified, non-custodial sentences are found to produce a net-benefit when compared with custodial sentences. Specifically, residential drug treatment, surveillance and surveillance combined with drug treatment are found both to cost less and to reduce offending when compared to prison.

Marsh and Fox (2008) identify a number of caveats which must be borne in mind when applying these results to policy-making. First, while the study attempts to focus on UK-based data, the majority of evidence of effect comes from studies undertaken in the USA, calling into question the transferability of the results to the UK context. Second, there are a limited number of studies which assess the relative effectiveness of custodial and non-custodial sentences and which also met the tight methodological criteria used during the literature review. Third, there is heterogeneity in the effects identified in these studies, which is to say the evidence is sometimes inconclusive.

Generally JR seems to work best when it is applied at a local or regional level. Indeed Allen argues:

> Inherent in the concept of JR is a greater emphasis on local ownership of those in trouble with the law and the development of local solutions.
>
> (Allen 2007: 7)

This approach is clearly evident in much of the USA experience. For example, in Oregon the state government turned over funds equal to the costs of keeping young offenders in state criminal justice institutions to the local level county administration. The county was given the flexibility to invest the funds in community-based supervision programmes and neighbourhood improvement projects. An incentive was created for the local administration to reduce the use of youth custody. Allen (2007) goes on to suggest that this locality-based analysis and approach style is consistent with recent developments in the local delivery of services in England and Wales, giving the example of local public service agreements and local area agreements. Since Allen's (2007) publication, the Policing and Crime Act 2009 has added 'reducing re-offending' to the statutory responsibilities of local Crime and Disorder Reduction Partnerships and made the probation service a responsible authority in those partnerships. However, there is evidence that devolution of authority is not sufficient for successful JR; devolution of resource must follow.

For example, a recent attempt to introduce the concept of Justice Reinvestment in Gateshead met with only limited success. Allen *et al.* (2007) describe two main problems faced here. The first is that limitations in the availability of data made accurate mapping of the numbers and characteristics of people in Gateshead difficult. Second, and less explicitly articulated, the project seems to have struggled with the limited financial incentives available to encourage local agencies, particularly local authorities, to invest in preventative programmes or community-based alternatives to prison. Two further problems which might have limited the success of the Gateshead project can also be identified. The first of these, suggested by a close reading of Allen *et al.* (2007), is that the project team did not develop the kinds of sophisticated economic modelling of different options which is characteristic of some Justice Reinvestment projects in the USA, for instance in the work of the Washington State Institute for Public Policy Research (see Aos *et al.* 2006). Such analysis might have been useful in pressing the Justice Reinvestment case. A further and related problem is to do with the scale of the project. Arguably, it was unrealistic, given the organisation of criminal justice and crime reduction services in England and Wales, to expect that such an approach would or could work effectively at the level of a single local authority, given that funding decisions about the criminal justice system are made primarily at a national and regional level.

More recently the Diamond Initiative – a scheme being piloted by London Probation and the Metropolitan Police Service (MPS), working as part of the London Criminal Justice Board – is using elements of the Justice Reinvestment approach. It brings together multi-agency teams of police, probation and local authority officers to resettle offenders back into the community following a prison sentence of less than 12 months. The local project teams undertake a case management role with non-statutory offenders through a nominated Lead Liaison Officer (Dawson and Stanko 2010). However, claims by the Deputy Commissioner of the Metropolitan Police, Tim Godwin, as reported in the press (*The Guardian*, 13 July 2010), that the initiative is based on JR seem questionable. From a methodological perspective, the main element of the JR process that the Diamond Initiative uses is justice mapping (London Criminal Justice Board 2009). However, an assessment of published material on the project suggests that, while the project has sought to draw on robust evidence of what works (Allen 2008; Dawson and Stanko 2010), it has not involved a systematic review of evidence or the long-run economic modelling of the more methodologically sophisticated approaches in the USA (e.g. Aos *et al.* 2006). From a procedural perspective, it has required substantial central funding and is driven primarily by police and probation (Justice Committee 2009). The project is focused primarily on the custodial and post-custodial end of the offending career (Allen 2008) rather than taking the broader view, characteristic of some projects in the USA, of offenders' criminal careers being rooted in deprived communities. Thus the Commission on English Prisons Today (2009) argues rather than re-directing resources into communities, Diamond Initiative resources are used for the management of individual offenders. In this sense, the Diamond Initiative is simply a reinvention of after-care schemes for short-term prisoners and an extension of Multi-Agency Public Protection (MAPPA) arrangements.

Public versus private prisons

Both in the USA and the UK, prison provision is increasingly delivered in a 'mixed economy'. Some prisons are owned and run by the state. Others are owned and/or run by the private sector. To date, the UK government has not, to the knowledge of the authors, commissioned and certainly hasn't published any robust impact studies of the relative impact of privately and publicly managed prisons. Such research has, however, taken place in the USA. In a recent systematic review and meta-analysis Lundahl *et al.* (2009) identify 12 high quality impact studies that involve directly comparing a specific, identifiable, private prison(s) with a closely matched, identifiable public prison(s). All comparisons were contemporaneous (ibid.). Lundahl *et al.*'s conclusion from their meta-analysis is:

> Cost savings from privatising prisons are not guaranteed and appear minimal. Quality of confinement is similar across privately and publicly managed systems, with publicly managed prisons delivering slightly better skills training and having slightly fewer inmate grievances.
>
> (Lundahl *et al.* 2009: 383)

Can economists make a difference to criminal justice policy?

There are many reasons for the relative lack of an economic dimension to the debate on imprisonment. Some of these are methodological, but, as we have seen in the course of this chapter, recent years have seen significant advances in methodological development. However, for economics to have a significant influence on criminal justice policy, two non-economic factors must be considered: judicial independence; and public opinion.

Judicial independence

Consider the 'market' for prison places: in a regular market, those who demand goods or services make adjustments to the level required by considering the price of the commodity – higher prices generally reduce demand. However, the 'demand' for criminal justice services is driven by the decisions sentencers make. Until recently it has been widely accepted these decisions are driven by considerations of justice and are made independently of considerations of the resource implications which are implied.

However, over recent years, greater awareness of economic arguments for and against different sentencing options have grown. An example is the debate around sentencing which resulted from Patrick (now Lord) Carter's first report on the criminal justice system. Faced with clear evidence of the problems posed by a rising prison population Carter noted the criminal justice system is demand-led: 'The system serves and is driven by the judiciary' (Carter 2003: 20). Clearly, it cannot be assumed supply of prison places will respond passively to demand. Carter is concerned sentencing practice is unable to take account of this and hence the capacity of the criminal justice system to deliver sentences will lag behind demand. While noting the importance of judicial independence in making individual sentencing decisions, Carter also notes prison capacity is largely fixed in the short to medium term. Therefore:

> Judges and magistrates need to be able to discharge their responsibility for managing demand for probation and prisons to ensure the consistent and cost effective use of existing capacity.
>
> (Carter 2003: 25)

For Carter, the introduction of the National Offender Management Service together with the establishment of the Sentencing Guidelines Council and Sentencing Advisory Panel will facilitate the development of an overall approach to sentencing which takes better account of criminal justice system capacity and the effectiveness of different sentencing options. A system which better matches supply and demand – weighing the costs and benefits of both – will ultimately be more cost-effective. A clearer split between purchasers and providers of custodial and community sentences, together with a stronger evidence base, will lead to the more efficient use of resources and a stabilisation or even a reduction in prison numbers and, potentially, criminal activity might be expected to follow.

Perhaps the biggest obstacle to this approach might have been opposition in response to a perceived threat to judicial independence. If sentencing had to be constrained by available capacity, the judiciary might have argued that this would limit their independence – even if this consideration were made at a system-wide level, rather than at the level of individual sentences. However, the judiciary recognise sentencing decisions have economic consequences; resources put into the criminal justice system are resources which cannot be put into other parts of the public sector. In economic terms this is known as opportunity cost; the foregone benefit of an alternative use of the resource. In a series of speeches, leading members of the judiciary have started to introduce a more direct consideration of resources into discussions of sentencing policy. For example, in a speech in 2006, Sir Igor Judge, President of the Queen's Bench Division, argues:

> There is only so much public money available. No one begrudges the cost of a prison to incarcerate those convicted of the most dreadful crimes, even if that might delay the building of a new hospital, or a new school. But people do question, although they would all come up with different answers, whether the cost of building a new prison at the expense of a new hospital is appropriate, if those incarcerated in the new prison, might reasonably have been dealt with by way of a community punishment.
>
> (Judge 2006: no page numbers)

The following year Lord Phillips of Worth Matravers, the Lord Chief Justice, argued that:

> If you decide to lock up one man for a minimum term of 30 years, you are investing £1 million or more in punishing him. That sum could pay for quite a few surgical operations or for a lot of remedial training in some of the schools where the staff are struggling to cope with the problems of trying to teach children who cannot even understand English.
>
> (Phillips 2007: 6)

Phillips went on to suggest that the government will need to establish a sentencing framework that takes account of the capacity of the criminal justice system to deliver different sentences:

Unless Parliament is prepared to provide whatever resources are necessary to give effect to the sentences that judges choose, in their discretion, to impose, Parliament must re-examine the legislative framework for sentencing. I do not believe that these simple propositions have been fully appreciated by those responsible for formulating criminal policy to which Parliament is invited to give effect.

(Philips 2007: 5)

Recently a series of Court of Appeal rulings in the UK has made clear judges can take account of resources in the prison system when deciding a sentence in cases where they have a choice of penalty and custody is not needed for the protection of the public (*The Times* 2007).

Public opinion

In any democracy, the likelihood of policy-makers acting on economic evidence when formulating criminal justice policy will be influenced by public opinion. Ultimately it is for society to decide how its own mores should be formulated and enforced. However it should be noted not all public opinion is as well informed as criminal justice specialists. The Justice Committee (2009) conclude that:

> Wider factors, such as the media, public opinion and political rhetoric, contribute to risk averse court, probation and parole decisions and hence play a role in unnecessary system expansion.
>
> (Justice Committee 2009: 91–2)

The orthodoxy is that the British public are broadly punitive in their approach to criminal justice. According to the British Crime Survey many people think that the criminal justice system is on the side of the offender, not the victim.[13] However, in its evidence to the Justice Committee, the International Centre for Prison Studies argued that when:

> asked a simple question, a majority will always tell pollsters that sentencing is too soft, whatever the objective sentencing levels are. This is largely because the public systematically underestimate the severity of sentencing. When respondents are properly informed about sentencing levels, and given detailed information about cases, a different picture emerges.
>
> (Justice Committee 2009: 96)

A poll for Rethinking Crime and Punishment (MORI 2004, reported in Justice Committee 2009) found, when given options:

• Five times as many people favour better parenting (57 per cent) than putting more offenders in prison (11 per cent) as the best way to reduce crime.

- The public do not rank prison highly as a way of dealing with crime. Most think that offenders come out of prison worse than they go in.
- Only 2 per cent would choose to spend a notional £10 million on prison places.
- Over half think residential drug treatment and tougher community punishments are the way forward.

The influence of media should also be considered, although there is debate about whether the media shape the views of the public or reinforce them (Justice Committee 2009). Nevertheless, there is a substantial evidence base to suggest that media reporting of crime is disproportionate (Justice Committee 2009; Reiner 2001). The Justice Committee (2009), in its review of public opinion and the influence of the media, concluded that more political leadership was required and that government should do more to challenge public perceptions and lead the debate on criminal justice policy.

Clearly, political leadership is required and in its review of the case for Justice Reinvestment the Justice Committee (2009), while critical of a lack of political leadership in shaping a more rational and evidence-based debate on crime and criminal justice, also suggested that, in the future, there is potential for political consensus:

> There appears to be most potential for [political] consensus around two issues: first 'what works' (evidence-based practice) in order to reduce crime and re-offending; and secondly, the most effective use of limited resources to achieve this.
>
> (Justice Committee 2009: 104)

> In basing arguments for reform on the best use of taxpayers' money, the political argument could be shifted away from notions about which party is 'harder' or 'softer' on crime and criminals to questions about the most effective use of scarce resources to reduce offending and re-offending. It is time for an objective consideration of what is in the best interests of society.
>
> (Justice Committee 2009: 104)

Conclusion

The use of custody is relatively costly compared to other forms of sentence. On both sides of the Atlantic these costs have risen rapidly over recent years. From an economic perspective different rationales for punishment can be advanced, but the evidence for the effectiveness and cost-effectiveness of custody is quite limited.

At the time of writing, the groundswell of political opinion in the UK seems to be moving to consider and address the challenges and to reap the benefits of the Justice Reinvestment experience of the USA. Justice Reinvestment is a multi-method, multi-disciplinary exercise that usually involves some level of economic analysis. As such it is an approach that has the potential to bring together available evidence both on methods which are effective in reducing re-offending and methods effective in reducing crime in local communities. Evidence from the USA shows that, properly applied, JR may lead to large savings in both national/state budgets and the intangible costs of crime to society. Development of Justice Reinvestment in the UK is still in the relatively early stages. It will be interesting to see how this movement develops.

10 Organised crime

Perhaps the Vatican is the only country in the world that does not have gangs or mafias in its midst, but we cannot even be sure of that as some Swiss guards have been engaging in strange behavior lately.

(Skaperdas 2001)

Introduction

In this chapter we focus on the contribution economics has made to understanding organised crime, the economic harm done by organised crime and, finally, we briefly look at some of the responses to organised crime that are most closely related to economic thinking. In particular we concentrate on asset confiscation.

First, a word of caution: study of many of the topics in this book has been hampered by a lack of data and a tendency for ideology or popular sentiment to 'cloud' the evidence. For no topic is this more true than the study of organised crime. The reader new to the topic is advised to put aside any preconceptions they may have developed based on media representations of organised crime, for example the 'Godfather' films.

Organised crime has been studied extensively in the USA since the 1950s and in many other parts of the world since the 1980s. However, as Paoli notes:

Both the recent waves of international interest and the previous [USA] debate are, in fact, inspired and at the same time, polluted by a moral panic that fuels the thriving curiosity of Americans and the rest of the world for the mafia and organised crime. Issues shaped by moral panic are not likely to be handled in a rational, matter-of-fact way, and organised crime has certainly been no exception to the rule.

(Paoli 2002: 52)

Indeed, van Duyne notes the appeal of organised crime to the media, and suggests in some cases authorities manipulate the media to make the problem appear worse than it is, 'abusing the generated fear to increase the powers of state and to erode the willingness to weigh the requirement of "organised crime" reduction against the maintenance of civil rights' (van Duyne 2004: 22). This is not to say that organised crime is not indeed a threat. However, according to van Duyne (1996: 274), the 'challenge of certain forms of organised crime is greatest where its possibilities to cloak its real nature are biggest'.

The scope of organised crime

Organised crime can cover a wide range of activities including illegal arms trafficking, drug trafficking, people smuggling, the sex trade, protection rackets, contraband, the human organ trade, vehicle theft, loan sharking, fraud, and money laundering (Rawlinson 2009). However, defining organised crime is not straightforward. As noted by van Duyne (1996), there is no agreed-upon definition; indeed, von Lampe (undated)[1] lists 150 competing definitions. We start by looking at some of the 'operational' definitions which have been developed by government agencies attempting to track and tackle organised crime.

Operational definitions of organised crime

The United Nations Convention against Transnational Organised Crime, adopted in 2000, is, according to the United Nations,[2] the main international instrument in the fight against transnational organised crime. It is supplemented by three Protocols, which target specific types of organised crime in the areas of: people trafficking; smuggling of migrants; and firearms trafficking. Article 2 of the Convention states that an:

> 'Organised criminal group' shall mean a structured group of three or more persons, existing for a period of time and acting in concert with the aim of committing one or more serious crimes or offences established in accordance with this Convention, in order to obtain, directly or indirectly, a financial or other material benefit.
>
> (United Nations 2004: 5)

'Serious crime' is defined as an offence punishable by a 'maximum deprivation of liberty of at least four years or a more serious penalty' (United Nations 2004: 5). A 'structured group' is defined as 'a group that is not randomly formed for the immediate commission of an offence and that does not need to have formally defined roles for its members, continuity of its membership or a developed structure' (United Nations 2004: 5).

Thus the United Nations concentrates on describing the structures and processes of organised crime, rather than specifying the types of activities involved. Similarly the definition used by the European Union focuses primarily on the organisation. The European Union, Article 1 of the 'Joint Action of December 1998 against Organised Crime' states that:

> A criminal organisation shall mean a structural association, established over a period of time, of more than two persons, acting in concert with a view

to committing offences, which are punishable by deprivation of liberty or a detention order of a maximum of at least four years or a more serious penalty, whether such offences are an end in themselves or a means of obtaining national benefits and, where appropriate, of properly influencing the operation of police authorities.

(quoted in Rawlinson 2009)

Agencies in the USA use a variety of definitions. Finklea (2010) notes that the statutory definition of organised crime stems from the Omnibus Crime Control and Safe Streets Act of 1968, as amended. This current definition of organised crime is:

the unlawful activities of the members of a highly organised, disciplined association engaged in supplying illegal goods and services, including but not limited to gambling, prostitution, loan sharking, narcotics, labor racketeering, and other unlawful activities of members of such organisations.

(quoted in Finklea 2010: 3)

This definition describes organised crime in terms of the illegal activities rather than in terms of what constitutes a criminal organisation (Finklea 2010).

These are all very broad definitions which, as Rawlinson (2009) notes, might be useful in providing a general framework for understanding organised crime, but in practice might undermine effective law enforcement. Thinking about the United Nations definition, he argues that:

According to this [UN] definition an organised crime group can include anything from a four-person, low-level racketeering outfit to highly complex, international networks engaged in human smuggling or money laundering.

(Rawlinson 2009: 325)

Rawlinson (2009) is concerned that broad definitions will leave the police to prioritise cases according to perceived threat at the local level rather than following national priorities. It will also make analysis of the threat difficult at an international level and impact on the development of appropriate responses. Referring to the EU definition, Rawlinson asks:

If, for instance, one country records the presence of one hundred crime groups, which comprise small numbers while another has twenty or thirty groups with larger memberships how is it possible to measure the actual influence of organised crime in the different jurisdictions (and hence appropriate responses by law enforcement) from the criteria posited in the definitions?

(Rawlinson 2001: 5)

Rawlinson (2001, 2009) favours a definition employed by the Dutch police which states:

We speak of organised crime if groups which focus primarily on illegal gains commit crimes with serious consequences for society, and are able to screen these crimes in a relatively successful manner, in particular by showing that they are prepared to use physical violence or by ruling out persons by corruptive means.

(quoted by Rawlinson 2001: 6)

Rawlison approves of the inclusion of the phrase 'serious consequences for society' which highlights the importance of considering the impact on society of illegal activities committed by persons employing certain techniques and behaviours in the execution of these acts. Defining and quantifying harm is an area where economists have made a contribution to the study of organised crime and we return to it later in this chapter. For Rawlinson the Dutch definition:

[A]llows for non-static, culturally specific and simultaneously internationally broad constructions of the term 'organised crime', an expedient approach at a time when national and international interests intersect.

(Rawlinson 2001: 6)

Threat assessments – Europe and the USA

Not only are definitions of organised crime contentious, but the extent to which the threat posed by organised crime is increasing is also unclear. For example, Paoli suggests that in order to justify its intervention into the area of organised crime 'the EU Council presents organised crime as a new threat, whose novelty lies in the increasing involvement of the criminal organisations in the supply of criminal goods and services' (Paoli 2002: 62).

As we have seen, the EU definition of organised crime is very broad, requiring joint action between only more than two people. Paoli thus asks:

If only three people are sufficient to form a criminal organisation, one might justifiably ask if the (alleged) increasing presence of these entities in the illegal arena really represents a major innovation in regard to the past and the threatening menace that the [EU] Plan assumes it to be.

(Paoli 2002: 62–3)

The addressing of such issues requires extensive data collection, and many nations regularly produce organised crime threat assessments. As well as monitoring the impact of crime on society, such assessments may be used in the efficient use of actions, force and sanctions to create disincentive structures which will reduce the threat.

In the UK, the Serious Organised Crime Agency (SOCA) produces an annual United Kingdom Threat Assessment (UKTA) which describes and assesses the threats posed to UK society by organised criminals, and considers how these threats may develop. In the 2008 threat assessment SOCA states:

In terms of the scale of serious organised criminal involvement, drug trafficking, especially Class A drugs, poses the single greatest threat to the UK. The profits made from drugs are a critical factor in the success and spread of serious organised crime, enabling more drugs to be bought, funding other forms of crime, and supporting criminal lifestyles.

(SOCA 2008: 5)

The 2009 threat assessment states: 'The overall threat to the UK from organised crime is high' (SOCA 2009a: unnumbered). The 2009 threat assessment reports 'As far as the relative scale and significance of the threats, it is still the case that most of those identified as involved in organised crime are engaged in drugs trafficking and distribution' (SOCA 2009a: unnumbered). Other organised crime activities which feature prominently in the 2009 threat assessment are: organised immigration crime and various kinds of fraud.

It should be borne in mind, according to van Duyne (1996), that organised crime in the Northern European context is essentially an international phenomenon. Indeed, Glenny (2009: 206) suggests, 'On the whole, Western and Northern Europeans are not associated with large-scale criminal activities except in their crucial role as consumers'.[3] Van Duyne (1996) reviews existing evidence and draws on a Dutch survey of organised crime enterprises to argue that the threat needs to be kept in context:

> The evidence suggests that while organised crime enterprises conduct trade across national boundaries, they do not constitute an international authority structure. Crime entrepreneurs constitute a challenge, not to the basic structure of society itself, but rather a more subtle kind of challenge to basic values and morals, particularly when criminal enterprise is linked to power at higher levels of society.
>
> (van Duyne 1996: 341)

According to the definition of organised crime adopted by the German Federal Crime Intelligence Office, the BKA, organised crime need not be concerned simply, solely or even primarily in the pursuit of profit, but may exist to pursue political or economic power.[4] The issue of how to measure the impact of such on society is an open and complex question.

In the USA, various agencies produce threat assessments. The USA Organized Crime Council (OCC) was convened in 2008 to address the evolving threats from organised crime. As well as noting individual illegal activities committed by organised crime groups such as: gambling; prostitution; racketeering; smuggling; trafficking; theft; murder; extortion; and money laundering, the OCC indicated these organisations might:

- penetrate the energy and other strategic sectors of the economy;
- provide logistical and other support to terrorists, foreign intelligence services, and governments;

- smuggle/traffic people and contraband goods into the United States;
- exploit the United States and international financial systems to move illicit funds;
- use cyberspace to target US victims and infrastructure;
- manipulate securities exchanges and perpetrate sophisticated frauds;
- corrupt or seek to corrupt public officials in the United States and abroad; or
- use violence or the threat of violence as a basis for power.

Such threat assessments are subject to debate. Zoutendijk (2010) reviews nine organised crime threat assessments produced by law enforcement agencies in different countries. He notes that some focus on organised crime groups, others on activities, markets or phenomena. Different reports use different attributes to determine the threat of an organised crime group. By comparing and contrasting the different reports Zoutendijk (2010: 63) suggests 'establishing what constitutes a threat is at its core a normative decision that cannot be left to intelligence analysts or scientists alone'. Levi (2007) suggests comparing organised crime in Europe and the USA may not be appropriate; Europe has its own set of 'economic and social landscapes in which organised crime *trade* takes place' (Levi 2009: 785, original emphasis).

Theorising organised crime

Study of organised crime is an area of increasing interest and a large and growing body of work which cuts across a number of disciplinary boundaries. Attempts to explain organised crime have drawn on a number of different academic traditions including criminology, sociology, political science, law and economics. Von Lampe argues:

> [S]tudents of organised crime have borrowed concepts and theories from a variety of academic disciplines. However, the multidisciplinary dimension has not necessarily ensured a high level of theoretical penetration of the objects of study. Despite recent advances, the theoretical literature on organised crime remains fairly thin and fragmented. In fact, one might even go so far as to say that 'organised crime theory,' to the extent it exists at all, is largely an eclectic patchwork and that the various references to other disciplines have added to the confusion that already existed.
>
> (von Lampe 2006: 77)

As von Lampe (2003) describes, Albanese (1989) has elaborated three influential models of organised crime: a 'hierarchical model'; a 'patron–client' model; and an 'enterprise model'. These models are both descriptors and products of their time and reflect both the changing nature of organised crime and the public's perception of it. Broadly speaking, the former two approaches emphasise the organisation and describe how it may deal in illicit and licit markets, while the latter approach considers organised crime to be a market-driven phenomenon, similar to a legitimate business, but operating outside the law. None of these approaches in isolation perfectly describes all criminal organisations, as we shall see.

The political and economic foundations of organised crime

Criminals organise for the same reasons societies organise, because the processes of life – production, supply, demand and consumption – and who gets to decide which goods or services are to be traded and how, cannot be determined efficiently at an individual level. As we shall see, organised crime flourishes in countries where social trust and enforcement of mores are weak. The earliest (what are now described as) criminal organisations were founded, not necessarily to exploit the gaps in the market created by legal and criminal process, but to facilitate the running of a localised political economy, albeit not necessarily to the benefit of the society as a whole.

Paoli (2002) considers mafia-like groups to be the result of a centuries-old process of social construction, not necessarily for the purpose of pursuing criminal ends, but also political and revolutionary or counter-revolutionary ends. Considering the development of the long-lasting organisations such as the Triads, Yakuza and Mafia (Casa Nostra), she notes they all arose 'before the consolidation of modern illegal markets' and are founded on strong social, not economic ties:

> Far from resembling a modern business firm, all the . . . associations are founded on relations of ritual kinship, which means that they do not bind their members to the respect of a mere purposive contract as a 'modern' firm or bureaucracy would normally do – but are founded on what Max Weber called 'status contracts'.
>
> (Paoli 2002: 76)

Paoli (2002: 81) argues that these 'ritual kinship ties are necessary to build large-scale illegal organisations' and hence:

> The most stable illegal enterprises are those relying on pre-existing non-economic ties. This realisation also explains the paradoxes of organised crime. While the logic of illegal markets does not promote the development of large-scale, modern bureaucracies, the most stable and structured illegal enterprises are those that are not exclusively oriented towards the marketplace and are able to embed their economic activities in non-economic relationships . . .
>
> (Paoli 2002: 84)

Paoli suggests (drawing on Powell 1990) that, in this sense, organisations such as the Italian Cosa Nostra, the American La Cosa Nostra, the Chinese Triads and the Japanese Yakuza have their roots in pre-modern, mediaeval structures of commerce made up of family businesses, guilds, cartels and extended trading companies – enterprises with loose and permeable boundaries.[5] In this way, what we now call racket enforcement can be likened to the formation of a proto-state or, indeed, vice versa.

As the power of the state and associated criminal justice system increases, the relative benefit to society from criminal organisation, compared to state organisation, decreases:

> When state apparatuses started to systematically provide the basic public goods – and primarily law and order – that enabled the functioning of national markets, these polyhedric, multivalent institutions became largely superfluous. Modern capitalistic enterprises progressively emerged from the dense webs of political, religious and social affiliations that had enveloped economic activity for centuries. The economy thus became an increasingly separate, differentiated sphere of modern society, with economic transactions defined no longer by the social or kinship obligations of those transacting but by rational calculations of individual gain.
>
> (Paoli 2002: 85)

For organisations such as the Italian Cosa Nostra, the American La Cosa Nostra, the Chinese Triads and the Japanese Yakuza this was not the case:

> The exclusion from state protection has not allowed illegal enterprises to follow such a path and thus benefit from the processes of functional differentiation. For this reason, the most lasting enterprises of the illegal arena today remain those that are founded on pre-existing noneconomic ties.
>
> (Paoli 2002: 85)

The 'hierarchical' ('alien conspiracy') model

As a result of their genesis in political economic terms, long-standing criminal organisations are initially mono-ethnic. As we shall see, this is both a strength and weakness of their structure in a newly globalised economy; notwithstanding it is globalisation and migration which has arguably given rise to the recent growth in organised crime.

The first wave of popular migration in modern times took place in the late industrial age as the 'New World' increasingly attracted immigrants from the old. Ethnic immigrants brought with them pre-conceptions of how societies were organised, including their traditional, quasi-political power structures, much to the consternation of the authorities of their new nations. This conflict between the governance expected by, and to some extent promoted by, immigrants to the USA and existing USA governance structures led early analysts of organised crime to describe it as an 'alien conspiracy' model or 'hierarchical' model (Smith 1980).

Paoli suggests this model was first put forward (though not by that name) in 1890 after the murder of a group of 11 Italians in New Orleans. The murder was described at the time as being carried out with 'cool deliberation' (Lodge 1891: 602) by 'men of good standing in the community' (ibid.). The supposed cause of this crime was that the Italians had been complicit in the murder of the New

Orleans Superintendent of Police. Describing the accompanying riot as 'wild justice', Lodge goes on to lay the blame squarely at the feet of USA immigration policy which (according to him) allowed into the nation: the Mafia; the Molly Maguires in Pennsylvania; Anarchists in Chicago; and, according to the *New York Times* (quoted by Lodge), the Secret Polish Avengers.[6]

The views of Lodge were not atypical for the time. Notwithstanding that immigrants to the USA were proportionally under-represented in committing crime – though not necessarily under-represented in suffering from it (see Abbot 1915) – in the southern states of the USA, there was much resistance to immigration, as noted by Berthoff (1951). This prevailing attitude to immigration, fostering an 'us and them' dichotomy between ethnic immigrants and locals, would tend to favour the longevity of ethnically based quasi-political power structures.[7] Indeed, the human condition is such, immigrant groups may perceive discrimination even where none exists (see Jensen 2002 for an example of this in the case of Irish immigration to the USA).

The 'hierarchical' model draws on influential enquiries into organised crime in the USA. For example, the Special Committee to Investigate Organised Crime of the Interstate Commerce Commission, chaired by Senator Kefauver, concluded that there was a nationwide crime syndicate, known as the Mafia, with a presence in many large USA cities (Paoli 2002). Cressey acted as a consultant to The President's Task Force on Organised Crime in 1967 and subsequently wrote a book (Cressey 1969) which identified the Cosa Nostra as a nationwide, hierarchical, bureaucratic organisation responsible for 'all but a tiny part of organised crime' in the USA (Paoli 2002).

While the origins of the model are based on concern about the activity of the (Italian) Mafia in the USA, the focus of American law enforcement agencies has subsequently turned to organised criminals from other ethnic and cultural groups. The President's Commission of Organised Crime in 1983 listed, in addition to the Mafia (La Cosa Nostra), other organised crime gangs including: outlaw motorcycle gangs; Columbian drug cartels; the Japanese Yakuza; and Russian gangs. This analysis of organised crime based on cultural or ethnic background has also been influential in other parts of the world. Van Duyne (1996), for example, suggests the European nations have replaced their (Cold War) concern over the Soviet empire with a new 'bogey', to wit, organised crime.

However, such a view of organised crime, as something external to society which might easily be excised, is arguably an oversimplification of the problem. Referring to the USA, van Duyne (2004) suggests the issues raised by organised crime have not been explained, but have rather been clouded with 'xenophobia and outright racism' (van Duyne 2004: 22). A focus on particular ethnic groups has been fostered, arguably, with a view to maintaining the authority of dominant American values by characterising organised crime as outside the mainstream (Rawlinson 2009).[8] Rawlinson (2001: 4) also notes 'the apparent eagerness with which the "Russian Mafia" became the new global *bête noire* in a flurry of media hype and scare mongering during the early to mid 1990s'.

The 'patron–client' model

Research has called into question the hierarchical and monolithic structure attributed to the Mafia organisations which led to the 'alien conspiracy' model. As various commentators (Paoli 2002; Rawlinson 2009) note, subsequent research studies have suggested that the Mafia is based on individuals or family-based networks engaged in both legal and illegal business. Such an emphasis on political, as well as economic, goals has led to the refining of the 'hierarchical' model into a more socio-political 'patron–client' model which sees the Cosa Nostra and other similar groups as a 'web of asymmetric ties embedded in local or ethnic networks' (von Lampe 2003: 2). Such groups may, but do not necessarily, engage in crime; they may equally use political power to manipulate legitimate markets in their favour – so called rent-seeking behaviour (see Chapter Two). For example, in southern Italy the Mafia have struggled to take control of the market for public works (Paoli 2004). In this context, a defining attribute of a criminal organisation is the use of violence and ritual kinship ties to enforce a sense that the morals of the group take precedence over the mores of society at large (Paoli 2002).

The 'enterprise' model

Simultaneously with the collapse of communism in Europe, a new age of globalisation has arrived. Alongside the increasing globalisation of legal markets has come increasing globalisation of illegal markets and competition from new players. Under such pressures, an increasing emphasis is placed on the pure profit motive of organised crime, as described by the 'enterprise model' proposed by Smith (1980) which analyses organised crime in terms of the market.

> [T]he essential motivation of those engaged in organised crime is clear: business. Business takes many forms and involves different actors, but irrespective of which side of the legal divide it lies, its main preoccupation is seeking profit-making opportunities, in other words, enterprise.
>
> (Rawlinson 2009: 326)

Drawing on earlier studies Rawlinson (2009) suggests that, as a provider of illegal goods or services, organised crime might be argued to be primarily reactive: exploiting gaps in a diverse and lucrative market where the clientele are, for the most part, ordinary people. Originating in the USA the 'enterprise' model has also become dominant in Europe where, in particular, it has influenced studies of the Italian Mafia (Paoli 2002).

Paoli (2002: 87) also notes that, over the last 40 years, the ties of kinship and group solidarity in the Mafia have been weakened by members' personal ambitions and 'economics activities'. As Western society at large has increasingly rejected 'fraternalism' as a social construct in favour of individualism, so too have the cultures from which mafia-style organisations draw their supporters. This has led to the 'exponential growth of mafia turncoats' (Paoli 2002: 87). A similar process has been observed in the USA, with an increasing number of ex-mafiosi going so far as to publish memoirs and auto-biographies (Firestone 1993). According to Firestone, '[w]hat made the Mafia so successful for so long was its ability to create and maintain a level of trust which allowed its members to avoid the prisoner's dilemma' (Firestone 1993: 216); however, self-interest is increasingly supplanting the interest of the collective as a motivating force. So far has suspicion and mistrust undermined the '*omerta*' (code of silence) of the American mob, the FBI witness protection programme is now rationally a safer bet for those arrested than reliance on the honour of the organisation (ibid.).

Somewhat ironically, the inroads the Italian state made in the 1990s in controlling the Mafia in the centre and north of Italy have led to power vacuums that the new '*criminalita organizzate straniere*' (foreign organised criminalities) have exploited (Paoli 2004). In Italy at the least, and with unconscious echoes of Lodge (1891), Paoli puts the blame for the return of organised crime squarely at the feet of 'considerable migration flows' (Paoli 2004: 26), singling out, in particular, the 'former Soviet Union and Eastern Europe'. Paoli concludes:

> If mafia groups do not receive the political support they desperately need, in the middle-term Italy might end up having the same type of organised crime that is widespread in the rest of Europe: namely, a myriad of criminal enterprises selling prohibited commodities with no ambitions to exercise a political power of any sort.
>
> (Paoli 2004: 28)

This is not to say organised crime no longer displays attributes which might be described by the 'hierarchical' or 'patron–client' models; there is, however, evolution in its form in response to the pressures of socio-economic competition – those organisations which compete most effectively in the market are the more likely to prosper. Currently not only is it the 'enterprise' model of organised crime which has the ascendancy over earlier models, it is those organisations which practise it most strongly which have seemingly won out over those described by more traditional models.

The economic drivers of organised crime

Why organise?

From an economic perspective, the presence of criminal organisations and societies is no more or less to be expected than the presence of societies in general. They are simply the most efficient way of organising certain operations (or, at least, perceived to be so). As discussed by von Lampe (2006), Smith (1994), drawing on Williamson (1985), argues firms exist where transactions costs are reduced by their existence. In this context, transaction costs include the cost of making – and (ideally) enforcing to an optimal level – contracts to buy or sell goods and services. Smith argues the factors which determine transaction costs in the legal sphere (bounded rationality, opportunism and asset specificity) are also decisive in an illegal setting (von Lampe 2006). According to Smith when the parties of a transaction, legal or otherwise, operate under conditions of uncertainty, when they are prone to self-interest seeking with guile, and when they are making investments that cannot be easily redeployed to other purposes, some form of organisation is inevitable (von Lampe 2006).

The problem of enforcement is especially pertinent in the illegal market, as noted by Paoli (2002). Illicit transactions cannot rely on the public good of the state legal system to enforce compliance with agreements. There is, thus, a need to enforce existing criminal contracts if the illicit market is to operate. Similarly if the criminal organisation has sufficient longevity so that future mutually beneficial agreements and contracts are likely to be made (from which one party or other will be excluded if they cheat on this contract) there is an economic incentive for all parties to honour contracts so as to continue to be party to mutually beneficial agreements. Thus protection of contracts is a defining attribute of organised crime (Skaperdas 2001), as it is a defining attribute of the state.

Similarly, there is little use in a petty criminal complaining to the state if their illegal entrepreneurial activity becomes prey to an extortion racket. Thus small independent criminals may become prey to larger organisations without recourse to law. Where a need arises, economic forces exist to provide an enterprise or business to meet the need (for a small consideration); in this case an overarching power structure to enforce 'contracts' and provide 'protection'. Von Lampe (2006) refers to Schelling (1967, 1971) and Reuter (1983) in this context. These use economic concepts to explain the emergence of 'power syndicates' in the context of conflict resolution. By paying 'protection' to a power syndicate, a petty criminal creates an incentive structure to ensure their survival at some level. The power syndicate, benefiting from the profits of smaller enterprises, will not wish to take so much in 'tax' as to drive them out of business thereby effectively killing the goose which lays the counterfeit eggs. Both the petty criminal and the power syndicate have an incentive structure which ensures low-level 'protected' criminality thrives.

In sum, where criminal activity exists, enforcement is required. In this context, criminal enterprise is formed to 'organise' pre-existing crime and, potentially, to streamline its operations. As noted by Schelling there is a general market advantage in 'internalising' the costs of violence, which is to say that those involved in low-level criminality pay the monetised costs of enforcement, which rationality indicates will be set at such a level as to allow them to continue making economic rent. Reuter (1983) argues that the demand for such arbitration may vary between market levels and between different types of illegal markets (von Lampe 2006) and, indeed, different sectors will achieve larger or lesser surpluses and thus be able to sustain higher costs.

In the same way that legitimate industry seeks to increase efficiency through specialisation, illicit enterprise may also choose to specialise. Indeed, this is likely to be further accentuated by the effect, noted by Paoli (2002), of the lack of vertical integration of illicit enterprises. Arguably the enforcement role of an organised criminal network will operate at its most efficient if it does not itself trade in the same market which it enforces, otherwise it will seek to promote one player (itself) at the expense of others, and market efficiency will be compromised. Moreover, the market is unlikely to have room for two rival 'governments' (or at least, not if one aim of all players is to minimise overt violence) thus, as discussed by Skaperdas and Syropoulos (1995) (cited in von Lampe 2006), the use of Game Theory can explain the emergence of criminal groups specialising in the monopolistic use of violence.

As von Lampe (2006) notes, a tendency towards monopolisation is often considered inherent in illegal markets (p. 84):

> Perhaps the most long lasting and most broadly based discussion within the parameters of the economic analysis of organised crime is about the monopolisation of illegal markets . . .
>
> (von Lampe 2006: 84)

For von Lampe (2006) two issues are at the centre of the debate: one issue concerns the degree to which illegal markets foster monopolisation; the other relates to the social costs and benefits of such monopolies in illegal markets. However, he notes that empirical (i.e. data-based) studies of illegal markets tend to find monopolies are an exception rather than the rule.

Reuter (1985) argues market forces will tend to work against the formation of monopolies. He argues that illegal markets tend to be populated by small, ephemeral enterprises in which relationships are marked more by competition than collusion. There are several reasons for this. First, the use of violence to maintain centralised control can be expensive and risky. Second, illegal enterprises lack external credit markets and the ability to advertise to create good will – both factors which limit their ability to expand. Finally, the increased visibility of large, centralised illegal enterprises make them more vulnerable to official detection and control. This is especially the case when there is no centralised regulatory authority affording a feasible target for corruption.

Recruitment

Those involved in organised crime differ in their demographic to the general criminal population. The standing decision[9] to become a criminal may be a life-long choice as well as a lifestyle choice. Such decisions may be formalised as a ritual kinship and criminal organisations may claim 'an absolute power over their members' (Paoli 2004: 22). In contrast to the age–crime profiles generally observed – where criminality generally declines with age beyond the early teens – there is evidence (van Koppen *et al*. 2010) that those involved in organised crime are late starters (or perhaps late in coming to the attention of the police). In their study of 854 individuals known to be involved in such crime, nearly 60 per cent were adult-onset offenders. Van Koppen *et al*. imply the late onset of criminality may be explained by the slow building of the relationships necessary to access high value crime and the transnational nature of such crime involving, as it does, logistic complexities.

The drivers behind the establishing of a criminal enterprise are relatively well established: market opportunity; and potential for collective efficiency. In order to expand, however, the enterprise must recruit further members. According to Firestone (1993) the attractors differ little from the attractors of crime in general, though perhaps the effects may be emphasised in the case of the decision to join a (perceived) successful criminal organisation.

Firestone (1993) summarises gangster biographic testimony into three main drivers, so far as the US mafia is concerned at any rate. First, 'strain' as discussed in Chapter Five: criminality provides an alternative path to 'success' for those who are unable to access socially legitimate means. Firestone, quoting Merton (1968), notes:

> Crime and vice constitute a 'normal' response to a situation where the cultural emphasis upon pecuniary success has been absorbed, but where there is little access to conventional and legitimate means for becoming successful.
> (Firestone 1993: 198)

The implication of strain theory in this context is that people join organised crime networks having seen their best efforts to succeed in society frustrated. However, Firestone notes, in the USA there is little sense of early-years deprivation amongst former mafiosi.

Second, Firestone considers 'control theory' (see Chapter Four). Proponents of control theory argue individuals' involvement with society forms a set of mores in proportion to shared: attachment; commitment; involvement; and belief. Thus crime results from weak societies when individuals suffer 'alienation from the surrounding social institutions'. In the case of former USA mafiosi, however, there is a deal of evidence it is the influence of the sub-culture around them which causes them to adopt a lifestyle that, while at deviance with society in general, is nevertheless accepted by their immediate community.

Third, 'criminal deviance' or 'criminal sub-culture' theory is suggested as the best explanation of recruitment to organised crime for the majority of individuals. In essence, people who grow up in societies dominated by organised crime are more likely to become members. Aspiration to the criminal way of life, emulation of (criminal) role models and access to recruitment provide an easy, and desirable, route into crime:

> 'it was an environment . . . I just grew with it. It didn't seem wrong. The whole life style didn't seem wrong.'
> (Sammy 'the Bull' Gravano from Blumenthal and Miller 1992: 293; quoted in Firestone 1993: 201)

Given the theoretical discussion above, it is perhaps understandable that there is increasing interest in using the concept of networks to explain organised crime. As Levi argues:

> The organisation of crimes results from the interaction of crime opportunities, offender and prospective offender motivations, skills, networks, and control

efforts (whether through the criminal law, administrative law or disruption). It is thus a *dynamic* process that evolves as offenders adapt (or fail to adapt) to their changing environment . . . .

(Levi 2007: 795, original emphasis)

The concept of a social network, it is argued, provides a more efficient and effective means of identifying, analysing and explaining the phenomenon of organised crime (McIllwain 1999). The advantages of understanding organised crime in terms of social networks are that they are never static and transcend culture, time and space, helping to explain how professional criminals engage in activities on a global scale (McIllwain 1999).

Globalisation and transnational organised crime

Recent factors associated with globalisation such as technological advances, the extension of the free-market and political change following the end of the Cold War have meant that national boundaries have begun to lose their significance (Rawlinson 2009) and as a result the nature and reach of organised crime has developed.

The United Nations Convention against Transnational Organised Crime defines an offence as transnational if: it is committed in more than one State; it is committed in one State but a substantial part of its planning, direction or control takes place in another State; it is committed in one State but involves an organised criminal group that operates in more than one State; or it is committed in one State but has substantial effects in another State (United Nations 2004). Drawing on a range of sources Rawlinson (2009) questions this definition, pointing out that:

[W]hile organised crime is increasingly exploiting opportunities offered on an international scale, such as drugs and human trafficking, these activities and the actors involved are locally based and will be affected by local conditions.

(Rawlinson 2009: 330)

Even if the concept is accepted numerous issues are raised such as how 'victims' and 'threats' are defined and how transnational organised crime might be measured when different states have different legal codes, different law enforcement practices and different recording practices (Rawlinson 2009). Criminals are well aware of these differences and are able to structure their activities on the global stage so as to exploit the comparative advantage of one regime over another. Shelley (2002: 91) notes 'The enormous discrepancies in regulation in a globalized world allow criminals and terrorists to exploit this lack of consistency to their advantage'.

According to Chatterjee (2005), organised crime in the twenty-first century has reacted to improvements in transport links, communications and technology in much the same way as legitimate business. Those organisations which emphasise fluidity and flexibility, an ability to react to the needs of the international market and law enforcement are increasingly the more prevalent compared to 'popular stereotypes' (i.e. those organisations which adopt a strict hierarchical structure).

If 'vertically integrated', bureaucratic organised criminal networks did ever exist, it is likely that they have been superseded by looser networks better able to adapt to the fast-moving challenges of globalisation:

> The global environment of myriad cultures, different markets (regulated and unregulated), and numerous languages also requires structural adjustments by organised crime. Traditional hierarchies and centrally managed structures, if they ever existed, cannot survive in these conditions. The international market demands flexibility, short-term but effective collaborations, more complex forms of communication and safeguards against successful police operations, and the engagement of an increasing number of different actors in different locations. Networks are therefore less likely to attract attention and can be disassembled and reconstructed quickly and in different forms. The most powerful position is no longer the head or leader of a structure, but with those who occupy certain 'nodal' points within the networks which give them the greater overall knowledge of an operation or series of operations.
>
> (Rawlinson 2009: 331)

The paradox of organised crime

Whether there is a natural limit to the size of criminal organisations, and an economic disincentive from the creation of monopoly, is an issue considered further by Paoli (2002). In particular she highlights a paradox she considers implicit within the 'enterprise model'. A number of factors, stemming from the illegality of the product or service, tend to prevent the development of large-scale enterprises in illegal markets.

First, where trade in certain goods and services is prohibited, illegal market suppliers cannot resort to state institutions to enforce contracts and there is no alternative sovereign power from which a wronged party may seek redress (Paoli 2002). Therefore property rights are poorly protected, employment contracts cannot be formalised and the development of large, formally organised and enduring companies is made difficult (ibid.).

Second, the absence of a formal apparatus guaranteeing the security of contracts has prevented the rise of external capital markets. Illegal enterprises are unlikely to have audited accounts and potential creditors are unlikely to lend when they lack court protection (ibid.).

Third, in order to minimise the risk of arrest and asset confiscation, entrepreneurs in the illegal market are likely to organise their activities to minimise the risk of law enforcement detection. This is likely to lead to segmented enterprises with a small number of employees and customers (ibid.).

Fourth, to minimise the risk of law enforcement detection, illegal organisations have few incentives for vertical integration. Vertical integration might be 'upstream' (producing semi-fabricated goods and raw materials that might otherwise have to be purchased from suppliers) or 'downstream' (finishing semi-fabricated goods and raw materials and moving further towards wholesaling and retailing) but in either direction the internalisation of additional functions increases risks (ibid.).

Fifth, the constraints of product or service illegality also reduce the geographical scope of illegal enterprises because of the difficulty of monitoring distant agents and the higher risks associated with transportation and communication to distant locations.

Sixth, due to the risk of detection by law enforcement agencies, illegal enterprises are likely to take a relatively short-term approach to planning, when compared to legal enterprises (ibid.).

Finally, operating in an illegal market prevents enterprises from marketing their products. As Paoli notes, marketing is associated with economies of scale and marketing is recognised as an important factor in the rise of modern large-scale corporations (ibid.). Paoli therefore concludes that while illegal markets do have much in common with legal markets in the sense that both have buyers, sellers, wholesalers, retailers, profits and losses, etc., the analogy between illegal and legal firms should not be 'pushed too far' (Paoli 2002: 64).

Illegal organisations described by the 'enterprise model' are more likely to be characterised as networks: 'loose associations of people which form, split and come together again as opportunities arise' (Paoli 2002: 67), 'most correctly described as "crews"' (Paoli 2004: 26). The strength and cohesion of these networks should not be overestimated (Paoli 2002).

Notwithstanding the strength of such non-economic ties, the reliance on kinship ties also places constraints on such illegal businesses as such groups have a restricted pool of people from which to recruit and, as a result, are often unable to internalise specialist functions needed for involvement in some of the most profitable sectors of the world economy (Paoli 2002).

Thus Paoli concludes that the very non-economic ties which guarantee the long-lasting success of a criminal organisation are an inherent constraint, while those organisations which rely simply on market forces and self-interest lack a means of enforcing contracts. This, she feels, 'leaves some space for optimism' (Paoli 2002: 88).

Notwithstanding the force of Paoli's argument, it should be noted that all the points she raises pre-suppose a strong stable state, for example, a Western democracy, the mores of which are generally approved by the population at large. If organised crime is, to some extent, ranged against the criminal justice system of a state with efficient and generally respected security forces and policing, there may well be inherent checks on the size of the criminal organisation. If, however, the criminal organisation manages to subvert, weaken or even to become the state (or if the state is inherently weak, thus giving an opportunity for crime to organise) these checks may be insufficient to restrain organised crime. Further, it is clearly not the case that criminal organisations lack the skills necessary to become involved in the most profitable sectors of the world economy – indeed one of the most profitable sectors of the world economy, the international trade in drugs, is, in fact, illicit.

The legal/illegal nexus

This permeable membrane between what is, and what is not, illicit – and the interactions between legal and illegal markets – give rise to what von Lampe (2006) terms the 'legal/illegal' nexus. The individuals, structures and events associated with organised crime do not exist in a social vacuum, but instead are linked to their surroundings.

Organised crime and legitimate business

The most obvious fashion by which organised crime effects legitimate business is through extortion. If the state is too weak to protect them, small business may be 'taxed' by criminal enterprise which will provide 'protection' – generally from members of the taxing organisation. The effect of any such tax is to reduce the incentive to work, and thus the level of income in the economy will be reduced – even if the threats do not actually result in violence. Further, as will be true of any criminal activity, those engaged in illicit work are denying society at large the benefit of their labour. Those engaged in driving getaway cars are not simultaneously serving the public as taxi drivers, for example. Hence, the greater the strength of the illicit economy, the less wealth a nation will have, in general.

However, it may be the case that legitimate and illicit businesses cooperate in certain areas to their mutual benefit – for example, the real-estate entrepreneurs of late 1980s Japan who used the Yakuza to 'clear' recalcitrant tenants (and owners) from property they wished to develop (Glenny 2009: 33 citing Delfs 1991: 29 citing Skaperdas 2001). The areas where criminal and legal organisations interact for their own economic benefit are termed by Ruggiero (1997) 'dirty economies'. He considers two specific markets to illustrate this cross-over: the trafficking of human beings; and international arms shipments. In each case the so-called legal sector is prepared to cooperate with, or even to perform the role of, organised crime to achieve its economic ends. According to Ruggiero, it is legally registered agencies rather than organised crime which dominate the market in illegal immigration in the UK. He notes the involvement of 'tourist agents, employment mediators, transport entrepreneurs and drivers' (Ruggiero 1997: 31), none of which had any affiliation with conventional criminal groups.

Similarly, Ruggiero suggests, while arms manufacturers have formerly dealt with organised crime as a means of transporting restricted goods, more recently '[t]he illicit arms business seems too lucrative a trade to be left in the hands of conventional criminals' (Ruggiero 1997: 33). Rather disconcertingly, according to Ruggiero, 'official economic actors' increasingly find it so much more efficient to provide illegal services themselves, rather than rely on criminal organisations, they are actually driving the latter out of the market. To Ruggiero (1997) the boundaries between organised crime and corporate crime are increasingly blurred as the larger corporations 'negotiate the degree of morality embedded in their practices' (Ruggiero 1997: 36).

It may well be the case that, in some sectors of the economy, legitimate business has no alternative but to deal with criminal organisations, as the latter may control the factors of production. Consider, for example, the case of labour unions in the USA. The re-organisation of labour unions by the Mafia in the prohibition era, termed 'racketeering' by the Employers' Association of Chicago in 1927, persists to this day and has arguably resulted in higher costs for legitimate industry and the failure of unions to achieve the aspirations of their members. So widespread is alleged Mafia involvement with labour unionisation in the USA, Jacobs (2006: 21) asks his readers to imagine 'What might America look like today if at least part of the American labor movement had not been hijacked by labor racketeers?'. Von Lampe (2006) contends business and labour racketeering are 'the two areas where organised crime is most intrinsically linked with the legal economy' (von Lampe 2006: 85). Not all industries suffer the problem to the same extent, as noted by Reuter (1987) who reviews a number of industries in several cities in the US and concludes:

> The available evidence, though quite fragmentary, suggests that the problem is inherent in certain structural characteristics of the industries that are affected.
>
> (Reuter 1987: 1)

Ichniowski and Preston (1989) explore the strengths and weaknesses of economic reasoning in explaining, and suggesting remedies for the presence of racketeering in New York City construction. They explain its presence in terms of characteristics of the industry; transactions cannot be conducted efficiently either between a large number of firms or within a few large firms. Consequently, criminals can 'sell', and profit from, their ability to impose organisation on the industry (ibid.). Criminal activity can persist because of barriers to entry in certain markets within the industry and because of industry characteristics such as constant changes of, and restricted access to, work sites (ibid.). Ichniowski and Preston (1989) also suggest that the role of unions as a monopolising institution may also facilitate criminal control.

Organised crime and the state

A clash of cultures – a clash of objectives

Thinking first about the 'hierarchical model' of organised crime, wherever there is a sub-culture (whether ethnic, cultural or business) in a nation whose members owe allegiance to that sub-culture above allegiance to the nation state, the potential exists for the differing incentive structure to create behaviour of which the state will not approve. Recall, economists discuss the general level of satisfaction of an individual or economic unit using the concept of 'utility' (see Chapter 2). We

have discussed (Chapter Two) the conflict between each individual's utility max-
imisation and the overall good of members of the state and general public. Where
sub-cultures and secret societies exist, where members owe allegiance to the sub-
culture ahead of the nation at large, a similar conflict arises. Thus, insofar as a
criminal organisation may be described by the hierarchical model, a clear threat to
the general good of the nation is implied by that sub-culture (be it Hell's Angels,
La Cosa Nostra or similar).

The threat of the 'enterprise model' is at first sight more straightforward. A
criminal enterprise in general operates by a business model where the profit principle is simply unconstrained by the mores of society at large. The threat is amplified
by the size of the enterprise, simply because the larger and more successful it is,
the more the utility of the individuals of which it is comprised is promoted by the
success of the enterprise. Whereas in the hierarchical model gang members might
be selfless, promoting their societies' success ahead of their own, in the enterprise
model gang members have joined and promote the gang simply because, according to their utility function, it is 'worth their while'.

If, for whatever reason, a gang member is convinced the prosperity of the gang
is of more importance than the prosperity of the state in which it operates, conflict with the wider society legal code is almost certain to follow. Therefore, the
implication of both the hierarchical and the enterprise models is that, whether or
not criminality (or at least, behaviour of which society at large disapproves) is
the founding principle of an organisation, the likelihood of criminality is present.
Rationally, the response of the state is to demand allegiance to the state over and
above allegiance to ethnic, cultural and business groups.

In short, if someone puts being a good gang member ahead of (for example)
being a good American, that someone is likely not to be a good American, except
perhaps by coincidence. However, if members of a sub-culture are indeed prepared to put their nation first and their sub-culture second, it behoves the nation
state to respect that choice and attempt to minimise occasions when the conflict of
loyalty must be tested. If a nation systematically discriminates against members
of a particular group, it is only to be expected members of that group will tend to
congregate and discount the importance of the state.

In this context, the rise of criminal gangs in post-Soviet era Russia was fore-
shadowed by the brutality of the previous regimes. Describing the brutality of the
social structure of the Russian empire, Cheloukhine (2008) observes:

> By the second half of eighteenth century, about 20,000 peasants were taking
> flight every year to unknown lands to escape the wrath of their landown-
> ers. Many of these peasants formed veritable armies of robbers, thieves, and
> tramps, and it was just a matter of time before some of the more capable coun-
> trymen tried to establish a professional criminal network of these 'outlaws.'
> (Cheloukhine 2008: 355)

As well as by brutal landowners, the legitimacy of the Russian imperial state was
undermined by corrupt bureaucracy. Based on these foundations (Cheloukhine

2008) a professional criminal hierarchy had formed in Russia by the beginning of the twentieth century. By the time Stalin began to send 'enemies of the Soviet system' to concentration camps, the criminal organisation in the former Russian empire was already a state within a state. Infringement by a member of the underworld of the 'thieves' code' generally resulted in a sentence of death being imposed (ibid.).

The opportunities for organised crime in weak and failing states

The roots of the Mafia in Italy lie, as we have seen, in the provision of some form of law and order in mediaeval culture (Paoli 2002) – a proto-state within a state. In this sense, criminal organisations are engaged in competition with the state – not competition in a market as we would understand it, but competition at a meta-level between two different kinds of economic systems. The economic system which triumphs may not be that which leads to the greatest societal well-being; it will, however, be likely to be that which most readily harnesses the power of the market to reinforce it.

For example, so poorly organised was the communist economic system of the Soviet Union that, whereas in Western Europe, organised crime existed mainly to provide illegal goods and services, in the USSR, criminals would traffic in what would appear to be perfectly legitimate items through the shadow (or unofficial) economy (Cheloukhine 2008). According to Cheloukhine, organised crime was a direct product of the command economy. The Soviet Union had tried to legislate away the invisible hand of the market, only to force it underground.

At the time of Perestroika in 1988, all underground market activities became legal. However, as it was the criminal organisations which had the most experience of running any sort of capitalist economy, it was the criminal capitalists who were best placed to thrive in the new Russia. With economic power came political power, to the extent that, according to Cheloukhine (2008: 373), 'the Russian state transformed and now functions according to mafia laws'. Similar patterns, to one extent or another, have been observed in a number of former iron-curtain and former communist nations (see Glenny 2009).

As we have seen, the absence of legally enforceable contracts stifles trade and therefore specialisation. Virtually all goods and services required by a modern economy require specialised production and delivery if civilised society is to be maintained. Specialised production and delivery require, if not law, then at least workable logistics. If the state cannot maintain sufficient authority, manufacturers cannot rely on raw material deliveries; suppliers cannot rely on payment; retailers cannot rely on wholesalers or their customers. The collapse of the Soviet empire in the last years of the twentieth century created a political economic vacuum in which the power of the state to enforce contracts was significantly weakened. This power vacuum was obvious to the would-be entrepreneurs of the new Russia. According to Glenny (2009), between them the Russian mafia and oligarchs defined the criminal justice system of the time:

[t]he police and even the KGB were clueless as to how one might enforce contract law. The protection rackets and Mafiosi were not so clueless – their central role in the new Russian economy was to ensure that contracts entered into were honoured.

(Glenny 2009: 73)

Compared to anarchy, the Russian Mob 'ensured a degree of stability' (ibid.: 76). As Olson (1993: 568) suggests, 'the rational, self-interested leader of a band of roving bandits is led, as though by an invisible hand,[10] to settle down, wear a crown, and replace anarchy with government'.

Paoli (2004: 22) points out that until the middle of the twentieth century, the Mafia 'had a higher degree of effectiveness and legitimacy' than the Italian state. Indeed, she goes on to note 'the Italian state and the mafia long shared power in considerable parts of Sicily and Calabria and the power of mafia groups was accepted and even legalised by government representatives' (Paoli 2004: 22).

The case of societies in transition is addressed, in general, by Keren (2000) from an economic perspective. Keren uses a model of career choice to explain the weakening of state power by the underworld in Eastern European countries.[11] According to Sung (2004) there are two hypotheses which might explain such growth. The first is the failed state model, according to which criminal organisations gain some level of legitimacy by providing social goods with more certainty than the state: for example, justice and stability. The second is the economic failure hypothesis, under which criminal syndicates provide better economic prospects than legitimate industry. Considering evidence from 59 nations, Sung finds the former hypothesis has more empirical support than the latter. Unemployment in particular seems to have little influence on the growth of organised crime; anecdotal evidence, however (Glenny 2009), suggests poverty or relative poverty is a major driver.

Organised crime and corruption

Organised crime may also interact with the state through subverting civil servants, in effect to serve the ends of the criminal gang ahead of the legitimate ends of the society they represent. As Levi notes:

No profits can be made if potential customers are not aware of the existence of the unlawful service, and this generally means that in the long run, the police will come to know about it too. To ensure freedom from the law, the criminals must therefore subvert the police and/or the courts, and this is a major reason for concern about the impact of organised crime.

(Levi 1998: 339)

In essence, criminal gangs are able to exploit the principal–agent problem. Their financial resources are certainly sufficient to provide perverse incentives to state employees. As noted by Skaperdas (2001: 176), 'From the 1920s, the Mafia could buy up whole police departments and also had significant influence in local and city politics.' Indeed, Kugler *et al.* (2005) argue, trying to reduce the level of organised crime in society through the traditional economist's solution of deterrence (see, for instance, Becker 1968) without simultaneously reducing corruption in civil servants may even be counter-productive. As the likelihood of apprehension increases, sufficiently moneyed criminals will increasingly turn to bribery to circumvent legal codes. If they are successful in this, the 'economic cost' of further criminal activity is reduced. According to Kugler *et al.* (2005: 1656), '[b]eyond a threshold of corruption in the justice system, increasing returns in various types of crime may take off', leading to a general breakdown in the criminal justice system and in the most extreme cases, 'state capture' by organised crime (Buscaglia and van Dijk 2003). Thus, through corruption, a robust state may become a failing or failed state, and hence more vulnerable to increased criminal organisation.

We have seen that gangs working against the national interest through max-imisation of their own utility are almost certain to arise where group interests are placed above those of the state as a whole. A state in which criminal organisations find it most difficult to operate, then, is one which is stable, which balances the allegiance of societies and individuals to the nation with respect for those indi-viduals and societies. And which, of course, has a strong criminal justice sector which promotes adherence to national codes in those cases where allegiance is not forthcoming.

The links between organised crime and terrorism

The potential links between organised crime and terrorism have come to promi-nence over recent years as the West has become increasingly engaged in its 'war on terror'. It would indeed seem to be a truism that the skill set which must be drawn upon to evade detection by the state as a terrorist will be similar to the skill set required as a criminal. Drawing on the 'alien conspiracy' model of organised crime, there would seem to be a further link between the running of what might amount to an alternative legal-code – for example in the monopolisation of vio-lent enforcing – and the undermining of legitimate government and society by violent means. The 'alien conspiracy' and the 'hierarchical model', to one extent or another, assume political as well as economic goals for criminal organisations. The links are less well defined when organised crime of the 'enterprise' model is considered. Levi (2007) has also drawn parallels between the social construction of the 'alien conspiracy' model in the USA and the more recent concerns in the USA about the Al Qaeda terrorist network.

In the case of criminal enterprises, political involvement will be pursued only if it adds to the overall profitability of the racket. Even in this latter context, how-ever, there are two potential links: terrorists might themselves resort to organised criminal activities to raise revenue; or they might consort with organised criminal networks, in effect purchasing illegal goods and services required for the success-ful completion of a particular task.

Considering the former, Dorn *et al.* (2005) set out a typology of upper-level drug traffickers, one type of which are 'politico-military traffickers' who use drug dealing as a means to achieve political change or power.[12] Western governments too recognise this threat and in recent years organised crime threat assessments have often highlighted potential links between organised crime and terrorists. For example, as Levi (2007) notes, the Provisional IRA and loyalist paramilitaries operating in Northern Ireland and the Republic of Ireland have traditionally obtained significant funds from crime ranging from extortion to cross-border smuggling. Levi (2007) distinguishes between the financing of (i) the infrastructure of global persuasion towards a particular religio-political doctrine, (ii) the infrastructure of terror (his examples include terrorist training camps), and (iii) operational expenditure on individual attacks. Levi (2007) points out that expenditure in the third category will often be relatively minimal, suggesting less than a thousand pounds for the London bombings of 2005 and US$400,000–500,000 for the attacks of September 2001. He therefore argues that it is:

> crucial to understand that financing a large movement and financing an individual suicide-bombing attack involve very different orders of magnitude of cost.
>
> (Levi 2007: 793)

Terrorists might also (in effect) sub-contract to organised crime certain aspects of their operation; making use of the goods and services offered by organised crime networks in the execution of terrorist activities. This might take the form of utilising established smuggling routes to move weapons or people into a country or acquiring forged identity documents. However, again, it is important not to overstate or sensationalise this relationship. The USA National Intelligence Council expects that between now and 2020:

> [T]he relationship between terrorists and organised criminals will remain primarily a matter of business, i.e., that terrorists will turn to criminals who can provide forged documents, smuggled weapons, or clandestine travel assistance when the terrorists cannot procure these goods and services on their own. Organised criminal groups, however, are unlikely to form long-term strategic alliances with terrorists. Organised crime is motivated by the desire to make money and tends to regard any activity beyond that required to effect profit as bad for business. For their part, terrorist leaders are concerned that ties to non-ideological partners will increase the chance of successful police penetration or that profits will seduce the faithful.
>
> (National Intelligence Council 2004: 96 quoted in Finklea 2010)

In 2001 the United Nations Security Council's Counter-Terrorism Committee invited member states to submit a report describing the links between organised crime and terrorism in their own economies. A comprehensive synthesis of the results of 193 of these is provided by Dandurand and Chin (2004). They note, only 14 of the 193 reports received made a connection between terrorism and organised criminality; the USA and the UK were amongst these. In the UK, the activity of sectarian paramilitaries in Ireland was highlighted. It was suggested that paramilitaries are involved in two-thirds of organised criminal groups. The particular types of crimes varied according to the religio-political affiliation of the terrorist group with (so-called) republicans favouring: tobacco fraud; oil fraud; and intellectual property crime; and (so-called) loyalists more likely to become involved in: extortion; tobacco fraud; drugs trade; and the illegal trade in arms.[13] In the USA, the primary links between crime and terrorism also involve drug-trafficking, although: medical insurance fraud; visa fraud; mail and wire fraud; and cigarette smuggling are also prevalent (Dandurand and Chin 2004). The link between drugs and terrorism is particularly marked as terrorist groups often win a double benefit through this trade, simultaneously funding their activities and weakening the moral fibre of their political enemies (ibid.).

In sum, Dandurand and Chin conclude there are few instances of organised criminals becoming involved in terrorism. Where hybrid groups exist, it is the political/terrorist groups which have evolved a business case as well as (or instead of) a political rationale for their existence.

Estimating the size and value of illegal markets

There are few attempts to measure the economic consequences of organised crime. Studies take two broad perspectives: the value in the market of illicit activities; and the cost of that activity to the society where it occurs. Economic theory would suggest the latter effect is greater than the former.[14] We look at an attempt to estimate the size and value of illegal markets in the UK and also look at valuations of the 'shadow economy' in a number of nation states.

As we have seen, international agencies cannot readily agree on a definition of organised crime; the measuring of its scale has proved even more difficult. As Fijnaut *et al.* point out:

> the seriousness of organised crime should not be solely assessed according to its nature and scale, but also to the damage it causes (Maltz 1990). So ideally, to determine the seriousness of organised crime in a country or city, the damage it causes should be assessed alongside its nature and scale. This is an ideal that has never been fully achieved anywhere is the world, not in qualitative terms, let alone in quantitative ones.
>
> (Fijnaut *et al.* 1998: 203)

Valuing organised crime in the UK

In the most comprehensive study to date in the UK, Duborg and Prichard (2007) present the results of a UK Home Office project which pulls together and further develops data and analysis on the revenues and costs of organised crime. The project looks at the most serious forms of organised crime: supplying of illicit drugs; people smuggling; people trafficking; excise fraud; fraud and non-excise intellectual property theft. The methodologies used to reach the estimates vary between organised crime types. For all the types of organised crime examined there are important caveats, most of which relate to a lack of reliable data and some of which relate to conceptual or definitional problems. In each case the 'value' of the crime is broken down into the benefits realised by organised criminal groups and the cost to society of their actions.

For example, the size of the UK market for people smuggling is estimated by Duborg and Prichard to be around £250 million per annum in 2003. This estimate is derived by estimating the number of people smuggled into the UK in 2003 and multiplying this by the average cost of 'facilitation' (the amount charged for their services by smugglers). However, there is no reliable data on the number of people smuggled into the UK; many will remain undetected. The estimates are based only on those who are detected at some point. Also there is limited data on the proportion of people smuggling which involves organised crime groups. Finally, there is limited data on the cost of 'facilitation'. Wherever data is incomplete, informed judgements must be made. The costs to society of this 'enterprise', that is, economic and social costs of people smuggling, are estimated based on the costs of support for smuggled asylum seekers during their claims for asylum; the costs of removing failed asylum seekers and other smuggled immigrants; the health costs of fatal accidents occurring in transit; and the costs of border control and counter-smuggling operations. In total these costs amount to an estimated £1.4 billion in 2003/04. It will be noted that the costs and benefits of any activities undertaken by immigrants once they have arrived are not considered; that is to say, whether they engage in work (potentially benefiting society) or further criminal activity (which will not).

Duborg and Prichard estimate the size of the UK market for people trafficking for sexual exploitation was up to £275 million in 2003. All of this is assumed to be attributable to organised crime. The estimate is derived by estimating the number of women involved in prostitution in the UK, making an informed judgement about the proportion that is trafficked and then multiplying this by the assumed revenue per victim. Caveats include the limited number of groups included in the estimate; for example, women trafficked to work 'on the street' are excluded. The total economic and social costs of people trafficking for sexual exploitation in the UK was estimated to be up to £1 billion in 2003. This was estimated by quantifying and then monetising the amount of physical and sexual abuse of trafficked women.[15] In addition the researchers estimated and monetised the deterioration in the quality of life suffered by those trafficked. Caveats include the limitations inherent in estimating the harms to trafficked women. For example, harms experienced by women before they reach the UK and on return to their home country are not included.

Excise smuggling involves buying tobacco, alcohol and oils[16] outside the UK and selling them in the UK without paying duty and (in some instances) value-added tax. Excise fraud typically involves goods which are nominally in transit between countries – and therefore exempt from duty – being diverted to the UK market. The size of the market for excise fraud and smuggling by organised crime groups is estimated by Duborg and Prichard to be approximately £2.9 billion in 2003/04. This is based on HM Revenue and Customs, HMRC, estimates of total consumption compared with consumption for which duty has been paid, making allowances for legitimate cross-border shopping, and combining this with estimated street prices. A key caveat is that estimates of consumption are based on surveys which are subject to two potential sources of uncertainty: random variation in sample data; and the possibility that people systematically under-report their consumption. Estimates also have to be made about the proportion of excise fraud committed by organised crime groups. For instance, it is assumed that all alcohol smuggling is organised, but only 80 per cent of hand-rolled tobacco smuggling and 90 per cent of cigarette smuggling is organised. It is estimated that the social and economic costs associated with excise fraud and smuggling by organised crime groups is approximately £3.7 billion in 2003/04. The biggest component of loss was lost tax revenue although there is also potentially damage to the profitability of legitimate retailers selling goods which have attracted excise-tax.

The size of the market for organised non-benefit fraud is estimated by Duborg and Prichard to be about £1.9bn in 2003/04. It is based primarily on HMRC and industry estimates of their losses. A key caveat is that fraud is under-reported because not all fraud is detected and not all fraud is reported (a company may not report a fraud for fear of the impact on its reputation). There is only limited data on the involvement of organised criminals in different sectors and therefore informed judgement has been used where necessary. The total economic and social costs of organised non-benefit fraud is estimated to be about £2.7 billion in 2003/04. The biggest component is fraud losses. Costs are also incurred in preventing and dealing with the after effects of fraud. A key caveat is that costs of fraud experienced by consumers have not been estimated. These are costs incurred by consumers attempting to avoid fraud and the emotional costs of having been defrauded.

Non-excise intellectual property theft covers the market for pirated, counterfeited and bootlegged goods in the UK and includes sectors such as computer games, computer software, films and music. Using music as an example, piracy involves infringement of copyright licensing, counterfeiting involves infringement of associated trademarks and bootlegging involves recording copyright material and reproducing it. Duborg and Prichard's estimate the size of the organised non-excise intellectual property theft market is circa £840 million per annum and is based primarily on industry estimates. The economic cost to the UK is estimated to be about £300 million per annum and is based on estimating the losses to the legal market of expenditure in illegal markets. Caveats include that different methods are used in different sectors and assumptions are made about the proportion of illegal activity attributable to organised criminals.

Duborg and Prichard's discussion of the size and costs associated with the illicit drugs market summarises the research undertaken by Pudney *et al.* (2006). This is discussed in Chapter Eleven.

A summary of the values that are estimated for the revenue accruing from each market and the economic and social costs associated with the market are set out in Table 10.1 along with a summary of key caveats.

Table 10.1 Valuations of market sizes, and economic and social costs

Sector	Market size	Key caveats	Economic and social costs	Key caveats
People smuggling	£250m	Based mainly on data on asylum claimants, so limited in scope.	£1.4bn	Based mainly on the costs of running the asylum system, so again, limitations apply.
People trafficking	£275m	Very poor data around the number of people trafficked, and hence large margins for error.	£1bn	Extremely difficult area to quantify and therefore estimate is very approximate.
Drugs	£5.3bn	Based solely on a detailed study by Pudney *et al.* (2006). Relies on self-reporting so may understate market size.	£15.4bn	Based solely on studies by Godfrey *et al.* (2002) and Gordon *et al.* (2006).
Excise fraud	£2.9bn	Relies solely on estimates produced by HMRC. Subject to large margins of error, but no reason to think there is a bias.	£3.7bn	Key component is loss of excise tax revenue.
Fraud	£1.9bn	Very conservative estimate of organised crime involvement. Relies on industry and HMRC data. Private sector data often thought to be poor, because of low reporting.	£2.7bn	Consists mainly of direct financial losses, so caveats attached to market size apply equally to economic costs.
Non-excise intellectual property theft	£840m	Uses industry data on scale of IPT market. It is well known that it is difficult to get reliable data on this issue, so large margins of error exist. Market size figures based on 'street values' of counterfeit goods, not full retail price of legal goods.	£300m	Allows only for the lost 'value-added' which would have been spent in the legal sector, had the IPT market not existed. Because of a lack of data no attempt has been made to value harms to brand image, or incentives to innovate, so value likely to be an underestimation.

Source: based on Duborg and Prichard (2007: Table S.1).

Note: this table is presented by Duborg and Prichard (2007) with the caveat that the market size and economic and social costs should not be added together because this would involve double counting. In some cases the values overlap. The revenue accruing to the organised criminal may be a component of the economic and social cost.

The size of the shadow economy

To the authors' knowledge, no nation other than the UK has comprehensively sur-veyed the size of illegal markets and the impact of the crime involved on the state. However, there are a number of studies which consider the size of what is known as the 'shadow economy' across nation states. Those activities carried out by organised criminal organisations are not all in the shadow economy as the shadow economy is defined as 'all market-based legal production of goods and services that are deliberately concealed from public authorities' (Schneider 2006: 4). It will be noted, then, that the trade in illicit commodities is excluded from this defini-tion, as is the offering of 'protection' and the trafficking of humans and protected species. Thus the size of the illegal economy is likely to be far greater than the size of the shadow economy. However, as one of the means used to measure the size of the shadow economy is the discrepancy between National Expendi-ture and National Income (Schneider and Enste 2000), it is clear some element of the gains made from illegal trade may be captured. Note that this cannot hope to determine the cost to society of the shadow economy, merely the amount of money which is made in that sector. Schneider and Enste note, however, that as well as illicit activities, this approach will also capture statistical irregularities and omissions. In addition, government statistical agencies will seek to reduce this discrepancy in published figure (reasoning they are reducing irregularities and omissions), and so the finally published data may be 'of questionable reliability' (Schneider and Ernste 2000: 93).

A related approach is to consider the level of cash demanded in the economy. Those purchasing illicit commodities are unlikely to want to use a cheque or credit card which may be traced back to them, hence illicit and shadow transactions are more likely to involve the use of cash than licit transactions. If it is assumed that the requirement of cash for licit transactions is able to be taken into account, any further increases in the demand for cash may be taken to indicate a growing demand for illicit and shadow activities. See Giles (1999) for a useful technical discussion of the issues involved.[17]

Using the 'currency demand' method, Schneider (2006) estimates the size of shadow economies for the majority of nations in the world. The reader is referred to his paper for a country by country breakdown. We present sum-mary data in Table 10.2. It should be borne in mind that the currency demand approach is only a rough estimate of the level of transactions for illegal goods and services as it also includes shadow markets for perfectly legal goods and services.[18] The estimates are likely to capture much more than organised criminal activities.

Tackling organised crime

Efforts to tackle organised crime at the level of the enterprise have met with mixed results, as the removal of key players has often resulted in little more than a 'job vacancy'. Notwithstanding, the symptoms of organised crime may be attacked

Table 10.2 Average size of the shadow economy for developing, transition and OECD countries as a percentage of official GDP

Countries/year	Average size of the shadow economy – value added in per cent of official GDP using DYMIMIC and currency demand method (number of countries)		
	1999/2000	*2000/2001*	*2002/2003*
Mostly developing countries:			
Africa	41.3	42.3	43.2
	(37)	(37)	(37)
Central and South America	41.1	42.1	43.4
	(21)	(21)	(21)
Asia	28.5	29.5	30.4
	(28)	(28)	(28)
Transition countries	38.1	39.1	40.1
	(25)	(25)	(25)
Highly developed OECD countries*	16.8	16.7	16.3
	(21)	(21)	(21)
South Pacific Islands	31.7	32.6	33.4
	(10)	(10)	(10)
Communist countries	19.8	21.1	22.3
	(3)	(3)	(3)
Unweighted average over 145 countries	33.6	34.5	35.2

Source: a summary of Schneider (2006: Table 4.1).

* The figures for the UK are 12.7 per cent, 12.5 per cent and 12.2 per cent respectively for 1999/2000, 2000/2001 and 2002/2003. The figures for the USA are 8.7 per cent, 8.7 per cent and 8.4 per cent respectively.

using a similar approach to that used to police any illicit activity; however, to tackle the cause requires an altogether more subtle approach. Here we take a selective look at efforts to tackle organised crime. We focus on two key strategies based on analysis of the economic incentive structure underlying criminal organisations: asset seizure and strategies to tackle money laundering. These two are increasingly being employed in, for example, the USA (Finklea 2010). Congress has recently enacted legislation regarding asset forfeiture and money laundering, with a view to increasing the federal government's ability to combat organised crime. According to Finklea (2010) the Department of Justice and Federal Bureau of Investigation have indicated that two of the three most prominent tools relied upon when investigating and prosecuting organised crime are the money laundering and asset forfeiture statutes. As we shall see, both these tools aim to reduce the incentive for criminals to become organised by reducing the returns to crime.

Money laundering

It might seem counterintuitive, but the possession of too much money (or at least money of the wrong kind) can cause a problem for criminal organisations. Compared to legal transactions, which may take place using debit/credit cards or cheques, illegal transactions are more likely to involve cash. Thus organised criminals potentially have access to a great deal of cash money. Before cash can be used, however, it has to be 'cleaned' so it cannot be traced back to its source. Consider: if you were to make regular cash deposits totalling hundreds of thousands of pounds at your local bank; if you were to buy sports cars paying for them in cash; if you paid cash for first class flights for a holiday (and settled your five-star hotel bill in cash), it would not be long before the authorities would be knocking on the door of your house (which you had paid for in cash) with a view to finding out from where you were accessing these funds. This is not a new problem; Gelemerova (2009) dates the origins of money laundering back 2,000 years to practices among Chinese merchants. In essence, modern money laundering involves moving cash generated in an illicit market into the legal economy so that criminals can use it to buy legitimate goods and services without exciting the suspicion of the authorities.

Wilson and Stevens (2008) note that high-level drug dealers face significant costs in moving their profits into the legitimate financial system. Currently, drug-dealing businesses are likely to launder their money through making numerous small deposits or using cash-based businesses as a front for their operations. Cash is also moved internationally either by use of money couriers or electronic transfer using money service businesses. Investing in property overseas can also be a means of hiding assets. Contacts within financial institutions who can assist with these transactions are valuable (ibid.). SOCA (2009a), in its UK organised crime threat assessment, notes that the United Arab Emirates, the Far East and South East Asia (particularly Hong Kong, Singapore and Shanghai) and Spain are attractive locations for money-laundering enterprises.

In the USA money laundering was established as a federal criminal offence in the Money Laundering Control Act of 1986. According to Finklea (2010) and Gelemerova (2009), the USA has been the main driving force behind the introduction of anti-money-laundering regulations worldwide. Key stages in developing an international strategy to tackle money laundering were, according to Gelemerova (2009): the 1988 agreement of the international community to the UN Convention Against Illicit Trafficking in Narcotic Drugs and Psychotropic Substances (1988); the Basle Statement of Principles on the Prevention of Criminal Use of the Banking System for the Purpose of Money Laundering (1988); and the establishment of the Financial Action Task Force on Money Laundering (FATF). Subsequently the FATF has evaluated countries' performance on money laundering, listing as 'non-cooperative' those that didn't meet FATF standards (Gelemerova 2009).

The global network of Financial Intelligence Units (FIUs) fed by a host of auxiliary (primarily financial) institutions required to report suspicious transactions

(Gelemerova 2009) has been particularly important in the arsenal of governments internationally. An FIU is a:

> central, national agency responsible for receiving (and, as permitted, request-
> ing), analysing and disseminating to the competent authorities, disclosures
> of financial information: (i) concerning suspected proceeds of crime, or (ii)
> required by national legislation or regulation, in order to counter money
> laundering.
>
> (Egmont Group 2003: 2 as quoted by Gelemerova 2009: 37)

Gelemerova (2009) lists some early challenges faced by the international network of FIUs as including issues around human rights, data protection and difficulties in sharing information stemming from the different legal statuses of FIUs in different countries. However, it is now generally recognised that the benefits which may result from the reduction of incentives for organised crime outweigh the costs imposed on society by such policing.

Once established, changes in international strategy on money laundering over the years have led to the broadening of the scope of the network of FIUs (Gelemerova 2009). For example, whereas originally money laundering was associated primarily with the illicit drug trade, the list of crimes covered has come to include 'practically all types of crimes-for-profit' (Gelemerova 2009: 39). At the same time the group of entities obliged to report suspicious transactions has expanded beyond financial institutions such as banks, to cover institutions such as: casinos; brokerage and securities firms; lawyers; notaries; auditors; real estate agents; etc. (Gelemerova 2009). For Gelemerova the stretching of the meaning of money-laundering, combined with variation in the guidance provided by FIUs, increases the risk that financial institutions will fail to fulfil their obligations properly. Taking the guidance issued in 2006 (updated in 2007) by the UK Joint Money Laundering Steering Group, Gelemerova (2009: 41) concludes: 'almost any customer from Eastern Europe, Russia or the Middle East could be regarded as a potential risk factor, irrespective of the type of transactions they undertake'.

The greater is the potential role of FUIs in monitoring transactions, the more data is collected and the more careful organisations have to be in handling it so the salient aspects are not lost in an ocean of facts. Gelemerova, after providing other, similar types of example, concludes:

> What is increasingly important now is for FIUs and other law enforce-
> ment agencies to create a more efficient way of feeding information back
> to reporting institutions. Otherwise the long awaited victory against money
> laundering will remain a fanciful and distant aim. . . . The system as it stands
> now is far from ideal. One can only speculate as to how much of the infor-
> mation that reporting institutions gather on their customers is actually used
> by FIUs. There are massive flows of reports about suspicious transactions,
> but how many of these are of good quality remains an issue. In addition, in
> the absence of proper definitions of 'suspicion' and 'risk', it is likely that

substantial amounts of quality intelligence remains in-house and is never passed onto the relevant FIUs.

(Gelemerova 2009: 53)

Asset forfeiture

Assuming the dominance of the 'enterprise model', the accumulation of large cash reserves is not likely to be the primary incentive for individuals to engage in a life of organised crime. It is what can be purchased with those cash reserves which provide the enticement. Conspicuous consumption serves both as the reward of criminal enterprise and the attractor of new recruits:

> '[m]any in Hell's Kitchen viewed [the local] Irish gangsters as Robin Hoods . . . [they] drove Buicks, Lincolns, and Cadillacs . . . seemed quite glamorous, and were apparently able to acquire anything they wanted. On a subconscious level . . . I wanted to be like them.'
>
> (Hoffman and Headley 1992: 21 quoted in Firestone 1993)

Both natural justice and economic theory (particularly the 'enterprise model' of organised crime described above) supported by limited empirical data would thus suggest asset confiscation is a potentially effective strategy for disrupting organised crime.

In the UK, the courts have for some time had the power to order the seizure of assets belonging to convicted drug traffickers. The scope of asset recovery was extended by the Proceeds of Crime Act (2002) (Matrix Knowledge Group 2007). The Act enables the retrieval of criminals' financial gains through civil as well as criminal courts and created the Assets Recovery Agency (ARA) which subsequently merged with the Serious and Organised Crime Agency (SOCA). An indication of the importance of asset recovery in tackling serious crime comes from SOCA's Annual Report for 2008/09 which notes that one in eight staff at SOCA were involved with asset recovery (SOCA 2009b). The Matrix Knowledge Group (2007) finds asset recovery appears more troubling for dealers than risk of prison. Dealers who are subject to confiscation orders described potentially losing significant sums of money which they had assumed could not be taken from them. However, progress in asset confiscation is slow and the ARA is subject to criticism. In 2007 the National Audit Office reports the ARA has, since its creation in 2003, spent £65 million and recovered assets worth only £23 million. Further, half of all cases the Agency took on in 2003/04 were still ongoing by August 2006; it had recovered assets in just 52 cases (National Audit Office 2007). Notwithstanding, by 2009, SOCA (2009b) is reporting substantial increases in the value of assets recovered or restrained.

In the USA, although many federal and state departments and agencies are involved in fighting organised crime, the agency with primary responsibility is the Federal Bureau of Investigation (FBI) (Finklea 2010). As its key analytical tool, the FBI uses the Enterprise Theory of Investigation (ETI) to investigate organised crime (ibid.). ETI involves two steps: (1) identifying a criminal organisation and the criminal activities of this organisation and (2) identifying the financial assets of the criminal organisation for possible forfeiture (Finklea 2010).

The scale of assets available for recovery

To estimate the value of new criminal assets available for seizure in the UK each year Duborg and Prichard (2007) set out a four-stage 'bottom-up' methodology.

First they estimate the total revenue accruing from organised crime in the UK. These are the same estimates described above in this chapter and summarised in Table 10.2. They focus on the sectors where asset recovery is likely to be an issue and where there is some data: drug markets; fraud (including excise fraud); intellectual property theft; people smuggling; and people trafficking.

Second, Duborg and Prichard (2007) make assumptions concerning the split of this revenue between different parts of the supply chain. They split each market into four elements: the UK retailer; UK middle market/wholesaler; UK producer (if there is one); and overseas suppliers, refiners and distributors. They also state that evidence is weak for this stage of the model.

Third, Duborg and Prichard (2007), again pointing out that evidence is very limited, estimate the proportion of this revenue associated with running a criminal enterprise. They draw primarily on Caulkins and Reuter (1998) who estimate the costs associated with retailing cocaine in the US in 1990[19] taken up by illegal business running cost.

Finally, they make assumptions about the proportion of the remaining profits that is stored in assets available for seizure. Again data is limited and so they make assumptions based on general household financial behaviour. The overall model leads to an estimate that the value of new criminal assets theoretically available for seizure is about £2 billion per year in the UK with more than £3 billion of revenue sent overseas annually. They contrast this with actual asset recovery in the UK of about £125 million in 2006/07.

Conclusion

The study of organised crime remains an area of uncertainty. Data is, understandably, limited and theory is still developing. Organised crime is also prominent in the public consciousness, permeates popular culture and is prone to media scaremongering. These factors do not make careful analysis easy. Economic analysis can, perhaps, bring clarity by helping us to understand organised crime as a part of commercial, political and social life, rather than as an 'alien other'. Economics will also provide insights into strategies for tackling organised crime.

11 Illicit drugs

Introduction

The study of illicit drugs is a wide field, many aspects of which have been examined by economists. In this single chapter it is not possible to cover all related material in detail so we are, necessarily, selective. We divide the chapter into two main sections: one examines issues which, in broad terms, are linked with the supply of drugs; the other concentrates on issues linked with the demand for drugs.

A recurring theme throughout this chapter is the lack of reliable data on drug-related issues. This is particularly apparent when we examine the supply side. Reliable data on the nature of drug markets is inevitably limited, although some ground-breaking studies have been undertaken in recent years; The Matrix Knowledge Group (2007) and Desroches (2007) have provided new insight. Reuter and Greenfield discuss this issue in a paper examining estimates of the value of global drug markets. They note that current estimates of: the number of drug users; their distribution across countries; per capita consumption of drugs; and prices paid are all 'very rough' (Reuter and Greenfield 2001: 169). As they go on to explain, in gathering data:

> The principal conceptual problem is that buyers cannot report a price in dollars per standardised unit, but only how much they spent on some quantity of white powder, the contents of which is unknown. Even after they have consumed their purchase, they cannot tell whether what they purchased was 30% pure or 70% pure, since their subjective experience with a given quantity of drug is highly variable, depending on many factors such as how recently they used and the setting in which they take it. The range of purities within cities is huge for heroin . . . Nor is the price strongly related to purity; the range of pure gram prices at the retail level is also huge.
>
> (Reuter and Greenfield 2001: 169–70)

On the demand side, there are also limits to our knowledge. Estimates of: the number of drug users in a country; the extent of their usage; and their reliance on the proceeds of crime to fund their consumption are all subject to some uncertainty. In the UK, extensive studies of those seeking drug treatment have provided fairly reliable data in relation to drug users in treatment (for instance Donmall *et al.* 2009); however, uncertainty remains about those drug users who are not known to the criminal justice system and are not in treatment. In the absence of reliable data many studies rely on some form of modelling where available data is combined with defensible assumptions in order to develop answers to key questions.

Before looking in more detail at supply and demand we set the context for the chapter by looking at the size and prevalence of illicit drug markets and the harm they do.

The size of the market for illicit drugs

Estimating the size of the world-wide market

In 2000 the United Nations Drug Control Program (UNDCP) estimated the world trade in illicit drugs was in the range of $300 to $500 billion (UNDCP 2000). However, Reuter and Greenfield (2001) argue this is in fact an over-estimate of total revenues because drugs are valued at their retail rather than their wholesale values. Even as an estimate of retail expenditures the value is too high as it uses USA street prices whereas Reuter and Greenfield (2001) estimate roughly three-quarters of heroin is consumed in poor nations in Southwest Asia (Pakistan, Afghanistan and Iran) and Southeast Asia (Burma and Thailand; possibly Malaysia). Street prices in these countries are far lower than street prices in the USA. Reuter and Greenfield estimate the size of illegal drugs market is $20–$25 billion (for cocaine, heroin, cannabis and synthetic drugs), or roughly equivalent to the global trade in coffee or tea. The United Nations Office on Drugs and Crime (2005) put the value of illicit drug markets at: US$13 billion at the production level; $94 billion at the wholesale level; and US$332 billion based upon retail prices.

Estimating the size of the UK market

The Matrix Knowledge Group (2007) summarise internal Home Office figures which suggest there are 300 major importers into the UK, 3,000 wholesalers, and 70,000 street dealers. Pudney *et al.* (2006) estimate the total size of the illicit drug market[1] for the UK was £5.3 billion in 2003/4. To put this figure into context, Pudney *et al.* (2006) note that it is roughly a third of the size of the tobacco market. Based on street value, crack cocaine accounted for 28 per cent, heroin for 23 per cent, cannabis for 20 per cent and powder cocaine for 18 per cent of expenditure (ibid.). Estimates are also made of the quantity of different drugs consumed. The quantity of cannabis consumed far outweighs the quantity of all the other drugs combined. These estimates of price and quantity were generated by using data from existing government sponsored surveys of three different groups of users: juveniles, non-arrestee adults and adult arrestees. Thus, estimates are based on a demand-side approach. Survey data were used to derive average frequencies of drug use in each of the three groups with allowances made for non-respondents. Pudney *et al.* (2006) note that, while the surveys provide good

248   *Illicit drugs*

information about the frequency of drug use, only incomplete and unreliable data is available on drug prices, quantities used and purity. They make assumptions about these factors based on previous research and combine assumptions about price, quantity and purity with the estimates of frequency of use to calculate the volume of drugs consumed and their price. The estimates were checked against supply-side data on drug seizures. Through this process a number of assumptions are made; therefore quite wide error margins are quoted. For instance, the estimate of the size of the illicit market in the UK is £5.3 billion plus or minus £1.3 billion; that is, the actual figure is estimated to fall between £4.0 billion and £6.6 billion (ibid.).

Estimating the size of the US market

The United States Department of Justice (2010) reports the overall availability of illicit drugs in the United States is increasing – the main exception being cocaine where there are shortages in many markets. Increased heroin availability is evidenced by higher purity, lower prices, and elevated numbers of heroin-related overdoses and overdose deaths (ibid.). This increased available is partly attributable to increased production in Mexico. The US government estimates Mexican production has more than doubled from 17 pure metric tons in 2007 to 38 pure metric tons in 2008 (ibid.). Cocaine shortages have persisted in many USA drug markets since early 2007, primarily because of decreased cocaine production in Colombia, but also because of increased worldwide demand for cocaine, especially in Europe (ibid.).

The harm associated with illicit drugs

Illicit drugs have the potential to cause three main types of harm. First, there is the direct harm drug consumption might do to drug users. Harms might include the impact on a drug user's physical or mental health or on their ability to work. Second, there is the harm that drug use might do to wider society. This might take the form of the costs incurred by the victims of drug-related crime, the criminal justice system or health services. Third, there is the harm that drug markets might cause to society at large – even those who are not directly engaged in the market. This might include violence resulting from conflict between rival drug dealers or the corruption of officials by drug traffickers. Economists refer to these kinds of harm as market externalities. See Chapter Two for a brief discussion on externalities in general.

Thinking specifically about the relationship between drugs and crime, a widely recognised typology suggests three categories of drug-related crime (Goldstein 1985):[2]

1. Psychopharmacological crime is caused directly by drug use.
2. Economic-compulsive crime is driven by drug users' need for money to buy drugs.

Table 11.1 Crime associated with cocaine consumption and spending

	Psychopharmacological crimes per metric ton	Economic-compulsive crimes per billion $	Systemic crimes per billion $	Economic-compulsive plus systemic crimes per billion $
Homicide	3	19	95	110
Sexual assault	24			
Aggravated assault	480	1,800	7,400	9,200
Simple assault		3,400	14,000	17,000
Robbery	700	7,300		7,300
Burglary		28,000		28,000
Larceny		120,000		120,000
Auto theft		2,700		2,700

Source: Caulkins *et al.* (1997: Table 4.1).

3. Systemic crime is crime that results from interaction between those who operate drug markets and might include violent disputes about drug-dealing territory or the enforcement of contracts.

For cocaine in the USA, these three components account for roughly one-sixth, one-third and half of drug-related crime (Caulkins and Reuter 2006; Caulkins *et al.* 1997). The numbers and types of crime are described in more detail in Table 11.1.

The harm done by and to illicit drug users

The economic and social costs of Class A drug use in the UK are estimated to be around £15.4 billion (Gordon *et al.* 2006). Class A drug users are categorised by type of user: young recreational; older regular; and problematic. Occasional drug use is not the principal cause of Britain's drug problems. Rather, the bulk of drug-related harm occurs among a relatively small group of problematic Class A drug users – predominantly heroin and cocaine users (Reuter and Stevens 2007). Thus, problematic Class A drug users account for 99 per cent of the £15.4 billion costs.

From the point of view of incidence, 90 per cent of the £15.4 billion costs are attributed to drug-related crime (Gordon *et al.* 2006), the vast majority of which is acquisitive crime. Fraud accounts for 32 per cent and burglary for 26 per cent of the £15.4 billion. The large scale of drug-related crime in the UK was initially suggested by anecdotal reports from police officers, who noticed that their custody suites were perpetually filled with persistent, heroin-addicted thieves (Reuter and Stevens 2007). This evidence was formalised by the New-ADAM (arrestee drug abuse monitoring) study, which found high rates of drug use by arrestees tested in its sampled sites, suggesting that a high proportion of crime is committed by drug users. However, this has been criticised for the unrepresentative nature of the sampled sites (Reuter and Stevens 2007). More recent research on a large and broadly representative sample of drug users seeking drug treatment found, at the point at which treatment was first accessed: the mean weekly value of drugs used was £169; 40 per cent of those seeking treatment reported committing acquisitive offences in the four weeks prior to interview; and 22 per cent reported committing crime specifically in order to fund their drug use (Jones *et al.* 2009).

The basic methodology used to generate the cost estimate of £15.4 billion (Godfrey *et al.* 2002) relies on a range of existing data sources. Class A drug users are first identified by type of user and then prevalence estimates are derived for each type of drug user using various existing surveys. Consequences by type of drug user are derived from available treatment data. The range of consequences is wide as illustrated in Table 11.2. Unit costs are then applied to the consequences where reliable data are available – mainly health-care services, the criminal justice system and state benefits (Godfrey *et al.* 2002). Total economic costs, defined as government reactive expenditure, are estimated by adding all the various cost consequences identified for each drug user type. Adding victim costs of crime and value for premature deaths to other resource costs results in total economic and social costs (Godfrey *et al.* 2002). This approach means that some assumptions are made at various stages in the process of reaching the estimate and therefore the final estimate of £15.4 billion falls within a confidence range of between £15.3 billion and £16.1 billion. It also opens the approach to criticism. For example, Reuter and Stevens (2007) note that some of the estimates used are debatable. One of the surveys from which estimates of the prevalence of drug use are derived is the National Treatment Outcome Research Study (NTORS). Reuter and Stevens (2007) argue that NTORS focuses on a relatively small number of highly criminally active drug users and extrapolating from this survey to the much larger population of problematic drug users is questionable.

The harm done by illicit drug markets

It is widely recognised that attempts by governments to control and eradicate illicit drug markets have had unintended consequences: the creation of a black market in illicit drugs and the violence and corruption this market generates (United Nations Office on Drugs and Crime 2009).

> Given the money involved, competition to sell is often fierce, resulting in small wars on the streets of marginalised areas in the developed and developing world alike. Profits are plunged back into increasing the capacity for violence and into corrupting public officials. Together, violence and corruption can drive away investment and undermine governance to the point that the rule of law itself becomes questionable.
>
> (United Nations Office on Drugs and Crime 2009: 165–6)

Table 11.2 Potential consequences of Class A drugs

Group – bearer of cost	Examples of cost
Users	Premature death Loss of quality of life – mental and physical health, relationships, etc. Impact on educational achievement, training opportunities etc. Excess unemployment and loss of lifetime earnings
Families/carers	Impact on children of drug users Transmission of infections Intergenerational impact of drug use Financial problems Concern/worry for users Caring for drug users or drug users' dependants
Other individuals directly affected	Victims of drug driving, drug-related violence, drug-related crime Transmission of infections from drug users
Wider community effects	Fear of crime Environmental aspects of drug markets – needles, effects of drug dealing in community, etc.
Industry	Sickness absence Theft in the workplace Security expenditure to prevent drug-related crime Productivity losses Impact of illicit markets on legitimate markets
Public sector	Health care expenditure Criminal justice expenditure Social care services Social security benefits

Source: Godfrey *et al.* (2002: Table 1.1).

These market externalities are wide ranging. The most obvious market externality is perhaps the violence associated with 'turf wars' between rival drug-selling gangs or the violent enforcement of agreements between buyers and sellers in the drug supply chain (or retribution for broken agreements). Other market externalities may be less immediately obvious. Reuter and Stevens (2007) provide two such examples. The first is the destabilising effect drug markets may have on the poorer communities where they sometimes flourish. In the UK several research projects (May *et al.* 2005; Pearson and Hobbes 2001) have shown the high earnings that mid-level drug dealers may generate. Although most dealers earn very little, young men in communities with high levels of drug selling may be attracted to that activity and away from education and legitimate, if low wage, jobs (Reuter and Stevens 2007). Second, the supply of illicit drugs in the country of final sale is associated with serious harms in the countries of production and transit (ibid.). Harms include crime, conflict, corruption, environmental damage and the destabilisation of local economies. Reuter and Stevens (2007) give the example of Colombia where the cocaine trade financed the growth of criminal cartels which have engaged in very high levels of violence and murder. Both the FARC, Colombia's Marxist guerrilla force, and the AUC, its paramilitary opponents, have used cocaine to finance activities including kidnapping and massacre (ibid.).

Not all of these costs are reflected in attempts to estimate the social and economic costs of crime. The work of Godfrey *et al.* (2002) and Gordon *et al.* (2006) focuses on harms which occur within the UK and which are more directly linked to individual drug users. They do not consider the cost to the legitimate sector of the economic power drugs money gives to the criminal sector. As we shall see later in the chapter, it is concern about externalities that underpins most economic arguments for drug legalisation.

Supply

As The Matrix Knowledge Group (2007) note, the facts that individuals are able to produce and sell illegal drugs and that people are willing to consume them implies that the trade in illegal drugs operates in the context of a market. The first part of this chapter sets out to understand how the supply of illegal drugs works. There is an extensive literature on this issue, not all of which can be covered here. We therefore concentrate on the supply of heroin and cocaine and in particular the activities of higher-level drug traffickers. These are the individuals and organisations which are responsible for purchasing the raw materials from which illicit drugs are made, refining them and transporting them across international boundaries for distribution within specific countries and regions. We draw on a range of sources, but in particular on a paper by Laura Wilson and Alex Stevens (Wilson and Stevens 2008), *Understanding Drug Markets and How to Influence Them*, which provides an excellent overview of the topic.

While there is much theoretical and empirical work to suggest illicit drug markets operate in much the same way as markets for other, licit, goods, there is also evidence to suggest illicit drug markets are in some ways unique and economic analysis will sometimes lead to counter-intuitive results (Caulkins and Reuter 2006). For example, it is generally held in economics that there should be one world price for any globally traded commodity. This rule seems not to hold. Indeed, the pricing structure as a whole seems very idiosyncratic.

Why are illegal drugs so expensive?

The United Nations Office on Drugs and Crime (2009) estimated the retail price of heroin in Western Europe in 2007 to be 52 euros per gram and in the USA to be 131 dollars per gram. For cocaine retail prices in 2007 were 68 euros per gram in Western Europe and 106 dollars per gram in the USA (ibid.).

Superficially, there is little to distinguish the production of heroin and cocaine from the production of tea and coffee. Indeed several studies that seek to better understand drug markets draw parallels with the coffee market in particular (Reuter and Greenfield 2001; Matrix Knowledge Group 2007). On the face of it the comparison seems reasonable. Heroin, cocaine, tea and coffee are all stimulants, grown in similar regions of the world, all subject to some refinement and processing prior to consumption and all consumed in relatively small quantities by large numbers of consumers in markets around the world. However, retail prices are dramatically different. For instance, the United Nations Office on Drugs and Crime (2009) estimated the retail price of heroin in Western Europe to be 52 euros per gram or £35.13 per gram.[3] In 2010 one of the UK's most popular brands of tea was retailing in one of its most popular supermarkets for £1.98 for a 250 gram packet of loose leaf tea,[4] the equivalent of £0.0079 per gram. This is a vast difference in price. As Wilson and Stevens (2008) note, it has been estimated that the retail price of heroin is 30 times higher per unit weight than gold.

An obvious starting point when considering why illicit drugs are so much more expensive than comparable licit substances is to look at the cost of producing opium (the main, raw ingredient used to make heroin) and the coca leaf (the main raw ingredient used to make cocaine). In 2008 the farm-gate price for dry opium in Afghanistan was 70 US dollars per kilogram and in Myanmar 301 US dollars per kilogram (United Nations Office on Drugs and Crime 2009). In Colombia, coca leaf is traded as fresh leaf, and the average per kilo price in 2008 was 1.1 US dollars (United Nations Office on Drugs and Crime 2009). In Peru, the average farm-gate price of coca paste was 723 US dollars per kilogram in 2008 (United Nations Office on Drugs and Crime 2009). These farm-gate prices are far removed from the retail prices quoted above and so it is obviously not the cost of growing, harvesting and processing the raw materials which explains why heroin and cocaine are so much more expensive than tea and coffee (see Figures 11.1 and 11.2).

Why then are illegal drugs so expensive? The short answer is because they are prohibited. As Wilson and Stevens argue:

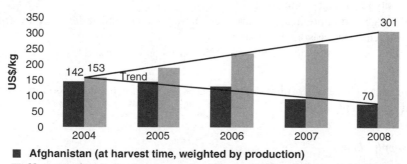

■ **Afghanistan (at harvest time, weighted by production)**
▨ **Myanmar (annual average, weighted by production, last year: at harvest time)**

Figure 11.1 Annual farm-gate prices for dry opium in Afghanistan and Myanmar, 2004–2008 (US$/kg).

Source: taken from United Nations Office on Drugs and Crime (2009: Figure 3).

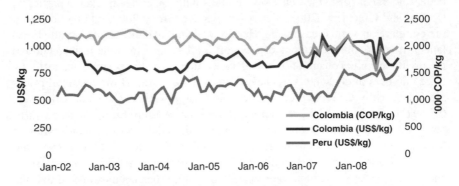

Figure 11.2 Monthly prices for coca paste in Peru and Columbia, 2002–2008.

Source: taken from United Nations Office on Drugs and Crime (2009: Figure 25).

> Prices are high because heroin and cocaine are scarce, but not in the sense that diamonds are. They can easily be cultivated in many different regions of the world. They are scarce because they are legally prohibited.[5]
>
> (Wilson and Stevens 2008: 1)

There are many reasons why illicit drug-dealing transactions are inefficient and therefore could incur more costs compared to licit commodity trading. These reasons can be considered to arise from indirect effects of law enforcement and include:

- the potentially many layers separating producers and consumers (although see Pearson and Hobbs 2001 for a counter view);
- the high cost for buyers and sellers of finding each other coupled with limited ability to advertise; and
- the high and unpredictable 'turnover' among buyers and sellers as they are arrested and imprisoned.

> (Wilson and Stevens 2008 based on Reuter and Caulkins 2004)

To understand better why illicit drugs are so expensive it is useful to look in more detail at the supply chain.

The supply chain

A 'supply chain' is the path a product – licit or illicit – takes from its production to being consumed (Wilson and Stevens 2008). The concept of the supply chain is as relevant to illicit drugs as it is to explaining how tea farmed in India ends up in your teacup. One of the things which makes the supply chain for illicit drugs such as heroin and cocaine so interesting is the 'mark-ups' which occur along it.

A number of studies examine these supply chains. One of the most groundbreaking is a study by The Matrix Knowledge Group (2007) in which a face-to-face interview programme was undertaken with 222 individuals in prison convicted of serious drug-related offences. The aim of the study was to identify and obtain data from 'high-level' drug dealers and the study identified a large number of these along with individuals who were classified by the research team as either 'mules', 'transporters' or 'storers', i.e. individuals involved in the movement of drugs, but who do not purchase or sell them.

Combining data from The Matrix Knowledge Group (2007) study with data from Reuter and Greenfield (2001), Wilson[6] and Stevens (2008) develop an overall picture of the typical supply chains for heroin and cocaine destined for retail in the UK (see Figure 11.3). They estimate farm-gate prices for heroin of £450 per kilo and for cocaine of £325 per kilo. The overall mark-ups along the supply chain from farm-gate to the UK street are about 16,800 per cent for heroin and 15,800 per cent for cocaine (Wilson and Stevens 2008). Compare this with coffee. The Matrix Knowledge Group (2007) compare the high mark-ups for cocaine and heroin with those earned on licit products to give a sense of the

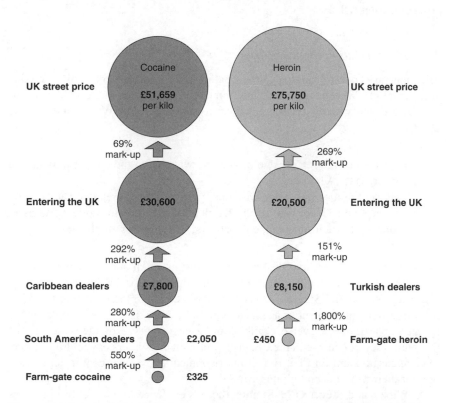

Figure 11.3 Supply chains and subsequent mark-ups for cocaine and heroin in the UK.

Source: Wilson and Stevens (2008: Figure 1).

effect of law enforcement activity on drug prices. They cite a model by Fritter and Kaplinsky (2001) of the coffee supply chain, estimating the price per kilogram as $3.00 (1994 prices) at the factory door in the producing country, $4.72 at the wholesale level in the consuming country, and $9.70 at the retail level in the consuming country. These prices suggest a mark-up between leaving the factory in the producing country and being sold in retail markets in the consuming country of 223 per cent in comparison with circa 16,000 per cent for heroin and cocaine in the UK. However, The Matrix Knowledge Group note that the difference in mark-ups between illicit and licit goods is primarily at the import and export stages. The mark-ups once in the importing country are more similar (105 per cent for coffee compared to 69 per cent for cocaine and 269 per cent for heroin).

It is interesting to note that mark-ups at different points in the supply chain vary between heroin and cocaine. For instance, the mark-ups associated with importing cocaine into the UK are greater than those associated with importing heroin, while the mark-ups associated with selling heroin at street level are greater than for dealing cocaine (Wilson and Stevens 2008). These differing mark-ups imply differing levels of risk or cost to the dealer with higher mark-ups implying relatively greater costs or greater risks.

The costs and risks of supplying drugs

The monetary costs of running a drug-dealing enterprise are very small. Caulkins and Reuter (1998) estimate the proportion of the retail price in the USA contributed by different costs. They estimate that (as summarised by Wilson and Stevens 2008):

- 12 per cent of the retail value of cocaine was due to the cost of moving the drug across USA borders;
- 13 per cent of the retail value was due to the earnings of retailers; and
- between 8 and 11 per cent of the retail value was due to product and asset seizures by law enforcement, competitors, customers or employees.

Non-monetary costs of drug dealing are more substantial and include risks such as imprisonment and the risks of dealing with other criminals which may result in violence (Wilson and Stevens 2008). Standard economic theory suggests higher rewards are required to entice agents to undertake more risk – this is true even for agents who are not risk-averse. Caulkins and Reuter (1998) estimate 24 per cent of the retail price of cocaine in the USA is a premium consumers pay to drug dealers to compensate them for their risk of imprisonment and 33 per cent is compensation for their risk of death of injury.

As Wilson and Stevens (2008) note, there is evidence high-level drug dealers take active steps to reduce non-monetary costs such as the risk of violence and that it is possible to operate as a high-level drug dealer without using violence.

An interesting example of risk-management, albeit from the lower levels of the supply chain, comes from Bowling's (1999) account of the rise and fall of the New York murder rate in the late 1980s. Bowling draws on a range of sources to describe the impact of the rapid and unstable expansion of the crack cocaine market in poor communities in New York. He argues the explosion of demand for crack cocaine in New York and the seizing by young and inexperienced drug dealers of the opportunities presented by dealing the new drug led to violent competition for territory in street markets. This was an important factor in the rise of the New York murder rate. By the early 1990s, however, crack cocaine was starting to go out of fashion and as the market matured it shrank in size and changed structure:

> The 'stories' told by police and community informants suggests that the market started out chronically unregulated, fed by supplies from new sources and involving groups of suppliers and distributors who were either new to the market or had previously traded in heroin or marijuana. By the early 1990s, the market had become much more clearly structured and organized. Ethnographic research suggests that the market 'downsized' . . . When the market was at its peak, many street-sellers were laid-off, dead or incarcerated. The streets were dangerous and the violence attracted unwanted attention to senior level drug suppliers and distributors consolidating businesses. Consequently, much of the drugs trade moved indoors to pool halls, bodegas, video stores, groceries and the like. Rather than having large numbers of people milling about on street corners carrying drugs, intermediaries were now used just to steer clients to an indoor location where there would be a seller behind a fortified counter and a security guard . . . The shift indoors reduced the risk of being 'ripped off', including murderously by other interests in the drug business and reduces the visibility of the operation to the police.
>
> (Bowling 1999: 540)

Why are drugs getting cheaper and does it matter?

The prices of both heroin and cocaine have dropped substantially over recent years. Between 1990 and 2007, heroin prices dropped by 62 per cent in Western Europe and 42 per cent in the USA (United Nations Office on Drugs and Crime 2009). Equivalent drops for cocaine were 27 per cent and 31 per cent (ibid.) (see Table 11.3). However, this long-term trend disguises seasonal peaks and troughs. For example, dealers interviewed by The Matrix Knowledge Group (2007) reported there were periodical and seasonal peaks in demand (but few, if any, peaks in supply) which affected price. A national heroin distributor described how prices for kilogram transactions of heroin could increase by as much as £1,000 around Christmas, if the high demand around the Christmas period coincided with increased security at points of entry into the UK (Matrix Knowledge Group 2007).

Table 11.3 Retail price per gram

Drug	Region (currency)	1990	2007	Percentage reduction between 1990 and 2007
Cocaine	US (dollars)	154	106	31
	Western Europe (euros)	92	67	27
Heroin	US (dollars)	224	131	42
	Western Europe (euros)	136	52	62

Source: data from United Nations Office on Drugs and Crime (2009: Figures 11, 12, 41 and 42).

Ignoring seasonal variations, it is clear that illicit drugs are getting relatively cheaper over recent years. Wilson and Stevens (2008) suggest this is because dealers may have become more efficient over time, finding ways to reduce the financial and non-financial costs associated with drug dealing. These might include taking advantage of the globalising economy to seek out cheaper distribution channels and finding more individuals from developing countries willing to act as drug couriers for less money (Storti and De Grauwe 2007). Wilson and Stevens also point to other possible effects of globalisation. For example, globalisation may lead to increased competition amongst producers and those willing to be drug dealers. New technology, particularly new means of communication, might afford new opportunities to streamline supply chains and increase the efficiency of operation.

Recall the market structure described in Chapter Two. Increases in efficiency, new technology and/or new supplies have the effect of increasing the level of supply at all prices. If demand does not change, this will lead both to a decline in price and an increase in the quantity traded.

One interesting possibility (which we explore in more detail later in this chapter) is that it may be drug dealers do not respond to risk the way we expect if they acted rationally (Wilson and Stevens 2008). Inefficient business decisions in the form of irrational pricing strategies adopted by drug dealers may have contributed to price reductions (Caulkins and MacCoun 2003).

As we have seen, it is generally accepted the higher the price of a commodity the lower its level of demand, and hence the lower is consumption. This would suggest, consumption will increase if drug prices drop. However, as Winter (2008) notes, the key question is 'by how much?' Or, to put it another way, how sensitive is drug consumption to changes in price? This sensitivity is summarised by economists into a single numerical measure, so-called elasticity. Suppose the price of a commodity decreases by 1 per cent. We expect to see consumption increase. If the percentage increase in demand is greater than 1 per cent the demand is *elastic*. If it is less than 1 per cent the demand is said to be *inelastic*.

Winter (2008) reviews a number of studies and finds estimates of elasticity for heroin between −0.25 and −1.80. The elasticity of demand for cocaine is estimated to be between −0.72 and −2.51. In other words estimates of elasticity of demand are broad and range from inelastic to elastic. In general, the greater in absolute value are these figures, the more buyers respond to increases in price by reducing demand, or respond to reductions in price by increasing demand. These figures can be contrasted with demand for cigarettes; these have an estimated price elasticity of –0.4 (MacCoun and Reuter 2001).

In drawing out the implications of studies on the elasticity of demand for drugs Winter suggests that:

> In evaluating drug control policies to reduce consumption, it is encouraging that the evidence suggests drug users are indeed sensitive to price, at least to some extent. But it may be crucial to distinguish between elastic demand responses and inelastic demand responses.
>
> (Winter 2008: 90)

This has certainly been the case in studies of cigarette price elasticity where, with more easily available data, researchers have been able to distinguish between short- and long-run elasticity and between different sub-groups of smokers.

Do drug markets follow general economic principles?

In the sections above we have drawn on economic concepts to explore how illicit drug markets operate. An assumption running through these sections is that individual drug users and drug markets follow general economic principles. Before we look in more detail at potential policy responses to drug markets we need to revisit this assumption, first by looking in more detail at the decisions individual drug consumers make and then through an examination of illicit drug markets themselves.

Drug users

Underlying much of the analysis of drug markets is the assumption that drug consumers behave rationally, a concept that raises many questions:

> Just as with any rational criminal, the potential drug user can weigh the costs and benefits of using an addictive substance and choose to consume the product if the benefits exceed the costs. Economists refer to this as *rational addiction*. But is this an oxymoron? Can an addict ever be rational?
>
> (Winter 2008: 83, emphasis in original)

As Winter (2008) explains, a rational addict's choice to consume a product today depends on how much of the product was consumed in the past and how much will be consumed in the future. When consumption in one period directly affects consumption in another period this is known as the reinforcement effect. In the rational addiction framework, a product is defined as addictive if it exhibits the reinforcement effect:

The single most important implication of the rational addiction model is that addicts are not 'trapped' by an addictive product. Instead, they make informed, conscious decisions to consume a product with the knowledge that current consumption in and of itself will affect future consumption.

(Winter 2008: 83)

The rational addiction model

The rational addiction model was first put forward by Becker and Murphy (1988) and considers an individual's choice of consumption of a particular consumption good, so as to maximise their utility (enjoyment) over time. However, the good in question has the characteristic that previous consumption affects current utility in two ways. The greater the level of past consumption, the less satisfying is the current level – this is known as the tolerance effect. Also, the greater the level of past consumption, the greater is the marginal utility of current consumption – this is known as the reinforcement effect. Clearly the two effects offset each other, and whether or not addiction results for an individual depends on the relative strength of the two effects. The impact of past consumption also varies with agent's general well-being and with negative life events, for example stress or anxiety, increasing the marginal utility of consumption. The level of 'consumption capital' measures the current level of addiction, and declines over time if no further consumption of the good takes place.

The rate at which reinforcement and tolerance change, the decay of consumption capital and the rate at which the future is discounted vary between individuals. In general, the more heavily the future is discounted, the more likely an individual is to become addicted. Becker and Murphy assume that agents' preferences are stable over time, and thus agents are rational in the sense that, with full knowledge, they choose whether or not to consume the good.

Becker and Murphy show there are several unstable points of equilibrium in the model. For example, a low level of consumption is generally unstable as a negative life event; temporarily increasing the utility of the good will cause consumption to increase permanently to a higher level; while a positive life event will lead to a decline in use to a lower level (or complete abstinence).

The model has several important implications including that 'cold turkey' (i.e. complete abstention) is the best way for the agent to eliminate their use of the good and that agents' demand will respond to long-term prices changes, rather than those which are perceived to be transitory. Indeed, anticipated future increases in price will reduce current consumption for the reason that agents will choose not to become addicted to goods which they perceive will become relatively expensive. See MacDonald (2004) for further discussion of this model.

Empirical evidence in support of the rational addiction model

If addicts are rational, then the implication is that they adjust their consumption levels based on current and future changes in their environment, including price.

Although, as we have discussed, the evidence on drug users' sensitivity to price is not conclusive, there is some evidence to suggest for some drug users, it is a factor which is taken into account. Further support for the hypothesis of rational addiction model is provided by qualitative studies of drug use. A study by Bennett (1986) based on a literature review and interviews with 135 opioid users found elements of rational choice in decisions to start, continue and cease use. More recently Warburton *et al.* (2005) used in-depth, qualitative interviews and an internet survey to research patterns of heroin use among a population of non-dependent and controlled dependent heroin users who saw their use as relatively problem-free. They found that this largely hidden population maintained stable and controlled patterns of heroin use. Non-dependent users tended to follow rules which enable them to restrict the frequency with which they used, while dependent users aimed to contain the amount of heroin that they used on a regular basis, to ensure that their use did not intrude into their everyday work and social routines. Most of the group studied were in work or studying and owned or rented their homes, making them much more affluent than typical Class A drug users normally described in studies based on those seeking drug treatment. They also tended to maintain a 'distance' from typical drug-taking sub-cultures and have non-drug-using friends. Hence they had life-structures and commitments that provided strong incentives for regulating their heroin use (Warburton *et al.* 2005).

The argument for rational addiction has important policy implications. If users are economically rational it could be assumed that they take potential individual costs and benefits of the drug use into account when making their decisions. This might imply that governments should not concern themselves with private individual costs of drug use but only be concerned about those consequences that impact on the rest of society (Godfrey *et al.* 2002).

Drug markets

Unlike legitimate commodity markets where price variations tend to be relatively small, the price of heroin and cocaine has been shown to vary substantially between and within cities in the same country (Reuter and Caulkins 2004). This insight gives us a clue as to some of the more obvious ways in which drug markets might differ from markets for legitimate commodities. Law enforcement means information about different outlets from which illicit drugs may be purchased and the price being charged at those different outlets is not easily available to purchasers. The same is true for drug dealers who may learn about market conditions through their network of contacts but who will not be able to gather information systematically (Matrix Knowledge Group 2007; Wilson and Stevens 2008). Therefore drug markets might best be understood as operating at local and regional levels rather than nationally (Caulkins and Reuter 1998).

As in legitimate markets when competition is limited, as prices of drugs fluctuate, price increases will tend to be passed on to lower levels of the supply chain (Wilson and Stevens 2008). However, whereas in a legitimate market this might typically result in the price paid by the consumer increasing, this will not always be the case in an illicit drug market. In practice it is more likely that the price will remain the same but the purity of the drug will reduce. This is partly because of the importance of completing transactions quickly and surreptitiously and therefore transaction amounts need to remain as 'round prices', e.g. $10 or $20 dollars, not $14.97 (Caulkins and Reuter 2006).

Indeed, that the drug market may further such 'idiosyncracies' is contended by Reuter and Caulkins (2004). They suggest that, while drug markets are amenable to analysis through economic principles, the application of these principles without careful thought – particularly if drug markets are viewed as being similar to regular goods markets – may lead to incorrect conclusions.

For example, one of the common tenets of economics is that supply curves generally slope upwards (see the discussion in Chapter Two). Reuter and Caulkins consider realistic situations where this might not hold at either primary production or retail level. Considering the latter, they characterise street level drug dealers as 'jugglers'. By this they mean that the dealer finances their own consumption of both the drug and the other necessities of life (e.g. food) through retail drug-dealing. If this is the case, when the price of the drug declines relative to food, the 'juggler' must curtail their own use in order to sell more of the product. Otherwise they will earn insufficient to buy food. Thus, as the (street) price falls the 'juggler' supplies more. In other words, the (retail) supply curve is sloping down – at least in the short-term.

Similarly, in the area of primary production, Reuter and Caulkins (2004) suggest that, as the price paid to the growers of opium poppies in Afghanistan increases, supplies might decline. Growers, not having access to banks, may respond to times of high prices by stockpiling finished product as a means of evening out incomes over growing seasons. Conversely, where prices are low, product from the stockpile will be released onto the world market to maintain incomes. Hence, in order to reduce income variability, lower prices are associated with greater amounts being made available – again leading to a downward sloping supply curve – at least in the short-term. Reuter and Caulkins suggest that controlling the drug at source is easier where there is a healthy banking sector so that inter-temporal transfers of wealth do not require growers to accumulate stocks of raw material.

Finally, noting the problem of prison-overcrowding and 'court-imposed caps' on the number of new criminals incarcerated, Reuter and Caulkins (2004) contend the industry-wide tax on the market imposed by authorities through enforcement activities might actually lead to an increase in supply. Reuter and Caulkins note the risk of imprisonment makes up about one-quarter of the cost of cocaine. One clear way of reducing imprisonment risks, at least in the short-term, is simply for the industry to increase output. As the number of prison places is approximately constant, the greater market size will lead to a reduced risk, per market participant.

In these examples, Reuter and Caulkins (2004) are not suggesting drug markets are not amenable to economic analysis at all, but rather to show they require carefully considered analysis. Their point is to highlight how the application of incentives may lead to perverse results. Reuter and Caulkins conclude examination of how drug markets differ from the standard paradigm is a necessary part of efficient drug policy.

Policies for tackling supply

There are many different policies that can be adopted to tackle the supply of drugs. In this section we outline three broad approaches. First there is the response of the criminal justice system to drug traffickers and drug dealers. Central to this approach is the use of custodial sentences and, increasingly, asset confiscation. Second, there are policy responses that focus on disruption of the supply chain. Third, there are harm reduction approaches to law enforcement where the emphasis is not on preventing the supply of all drugs, but on tackling the most harmful aspects of drugs markets. We draw on a range of sources in this section, but are particularly indebted to a monograph prepared for the UK Drug Policy Commission by Peter Reuter and Alex Stevens titled *An Analysis of UK Drug Policy* (Reuter and Stevens 2007) which provides an excellent overview of the topic.

Criminal justice system responses

Substances such as cocaine, heroin and other widely used illicit drugs have not always been illegal. Until 1916 there was very little control of what are now illegal drugs (Reuter and Stevens 2007). Up until the 1960s criminalisation of the distribution and use of cocaine and morphine (and later cannabis) were combined with the availability of cocaine and heroin to addicts through doctors in a system that separated the treatment of dependent drug users from the punishment of unregulated use and supply (Reuter and Stevens 2007). However, since then 'both international and British legal developments show a punctuated but inexorable increase in the level of legal control of drugs' (Reuter and Stevens 2007: 14). The result is that in both the UK and the USA, the supply of most illegal drugs is an offence that carries long prison sentences of many years or even life imprisonment.

Drawing on various sources Reuter and Stevens (2007) describe how 7,981 prison sentences were given for drug law offences in England and Wales in 2004 (Nicholas *et al.* 2005). The majority of these sentences were for dealing (58 per cent) and when trafficking offences are added (9 per cent) supply-side offences account for two-thirds of the prison sentences given for drug law offences. There were increases between 1994 and 2004 in the absolute numbers of drug offenders imprisoned, the proportion of offenders imprisoned for each of the categories of drug offence and the average length of sentence for drug offences (Reuter and Stevens 2007). As we saw in Chapter Nine the proportion of imprisoned offenders who are given longer prison sentences has also been increasing for all offences. Nevertheless, the use of imprisonment has generally grown especially rapidly for drug dealers and distributors (Reuter and Stevens 2007). As we discuss elsewhere in this chapter, that decade (1994 to 2004) has not generally seen reductions in drug usage nor have prices risen, suggesting that this increasingly punitive approach has had no impact on the supply of drugs. This is not surprising. In Chapter Nine we examined the effect of sentencing on crime in general and found that the evidence for a direct link between the use of custody and levels of crime are inconclusive. As we have also seen, evidence suggests that sentence severity is probably less important than certainty in creating an effective deterrent (von Hirsch *et al.* 1999). This is borne out by some empirical evidence from high-level drug dealers; the Matrix Knowledge Group (2007) found dealers viewed prison as either an occupational hazard or an unlikely risk.

Not only is the use of imprisonment ineffective in reducing the supply of drugs, it is also expensive. Reuter and Stevens (2007) estimate the cost to the taxpayer of the 7,981 prison sentences given for drug offences, two-thirds of which were for supply-side offences, exceeds £453 million.[7] Similar conclusions have been reached in the USA. For example, looking specifically at cocaine Caulkins *et al.* developed economic models that showed that:

> *Mandatory minimum sentences are not justifiable on the basis of cost-effectiveness at reducing cocaine consumption, cocaine expenditure or drug-related crime.* Mandatory minimums reduce cocaine consumption less per million taxpayer dollars spent than does spending the same amount on enforcement under the previous sentencing regime. And either type of incarceration approach reduces drug consumption *less* than does putting heavy users through treatment programs, per million dollars spent.
>
> (Caulkins *et al.* 1997: xvi, original emphasis)

A promising addition to the use of custody is asset confiscation, which we discuss in more detail in relation to organised crime (in Chapter Ten).

Disrupting the supply chain

There are different points of the supply chain at which disruption might take place. In this section we discuss briefly the evidence for attempting to stop the supply of drugs at source, for intervening as drugs are moved across and between countries and for disruption of local drug markets.

Disruption of production and/or the early stages in the supply chain

In an extensive, systematic review of the literature Mazerolle *et al.* (2007b) identify evaluations of interventions that attempted to eradicate crops from which drugs are derived and others that sought to seize large quantities of drugs in the early stages of the supply chain.

Crop eradication generally involves large-scale efforts to identify and destroy or seize large quantities of drugs, often involving air interdiction, e.g. spraying pesticide (Mazerolle *et al.* 2007b). Only two crop eradication intervention evaluations were identified, both involving cannabis. Mazerolle *et al.* conclude that:

There was not a lot of support to suggest that crop eradication has a positive impact on supply and availability of cannabis.

(Mazerolle *et al.* 2007b: 123)

This is not surprising. As we note earlier in this chapter, the farm-gate price of the drug is only a small element of the street price of a drug. Thus Reuter and Stevens (2007) conclude even major changes in production and seizure levels are likely to have only minor effects on the price to drug users as increases in smuggling costs can be passed on with minimal consequences for consumption. However, as we discuss above some research does suggest demand for drugs is price elastic and Reuter and Stevens note it is this idea which motivates the use of border interdiction to restrict supply, increase price and therefore reduce drug use. Notwithstanding, they conclude:

it is very difficult indeed to achieve large enough reductions in supply to increase the retail price and so affect drug use.

(Reuter and Stevens 2007: 64)

Drug seizure further down the supply chain

The interventions to seize drugs identified by Mazerolle *et al.* (2007b) involved the seizures of large quantities of drugs intended for trafficking and dealing rather than individual use. Such seizures might result from such interventions that included interdiction, investigations and other undercover operations. Mazerolle *et al.* (2007b) identify five studies which evaluate five separate interventions. The typical drug targeted by these evaluations was heroin (four of five studies identified). Again there is little evidence to suggest drug seizures were effective. Four studies assessed the impact of drug seizures on the price, purity or availability and in three of these studies drug seizures did not appear to have a street-level effect on the price, purity or availability of heroin. Neither did they suggest an effect on drug-use patterns, drug-related deaths or overdoses, treatment enrolment or rates of crime and arrest. Only one study suggested associated harm reductions as a result of seizures, reporting a reduction in heroin overdose deaths (Mazerolle *et al.* 2007b). There is also some evidence from The Matrix Knowledge Group research with high-level drug dealers that law enforcement can influence prices.

One dealer operating in the national level distribution of multiple drugs, described that the main reason price would vary is because of availability. If there had been a large drug bust the price would go up by a 'couple of grand a kilo'. Similarly, a dealer operating in the retail market for cocaine in the 1980s described watching the news to see what the prices would be like. 'If security was up or there had been a big raid, prices would go up.'

(Matrix Knowledge Group 2007: 22)

However, the stark contrast between rising drug seizures and falling drug prices in the UK (see Figures 11.4 and 11.5) suggest that seizure is generally unsuccessful as a strategy for tackling drugs markets.

Disrupting street-level drug markets

The final stage in the supply chain of illicit substances is the street; targeting distributors and retailers of illicit drugs for arrest. However, Reuter and Stevens

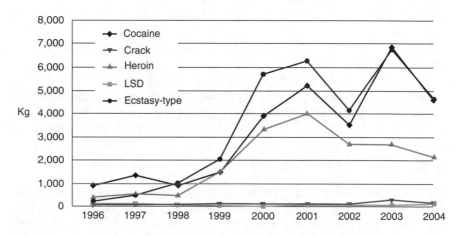

Figure 11.4 Quantities of drugs (kg) seized in England and Wales by year.

Source: Reuter and Stevens (2007: Figure 4.4), which in turn draws on Home Office data.

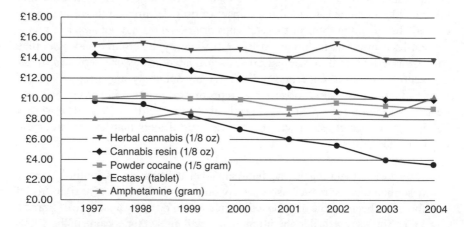

Figure 11.5 Average prices (£) reported by drug users for the purchase of different illegal drugs by year.

Source: Reuter and Stevens (2007: Figure 4.5), which in turn is based on data from the Independent Drug Monitoring Unit.

(2007) argue that there is little evidence of reductions in drug use from enforcement operations. They conclude available studies, while not generally of very high methodological quality, suggest crackdowns tend to lead to changes rather than reductions in drug selling and using. Thus drug-dealing activities might be displaced to areas outside the crackdown area only to move back in once the operation is over (Reuter and Stevens 2007). Even where police efforts have led to numerous arrests of dealers and seizures of large quantities of drugs, it has been difficult to discern sustainable impacts in reducing drug use or other crimes (Reuter and Stevens 2007). In a systematic review of the available evidence Mazerolle *et al.* (2007a) identify four broad strategies for police enforcement activities in local drug markets:

- Community-wide policing approaches which involve a wide array of diverse interventions that rely on the police forging partnerships (e.g. with other police agencies, community entities, regulators, city inspectors).
- Geographically-focused policing approaches, targeted at hot-spots, that typically involve the use of problem-solving models and/or partnerships with third parties and include a wide array of interventions.
- Hot-spots policing (directed patrols, crackdowns, raids) that involve police-only activities.
- Traditional approaches to drug law enforcement that arc unfocused and rely principally on law enforcement resources (e.g., routine patrols, arrests).

Their review concludes approaches with a strong geographical focus and which involve partnership between the police and a range of other agencies are most effective at disrupting street-level drug markets through the use of enforcement. Of the approaches they review:

> Unfocused law enforcement-only approaches to dealing with drug problems are a distant last.
>
> (Mazerolle *et al.* 2007a: 7)

Another approach is to reduce the incentives to deal drugs. A number of studies highlight the extremely low wages of street-level drug dealers, particularly when the risks of arrest and violence to which they are exposed are taken into account. For example Levitt and Venkatesh (2000) use a unique data set detailing the financial activities of a drug-selling street gang in Chicago to analyse gang economics. Their data is for one neighbourhood level gang, part of a larger organisational structure. That gang is overseen by a local gang leader, and has one enforcer,[8] one treasurer and one runner[9] at any given point in time. The number of foot soldiers[10] ranges between 25 and 75 over the period examined. At any given point in time, roughly one-fourth of the males aged 16–22 in the neighbourhood are foot soldiers. This study finds foot soldiers earn just $3.30 an hour, less than the minimum wage – thereby answering the question 'why do drug dealers still live with their moms?' posed by Levitt and Dubner (2005) in the popular book *Freakonomics*. Levitt and Venkatesh (2000) find, on average, earnings in the gang are somewhat above the legitimate labour market alternative for the poor area of Chicago where the gang is based; however, the enormous risks of drug selling more than offset this small wage premium. Levitt and Venkatesh (2000) conclude compensation within the gang is highly skewed, and the prospect of future riches, not current wages, is the primary economic motivation. As Levitt and Dubner put it in *Freakonomics*:

> a crack gang works pretty much like the standard capitalist enterprise: you have to be near the top of the pyramid to make a big wage.
>
> (Levitt and Dubner 2005: 93)

If dealing pays so little, it is reasonable to suppose that some individuals are drawn into this career solely because of a lack of legitimate and better paying work. Indeed, Reuter and Stevens (2007) report on a US study to decrease drug use and dealing by increasing opportunities for unemployed young men who are most at risk of getting involved in the trade. The study found that even modest improvements in the accessibility of jobs for young men can have significant effects in reducing drug dealing in poor neighbourhoods (Ihlanfeldt 2007). It is, of course, also the case that employed individuals have more to lose if they become addicted, and so the provision of employment is also likely to reduce the demand side of the market. See also the discussion on crime, poverty and the labour market in Chapter Five.

A harm reduction approach to enforcement

Enforcement spending by the US and the UK governments

An enormous amount is spent by governments on drug enforcement. Quoting various sources, Mazerolle *et al.* (2007b) note US federal expenditures on the control of illegal drugs surpassed $17 billion in 1999 and the combined expenditures by federal, state and local governments exceeds $30 billion. In 2002, more than 50 per cent of the total federal expenditure on the control of illegal drugs is spent on domestic law enforcement, and more than two thirds (67.4 per cent) of the total expenditure is spent on supply-reduction efforts.

Similarly, in the UK, Reuter and Stevens (2007) estimate in 2004 the annual spending on enforcement of the Misuse of Drugs Act by the criminal justice system in England and Wales might have been in the order of £2 billion. Given the substantial sums of public money being spent and the obvious limitations of attempts by the police and criminal justice system to disrupt drug markets and reduce drug use, experts in the field are increasingly advocating a harm reduction approach to enforcement. For instance, Caulkins and Reuter (2009: 16) argue 'not all dealers are equally destructive' and that one aim for enforcement agencies such as the police could be to attempt to *shape* the drug market rather than to eradicate it, by making the most noxious forms of selling uncompetitive relative to less harmful practices. Caulkins and Reuter (2009) suggest:

There are ways of manipulating the market into achieving more of what law enforcement wants (less harm) without inducing push-back by the market.

> (Caulkins and Reuter 2009: 17)

This approach is clearly based on an economic analysis of drug market dynamics. In particular, it recognises the economic concept of market externality. Market externalities are the (harmful) by-products of the market; in this case violence:

> markets have an intrinsic desire to meet demand, that is, to provide whatever quantity of drugs is desired at the going price. Trying to block that desire is like trying to sweep back a flood. But markets have not similar innate need to create externalities (harms suffered by others). By definition, market participants are indifferent to the level of externalities . . .
>
> (Caulkins and Reuter 2009: 17)

For enforcement to suppress a particularly noxious part of the market, it is not necessary to make that submarket or that selling practice uneconomical; it is only necessary to make it uncompetitive relative to other, less noxious forms of selling (Caulkins and Reuter 2009). There are at least three broad policing strategies which may be employed for achieving this form of market regulation (Caulkins and Reuter 2009):

- specific deterrence, in which police target particular individuals;
- place-based enforcement, e.g. targeting markets in areas that are particularly accessible for youth; and
- targeting behaviours such as use of juveniles in selling or use of violence in disputes.

An example of the first strategy, cited by Caulkins and Reuter (2009), is the well-known Boston Gun Project. In that case the market externality of violence between gangs fighting for territory arose as a by-product of drug dealing. The police gathered evidence on gangs' drug dealing with a view to reducing inter-gang violence. The cooperation demanded by the police from the gangs in return for non-prosecution for known offences was to refrain from lethal violence. This approach led to substantial reductions in youth violence and homicide.

Demand

We have thus far considered drivers and inhibitors of the world drug market from the supply side; in this section we look at strategies for reducing demand for illicit drugs. These include the use of prevention, drug treatment, criminal justice system sanctions and harm reduction. First, however, we look briefly at the current state of knowledge about the prevalence of drug use.

The prevalence of drug use

In the USA, the National Survey on Drug Use and Health (NSDUH) estimates that, in 2008, 14.2 per cent of individuals 12 years-of-age and older used illicit drugs during the preceding year; the most commonly used illicit drug being marijuana. Approximately 5.3 million individuals aged 12 and older were estimated to have used cocaine in the past year and 453,000 individuals to have used heroin (National Drug Intelligence Center 2010). In the UK, the British Crime Survey (Hoare 2009) estimates 3.2 million people aged 16–59 used illicit drugs in the previous year and 1.2 million used a Class A drug. It is estimated that cocaine powder and ecstasy were the most commonly used Class A drugs. Of the 1.2 million people who used any Class A drug in the last year, the majority had used cocaine powder (974,000) and around half used ecstasy (586,000). International comparisons show that the UK has the highest rates of self-reported drug use in Western Europe (see Figure 11.6).

However, despite the availability of data from self-report studies and data from drug treatment services, it is difficult to estimate the number of people who use drugs, the frequency of their drug use and the amount of drugs they consume. It is generally recognised that sources such as these self-report studies are not sufficient to generate reliable estimates of the number of drug users – particularly Class A drug users – because, by their very construction, they do not take sufficient account of users who are not in drug treatment and are not captured in household surveys.

In their UK study, Hay *et al.* (2008) derive estimates of 'problem drug users' (defined as those who use opiates and/or crack cocaine) from two indirect

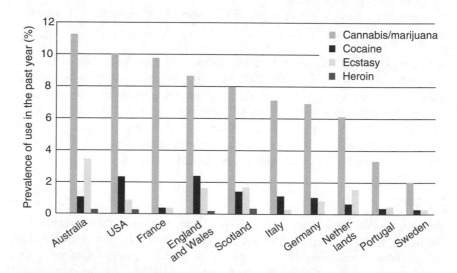

Figure 11.6 Prevalence of drug use in the previous year reported by adults.

Source: Reuter and Stevens (2007: Figure 2.5).

measurement techniques: the capture–recapture method; and the multiple indicator method. The former, the capture–recapture method, uses information on the overlap between data sources which provide information on drug users at the local level to generate estimates of the size of the hidden population (i.e. problem drug users not identified from any data source). The multiple indicator method models the relationship between the prevalence of problem drug use and readily available indicators such as aggregate numbers of drug users in treatment or committing drug-related crimes in those areas where these prevalence estimates are available. It can therefore provide prevalence estimates for areas where capture–recapture estimates are not available (Hay *et al.* 2006). Hay *et al.* (2008) estimate that there were 328,767 problem drug users in England in 2006/07. This corresponds to 9.76 problem drug users per thousand of the population aged 15–64. Of these 273,123 were opiate users and 180,618 were crack users.

Reuter and Stevens (2007) estimate prevalence of problem drug use for different countries and find that while the USA has the highest rates per head of population, the UK has the highest rates in Europe (see Figure 11.7).

Reducing demand through prevention

Drug use prevention approaches tend to fall into two categories – universal and targeted (Canning *et al.* 2004). Universal approaches are designed to reach everyone within a particular population regardless of their risk of drug misuse, while targeted approaches focus on high-risk groups of individuals or those already engaged in problematic drug-using behaviour. The main focus for the primary prevention of drug use has been young people in schools. Generally, programme

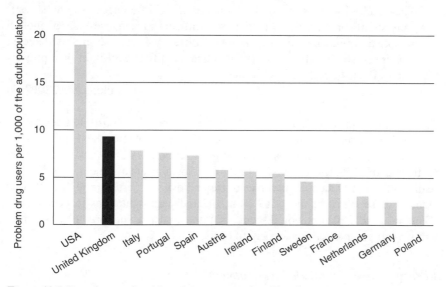

Figure 11.7 Prevalence of problem drug use at national level.

Source: Reuter and Stevens (2007: Figure 2.6).

effectiveness has been assessed in relation to so-called 'gateway' drugs such as alcohol, tobacco and marijuana[11] (Canning *et al.* 2004).

A 'review of reviews'[12] of evaluations of drug use prevention programmes for young people was undertaken by Canning *et al.* (2004). They reached the following broad conclusions:

- evidence shows school-based interventions aimed at young people can delay for a short time the start of substance misuse by non-users, and temporarily reduce use by some current users, although the effects decrease with time;
- universal prevention programmes appear to be more effective for lower-risk young people than those at higher risk;
- review evidence suggests that interactive educative programmes using peers are more effective than non-interactive interventions in preventing drug misuse; and
- information-based programmes led by police officers have not had much effect on substance misuse behaviour.

Overall, then, evidence suggests prevention programmes tend to have relatively small and short-term effects and are, therefore, unlikely to have major effects on drug use (Reuter and Stevens 2007). If, when robust evaluation has been carried out, the difference between young people receiving a drug prevention programme and a comparable group not receiving the programme is small, from an economic perspective, this raises an important question. Caulkins *et al.* pose it in relation to school-based drug prevention:

> The next logical question to ask is whether these differences that are 'statistically significant' are also 'practically significant'. If one uses a large enough sample and fine enough measurements, differences can be reliably detected that are so small as to be of little practical significance. Might then prevention's effects be real but irrelevant?
>
> (Caulkins *et al.* 2002: 1)

To answer this question Caulkins *et al.* (2002) estimated the costs and benefits of schools-based drug prevention programmes. They estimate that the benefit to society from one student's participation in drug prevention was $840 against a cost per participant of $150. Close to 40 per cent of the social value of drug prevention was realised through reductions in tobacco use and over a quarter through decreased alcohol abuse. Most of the rest was associated with reductions in cocaine use (Caulkins *et al.* 2002). It would seem, then, the evidence supports the use of prevention programmes on a cost–benefit basis.

Reducing demand through drug treatment

There is a fairly extensive evidence base on the economic case for drug treatment. In England the National Treatment Outcome Research Study (NTORS), an extensive longitudinal study of clients receiving both residential and community drug treatment interventions, showed 'clear economic benefits to treating drug misusers in England' (Godfrey *et al.* 2004: 1). For the 549 clients included in the economic evaluation, addiction treatment cost £2.9 million in the two years prior to the episode of treatment studied and a further £4.4 million in the subsequent two years. The researchers report that economic benefits largely accrue from reduced crime and victim costs of crime. Crime costs fell by £16.1 million during the first year and by £11.3 million during the second year. Health-care costs were relatively small but approximately doubled during the course of the study – not surprising as treatment itself has a cost and, while in treatment, drug users are more likely to receive health care for related health issues. The ratio of benefits to cost calculated for drug treatment ranged between £9.50 and £18 for each pound spent depending on assumptions used by the researchers (Godfrey *et al.* 2004).

The NTORS analysis describes the effectiveness of treating problem drug users between 1995 and 2000. Since the analysis there have been changes in the delivery of drug treatment (in particular the increasing use of referral into drug treatment through the criminal justice system) and changes in the population receiving treatment (in particular rises in the use of crack or cocaine) (Donmall *et al.* 2009). A further analysis, the Drug Treatment Outcomes Research Study (DTORS) continued the work of the NTORS, examining, among other things, the outcomes associated with drug treatment and the cost-effectiveness of drug treatment services (Donmall *et al.* 2009).

The DTORS was based on a longitudinal survey of a sample of 1,796 adults broadly representative of the population of Tier 3 and Tier 4 treatment-seekers in England from 342 treatment facilities across 94 Drug Action Team (DAT) areas. Follow-up surveys were conducted at between three to five months after the baseline interview, and again at between 11 and 13 months after the baseline interview. A total of 1,131 initial follow-up and 504 second follow-up interviews were achieved. Findings from the outcome study are too extensive to report here in detail but they include:

- Seventy-six per cent of all eligible treatment seekers – and 89 per cent of those starting treatment – were either retained for 12 weeks or completed planned treatment. However, 'new' clients (defined as those with no previous experience of structured treatment) were significantly less likely to start or be retained in treatment.
- The majority of improvement in outcomes was achieved within 12 weeks of treatment but the rate of improvement continued between three and six months. However, there was no significant further improvement thereafter.
- All drug types were used by significantly lower proportions of respondents at follow-up interviews compared to at the baseline interviews. The proportion using heroin, crack, cocaine, amphetamines or benzodiazepines approximately halved by the time of the follow-up.

- The mean weekly value of drugs used fell from £169 at baseline to £64 at first follow-up interview.
- The proportion who reported committing any acquisitive offences in the four weeks prior to interview fell from 40 per cent at baseline to 21 per cent at first follow-up and 16 per cent at second follow-up.
- The proportion who reported committing any crime specifically in order to fund their drug use fell from 22 per cent at baseline to 8 per cent at first and 7 per cent at second follow-up.

Based on these findings and others the authors conclude:

> The majority of treatment seekers reported significant reductions in drug use and, where applicable, offending, affirming the overriding message that treatment is an effective means of reducing the harmful behaviours that are associated with problem drug use. Where comparable, the positive DTORS outcomes are equivalent to, or better than, those observed a decade ago by NTORS.
>
> (Jones *et al.* 2009: v)

However, it is worth noting that the outcome study has some methodological limitations; key ones being high rates of attrition over the lifetime of the study, the use of self-report data to estimate service use, offending and health status and, most importantly, the absence of a control group not receiving treatment with which to compare the outcomes achieved by the intervention group (Davies 2009). The lack of a control group is of particular concern because it is possible, in a longitudinal study lasting some years, the changes observed are in part the result of the maturing of those receiving drug treatment which might have been observed in the absence of drug treatment. The lack of a control group is also an important limitation of the earlier NTORS. Reuter and Stevens (2007) note, in a later study analysis of criminal convictions of the NTORS sample, the pattern of convictions – peaking before and diminishing after treatment – is present for all age groups (Gossop *et al.* 2006). This suggests that NTORS post-treatment reductions were not just a product of maturation. This issue is particularly pertinent to the economic analysis. As we saw in Chapter Six a robust cost–benefit analysis requires a reliable estimate of intervention impact.

Data on 1,796 drug treatment seekers who participated in the NTORS baseline interviews was also used for an economic analysis by Davies *et al.* (2009). Their analysis drew on costs of drug treatment from the National Drug Treatment Monitoring System (NDTMS) and data collected in the DTORS survey. Unit costs of crime previously estimated by the Home Office (2005) were used to calculate costs of offending; other unit costs were estimated from published literature and databases. As no comparator group was available, costs were calculated for the treatment group and estimated for a constructed group based on what might have happened in the absence of structured drug treatment. The authors summarise their key findings as follows:

Overall, the net benefits of structured drug treatment were estimated to be positive, both overall and at the individual level in around 80 per cent of cases, with a benefit-cost ratio of approximately 2.5:1. Small sample size prevented the estimation of robust net benefits for sample subgroups. However, the results are broadly generalisable to the population of people seeking structured drug treatment in England and Wales.

(Davies *et al.* 2009: unnumbered)

Reducing demand through criminal justice policy

The use of criminal justice system sanctions

Society typically imposes criminal justice sanctions on those who use drugs, normally by criminalising the possession of illicit substances. However, the international evidence suggests that such approaches are not effective. Reuter and Stevens (2007) consider the example of cannabis. They note that, while much of the Western world enforces a policy of strict punishment for possession, a number of jurisdictions including 11 states in the USA and, in Europe, the Netherlands and Portugal have effectively decriminalised the possession of small amounts. Reuter and Stevens (2007) discuss various studies which have explored the impact of variations in the enforcement of such policies concluding:

- There were no greater increases in cannabis use or favourable attitudes towards the drug in the states of the USA which decriminalised its possession than were experienced in the states which did not (Single *et al.* 2000).
- Research on rates of cannabis/marijuana use in San Francisco and Amsterdam, two liberal cities with very different approaches to prohibition, found similar rates of use, although slightly higher in San Francisco (Reinarman *et al.* 2004).
- In the Netherlands the de-penalisation of cannabis use did not of itself lead to increased use, although the commercial promotion of the drug may have had such an effect (MacCoun and Reuter 2001).
- Research (Pacula *et al.* 2004) shows that decriminalisation in the USA has made only a limited difference, in part because criminal penalties remain for those who are caught using the drug even where such penalties have been eliminated for possession.
- In Portugal, the decriminalisation of small amounts of all types of drugs in 2001 was apparently followed by an increase in non-opiate drug-related deaths (from 19 in 1999 to 54 in 2003). Meanwhile, opiate drug-related deaths fell substantially (from 350 to 98). It is difficult to attribute causality in these trends to the change in drug laws. For example, the fall in opiate-related deaths has been attributed to a rapid increase in the capacity of opiate substitution treatment, and not to drug laws (Tavares *et al.* 2005).
- In Italy drug possession was illegal and repressed until 1975. That year, possession of small amounts of drugs for personal use was decriminalised,

while sanctions for trafficking were increased. In 1990, this law was repealed, and sanctions were reintroduced for personal possession. In 1993, a popular referendum took policy back to one of tolerance of possession for personal use, although administrative measures, such as suspension of driving licences and passports, continued to be used. Throughout all these changes in legislation, use of drugs tended to increase, with no apparent effect from either legal tolerance or repression (Solivetti 2001).

This brief review leads Reuter and Stevens to conclude:

> Overall, the international evidence suggests that drug laws do not have direct effects on the prevalence of drug use. However, enforcement of drug laws may have effects on other drug-related harms. For example, targeting drug users and dealers for arrest may encourage them to adopt practices that are dangerous for their health.
>
> (Reuter and Stevens 2007: 61)

In support of the latter point, they point to studies that jurisdictions with tougher approaches to enforcement have poorer levels of public health. For example, a study in the USA has shown those cities with a tougher approach to enforcement do not have lower levels of injecting drug use, but do have higher levels of HIV infection among injectors (Friedman *et al.* 2006 cited in Reuter and Stevens 2007).

Coerced treatment and drug courts

Possibly a more promising criminal justice approach is the use of coerced treatment. As discussed above, the Drug Treatment Outcomes Study from England shows positive effects and a favourable economic return on the use of drug treatment. The study found that referrals to drug treatment from the criminal justice system (i.e. referrals where there was an element of coercion) resulted in equivalent levels of change when compared to non-criminal justice system referrals across nearly all outcomes measured during the study (Donmall *et al.* 2009).

One approach to delivering 'enforcement–treatment' partnerships that has been particularly popular in the USA is the Dedicated Drug Court. These are courts which use the power and authority of a judge to keep a drug offender in treatment, providing rewards for successes and sanctions for failures (Wilson *et al.* 2006). Generally, the offender will return to court regularly during the period of their sentence and the judge will monitor their progress closely, imposing sanctions for infractions such as drug relapse or a failure to attend treatment and also encouragement to reward success. In the USA encouragement has sometimes included a reduction in formal requirements, dropping of charges upon successful completion and/or an award ceremony for successful 'graduation' (Wilson *et al.* 2006). Drug courts in the USA are now widespread. Wilson *et al.* 2006 report that, as of March 2005, there were over 1,300 established or recently implemented drug courts in the United States, with over 500 being planned (BJA Drug Court Clearinghouse Project 2005 cited by Wilson *et al.* 2006). A systematic review of existing evaluations identified 55 evaluations using either experimental or quasi-experimental evaluation designs. The reviewers conclude:

> The overall findings tentatively suggest that drug offenders participating in a drug court are less likely to reoffend than similar offenders sentenced to traditional correctional options.
>
> (Wilson *et al.* 2006: 459)

Their equivocation stemmed from the generally weak methodological nature of the research in this area, although they note that higher quality studies also observed positive results.

Drug courts have been piloted in the UK, most recently in West London and Leeds in a pilot sponsored by the Ministry of Justice (Matrix Knowledge Group 2008). Important elements of the UK model are reported to include 'specialism' (drug courts exclusively handle cases relating to drug-misusing offenders), 'continuity' (drug courts involve sustained continuity of magistrates' bench or district judge throughout the period an offender comes before the court), 'training' (sentencers and other court staff receive additional training on working with drug-misusing offenders and the drug court model) and 'partnership' (there is effective working between the court and other criminal justice system agencies and professionals) (ibid.). A key element of the model is continuity of judiciary and, although the evaluation of drug courts does not include a full impact study, there is some evidence to show that continuity of magistrates has a statistically significant impact on offenders. Offenders are less likely to miss a court hearing, more likely to complete their sentence and less likely to be reconvicted compared to a comparison group sentenced in a regular court. The evaluation of drug courts in England also includes an economic analysis. Because a full impact analysis was not completed a full cost–benefit analysis is not possible. However, the researchers undertook a break-even analysis in which they looked at the cost of the intervention (the cost ranged from £4,770 to £6,929 per offender, depending on the length of sentence) and the value of the outcomes that the intervention might potentially achieve. On this basis the researchers concluded that 8 per cent of offenders seen by the courts would need to stop taking drugs for five years or more following completion of the sentence to provide a net economic benefit to wider society and 14 per cent in order to provide a net economic benefit to just the criminal justice system.

Harm reduction

As it is traditionally understood, harm reduction is seen as a public health approach. Approaches which might broadly be classed as harm reduction include opioid substitution treatment (in the UK methadone is currently used) and needle and syringe exchange programmes. Key aims of harm reduction are to reduce harms such as deaths from drug overdose and the spread of infectious diseases associated with the most harmful drug-taking practices such as sharing needles.

Taking drug injecting as an example, Hay *et al.* (2007) estimate, in 2005/06, there were 129,977 users in England aged 15 to 64 injecting opiate and/or crack cocaine. The National Institute for Clinical Excellence (2009) reports the cost of providing health services to someone who injects drugs is estimated to be about £35,000 over their lifetime. One response to this substantial harm is to offer injecting drug users free and sterile injecting equipment to reduce the risk of harm to them and to discourage the sharing of drug injecting equipment which might pose a risk to others. In 2005 there were estimated to be 1,700 Needle and Syringe Programmes (NSPs) in England (ibid.). In addition to needles and syringes they often also supply other equipment used to prepare and take illicit drugs such as filters, mixing containers and sterile water (ibid.). NSPs often pro- vide other services including: advice on safer injecting practices; advice on how to avoid an overdose; information on safe disposal of injecting equipment; access to blood-borne virus testing, vaccination and treatment; access to drug treatment; and other health and welfare services (e.g. condom provision). NICE (2009: 44) reports that 'Overall, needle and syringe programmes were found to be cost effec- tive.' This is based on a review of existing economic studies (most of which are from the USA) and a modelling exercise. NICE (2009) modelling found that most cost-effective NSPs aimed *to reduce the number of people who are injecting drug users*. They can reduce costs of drugs misuse to society by reducing drug-related crime and reducing transmission of hepatitis C or HIV through injecting (ibid.).

Arguments for and against the legalisation of illicit substances

Having gained a better understanding of supply and demand and policies that might be adopted to tackle drug use we move finally to consider the arguments for and against the legalisation of drugs.

Arguments for legalisation

The legalisation movement has grown in influence over recent years. Different arguments for legalisation can be identified including:

- drug legalisation will allow governments to generate new tax income;
- illicit drug consumption drives a substantial proportion of acquisitive prop- erty crime, the result of drug users needing income to pay the relatively high price of drugs, the high price of which is due large part to their illegality;
- much of the harm resulting from illicit drugs results not from the drugs them- selves, but from market externalities (violence) that result, in part from their illegality; and,
- legalisation would allow for some of the harms to public health associ- ated with illicit drugs (disease and infection) to be more openly and easily managed.

The acceptance of some or all of these points has led many economists to conclude that a strong case can be made for legalising some or all illicit drugs (Winter 2008). The first three of these arguments are most strongly grounded in economic theory and argument. Therefore we focus on these in this section.

Legalise and tax

As we have seen, the market in illicit drugs is substantial. One argument in favour of legalisation is that this market could generate substantial tax revenue which could be used to ameliorate many of the harms caused by illicit drugs. This argument is sometimes linked to arguments that drug users are rational and to neo-liberal values upheld by many economists. As Winter notes:

> to the extent that drug users are rational and understand the nature of their consumption patterns, the benefits of drug prohibition may be overstated. By and large, the concept of paternalism is a tough sell to many economists.
>
> (Winter 2008: 93)

One argument against this approach is that, if currently illegal substances were made legal, their popularity would increase. The much higher levels of morbidity and mortality associated with licit substances such as alcohol and tobacco (compared to levels resulting from the use of illicit substances) are held as examples of what might happen should harder drugs become legal. Commenting on the much higher rates of death associated with alcohol and tobacco, when compared to illicit drugs, the United Nations Office on Drugs and Crime argues:

> [T]his greater death toll is not a result of the licit substances being pharmacologically more hazardous than the illicit ones. The greater death toll is a direct result of their being legal, and consequently more available.
>
> (United Nations Office on Drugs and Crime 2009: 164)

However, the evidence on exactly what might be the effect of legalisation on consumption is not clear. As noted above, studies of partial decriminalisation of cannabis generally do not suggest such a measure led to substantial increases in usage. The Transform Drug Policy Foundation (2009) illustrate the limited evidence on this debate by quoting first from a Parliamentary Select Committee[13] which examines the evidence prohibition provides a deterrent effect and second from the government's response, which seemed to rely on a 'belief' in illegality, rather than an evidence base. They conclude:

> We have found no solid evidence to support the existence of a deterrent effect, despite the fact that it appears to underpin the Government's policy on classification. In view of the importance of the drugs policy and the amount spent in enforcing the penalties associated with the classification system, it

is highly unsatisfactory that there is so little knowledge about the system's effectiveness.

(The Science and Technology Select Committee 2006 quoted in
Transform Drug Policy Foundation 2009)

The Government fundamentally *believes* that illegality is an important factor when people are considering engaging in risk-taking behaviour. The exposure to criminal sanction, in particular through sentencing influences perceptions and behaviours. It *believes* that the illegality of certain drugs, and by association their classification, will impact on drug use choice, by informing the decisions of dealers and users.

(Home Office 2006b quoted in Transform Drug Policy Foundation 2009,
emphasis added)

A second argument against the 'legalise and tax' strategy is, while developed countries might be able to gather tax revenues generated by drug legalisation and utilise them to ameliorate the harms caused by drugs, this would not be the case in developing countries:

Unfortunately, most of this thinking [on legalisation] has . . . been restricted to the developed world, where both treatment and capacity to collect taxes are relatively plentiful. It ignores the role that global drug control plays in protecting developing countries from addictive drugs. Without consistent global policy banning these substances, developing countries would likely be as afflicted by street drugs as they are currently afflicted by growing tobacco and alcohol problems.

(United Nations Office on Drugs and Crime 2009: 164)

The impact of legalisation on acquisitive crime

Based primarily on published Home Office research and criminal justice data the Transform Drug Policy Foundation argue that

It is a relatively small subset of the using population, made up of marginalised low income dependent users offending to fund their drug use, who are disproportionately responsible for creating the secondary £13.9 billion in acquisitive crime costs from the £3.7 billion turnover of the illicit market for heroin and cocaine. That the heroin and cocaine market, freed of the distorting influence of criminal market economic pressures, would likely be worth around one tenth of the £3.7 billion figure highlights this particular negative impact of prohibition economics even more starkly.

(Transform Drug Policy Foundation 2009: 5)

Based on the estimate that over half of all UK property crime is to fund drug misuse, primarily heroin and cocaine, the Transform Drug Policy Foundation (2009) estimate that the costs of crime associated with illegal drug use would contract by 75 per cent. The Transform Drug Policy Foundation go on to argue the drugs–crime dynamic would change dramatically if drugs were legalised and regulated. Drugs would be available on prescription or at affordable prices comparable to those paid for alcohol by dependent drinkers. This would mean levels of acquisitive crime related to fundraising would be negligible. The evidence cited to support this is the lack of evidence in the UK for acquisitive crime committed to fund either alcohol or tobacco usage.

The impact of legalisation on organised crime

As the United Nations Office on Drugs and Crime note, probably the strongest argument for legalisation relates to the market externalities associated with drug markets:

> The main problem is not that drug control efforts have failed to eliminate drug use, an aspirational goal akin to the elimination of war and poverty. It is that in attempting to do so, they have indirectly enriched dangerous criminals, who kill and bribe their way from the countries where drugs are produced to the countries where drugs are consumed.
>
> (United Nations Office on Drugs and Crime 2009: 163)

In a strongly worded discussion of the debate on legalisation, in which it argues strongly for maintaining the illegal status of currently illicit drugs, the United Nations Office on Drugs and Crime (2009) recognises that the argument for legalisation as a way of reducing the involvement of organised crime has some attractions but is adamant that the correct response is to find more creative ways simultaneously to control drugs and reduce crime in more cost-efficient ways. Ways to do this might include moving beyond reactive law enforcement, stopping imprisoning petty offenders and instead focusing law enforcement on high profile, high volume and violent criminals, be they dealers or users and adopting a harms-based approach to enforcement as discussed above (United Nations Office on Drugs and Crime 2009).

Conclusion

In this chapter we have used economic principles and economically-driven research to discuss and describe the market for illegal drugs. We have looked at a range of policy responses which might be used by governments seeking to disrupt the market – to reduce the supply of or the demand for illicit drugs. What then might we conclude about the so-called 'war on drugs'? If illegal drug markets behave in similar ways to legal markets then, taking into account the high demand for illegal drugs, the relative ease of production and their relatively high price, it is difficult to see a how a fundamental change in current market dynamics can be brought about through law enforcement. Wilson and Stevens argue:

When viewed in the context of a market, preventing the buying and selling of all illegal drugs is not an achievable goal of law enforcement.

(Wilson and Stevens 2008: 9)

Furthermore, established drug markets possess features that may make them more 'resilient' to law enforcement responses than other illegal or heavily regulated markets (as summarised by Wilson and Stevens 2008):

*   *Low vulnerability*: at a macro level, drug markets are able to insulate or protect themselves from law enforcement operations. The frequency of transactions does not appear to be affected by arrests or seizures.
*   *A high elasticity to external shocks*: when law enforcement does cause a disruption to supply, drug markets usually recover to pre-disruption levels quickly.
*   *A high capacity to adapt*: drug markets can respond to law enforcement disruptions by reconfiguring their structures to make themselves less vulnerable e.g. employing different transportation routes (Bouchard 2007).

On the demand side, evidence for prevention is relatively weak. There is evidence to show that drug treatment can be both effective and cost beneficial but there is little evidence to date to suggest that more widespread and effective drug treatment is sufficient to bring about a fundamental change in the dynamics of illegal drug markets. When the elasticity of demand is high, one substance misuse is likely to replace another in the market.

For a more fundamental change in market dynamics we perhaps need to look to more radical policy shifts. While legalisation might be a political 'step too far', perhaps approaches to enforcement based on harm reduction combined with widespread and effective drug treatment offer some possibility of substantially reducing the harms associated with illegal drug markets.

Notes

1 Introduction

1　Literally 'measuring economics'.
2　[1807 Mme de Staël Corinne III. xviii. v.] *tout comprendre rend très-indulgent.*

2 A brief introduction to economic theory

1　The exception is Chapter Five which examines the relationship between the economy and crime and draws to some extent on macroeconomic theory.
2　There is some dispute about the actual identity of Kautilya, the self-identified author of Arthashastra.
3　For a fuller discussion than we have space for here, see Basu and Sen (2008).
4　Economists might write this as $d = d(p)$, which says, in short, the amount demanded depends on the price which is paid per unit.
5　Economists might express this by writing $s = s(p)$.
6　It should be borne in mind that the Laffer effect is disputed. See, for example, Davidson and Davidson (1996: p. 85 and following).
7　In fact there are two main approaches to this question: positive economics, which considers how the economy works without incorporating value judgements or suggesting which of two policies might be desirable; and normative economics, which does include the consideration of value judgements. See Keynes (1891).
8　One might argue Pagliarini is not really talking about 'greed' in the usually understood sense, viz. 'an excessive desire for food or wealth' (OED).
9　In general, equality of consumption does not imply identical consumption. After all, people have a variety of preferences.
10　If you are reading this while standing in the bookshop and *not* buying, you should feel guilty.

3 Modelling criminal behaviour

1　The individual offender would (presumably) prefer not to be in prison, society at large pays the cost of the incarceration, and society loses out from not having the productivity of that individual.
2　Consider Sholam Weiss, sentenced in 2000 to 845 years in prison for multiple counts of fraud which cost National Heritage Life Insurance an estimated $450 million. After sentencing, while a fugitive, it is difficult to imagine the threat of an extra year which might be added to his prison term would have had much deterrent value to Weiss. Weiss's sentence does seem somewhat harsh when compared to Bernard Madoff's; a mere 150 years for fraud of a grossly (literally) greater $65 billion.

3 We shall see that some of the work which builds on Becker (1968) considers that some agents may prefer risk so strongly that an increase in the severity of punishment may even increase the level of crime. Becker, however, does not go so far.

4 Indeed, compensation is not even considered an issue for the court: viz. 'The assessment of compensation in cases of death will usually be complex, will involve payment of sums well beyond the powers of a criminal court, and will ordinarily be covered by insurance' (Sentencing Guidelines Council 2010: 7).

5 In theory, if the value of stigma were accurately known, an efficient sentence would take this into account. Indeed, as the costs of stigma fall on the perpetrator, rather than society, it is theoretically more efficient for society to stigmatise rather than incarcerate. See our further discussion on stigma below.

6 In psychological terms, 'closure' is achieved once a satisfactory conclusion to a difficult life event has been reached.

7 See Chapter Two.

8 The City referred to (note the capitalisation) is the square mile of London's financial district.

9 Walker claims one-sixth of one per cent of pedestrians killed on UK roads are struck by a bicycle – it is doubtful any third party deaths have occurred from people sleeping 'rough'.

10 This raises the issue whether the media is in fact performing a useful function in increasingly emphasising the more serious though less common crimes, in effect providing a societal counterbalance to the very many low-level crimes which are experienced every day cf. Reiner (2001).

11 It is not clear how we might distinguish an offender who ceases illegal activity as a result of the deterrent effect of punishment from one who ceases activity as a result of a relatively increased preference for legal activities (rehabilitation).

12 This is a necessary assumption as otherwise a risk-averse agent might choose to undertake illegal activity, even if the payout were no more than that of the legal activity, where the legal activity were extremely risky. To give a hyperbolic example, Moriarty might pocket a £20 note carelessly left by the previous user of an ATM, when he might not necessarily run out into a busy road chasing a £20 note he himself had dropped.

13 This insight is not new, of course, and is summed up in the aphorism 'I might as well be hung for a sheep as for a lamb'. Until the nineteenth century, capital punishment (or deportation) was the standard penalty under English law for stealing sheep, irrespective of the age of the animal. Similarly, the penalty of declaring criminals 'outlaw' (i.e. not protected by the rules of law and therefore liable to death on sight) in mediaeval England might well force specialisation in criminal activities from that point.

14 Less than GCSE grade A* to C or equivalent.

15 GCSE grade A* to C or equivalent and higher.

16 It might also be noted that young men are also likely, on average, to be stronger than older people or women, and thus have physical attributes which might make their success at crime (or, at least, crime against the person and property crime) slightly more likely.

17 Gestalt is a psychological term meaning 'wholeness' or 'completeness'.

18 In New York, at least, this is not a legal defence. See http://www.syracuse.com/news/index.ssf/2010/06/new_york_attorney_general_ever.html (accessed 20 July 2011).

4 Rational Choice theory in criminology

1 Taleb (2007: xxii).

2 While it is recognised the term 'positivism' means different things to different people, the aim here is to provide a very basic outline of the positivist position and no attempt is made to distinguish different philosophical or theoretical positions that exist within the broad church of the positivist approach.

3 Known variously as the hypothetic-deductive method or the logico-deductive method.
4 However, it is not being suggested that empirical research does not have a role to play. As Phillips notes:

> it is difficult to deny *some* role to empirical data or evidence in the growth of human knowledge; the issue centers on *what* role. Critics of positivism sometimes get carried away . . . and in their eagerness to celebrate its demise they throw the empiricist baby out with the positivist bathwater.
>
> (Phillips 1986: 43, emphasis in original)

5 The problem here is how can we, 'trapped' within our own minds, know what someone else is thinking? This dilemma is referred to as the problem of Other Minds.
6 This is not to say that his patients did not respond to rational incentives. One patient complained his 'trouble' had come on him again – the trouble in question being to break into, steal from and burn down churches. The rationality of the marginal decision was shown by the fact that churches were chosen as targets because 'churches were poorly secured, easy to break into, and contained valuable objects in silver'.
7 See Cornish and Clarke (1986b) for a fuller explanation of these criticisms.
8 See above discussion on satisficing.
9 This is one element of a broader project in which Garland looks at the various factors that have led to what he sees as a radical reorientation of crime control and criminal justice policy over the last 30 years.
10 It is, of course, not always the case that the visceral factors are at odds with the agents' long-term rational choice. My eating now in response to hunger is in accord with my long-term goal of not starving to death.
11 This insight, 'Lead us not into temptation', has been a useful source of guidance for a good many years prior to Loewenstein (2000).
12 The converse argument could also be made that agents, in addition to avoiding temptation, ought to take opportunities which might preserve them from transitory factors, or to mitigate their impact should they arise.
13 For instance, Johnson and Goldstein (2003).
14 Or, more cynically, whichever might benefit the one offering the choice – as anyone who has had to 'opt-out' of an on-line e-mailing list will know.
15 Mind you, they were writing in the context of investment bankers.
16 The Beirut Massacre which resulted in the death of between 400 and 3,500 civilians was carried out by Lebanese militia in refugee camps at Sabra and Chatilla. It was reported at the time the Israeli Army had allowed the militia access to the camps and, according to some reports, provided them with arms.
17 As has been noted before 'It is a capital mistake to theorize before one has data. Insensibly one begins to twist facts to suit theories, instead of theories to suit facts' (Conan Doyle 1891).

5 The labour market, poverty and crime

1 From the Greek: 'a' (without) and 'nomos' (law).
2 Home Office historic crime data available at http://rds.homeoffice.gov.uk/rds/pdfs/100years.xls (accessed 7 March 2010).
3 It is, of course, possible to search for different work while still maintaining one's current employment.
4 By 'real wage' we mean, the wage rate once we have allowed for changes in the costs of goods and services. For example, if food prices double, but the money wage stays unchanged, this will mean the real wage has reduced because workers will not be able to buy so much with their income.
5 'Auto-theft', despite the name, is not theft from oneself, but rather theft of an automobile, i.e. a car.

6 Monetarism refers to the hypothesis that a 'tight' control of the money supply is required for long-term macro-economic stability and control of price inflation. Monetarist macro-economic policies are often adopted by national governments alongside an increasing emphasis on the neo-classical school of economic thought which emphasises a market-oriented solution to structural problems. In the case of unemployment, this implies an emphasis on 'labour market flexibility', particularly flexibility in workers' real wages and conditions of employment (generally in the downwards direction). See Davidson and Davidson (1996).

7 That is to say, neo-classical.

8 MacDonald (2002) would appear to hold a different point of view on this. He concludes the decision whether or not to report crime varies with victim characteristics and over time.

9 Particularly consumption of beer.

10 Field (1999).

11 That is, adjusted for price inflation.

12 Levitt (2001) considers Greenberg's models might benefit from the consideration of poverty and imprisonment effects, implying Greenberg's results may also suffer from model under-specification.

13 Or vice versa, we might suppose.

14 It need hardly be said Cantor and Land do not necessarily agree with Greenberg's findings. See Cantor and Land (2001).

15 By 'national' Levitt means at the level of the United States, rather than state by state.

16 The first year of the twenty-first century was especially fruitful in the consideration of the relationship between unemployment and crime in the USA.

17 It is worth noting that changes in income are closely related to the changes in consumption suggested by Field (1990, 1999).

18 Office for National Statistics, Labour Market Statistics, Employment Levels by Country of Birth and Nationality (16+).

19 The improvement is somewhat slight. Compared to 1979, real wages in the unskilled sector were still 20 per cent lower in 1997 than they were in 1979.

20 The majority of regions saw an increase in violent crime – however, the increase was less for those areas where workers had benefitted more from the introduction of the minimum wage.

6 Economic tools: estimating the bottom line of criminal justice interventions

1 For instance, economists often make use of the findings from social experiments. We discuss social experiments in the section on cost–benefit analysis.

2 Economists would generally hold, philosophically, that nothing is 'free' – someone is paying. In this case we mean that the good service is not paid out of the intervention budget.

3 Generally known in the USA as 'offender re-entry'.

4 Indeed, from the economic point of view, one should continue to collect data until the marginal cost of collecting more data exceeds the marginal benefit expected from having that data.

5 The increase in your capital is slightly more in the second year as you are receiving interest on your initial £100, and also on the £5 gain you made in year one.

6 Mathematically, if we wish to discount any amount from a future year to the present, we may write

$$Present\ Value = \frac{A}{(1+r)^t}$$

where A represents the amount received t years in the future and the discount rate is represented by the letter r.

7 Thus we see that two birds in the bush should be discounted to one in the hand.
8 In practice, however, unless all the interventions have been assessed in the same way, comparing the results of different CBA studies is far from straightforward (Roman 2004).
9 This example is adapted from Blastland and Dilnot (2007: 45).
10 Occasionally it is suggested in the popular press that it would be simpler just to give the criminal £40,000 per year so long as they commit no further crime. It can't be denied this might well work on an individual basis. However, from an economic point of view, the incentive structure thus created – to wit that anyone can commit a crime and expect to be bribed by the rest of society to refrain from that crime in the future – is likely to lead to rather a lot of first offences.
11 Well, the physicist might not actually need $e = mc^2$, but it's always useful to put in somewhere.
12 It should also be borne in mind that these factors are not independent; for example, the player's blood alcohol level may depend, in part, on how much money is riding on the game.
13 Mathematically, the probability of being re-convicted in the 1st year after completing a sentence is p. The probability of being re-convicted in the jth year ($j \geq 2$) after completing a sentence is

$$p^j \prod_{k=1}^{j-1} \left(1 - p^k\right).$$

14 Suppose the (weighted) average cost of the offence leading to re-conviction is represented by the letter c and the total cost of the criminal career is represented with the letter y. It can be shown (Fox *et al.* 2010) the total expected (i.e. average) cost of future crime for a typical offender on completion of their sentence is

$$y = \omega(c + y),$$

where

$$\omega = \left(p + \sum_{j=2}^{r} \frac{p^j \prod_{k=1}^{j-1} \left(1 - p^k\right)}{\left(1 + r\right)^{j-1}} \right).$$

In other words

$$y = \left(\frac{\omega}{1 - \omega} \right) c.$$

15 Technically, the 'line of best fit' is defined as that which minimises the sum of the squares of the differences of the original data from the estimated relationship.
16 Those readers of an econometric bent may note, while the coefficients are estimated using Least Squares, which is unbiased in this context, the confidence intervals were estimated using Weighted Least Squares to correct for the innate heteroscedasticity in the random term.
17 Or, equivalently, insignificant with a size of 5 per cent – where the level of confidence and the size sum to 100 per cent. The size is the probability of finding a significant relationship when in truth the data are unrelated.
18 This is recognised by the Fifth Amendment to the United States Constitution, which states, in part, 'nor shall any person be subject for the same offense to be twice put in jeopardy of life or limb'.

19 To be precise, we may be 96.68 per cent confident – based on this data set alone.
20 Obviously if the book was written *before* the win on the lottery took place, we might place more trust in the strategy put forward.
21 To be more precise, 99.999999999999999539 per cent confident.
22 Or indeed that homicide leads to the consumption of wine?
23 Field (1990).
24 Levitt suggests it is reasonable to consider the local economy, etc., on both budgets and crime. For example, a cash-strapped local government might reduce fire and police budgets and other social services. It is the change in the latter which might influence crime rates. He controls for this by considering local economic variables.
25 In some cases the uncertainty is such the confidence interval is so narrow, it is hidden by the point which represents the centre of the range.
26 The effect of the size of the police force is not significant with 95 per cent confidence; it is, however, significant with 90 per cent confidence.

7 The costs of crime

1 In a subsequent publication the Home Office (2005) reduce their estimates of some of the sub-totals that go to make up this figure. Due to changes in methodology they are no longer able to provide a total figure; although it would presumably be less than £60 billion.

8 Crime reduction

1 This project is ongoing. The figures quoted here are taken from the project's website www.colorado.edu/cspv/blueprints/index.html (accessed 8 July 2010).
2 See for instance the Home Office 'mini sites' which provide guidance to practitioners on tackling a range of different types of crime and anti-social behaviour: http://tna. europarchive.org/20100413151441/http://www.crimereduction.homeoffice.gov.uk/ mini-sites.htm (accessed 20 July 2011) or the regular guidance documents the Home Office has published for Crime and Disorder Reduction Partnerships (latterly rebranded as Community Safety Partnerships).
3 Known between 1998 and 2010 as Crime and Disorder Reduction Partnerships.
4 ONS website: http://www.statistics.gov.uk/CCI/nugget.asp?ID=314 (accessed 20 May 2010).
5 Ibid.
6 It should be borne in mind, however, lack of evidence of effectiveness is not evidence of lack of effectiveness.

9 The economic analysis of prisons and community justice alternatives

1 Dodge does argue that prison should be reserved for the most dangerous offenders.
2 Community sentences require offenders to undertake rehabilitative programmes and work in the community whilst under the supervision of the probation service. The Criminal Justice Act 2003 introduced a single community sentence which allows judges and magistrates to combine different orders and tailor the sentence to fit the needs of the offender.
3 As economists have noted, 'In practice, the difference between theory and practice is greater than it was in theory'.
4 See, for example, Plous (1993).
5 That is to say, criminals' expected income falls as the probability of detection and/or severity of sentence increase.
6 Meaning, as criminal activities become more risky, relative to legitimate activities, agents will tend to adopt the latter.

7 It should also be noted they show that the effect varies somewhat with the type of crime. In general, however, setting aside the crime of rape (for which the incarceration effect becomes greater as the rate of incarceration increases), the 'less–less' hypothesis is accepted by Liedka *et al.*

8 It should be noted that we use the word deterrence here, not in the sense of 'dissuade (from future actions) through fear of the consequences', but rather in the sense of 'prevention' (of future actions). We would not wish the reader to conclude a community sentence is either more or less to be feared than a custodial sentence simply because the rehabilitation rates differ.

9 We discuss econometrics and their use in studies of crime and criminal justice in Chapter Six.

10 It is worth noting, in the context of the discussion on deterrence, Liedka *et al.* (2006) estimate that, had California further increased its incarceration rate in 1998, the level of crime would be expected to increase. See the above discussion about the non-linear effects of incarceration on deterrence.

11 By way of contrast to the estimated cost of one serious crime being $100,000 (Cohen 2007) based on willingness-to-pay, the Home Office (2005) estimates the cost of a typical crime of 'Violence Against the Person' to be £10,407 (2003 prices).

12 As Hedderman and Hough (2005) explain, regression to the mean involves extreme scores in the first observation shifting towards the mean on subsequent observations.

13 See, for example, Home Office (2006c).

10 Organised crime

1 Klaus von Lampe, 'Definitions of Organized Crime', www.organized-crime.de/OCDEF1.htm (accessed 20 July 2011).

2 See United Nations Office on Drugs and Crime, www.unodc.org/unodc/en/treaties/CTOC/index.html (accessed 11 August 2010).

3 This may not be grounds for complacency, however. Until the 1990s the same could have been said of the state of Israel. According to Glenny (2009), that changed after the decade of high immigration beginning 1989. See Glenny (2009) chapter 5.

4 Küster, D. (1991) Das Lagebild der organisierten Kriminalität in der Bundesrepublik Deutschland, illustriert anhand typischer Ermittlungsverfahren. In: *Organ isierte Kriminalität in einem Europa durchlässiger Grenzen, Wiesbaden, Bundeskriminalamt* (as quoted in van Duyne 1996).

5 Not all such societies have such historical roots – the Hell's Angels, for example. However, the point remains that the society itself did not come into existence purely to promote criminal activity. They have a political and social, rather than economic, base.

6 Lodge goes on to imply his nation also suffered from increasing numbers of Bohemians, Jews, Mormons (sic), Hungarians and in general, 'people removed from us in race and blood'.

7 It is interesting to note that Berthoff, writing 60 years after Lodge, implies the men killed in New Orleans were not involved in the murder of the police chief.

8 This may well be true; however, organised crime will only exist if it fulfils a role in the market, as we shall see. If a government wishes its citizens to cease trading with organised criminals, perhaps portraying the criminals as part of an alien conspiracy is a rational approach.

9 If indeed it has been a decision. As Paoli (2002) notes, organised criminal groups often operate as a 'compulsory organisation'.

10 That is to say, by market forces.

11 Of course, from a Marxist point of view, the turning from a socialist culture to a capitalist culture would be expected to increase crime in general (Sparks 1980).

12 The other two categories identified are 'business criminals' who are involved in drug dealing to make money for themselves and 'adventurers' who accept but do not fully

understand the risks they take because they enjoy the excitement or because they feel they have little alternative.

13 That the link between crime and terrorism is a constantly changing one is illustrated by the behaviour of terrorist groups since the general 'cease-fires' in Northern Ireland since the 1990s. Although presumably the need to fund operations has declined, the link between paramilitaries and involvement in criminal activities has remained (Dandurand and Chin 2004).

14 If an activity is valued at, for example, £10.00, but causes only £1.00 of damage, a clear chance for all to improve their position following trade exists; to wit, those who gain from the activity can afford to compensate those who do not.

15 The methodology used is the same as that used in Home Office (2005) as described in Chapter Seven.

16 Oils such as diesel for road vehicles.

17 Other approaches are also summarised by Schneider and Enste (2000). We summarise here those most likely to capture shadow markets for illicit activities, rather than legal activities.

18 These may range from, for example, paying a cub-scout for a 'bob-a-job' to getting a cut price rate from (say) a plumber or electrician so long as payment is made in cash, with no invoice or receipt.

19 We discuss these types of running costs in Chapter Eleven.

11 Illicit drugs

1 Defined as cannabis, amphetamines, ecstasy, powder cocaine, crack cocaine and heroin.

2 Originally, this categorisation related specifically to the relationship between drugs and violent crime, but it has been broadened subsequently to all crime (see for instance Caulkins and Reuter 2006).

3 This figure was based on 2007 data. On the week beginning 2 July 2007 a euro was worth 0.6756 pounds sterling.

4 A packet of PG Tips Loose Leaf Tea (250g) was quoted on Tesco.com at £1.98 on 22 May 2010.

5 They go on to acknowledge that demand is also important. Demand is considered below.

6 Wilson was project manager for The Matrix Knowledge Group (2007) study.

7 Their estimate is at 2001/02 prices and assumes that prisoners serve half their sentences, but with no overcrowding.

8 Whose role was to oversee gang members' safety.

9 Whose role was to transport quantities of drugs and money to and from the supplier respectively.

10 Dealers on the street.

11 Relatively innocuous addictive substances, the use of which may lead the individual to experiment with and become addicted to harder drugs.

12 Systematic reviews are studies that sift through existing evaluation studies, identify those that are relevant to the subject matter and that are most methodologically robust and then present their conclusions, sometimes after some form of statistical synthesis of their findings. Canning *et al.* (2004) is a 'review of reviews', i.e. they systematically identify and synthesise the findings from existing systematic reviews.

13 A cross-party committee of Members of Parliament which has the role of scrutinising government policy.

Bibliography

Abbot, G. (1915) 'Immigration and Crime (Report of Committee 'G' of the Institute)', *Journal of the American Institute of Criminal Law and Criminology*, Vol. 6, pp. 522–532.

Adams, J. (1982) 'The Efficacy of Seat Belt Legislation', *Society of Automotive Engineers, SAE paper no. 820819*, Warrendale, PA. Also published in SAE Transactions 1982, 2824–2838.

Albanese, J. (1989) *Organized Crime in America* (2nd Edition), Cincinnati: Anderson.

Allen, R. (2007) 'From Restorative Prisons to Justice Reinvestment', in Allen, R. and Stern, V. (Eds.) *Justice Reinvestment – A New Approach to Crime And Justice*, London: International Centre for Prison Studies.

Allen, R. (2008) *LCJB Neighbourhood Pathways Project Potential Interventions*, London: London Criminal Justice Board.

Allen, R. C. (1996) 'Socioeconomic Conditions and Property Crime: A Comprehensive Review and Test of the Professional Literature', *American Journal of Economics and Sociology*, Vol. 55, pp. 293–308.

Allen, R., Jallab, K. and Snaith, E. (2007) 'Justice Reinvestment in Gateshead – The Story So Far', in Allen, R. and Stern, V. (Eds.) *Justice Reinvestment – A New Approach to Crime and Justice*, London: International Centre for Prison Studies.

Aos, S., Phipps, P., Barnoski, R. and Lieb, R. (2001a) *The Comparative Costs and Benefits of Programs to Reduce Crime*, Version 4.0, Olympia: Washington State Institute for Public Policy.

Aos, S., Phipps, P., Barnoski, R. and Lieb, R. (2001b) 'The Comparative Costs and Benefits of Programs to Reduce Crime', in Welsh, B., Farrington, D. and Sherman, L. (Eds.) *Costs and Benefits of Preventing Crime*, Oxford: Westview Press.

Aos, S., Miller, M. and Drake, E. (2006) *Evidence-Based Public Policy Options to Reduce Future Prison Construction, Criminal Justice Costs, and Crime Rates*, Olympia: Washington State Institute for Public Policy.

Arrow, K. (1951) *Social Choice and Individual Values*, New York: John Wiley & Sons.

Arrow, K. (1997) 'The Benefits of Education and the Formation of Preferences', in Behrman, J. and Stacey, N. (Eds.) *The Social Benefits of Education*, Ann Arbor: The University of Michigan Press.

Ashraf, N., Camerer, C. and Loewenstein, G. (2005) 'Adam Smith, Behavioral Economist', *The Journal of Economic Perspectives*, Vol. 19, pp. 131–145.

Atkinson, G., Healey, A., Mourato, S. and Shepherd, J. (2001, unpublished) *Valuing Reductions in Violent Crime: A Stated Preference Approach*, Home Office Report.

Atkinson, G., Healey, A. and Mouratoz, S. (2005) 'Valuing the Costs of Violent Crime: A Stated Preference Approach', *Oxford Economic Papers*, Vol. 57, pp. 559–585.

Bacon, F. (1620) *The New Organon and Related Writings*, http://www.constitution.org/bacon/nov_org.htm (accessed 20 July 2011).

Barclay, G. and Tavares, C. (Eds.) (1999) *Information on the Criminal Justice System in England and Wales Digest 4*, London: Home Office Research, Development and Statistics Directorate.

Barrett, R. (2010) 'Disadvantaged Groups in the Labour Market', *Economic and Labour Market Review*, Vol. 4(6), pp. 18–24.

Basu, R. L. and Sen, R. K. (2008) *Ancient Indian Economic Thought, Relevance for Today*, New Delhi: Rawat Publications.

Bauman, Z. (1992) *Intimations of Postmodernity*, London: Routledge.

Beccaria, C. (1764) *On Crimes and Punishments*, translation published by Hackett Publishing Company, 1986.

Becker, G. (1968) 'Crime and Punishment: An Economic Approach', *Journal of Political Economy*, Vol. 76, pp. 169–217.

Becker, G. S. and Murphy, K. M. (1988) 'A Theory of Rational Addiction', *The Journal of Political Economy*, Vol. 96(4), pp. 675–700.

Belfield, C. R., Nores, M., Barnett, W. S. and Schweinhart, L. J. (2006) 'The High/Scope Perry Preschool Program: Cost-Benefit Analysis Using Data from the Age-40 Follow-Up', *The Journal of Human Resources*, Vol. 41(1), pp. 162–190.

Bennett, T. (1986) 'A Decision-Making Approach to Opioid Addiction', in Cornish, D. and Clarke, R. (Eds.) *The Reasoning Criminal*, New York: Springer-Verlag, pp. 83–102.

Bentham, J. (1789) *Introduction to the Principles of Morals and Legislation*, 1948 edition, New York: Hafner Publishing Company.

Berthoff, R. T. (1951) 'Southern Attitudes Toward Immigration, 1865–1914', *The Journal of Southern History*, Vol. 17, pp. 328–360.

Blanchard, O. and Summers, L. (1987) 'Hysteresis in Unemployment', *European Economic Review*, Vol. 31, pp. 288–295.

Blastland, M. and Dilnot, A. (2007) *The Tiger That Isn't: Seeing Through a World of Numbers*, London: Profile Books.

Blau, J. R. and Blau, P. M. (1982) 'The Cost of Inequality: Metropolitan Structure and Violent Crime', *American Sociological Review*, Vol. 47, pp. 114–129.

Blumenthal, R. and Miller, J. (1992) *The Gotti Tapes*, New York: Random House.

Boettke, P. (1990) 'The Political Economy of Utopia: Communism in Soviet Russia, 1918–1921', *Printemps*, Vol. 1.

Bouchard, M. (2007) 'On the Resilience of Illegal Drug Markets', *Global Crime*, Vol. 8(4), pp. 325–344.

Bowles, S. and Gintis, H. (2002) 'Social Capital and Community Governance', *The Economic Journal*, Vol. 112, No. 483, Features (Nov. 2002), pp. F419–F436.

Bowling, B. (1999) 'The Rise and Fall of New York Murder: Zero Tolerance or Crack's Decline', *The British Journal of Criminology*, Vol. 39(4), pp. 531–544.

Box, S. (1987) *Recession, Crime and Punishment*, London: Macmillan.

Brand, S. and Price, P. (2000) *The Economic and Social Costs of Crime, Home Office Research Study 217*, London: The Home Office.

Brantingham, P. J. and Faust, F. (1976) 'A Conceptual Model of Crime Prevention', *Crime and Delinquency*, Vol. 22, pp. 284–296.

Brewer, M., Goodman, A., Muriel, A. and Sibieta, L. (2007) 'Poverty and Inequality in the UK: 2007', *Institute for Fiscal Studies Briefing No. 73*, London: Institute for Fiscal Studies.

Britt, C. L. (1994) 'Crime and Unemployment Among Youths in the United States, 1958–1990', *American Journal of Economics and Sociology*, Vol. 53, pp. 99–109.

Britt, C. L. (1997) 'Reconsidering the Unemployment and Crime Relationship: Variation by Age Group and Historical Period', *Journal of Quantitative Criminology*, Vol. 13, pp. 405–417.

Browne, K. (1992) 'Deviancy Amplification, Moral Panics and the Media', in Kirby, M., Kidd, W., Koubel, F., Barter, J., Hope, T., Kirton, A., Madry, N., Manning, P. and Triggs, K. (Eds.) *Sociology in Perspective*, Oxford: Heinemann Educational Publishers.

Burlingame, M. (2008) *Abraham Lincoln: A Life*, Baltimore, MD: Johns Hopkins University Press.

Burtless, G. (1999) 'Effects of Growing Wage Disparities and Changing Family Composition on the US Income Distribution', *European Economic Review*, Vol. 43, pp. 853–865.

Buscaglia, E. and van Dijk, J. (2003) 'Controlling Organized Crime and Corruption in the Public Sector', *Forum on Crime and Society*, Vol. 3, pp. 3–34.

Campbell, S. and Harrington, V. (2000) *Youth Crime: Findings From the 1998/99 Youth Lifestyles Survey*, Research Findings No. 126, London: Home Office.

Canning, U., Millward, L., Raj, T. and Warm, D. (2004) *Drug Use Prevention Among Young People: A Review Of Reviews*, Wetherby: Health Development Agency.

Cantor, D. and Land, K. C. (1985) 'Unemployment and Crime Rates in Post World War II United States: A Theoretical and Empirical Analysis', *American Sociological Review*, Vol. 50, pp. 317–332.

Cantor, D. and Land, K. C. (2001) 'Unemployment and Crime Rate Fluctuations: A Comment on Greenberg', *Journal of Quantitative Criminology*, Vol. 17, pp. 329–342.

Cappelli, P. (1993) 'Are Skill Requirements Rising? Evidence From Production and Clerical Jobs', *Industrial and Labor Relations Review*, Vol. 46, pp. 515–530.

Carmichael, F. and Ward, R. (2000) 'Youth Unemployment and Crime in the English Regions and Wales', *Applied Economics*, Vol. 32, pp. 559–571.

Carmichael, F. and Ward, R. (2001) 'Male Unemployment and Crime in England and Wales', *Economics Letters*, Vol.73, pp. 111–115.

Carson, R. T. (2007) *Contingent Valuation: A Comprehensive Bibliography and History*, Northampton, MA: Edward Elgar.

Carter, P. (2003) *Managing Offenders, Reducing Crime: A New Approach*, London: Home Office.

Caulkins, J. P. and MacCoun, R.J. (2003) 'Limited Rationality and the Limits of Supply Reduction', *Journal of Drug Issues*, Vol. 33(2), pp. 433–464.

Caulkins, J. P. and Reuter, P. (1998). 'What Price Data Tell Us About Drug Markets', *Journal of Drug Issues*, Vol. 28(3), pp. 593–613.

Caulkins, J. P. and Reuter, P. (2006) 'Illicit Drug Markets and Economic Irregularities', *Socio-Economic Planning Sciences*, Vol. 40, pp. 1–14.

Caulkins, J. P. and Reuter, P. (2009) 'Towards a Harm-Reduction Approach to Enforcement', *Safer Communities*, Vol. 8(1), pp. 9–23.

Caulkins, J. P., Rydell, C., Shwabe, W. and Chiesa, J. (1997) *Mandatory Minimum Drug Sentences: Throwing Away the Key or the Taxpayers Money?*, Santa Monica: RAND.

Caulkins, J. P., Pacula, R., Paddock, S. and Chiesa, J. (2002) *School-Based Drug Prevention: What Kind of Drug Use Does it Prevent?*, Santa Monica: RAND.

Chambers, M., Ullmann, B. and Waller, I. (2009) *Less Crime, Lower Costs Implementing Effective Early Crime Reduction Programmes in England and Wales*, London: Policy Exchange.

Chatterjee, J. (2005) *The Changing Structure of Organized Crime Groups*, Ottawa: Royal Canadian Mounted Police.

Cheloukhine, S. (2008) 'The Roots of Russian Organized Crime: From Old-Fashioned

Professionals to the Organized Criminal Groups of Today', *Crime Law Social Change*, Vol. 50, pp. 353–374.

Chiricos, T. (1987) 'Rates of Crime and Unemployment: An Analysis of Aggregate Research Evidence', *Social Problems*, Vol. 34, pp. 187–211.

Chou, S.-Y., Grossman, M. and Saffer, H. (2004). 'An Economic Analysis of Adult Obesity: Results from the Behavioral Risk Factor Surveillance System', *Journal of Health Economics*, Vol. 23(3), pp. 565–587.

Clarke, K. (2010) *The Government's Vision for Criminal Justice Reform*, Speech to Centre for Crime and Justice Studies, 30 June, London: Ministry of Justice.

Clarke, R. (1992) *Situational Crime Prevention: Successful Case Studies*, New York: Harrow and Heston.

Clarke, R. (1995) 'Situational Crime Prevention', in Tonry, M. and Farrington, D. P. (Eds.) *Building a Safer Society: Crime and Justice: A Review of Research, Vol. 19*, Chicago: University of Chicago Press.

Clarke, R. (2005) 'Seven Misconceptions of Situational Crime Prevention', in Tilley, N. (Ed.) *Handbook of Crime Prevention and Community Safety*, Cullompton: Willan.

Clarke, R. and Eck, J. (2004) *Crime Analysis for Problem Solvers: In 60 Small Steps*, Washington DC: US Department of Justice, Office of Community Oriented Policing Services.

Cohen, M. A. (2000) 'Measuring the Costs and Benefits of Crime and Justice', in *Vol. 4: Measurement and Analysis of Crime and Justice*, Washington DC: National Institute of Justice, NCJ.

Cohen, M. A. (2007) *Valuing Crime Control Benefits Using Stated Preference Approaches*, paper prepared for a workshop on 'Cost-Benefit Analysis and Crime Control', 20 November 2006, sponsored by the National Institute of Justice, Home Office, Urban Institute Justice Policy Center and Matrix Research and Consultancy.

Cohen, M. A., Rust, R. T., Steen, S. and Tidd, S. T. (2004) 'Willingness-to-Pay for Crime Control Programs', *Criminology*, Vol. 42, pp. 89–109.

Cohen, S. (1972) *Folk Devils and Moral Panics*, London: Paladin.

Coleman, K., Kaiza, P., Hoare, J. and Jansson, K. (2008) *Homicides, Firearm Offences and Intimate Violence 2006/07 (Supplementary Volume 2 to Crime in England and Wales 2006/07)*, London: Home Office Statistical Bulletin 03/08.

Commission on English Prisons Today (2009) *Do Better Do Less: The Report of the Commission on English Prisons Today*, London: The Howard League for Penal Reform.

Conan Doyle, A. (1891) 'A Scandal in Bohemia', *The Strand Magazine*, London, July.

The Conservative Party (2009) *Prisons with a Purpose: Our Sentencing and Rehabilitation Revolution to Break the Cycle of Crime*, London: The Conservative Party.

Cook, P. J. and Ludwig, J. (2000) *Gun Violence: The Real Costs*, Oxford: Oxford University Press.

Cook, P. J. and Zarkin, G. A. (1985) 'Crime and the Business Cycle', *Journal of Legal Studies*, Vol. 14, pp. 115–128.

Cook, T. and Campbell, D. (1979) *Quasi-experimental Design and Analysis Issues for Field Settings*, Boston: Houghton Mifflin Company.

Corman, H. and Mocan, H. N. (2000) 'A Time-Series Analysis of Crime, Deterrence and Drug Abuse in New York City', *American Economic Review*, Vol. 90, pp. 584–604.

Cornish, D. and Clarke, R. (Eds.) (1986a) *The Reasoning Criminal*, New York: Springer-Verlag.

Cornish, D. and Clarke, R. (1986b) 'Situational Prevention, Displacement of Crime and Rational Choice Theory', in Heal, K. and Laycock, G. (Eds.) *Situational Crime Prevention: From Theory into Practice*, London: HMSO, pp. 1–16.

The Council of State Governments (undated) *Justice Reinvestment*, briefing paper downloaded from www.justicereinvestment.org (accessed 1 June 2010).

Crawford, A. (1997) *The Local Governance of Crime: Appeals to Community and Partnerships*, Oxford: Oxford University Press.

Crawford, A. (1998) *Crime Prevention and Community Safety: Politics, Policies and Practice*, London: Longman.

Cressey, D. (1969) *Theft of the Nation: The Structure and Operations of Organised Crime in America*, New York: Harper and Row.

Dahlberg, M. and Gustavsson, M. (2008) 'Inequality and Crime: Separating the Effects of Permanent and Transitory Income', *Oxford Bulletin of Economics and Statistics*, Vol. 70, pp. 129–153.

The Daily Telegraph (2009) 'British Policing "Has Lost Its Way in Target Culture"', 26 November.

Dalrymple T, (1994) 'The Knife Went In', *City Journal*, Autumn, www.city-journal.org/printable.php?id=1371 (accessed 20 July 2011).

Dalrymple, T. (2008) *Not With a Bang But a Whimper: The Politics & Culture of Decline*, Wolvey: Monday Books.

Dandurand, Y. and Chin, V. (2004) *Links between Terrorism and Other Forms of Crime*, Report to Foreign Affairs Canada and The United Nations Office on Drugs and Crime, Vancouver.

Davidson, G. and Davidson, P. (1996) *Economics for a Civilized Society* (2nd Edition), London: Macmillan.

Davies, L., Jones, A., Vamvakas, G., Dubourg, R. and Donmall, M. (2009) *The Drug Treatment Outcomes Research Study: Cost Effectiveness Analysis*, London: Home Office.

Dawson, P. and Stanko, B. (2010) *An Evaluation of the Diamond Initiative: Year One Findings*, London: Metropolitan Police Service/London Criminal Justice Partnership.

De Boer, L. and Seeborg, M. (1984) 'The Female–Male Unemployment Differential: Effects of Changes in Industry Employment', *Monthly Labor Review*, Vol. 107, pp. 8–15.

De Sardan, J. P. O. (1999) 'A Moral Economy of Corruption in Africa?', *The Journal of Modern African Studies*, Vol. 37, pp. 25–52.

Delfs, R. (1991) 'Feeding the System', *Far Eastern Economic Review*, Vol. 21, pp. 228–230.

Desroches, F.J. (2007) 'Research on Upper Level Drug Trafficking: A Review', *Journal of Drug Issues*, Vol. 7(4), pp. 827–844.

Devine, J. A., Sheley, J. F. and Smith, M. D. (1988) 'Macroeconomic and Social-Control Policy Influences on Crime Rate Changes, 1948–1985', *American Sociological Review*, Vol. 53, pp.407–420.

Dhiri, S. and Brand, S. (1999) 'Analysis of Costs and Benefits: Guidance for Evaluators', *Crime Reduction Programme – Guidance Note 1*, London: Home Office.

Dickens, R. and Manning, A. (2004) 'Has the National Minimum Wage Reduced UK Wage Inequality?', *Journal of the Royal Statistical Society. Series A (Statistics in Society)*, Vol. 167, pp. 613–626.

DiIulio, J. (1996) 'Help Wanted: Economists, Crime, and Public Policy', *Journal of Economic Perspectives*, Vol. 10, pp. 1–23.

Ditton, J., Chadee, D., Farrall, S., Gilchrist, E. and Bannister, J. (2004) 'From Imitation to Intimidation: A Note on the Curious and Changing Relationship Between the Media, Crime and Fear of Crime', *The British Journal of Criminology*, Vol. 44, pp. 595–610.

Dodge, C. R. (1979) *A World Without Prisons: Alternatives to Incarceration Throughout the World*, Lexington, MA: Lexington Books.

Dolan, P. and Peasgood, T. (2007) 'Estimating the Economic and Social Costs of the Fear of Crime', *The British Journal of Criminology*, Vol. 47, pp. 121–132.

Dolan, P., Loomes, G., Peasgood, T. and Tsuchiya, A. (2005) 'Estimating the Intangible Victim Costs of Violent Crime', *The British Journal of Criminology*, Vol. 45, pp. 958–976.

Donmall, M., Jones, A., Davies, L. and Barnard, M. (2009) *Summary of Key Findings from the Drug Treatment Outcomes Research Study (DTORS)*, London: Home Office.

Dorn, N., Levi, M. and King, L. (2005) *Literature Review on Upper Level Drug Trafficking, Home Office Online Report 22/05*, London: Home Office.

Downes, D. and Rock, P. (1995) *Understanding Deviance: A Guide to the Sociology of Crime and Rule Breaking*, Oxford: Oxford University Press.

Doyal, L. and Gough, I. (1991) *A Theory of Human Needs*, London; Macmillan.

Drummond, M., Sculpher, M., Torrance, G., O'Brien, B. and Stoddart, G. (2005) *Methods for the Economic Evaluation of Health Care Programmes* (3rd Edition), Oxford: Oxford University Press.

Duborg, R. and Prichard, S. (2007) *Organised Crime: Revenues, Economic and Social Costs, and Criminal Assets Available for Seizure*, London: Home Office.

Duclos, J.-Y., Esteban, J. and Ray, D. (2004) 'Polarization: Concepts, Measurement, Estimation', *Econometrica*, Vol. 72, pp. 1737–1772.

Duffy, B., Wake, R., Burrows, T. and Bremner, P. (2007) *Closing the Gaps – Crime and Public Perceptions*, London: Ipsos Mori.

Durkheim, É. (1893) *The Division of Labour in Society* (translated by Halls, W. D., 1984), New York: The Free Press.

Edin, K. and Reed, J. M. (2005) 'Why Don't They Just Get Married? Barriers to Marriage among the Disadvantaged', *The Future of Children*, Vol. 15, pp. 117–137.

Egmont Group (2003) *Information Paper on Financial Intelligence Units and the Egmont Group*, September.

Ehrlich, I. (1973) 'Participation in Illegitimate Activities: A Theoretical and Empirical Investigation', *The Journal of Political Economy*, Vol. 81(3), pp. 521–565.

Eide, E. (1999) 'The Economics of Criminal Behaviour', in Bouckaert, B. and De Geest, G. (Eds.) *Encyclopedia of Law and Economics, V. The Economics of Crime and Litigation*, Cheltenham: Edward Elgar.

Ekblom, P. (2000) 'The Conjunction of Criminal Opportunity', in Ballintyne, S., Pease, K. and McLaren, V. (Eds.) *Secure Foundations: Key Issues in Crime Prevention, Crime Reduction and Community Safety*, London: IPPR.

Elvick, R. (2001) *Cost-Benefit Analysis of Police Enforcement, Working Paper 1*, The 'Escape' Project.

Entorf, H. and Spengler, H. (2000) 'Socioeconomic and Demographic Factors of Crime in Germany: Evidence From Panel Data of the German States', *International Review of Law and Economics*, Vol. 20, pp. 75–106.

Euwals, R. and Hogerbrugge, M. (2004) 'Explaining the Growth of Part-Time Employment: Factors of Supply and Demand', *IZA Discussion Paper No. 1124*, April.

Farrall, S. and Gadd D. (2004, unpublished) 'Evaluating Crime Fears: A Research Note on a Pilot Study to Improve the Measurement of the "Fear of Crime" as a Performance Indicator', unpublished paper, Department of Criminology, Keele University.

Farrington, D. P. (1997) 'Human Development and Criminal Careers', in Maguire, M., Morgan, R. and Reiner, R. (Eds.) *Oxford Handbook of Criminology* (2nd Edition), Oxford: Oxford University Press.

Farrington, D. P. (2003) 'Methodological Quality Standards for Evaluation Research', *The ANNALS of the American Academy of Political and Social Science*, Vol. 587(1), pp. 49–68.

Farrington, D. P. (2007) 'Childhood Risk Factors and Risk-Focussed Prevention', in Maguire, M., Morgan, R. and Reiner, R. (Eds.) *The Oxford Handbook of Criminology* (4th Edition), Oxford: Oxford University Press.

Farrington, D. P. and Jolliffe, D. (2002) *A Feasibility Study into Using a Randomised Controlled Trial to Evaluate Treatment Pilots at HMP Whitemoor, Home Office Online Report 14/02*, London: Home Office.

Felson, M. (1986) 'Linking Criminal Choices', in Cornish, D. and Clarke, R. (Eds.) *The Reasoning Criminal*, New York: Springer-Verlag, pp. 119–128.

Felson, M. (1994) *Crime and Everyday Life: Insights and Implications for Society*, London: Pine Forge Press.

Felson, M. (1995) 'Those Who Discourage Crime', in Eck, J. and Weisburd, D. (Eds.) *Crime and Place: Crime Prevention Studies*, Vol. 4, Monsey, NY: Criminal Justice Press.

Field, S. (1990) *Trends in Crime and Their Interpretation: A Study of Recorded Crime in Post-War England and Wales, Home Office Research Study No. 119*, London: Home Office.

Field, S. (1999) *Trends in Crime Revisited, Home Office Research Study No. 195*, London: Home Office.

Fielding, N., Clarke, A. and Witt, R. (Eds.) (2000) *The Economic Dimensions of Crime*, Basingstoke: Macmillan.

Fijnaut, C., Bovenkerk, F., Bruinsma, G. and van de Bunt, H. (1998) *Organized Crime in the Netherlands*, The Hague: Kluwer Law International.

Finklea, K. (2010) *Organized Crime in the United States: Trends and Issues for Congress*, Washington, DC: Congressional Research Service.

Firestone, T. A. (1993) 'Mafia Memoirs: What They Tell Us About Organized Crime', *Journal of Contemporary Criminal Justice*, Vol. 197, pp. 197–220.

Fisman, R. and Miguel, E. (2008) 'Corruption, Norms, and Legal Enforcement: Evidence from Diplomatic Parking Tickets', *Journal of Political Economy*, Vol. 115(6), pp. 1020–1048.

Fox, C. and Albertson, A. (2010) 'Could Economics Solve the Prisons Crisis?', *The Probation Journal*, Vol. 57(3), pp. 263–280.

Fox, C., Williams, P., Albertson, K., Provan, A. and Woods, A. (2010) *Interim Findings from the Evaluation of Choose Change*, Manchester: Manchester Metropolitan University.

Friedman, M. (1968) 'The Role of Monetary Policy', *American Economic Review*, Vol. 58, pp. 1–21.

Friedman, S., Cooper, H., Tempalski, B., Keem, M., Friedman, R., Flom, P. and Des Jarlais, D. (2006) 'Relationships of Deterrence and Law Enforcement to Drug-Related Harms Among Drug Injectors in US Metropolitan Areas', *AIDS*, Vol. 20(1), pp. 93–99.

Fritter, R. and Kaplinsky, R. (2001) 'Who Gains From Product Rents as the Coffee Market Becomes More Differentiated? A Value Chain Analysis', *Institute of Development Studies Bulletin Paper*, University of Sussex.

Galvan, A., Hare, T., Voss, H., Glover, G. and Casey, B. (2007) 'Risk-Taking and the Adolescent Brain: Who is at Risk?' *Developmental Science*, Vol. 10, pp. F8–F14.

Garland, D. (1996) 'The Limits of the Sovereign State: Strategies of Crime Control In Contemporary Society', *The British Journal of Criminology*, Vol. 36(4), pp. 445–471.

Garland, D. (2001) *The Culture of Control: Crime and Social Order in Contemporary Society*, Oxford: Oxford University Press.

Gelemerova, L. (2009) 'On the Frontline Against Money-Laundering: The Regulatory Minefield', *Crime Law and Social Change*, Vol. 52, pp. 33–55.

Giddens, A. (1998) *The Third Way: The Renewal of Social Democracy*, Cambridge: Polity.

Giles, D. E. A. (1999) 'Measuring the Hidden Economy: Implications for Econometric Modelling', *The Economic Journal*, Vol. 109, pp. F370–F380.

Gilling, D. (1997) *Crime Prevention: Theory, Practice and Politics*, London: University College London Press.

Glaeser, E., Sacerdote, B. and Scheinkman, J. (1996) 'Crime and Social Interactions', *The Quarterly Journal of Economics*, Vol. 111, pp. 507–548.

Glenny, M. (2009) *McMafia: Seriously Organised Crime*, London: Vintage.

Godfrey, C., Eaton, G., McDougall, C. and Culyer, A. (2002) *The Economic and Social Costs of Class A Drug Use in England and Wales, 2000, Home Office Research Study 249*, London: Home Office.

Godfrey, C., Stewart, D. and Gossop, M. (2004) 'Economic Analysis of Costs and Consequences of the Treatment of Drug Misuse: 2-Year Outcome Data from the National Treatment Outcome Research Study (NTORS)', *Addiction*, Vol. 99, pp. 697–707.

Goldblatt, P. and Lewis, C. (Eds.) (1998) *Reducing Offending: An Assessment of Research Evidence on Ways of Dealing With Offending Behaviour, Home Office Research Study 187*, London: Home Office.

Goldstein, P. J. (1985). 'The Drugs/Violence Nexus: A Tripartite Conceptual Framework', *Journal of Drug Issues*, Vol. 39, pp. 143–174.

Gordon, L., Tinsley, L., Godfrey, C. and Parrott, S. (2006) 'The Economic and Social Costs of Class A Drug Use in England and Wales, 2003/4', in Singleton, N., Murray, R. and Tinsley, L. (Eds.) *Measuring Different Aspects of Problem Drug Use: Methodological Developments, Home Office Online Report 16/06*, London: Home Office.

Gossop, M., Trakada, K., Stewart, D. and Witton, J. (2006). 'Levels of Conviction Following Drug Treatment: Linking Data from the National Treatment Outcome Research Study and the Offenders Index', *Home Office Findings 275*, London: Home Office.

Gottfredson, M. R. and Hirschi, T. (1990) *A General Theory of Crime*, California: Stanford University Press.

Gould, E. D., Weinberg, B. A. and Mustard, D. B. (2002) 'Crime Rates and Local Labor Market Opportunities in the United States: 1979–1997', *The Review of Economics and Statistics*, Vol. 84, pp. 45–61.

Government Social Research Unit (2007) *Background Paper 7 – Why Do Social Experiments? Experiments and Quasi-Experiments for Evaluating Government Policies and Programmes*, London: Cabinet Office.

Granger, C. W. J. (1980) 'Testing for Causality: A Personal Viewpoint', *Journal of Economic Dynamic Control*, Vol. 2, pp. 329–352.

Gray, T., and Olson, K. W. (1989) 'A Cost Benefit Analysis of the Sentencing Decision for Burglars', *Social Science Quarterly*, Vol. 70, pp. 708–722.

Green, D. P., Glaser, J. and Rich, A. (1998) 'From Lynching to Gay Bashing: The Elusive Connection Between Economic Conditions and Hate Crime', *Journal of Personality and Social Psychology*, Vol. 75, pp. 82–92.

Greenberg, D. F. (2001) 'Time Series Analysis of Crime Rates', *Journal of Quantitative Criminology*, Vol. 17, pp. 291–327.

Grogger, J. (1998) 'Market Wages and Youth Crime', *Journal of Labor and Economics*, Vol. 16, pp. 756–791.

Groot, W. and Van Den Brink, H. (2007) 'The Effects of Education on Crime', *Applied Economics*, pp. 1–11.

Grünhut, M. (1952) 'Probation in Germany', *Howard Journal*, Vol. 8, pp. 168–174.

The Guardian (2002) 'Heads, Belgium Wins – and Wins', 4 October.

The Guardian (2005) 'Concern Over Rise of "Happy Slapping" Craze', 26 April.

The Guardian (2010a) 'Why Do Police Target Cyclists Who Jump Red Lights?', 16 April.

The Guardian (2010b) 'Police Chief Backs Scheme That Aids Ex-Prisoners and Cuts Reoffending', 13 July.

Hale, C. (1998) 'Crime and Business Cycle in Post-War Britain Revisited', *British Journal of Criminology*, Vol. 38(4), pp. 681–698.

Hale, C. (2009) 'Economic Marginalisation, Social Exclusion, and Crime', in Hale, C., Hayward, K., Wahidin, A. and Wincup, E. (Eds.) *Criminology* (2nd Edition), Oxford: Oxford University Press.

Halpern, D. S. (2001) 'Morals, Social Trust and Inequality: Can Values Explain Crime?', *British Journal of Criminology*, Vol. 41, pp. 236–251.

Hansen, K. (2003) *Male Crime and Rising Female Employment*, London: Centre for Longitudinal Studies, Institute of Education, University of London.

Hansen, K. and Machin, S. (2002) 'Spatial Crime Patterns and the Introduction of the UK Minimum Wage', *Oxford Bulletin of Economics and Statistics*, Vol. 64, pp. 677–698.

Hargreaves Heap, S., Hollis, M., Lyons, B., Sugden, R. and Weale, R. (1992) *The Theory of Choice: A Critical Guide*, Oxford: Blackwell.

Harper, G. and Chitty, C. (Eds.) (2005) *The Impact of Corrections on Re-offending: A Review of 'What Works'*, Home Office Research Study 291, London: Home Office http://www.homeoffice.gov.uk/rds/pdfs04/hors291.pdf (accessed 25 March 2010).

Harsanyi, J. (1955) 'Cardinal Welfare, Individualistic Ethics, and Interpersonal Comparisons of Utility', *Journal of Political Economy*, Vol. 63, pp. 309–321.

Haskell, W., Lee, I., Pate, R., Powell, K., Blair, S., Franklin, B., Macera, C., Heath, G., Thompson, P. and Bauman, A. (2007) 'Physical Activity and Public Health: Updated Recommendation for Adults from the American College of Sports Medicine and the American Heart Association', *Circulation*, Vol. 116, pp. 1081–1093.

Hay, G., Gannon, M., MacDougall, J., Millar, T., Eastwood, C. and McKeganey, N. (2006) 'Local and National Estimates of the Prevalence of Opiate Use and/or Crack Cocaine Use', in Singleton, N., Murray, R. and Tinsley, L. (Eds.) *Measuring Different Aspects of Problem Drug Use: Methodological Developments*, Online Report 16/06, London: Home Office.

Hay, G., Gannon. M., MacDougall, J., Millar, T., Eastwood, C. and McKeganey, N. (2007) *National and Regional Estimates of the Prevalence of Opiate Use and/or Crack Cocaine Use 2005/06: A Summary of Key Findings*, London: Home Office.

Hay, G., Gannon, M., MacDougall, J., Millar, T., Williams, K., Eastwood, C. and McKeganey, N. (2008) *National and Regional Estimates of the Prevalence of Opiate Use and/or Crack Cocaine Use 2006/7*, London: Home Office.

Hedderman, C. (2008) *Building on Sand: Why Expanding the Prison Estate is Not the Way to 'Secure the Future'*, London: Centre for Crime and Justice Studies.

Hedderman, C. and Hough, M. (2005) 'Diversion from Prosecution at Court and Effective Sentencing', in Perry, A. E., McDougall, C. and Farrington, D. P. (Eds.) *Reducing Crime: The Effectiveness of Criminal Justice Interventions*, Chichester: Wiley.

Her Majesty's Prison Service (2010) *Monthly Bulletin – January 2010*, available at http://www.hmprisonservice.gov.uk/assets/documents/100049F4population_bulletin_monthly_january_2010.pdf (accessed 24 March 2010).

Her Majesty's Treasury (undated) *The Green Book: Appraisal and Evaluation in Central Government*, London: TSO.

Hindelang, M., Gottfredson, M., and Garofalo, J. (1978) *Victims of Personal Crime: An Empirical Foundation for a Theory of Personal Victimisation*, Cambridge, MA: Ballinger.

Hirsch, B. T. (2005) 'Why Do Part-Time Workers Earn Less? The Role of Worker and Job Skills', *Industrial and Labor Relations Review*, Vol. 58, pp. 525–551.

Hirschi, T. (1969) *The Causes of Delinquency*, Berkeley: University of California Press.

Hirschi, T. and Gottfredson, M. (1983) 'Age and the Explanation of Crime', *The American Journal of Sociology*, Vol. 89, pp. 552–584.

Hoare, J. (2009) 'Drug Misuse Declared: Findings from the 2008/09 British Crime Survey (England and Wales)', *Home Office Statistical Bulletin 12/9*, London: Home Office.

Hobbes, T. (1943) *Leviathan*, London: Everymans Library.

Hoffman, W. and Headley, L. (1992) *Contract Killer: The Explosive Story of the Mafia's Most Notorious Hit Man*, New York: Avalon Publishing Group.

Hollis, M. (1977) *Models of Man*, Cambridge: Cambridge University Press.

Hollis, M. (1987) *The Cunning of Reason*, Cambridge: Cambridge University Press.

Hollis, M. (1994) *The Philosophy of the Social Sciences: An Introduction*, Cambridge; Cambridge University Press.

Home Affairs Committee (2007) *Police Funding. Fourth Report of Session 2006/7*, London: The Stationery Office.

Home Office (2003a) 'Modelling Crime and Offending: Recent Developments in England and Wales', *Home Office Occasional Paper 80*, London: Home Office.

Home Office (2003b) *Prison Statistics England and Wales 2002*, Cm 5996, available on-line at http://www.archive2.official-documents.co.uk/document/cm59/5996/5996.pdf (accessed 24 March 2010).

Home Office (2005) *The Economic and Social Costs of Crime Against Individuals and Households 2003/04*, *Home Office Online Report 30/05*, London: Home Office, available at http://webarchive.nationalarchives.gov.uk/20110218135832/rds.homeoffice.gov.uk/rds/pdfs05/rdsolr3005.pdf (accessed 20 July 2011).

Home Office (2006a) 'Problem-Oriented Policing', Home Office Crime Reduction Website, http://www.crimereduction.homeoffice.gov.uk/fearofcrime0208.htm (accessed 25 January 2010).

Home Office (2006b) *The Government Reply to the Fifth Report from the House of Commons Science and Technology Committee Session 2005–06 HC 1031*, London: The Stationery Office.

Home Office (2006c) *Criminal Justice System Review: Rebalancing the Criminal Justice System in Favour of the Law-Abiding Majority*, Home Office, London, available at http://www.homeoffice.gov.uk/documents/CJS-review.pdf/CJS-review-english.pdf?view=Binary (accessed 20 July 2011).

Home Office (2009) *Crime in England and Wales 2008/09*, London: Home Office.

Home Office (2010) *Recorded Crime Statistics 2002/03–2009/10*, available at http://www.homeoffice.gov.uk/publications/science-research-statistics/research-statistics/crime-research/crime-stats-2002-2010 (accessed 20 July 2011).

Home Office (2011) *A Summary of Recorded Crime Data from 1898 to 2001/02*, available at http://data.gov.uk/dataset/recorded-crime-data-1898-2001-02 (accessed 20 July 2011).

Homel, R. (2005) 'Developmental Crime Prevention', in Tilley, N. (Ed.) *Handbook of Crime Prevention and Community Safety*, Cullompton: Willan Publishing.

Hope, T. (1998) 'Community Crime Prevention', in Goldblatt, P. and Lewis, C. (Eds.) *Reducing Offending: An Assessment of Research Evidence On Ways of Dealing with Offending Behaviour*, London: Home Office.

Hopkins Burke, R. (2005) *An Introduction to Criminological Theory*, Cullompton: Willan Publishing.

Hough, M. and Roberts, J. (1998) *Attitudes to Punishment: Findings from the British Crime Survey, Home Office Research Study No. 179*, London: HMSO.

Ichniowski, C. and Preston, A. (1989) 'The Persistence of Organized Crime in New York City Construction: An Economic Perspective', *Industrial and Labor Relations Review*, Vol. 42(4), pp. 549–565.

Ihlanfeldt, K.R. (2007) 'Neighbourhood Drug Crime and Young Males' Job Accessibility', *The Review of Economics and Statistics*, Vol. 89(1), pp. 151–164.

Institute of Alcohol Studies (2010) *IAS Fact Sheet – Alcohol Consumption in the UK*, available at http://www.ias.org.uk/resources/factsheets/consumption-uk.pdf (accessed 20 July 2011).

Institute for Fiscal Studies (2010) 'Poverty and Inequality in the UK: 2010', *Commentary No. 116*, available at http://www.ifs.org.uk/publications/4877 (accessed 10 November 2010).

Jacobs, J. B. (2006) *Mobsters, Unions, and Feds: The Mafia and the American Labor Movement*, New York: New York University Press.

James, O. (1997) 'Curse of Comparison', *Prospect*, 23 October, www.prospectmagazine.co.uk/printarticle.php?id=4469 (accessed 20 July 2011).

Jensen, R. (2002) '"No Irish Need Apply": A Myth of Victimization', *Journal of Social History*, Vol. 36, pp. 405–429.

Johnson, E. and Goldstein, D. (2003) 'Do Defaults Save Lives?', *Science*, Vol. 302, pp. 1338–1339.

Johnston, P. (2003) *No Hysteria: Fears of Crime Are Rational*, The Edge, Issue 12, ESRC http://www.esrc.ac.uk/_images/The Edge 12_tcm8-8219.pdf (accessed 20 July 2011).

Jones, A., Donmall, M., Millar, T., Moody, A., Weston, S., Anderson, T., Gittins, M., Abeywardana, V. and D'Souza, J. (2009) *The Drug Treatment Outcomes Research Study: Final Outcomes Report,* London: Home Office.

JournalLive (2008) 'Heavy-Handed Police Fuel Football Violence', http://www.journal-live.co.uk/north-east-news/todays-news/2008/08/26/heavy-handed-police-fuel-football-violence-61634-21602089/ (accessed 20 July 2011).

Judge, I. (2006) *Public Protection*, Speech by Sir Igor Judge, President of The Queen's Bench Division at King's College London, 20 November.

Justice Committee (2009) *Cutting Crime: The Case for Justice Reinvestment*, London: The Stationery Office Limited.

Karoly, L. A. and Burtless, G. (1995) 'Demographic Change, Rising Earnings Inequality, and the Distribution of Personal Well-Being, 1959–1989', *Demography*, Vol. 32, pp. 379–405.

Keren, M. (2000) 'The Mafia as a Principal Actor in Transition: An Outline of an Evolutionary Game', *Economic Systems*, Vol. 24(4), pp. 360–364.

Kessler, D. and Levitt, S. (1999) 'Using Sentence Enhancements to Distinguish Between Deterrence and Incapacitation', *Journal of Law and Economics*, Vol. 42, pp. 343–363.

Keynes, J. (1891) *The Scope and Method of Political Economy*, London: Macmillan.

King, J. (1992) *No Such Thing As Society?: Individualism and Community*, Buckingham: Open University Press.

Krueger, A. O. (1974) 'The Political Economy of the Rent-Seeking Society', *The American Economic Review*, Vol. 64(3), pp. 291–303.

Kugler, M., Verdier, T. and Zenou, Y. (2005) 'Organized Crime, Corruption, and Punishment', *Journal of Public Economics*, Vol. 89, pp. 1639–1663.

Laffer, A. (2004) *The Laffer Curve, Past, Present and Future*, The Heritage Foundation http://www.heritage.org/Research/Taxes/bg1765.cfm (accessed 4 August 2008).

Laub, J. H. and Sampson, R. J. (2003) *Shared Beginnings, Divergent Lives: Delinquent Boys to Age 70*, Boston, MA: Harvard University Press.

Laub, J. H., Nagin, D. S. and Sampson, R. J. (1998) 'Trajectories of Change in Criminal Offending: Good Marriages and the Desistance Process', *American Sociological Review*, Vol. 63, pp. 225–238.

Leppel, K. and Clain, S. H. (1988) 'The Growth in Involuntary Part-Time Employment of Men and Women', *Applied Economics*, Vol. 20, pp. 1155–1166.

Levi, M. (1998) 'Organising Plastic Fraud: Enterprise Criminals and the Side-Stepping of Fraud Prevention', *The Howard Journal*, Vol. 37(4), pp. 423–428.

Levi, M. (2007) 'Organized Crime and Terrorism', in Maguire, M., Morgan, R. and Reiner, R. (Eds.) *The Oxford Handbook of Criminology*, Oxford: Oxford University Press.

Levitt, S. D. (1996) 'The Effect of Prison Population Size on Crime Rates: Evidence From Prison Overcrowding Litigation', *Quarterly Journal of Economics*, Vol. 111, pp. 319–351.

Levitt, S. D. (1997) 'Using Electoral Cycles in Police Hiring to Estimate the Effect of Police on Crime', *American Economic Review*, Vol. 87, pp. 270–290.

Levitt, S. D. (2001) 'Alternative Strategies for Identifying the Link Between Unemployment and Crime', *Journal of Quantitative Criminology*, Vol. 17, pp. 377–390.

Levitt, S. D. (2002) 'Using Electoral Cycles in Police Hiring to Estimate the Effects of Police on Crime: Reply', *The American Economic Review*, Vol. 92, pp. 1244–1250.

Levitt, S. D. and Dubner, S. J. (2005) *Freakonomics: A Rogue Economist Explores the Hidden Side of Everything*, New York: William Morrow/HarperCollins.

Levitt, S. D. and Miles, T. J. (2006) 'Economic Contributions to the Understanding of Crime', *Annual Review of Law and Social Science*, Vol. 2, pp.147–164.

Levitt, S. D. and Venkatesh, S. (2000) 'An Economic Analysis of a Drug-Selling Gang's Finances', *Quarterly Journal of Economics*, Vol. 115(3), pp. 755–789.

Liedka, R., Piehl, A, and Useem, B. (2006) 'The Crime-Control Effect of Incarceration: Does Scale Matter?', *Criminology & Public Policy*, Vol. 5(2), pp. 245–275.

Lodge, H. C. (1891) 'Lynch Law and Unrestricted Immigration', *North American Review*, Vol. 152(414), pp. 602–613.

Loewenstein, G (1996) 'Out of Control: Visceral Influences on Behavior', *Organizational Behavior and Human Decision Processes*, Vol. 65, pp. 272–292.

Loewenstein, G. (2000) 'Emotions in Economic Theory and Economic Behavior', *The American Economic Review*, Vol. 90, pp. 426–432.

London Criminal Justice Board (2009) 'Innovative Scheme Aims to Break the Cycle of Re-offending', *London Criminal Justice Board Briefing Note January 2009*, London: London Criminal Justice Board.

Lord, C., Ross, L. and Lepper, M. (1979) 'Biased Assimilation and Attitude Polarization: The Effects of Prior Theories on Subsequently Considered Evidence', *Journal of Personality and Social Psychology*, Vol. 37, pp. 2098–2109.

Lord, G., Lepper, M. and Preston, E. (1984) 'Considering the Opposite: A Corrective Strategy for Social Judgment', *Journal of Personality and Social Psychology*, Vol. 47, pp. 1231–1243.

Ludwig, J. and Cook, P. J. (2001) 'The Benefits of Reducing Gun Violence: Evidence From Contingent Valuation Survey Data', *Journal of Risk and Uncertainty*, Vol. 22, pp. 207–226.

Lundahl, B., Kunz, C., Brownell, C., Harris, N. and Van Vleet, R. (2009) 'Prison Privatization: A Meta-analysis of Cost and Quality of Confinement Indicators', *Research on Social Work Practice*, Vol. 19(4), pp. 383–394.

MacCoun, R. and Reuter, P. (2001). 'Evaluating Alternative Cannabis Regimes', *British Journal of Psychiatry*, Vol. 178, pp. 123–128.

MacDonald, Z. (2002) 'Official Crime Statistics: Their Use and Interpretation', *The Economic Journal*, Vol. 112, pp. F85–F106.

MacDonald, Z. (2004) 'What Price Drug Use? The Contribution of Economics to an Evidence-Based Drugs Policy', *Journal of Economic Surveys*, Vol. 18(2), pp. 113–152.

Machin, S. and Meghir, C. (2004) 'Crime and Economic Incentives', *Journal of Human Resources*, Vol. 339(4), pp. 958–979.

Maltz, M. D. (1990) *Measuring the Effectiveness of Organized Crime Control Efforts*, Chicago: US Department of Justice, Office of International Criminal Justice.

Market and Business Development (2010) *Press Release: UK CCTV Market Research Report*, http://www.mbdltd.co.uk/Press-Release/CCTV.htm (accessed 20 July 2011).

Marris, R. and Volterra Consulting (2000) *Survey of the Research Literature on the Criminological and Economic Factors Influencing Crime Trends. Technical Report*, London: Home Office.

Marsh, K. and Fox, C. (2008) 'The Benefit and Cost of Prison in the UK. The Results of a Model of Lifetime Re-offending', *The Journal of Experimental Criminology*, Vol. 4(4), pp. 403–423.

Marsh, P., Fox, K., Carnibella, G., McCann, J. and Marsh, J. (1996) *Football Violence in Europe*, Washington, DC: The Amsterdam Group.

Marsh, K., Chalfin, A. and Roman, J. (2008) 'What Does Economic Analysis Add to Decision Making? Evidence from the Criminal Justice Literature', *Journal of Experimental Criminology*, Vol. 4(2), pp. 117–135.

Marsh, K., Fox, C. and Hedderman, C. (2009) 'Do You Get What You Pay For? Assessing the Use of Prison from an Economic Perspective', *Howard Journal of Criminal Justice*, Vol. 48(2), pp. 144–157.

Marsh, K., Fox, C. and Sarmah, R. (2009) 'Is Custody an Effective Sentencing Option for the UK? Evidence from a Meta-Analysis of Existing Studies', *The Probation Journal*, Vol. 56(2), pp. 129–151.

Marshall, A. (1890) *Principles of Economics* (reprinted 1966), London: Macmillan.

Marvell, T. and Moody, C. (1994) 'Prison Population and Crime Reduction', *Journal of Quantitative Criminology*, Vol. 10, pp. 109–139.

Marvell, T. and Moody, C. (1996) 'Specification Problems, Police Levels, and Crime Rates', *Criminology*, Vol. 34, pp. 609–646.

Marx, K. (1844) *Contribution to the Critique of Hegel's Philosophy of Law*, Deutsch Französische Jahrbücher.

The Matrix Knowledge Group (2007) *The Illicit Drug Trade in the United Kingdom, Home Office Online Report 20/07*, London: Home Office.

The Matrix Knowledge Group (2008) *Dedicated Drug Court Pilots: A Process Report*, London: Ministry of Justice.

May, T., Duffy, M., Few, B. and Hough, M. (2005) *Understanding Drug Selling in Communities: Insider or Outsider Trading?*, York: Joseph Rowntree Foundation.

Mazerolle, L., Soole, D. and Rombouts, S. (2007a) *Crime Prevention Research Reviews No. 1: Disrupting Street-Level Drug Markets*, Washington, DC: US Department of Justice Office of Community Oriented Policing Services.

Mazerolle, L., Soole, D. and Rombouts, S. (2007b) 'Drug Law Enforcement: A Review of the Evaluation Literature', *Police Quarterly*, Vol. 10(2), pp. 115–153.

McDougall, C., Cohen, M., Swaray, R. and Perry, A. (2003) 'The Costs and Benefits of

Sentencing: A Systematic Review', *The ANNALS of the American Academy of Political and Social Science*, Vol. 587, pp. 160–177.

McIllwain, J. S. (1999). 'Organized Crime: A Social Network Approach', *Crime, Law and Social Change*, Vol. 32(4), pp. 301–323.

Mendes, S. M. and McDonald, M. D. (2001) 'Putting Severity of Punishment Back in the Deterrence Package', *Policy Studies Journal*, Vol. 29(4), pp. 588–610.

Mental Floss (2009) *How Superman Defeated the Ku Klux Klan*, http://www.mentalfloss.com/blogs/archives/39296 (accessed 20 July 2011).

Merton, R. K. (1938) 'Social Structure and Anomie', *American Sociological Review*, Vol. 3, pp. 672–682.

Merton, R. K. (1968) *Social Theory and Social Structure*, New York: The Free Press.

Miles T. J. and Ludwig, J. (2007) 'The Silence of the Lambdas: Deterring Incapacitation Research', *Journal of Quantitative Criminology*, Vol. 23, pp. 287–301.

Mills, H., Silvestri, A. and Grimshaw, R. (2010) *Police Expenditure, 1999–2009*, London: Centre for Crime and Justice Studies.

Ministry of Justice (2008) 'Appraisal of Prisoner Resettlement Projects for Short-sentence Prisoners', unpublished.

Ministry of Justice (2009) *Story of the Prison Population 1995–2009 England and Wales*, London: Ministry of Justice.

Morgan, R. and Liebling, A. (2007) 'Imprisonment: An Expanding Scene', in Maguire, M., Morgan, R. and Reiner, R. (Eds.) *The Oxford Handbook of Criminology* (4th Edition), Oxford: Oxford University Press.

Morley, B. and Thomas, D. (2005), 'Modelling Home Advantage and the Importance of the Toss in One-Day Cricket Matches', *Journal of Sports Sciences*, Vol. 23, pp. 261–268.

Nagin, D. S. and Paternoster, R. (1993) 'Enduring Individual Differences and Rational Choice Theories of Crime', *Law and Society Review*, Vol. 27(3), pp. 467–496.

Nagin, D. S., Piquero, A. R., Scott, E. S. and Steinberg, L. (2006) 'Public Preferences for Rehabilitation Versus Incarceration of Juvenile Offenders: Evidence From a Contingent Valuation Survey', *Criminology and Public Policy*, Vol. 5, pp. 627–652.

Narayan, P. K. and Smyth, R. (2004) 'Crime Rates, Male Youth Unemployment and Real Income in Australia: Evidence From Granger Causality Tests', *Applied Economics*, Vol. 36, pp. 2079–2095.

National Audit Office (2007) *The Assets Recovery Agency*, London: The Stationery Office.

National Drug Intelligence Center (2010) *National Drug Threat Assessment 2010*, Washington, DC: United States Department of Justice.

National Institute for Clinical Excellence (2009) *Needle and Syringe Programmes: Providing People Who Inject Drugs With Injecting Equipment, Public Health Guidance 18*, London: National Institute for Health and Clinical Excellence.

National Intelligence Council (2004) *Mapping the Global Structure*, National Intelligence Council, Report of the National Intelligence Council's 2020 Project, based on consultations with nongovernmental experts around the world, Washington, DC: National Intelligence Council.

New York Times (2009) 'Economists Try Target Practice in a Fun-House Mirror', 16 February, http://www.nytimes.com/2009/02/16/arts/television/16watc.html (accessed 20 July 2011).

Nicholas, S., Povey, D., Walker, A. and Kershaw, C. (2005) *Crime in England and Wales, 2004/2005*, London: Home Office.

Nordhaus, W. D. (2007), 'A Review of the "Stern Review on the Economics of Climate Change"', *Journal of Economic Literature*, Vol. 45(3), pp. 686–702.

Norris, C., McCahill, M., and Wood, D. (2004) 'Editorial. The Growth of CCTV: A Global Perspective on the International Diffusion of Video Surveillance in Publicly Accessible Space', *Society and Surveillance*, Vol. 2(2/3), pp. 110–135.

Office for National Statistics (2001) *Social Capital: A Review of the Literature*, London: ONS.

Office for National Statistics (2009) *Social Trends 39*, available at http://www.statistics. gov.uk/downloads/theme_social/Social_Trends39/Social_Trends_39.pdf (accessed 2 April 2010).

Office for National Statistics (2010) *Labour Market Statistics – Integrated FR*, http://www. statistics.gov.uk/statbase/tsdtimezone.asp (accessed 20 July 2011).

Olson, M. (1993) 'Dictatorship, Democracy, and Development', *The American Political Science Review*, Vol. 87, pp. 567–576.

Pacula, R., Chriqui, J. and King, J. (2004) *Marijuana Decriminalization: What Does It Mean in the United States?*, Santa Monica, CA: RAND.

Pagliarini, R. (2010) *Greed is Good: Why You Need to Tap Into Your Inner Gordon Gekko*, available at http://www.latimes.com/sns-jobs-pagliarini-your-inner-gordon-gekko,0, 2106881.story (accessed 10 November 2010).

Paoli, L. (2002) 'The Paradoxes of Organized Crime', *Crime, Law and Social Change*, Vol. 37, pp. 51–97.

Paoli, L. (2004) 'Italian Organised Crime: Mafia Associations and Criminal Enterprises', *Global Crime*, Vol. 6, pp. 19–31.

Pawson, R. and Tilley, N. (1997) *Realistic Evaluation*, London: Sage.

Pearson, G. and Hobbs, D. (2001) *Middle Market Drug Distribution, Home Office Research Study 227*, London: Home Office.

Pease, K. (1994) 'Crime Prevention', in Maguire, M., Morgan, R., and Reiner, R. (Eds.) *Oxford Handbook of Criminology* (1st Edition), Oxford: Clarendon Press, pp. 659–703.

PEW Center on the States (2008) *One in 100: Behind Bars in America 2008*, Washington, DC: PEW Charitable Trusts.

Phillips, D. L. (1986) *Towards a Just Social Order*, Princeton, NJ: Princeton University Press.

Phillips, L. J. (2007) *How Important is Punishment?*, Speech to the Howard League for Penal Reform, 15 November.

Piehl, A. M. and DiIulio, J. J. (1995) 'Does Prison Pay? Revisited', *Brookings Review*, Vol. 13, pp. 20–25.

Plato, *The Republic*, available at http://classics.mit.edu/Plato/republic.2.i.html (accessed 10 November 2010).

Plous, S. (1993) *The Psychology of Judgment and Decision Making*, New York: McGraw-Hill.

Popper, K. R. (1972) *Conjectures and Refutations: The Growth of Scientific Knowledge*, London: Routledge and Kegan Paul.

Powell, W. W. (1990) 'Neither Market Nor Hierarchy: Network Forms of Organization', in Thompson, G., Frances, J., Levaèiæ, R. and Mitchell, J. (Eds.) *Markets, Hierarchies and Networks. The Coordination of Social Life*, London: Sage.

Prison Reform Trust (2009) *Bromley Prison Briefing*, London: Prison Reform Trust.

Pudney, S., Badillo, C., Bryan, M., Burton, J., Conti, G. and Iacovou, M. (2006) 'Estimating the Size of the UK Illicit Drug Market', in Singleton, N., Murray, R. and Tinsley, L. (Eds.) *Measuring Different Aspects of Problem Drug Use: Methodological Developments, Home Office Online Report 16/06*, London: Home Office.

Pyle, D. J. and Deadman, D. F. (1994) 'Crime and the Business Cycle in Post-War Britain', *British Journal of Criminology*, Vol. 34(3), pp. 339–357.

Quinton, P. and Morris, J. (2008) *Neighbourhood Policing: The Impact of Piloting and Early National Implementation*, *Home Office Online Report 01/08*, London: Home Office.

Radzinowicz, L. (1939) 'The Influence of Economic Conditions on Crime', *Sociological Review*, Vol. 33, pp. 139–153.

Raphael, S. and Winter-Ebmer, R. (2001) 'Identifying the Effect of Unemployment on Crime', *Journal of Law and Economics*, Vol. 44, pp. 259–283.

Rasmussen, E. (1996) 'Stigma and Self-Fulfilling Expectations of Criminality', *Journal of Law and Economics*, Vol. 39, pp. 519–544.

Ratzinger, J. (1985) *Market Economy and Ethics*, available at http://www.acton.org/global/article/market-economy-and-ethics (accessed 10 November 2010).

Rawlinson, P. (2001) 'Russian Organized Crime and Baltic States: Assessing the Threat', *Working Paper 38/01*, ESRC Research Programme 'One Europe of Several'.

Rawlinson, P. (2009) 'Understanding Organized Crime', in Hale, C., Hayward, K., Wahidin, A. and Wincup, E. (Eds.) *Criminology*, Oxford: Oxford University Press.

Raynor, P. (2007) 'Community Penalties', in Maguire, M., Morgan, R. and Reiner, R. (Eds.) *The Oxford Handbook of Criminology* (4th Edition), Oxford: Oxford University Press.

Reilly, B. and Witt, R. (1992) 'Crime and Unemployment in Scotland', *Scottish Journal of Political Economy*, pp. 213–228.

Reinarman, C., Cohen, P. D. A. and Kaal, H. L. (2004) 'The Limited Relevance of Drug Policy: Cannabis in Amsterdam and San Francisco', *American Journal of Public Health*, Vol. 94, pp. 836–842.

Reiner, R. (2001) 'The Rise of Virtual Vigilantism: Crime Reporting Since World War II', *Criminal Justice Matters*, Vol. 43, pp. 4–5.

Reiner, R. (2007) 'Political Economy, Crime, and Criminal Justice', in Maguire, M., Morgan, R. and Reiner, R. (Eds.) *The Oxford Handbook of Criminology*, Oxford: Oxford University Press.

Reuter, P. (1983) *Disorganized Crime. The Economics of the Visible Hand*, Cambridge, MA: MIT Press.

Reuter, P. (1985) *The Organization of Illegal Markets: An Economic Analysis*, Washington, DC: National Institute of Justice.

Reuter, P. (1987) *Racketeering in Legitimate Industries: A Study in the Economics of Intimidation*, Santa Monica, CA: RAND.

Reuter, P. and Caulkins, J. P. (2004) 'Illegal "Lemons": Price Dispersion in Cocaine and Heroin Markets', *Bulletin on Narcotics*, Vol. 56, pp. 141–165.

Reuter, P. and Greenfield, V. (2001) 'Measuring Global Drug Markets: How Good are the Numbers and Why Should We Care About Them?' *World Economics*, Vol. 2(4), pp. 159–173.

Reuter, P. and Stevens, A. (2007) *An Analysis of the UK Drug Policy: A Monograph Prepared for the UK Drug Policy Commission*, London: UK Drug Policy Commission.

Robbins, L. (1945) *An Essay on the Nature & Significance of Economic Science* (2nd Edition), London: Macmillan.

Rock, P. (2007) 'Sociological Theories of Crime', in Maguire, M., Morgan, R. and Reiner, R. (Eds.) *The Oxford Handbook of Criminology*, Oxford: Oxford University Press.

Roman, J. (2004) 'Can Cost-Benefit Analysis Answer Criminal Justice Policy Questions, And If So, How?' *Journal of Contemporary Criminal Justice*, Vol. 20, pp. 257–275.

Roman, J. K., Reid, S. E., Chalfin, A. J. and Knight, C. R. (2009) 'The DNA Field Experiment: A Randomized Trial of the Cost-Effectiveness of Using DNA to Solve Property Crimes', *Journal of Experimental Criminology*, Vol. 5, pp. 345–369.

Rousseau, J. (1968) *The Social Contract*, Harmondsworth: Penguin.

Rowe, D. (2007) *Beyond Fear (20th Anniversary Edition)*, London: Harper Perennial.

Ruggiero, V. (1997) 'Criminals and Service Providers: Cross-National Dirty Economies', *Crime, Law and Social Change*, Vol. 28, pp. 27–38.

Sah, R. (1991) 'Social Osmosis and Patterns of Crime', *Journal of Political Economy*, Vol. 99, pp. 1272–1295.

Sampson, R. and Laub, J. (1993) *Crime in the Making: Pathways and Turning Points Through Life*, Cambridge, MA: Harvard University Press.

Sampson, R., Raudenbush, S. and Earls, F. (1997) 'Neighborhoods and Violent Crime. A Multi-level Study of Collective Efficacy', *Science*, Vol. 277, pp. 918–924.

Sampson, R., Raudenbush, S. and Earls, F. (1998) *Neighborhood Collective Efficacy – Does It Help Reduce Violence?*, Washington DC: National Institute of Justice.

Sayers, D. L. (1945) *The Man Born to be King*, London, Victor Gollancz.

Schelling, T. C. (1967) 'Economic Analysis and Organized Crime', in *Task Force Report: Organized Crime, Annotations and Consultant's Papers*, Washington, DC: Government Printing Office, pp. 114–126.

Schelling, T. C. (1971) 'What Is the Business of Organized Crime?', *The Journal of Public Law*, Vol. 20(I), pp. 71–84.

Schneider, F. (2006) 'Shadow Economies of 145 Countries All Over the World: What Do We Really Know?', *CREMA Working Paper 2006-01*, Basel: Center for Research in Economics, Management and the Arts.

Schneider, F. and Ernste, D. (2000) 'Shadow Economies: Size, Causes And Consequences', *Journal of Economic Literature*, Vol. 38, pp. 77–114.

Schnelle, J. F., Kirchner, R. E., Macrae, J. W., Mcnees, M. P., Eck, R. H., Snodgrass, S., Casey, J. D. and Uselton, P. H. (1978) 'Police Evaluation Research: An Experimental and Cost-Benefit Analysis of a Helicopter Patrol in a High Crime Area', *Journal of Applied Behavior Analysis*, Vol. 1(1), pp. 11–21.

Schweinhart, L. (undated) *The High/Scope Perry Preschool Study Through Age 40 Summary, Conclusions, and Frequently Asked Questions*, Ypsilanti: High/Scope Educational Research Foundation.

The Science and Technology Select Committee (2006) *Drug Classification: Making a Hash of It?*, London: The Stationery Office Limited.

Sellin, T. (1942) 'Crime', *The American Journal of Sociology*, Vol. 47, pp. 898–906.

Sen, A. (1977) 'Rational Fools: A Critique of the Behavioral Foundations of Economic Theory', *Philosophy and Public Affairs*, Vol. 6, pp. 317–344.

Sentencing Advisory Panel (2010a) *Overarching Principles of Sentencing*, available at http://www.sentencing-guidelines.gov.uk/docs/s_g_update_10_march/overaching_principles_of_sentencing.pdf (accessed 1 July 2011).

Sentencing Advisory Panel (2010b) *Sentencing for Domestic Burglary*, available at http://www.sentencing-guidelines.gov.uk/docs/s_g_update_10_march/sentencing_for_domestic_burglary.pdf (accessed 1 July 2011).

Sentencing Guidelines Council (2010) *Corporate Manslaughter & Health and Safety Offences Causing Death*, available at http://www.sentencing-guidelines.gov.uk/docs/guideline_on_corporate_manslaughter.pdf (accessed 1 July 2011).

Serious Organised Crime Agency (SOCA) (2008) *The United Kingdom Threat Assessment of Serious Organised Crime 2008/9*, London: SOCA.

Serious Organised Crime Agency (SOCA) (2009a) *The United Kingdom Threat Assessment of Serious Organised Crime 2009/10*, London: SOCA.

Serious Organised Crime Agency (SOCA) (2009b) *Annual Report 2008–9*, London: SOCA.

Shadish, R., Cook, T. and Campbell, D. (2002) *Experimental and Quasi-Experimental Designs for Generalized Causal Inference*, Boston: Houghton-Mifflin.

Shaw, A. (1950) (compiler and editor) *The Lincoln Encyclopaedia*, New York: Macmillan.

Shaw, C. R. and McKay, H.D. (1942) *Juvenile Delinquency and Urban Areas*, Chicago: University of Chicago Press.

Shaw, C. R. and McKay, H. D. (1969) *Juvenile Delinquency and Urban Areas: A Study of Rates of Delinquency in Relation To Differential Characteristics of Local Communities in American Cities* (Revised Edition), Chicago: University of Chicago Press.

Shelley, L. I. (2002) 'The Nexus of Organized International Criminals and Terrorism', *International Annals of Criminology*, Vol. 20 1/2, pp. 85–92.

Shepherd, J. (2006) 'The Imprisonment Puzzle: Understanding How Prison Growth Affects Crime', *Criminology and Public Policy*, Vol. 5(2), pp. 285–298.

Shepherd, J. P., Shapland, M., Pearce N. X. and Scully, C. (1990) 'Pattern, Severity and Aetiology of Injuries in Victims of Assault', *Journal of the Royal Society of Medicine*, Vol. 83, pp. 75–78.

Sherman, L. W., Gottfredson, D., MacKenzie, D., Eck, J., Reuter, P. and Bushway, S. (1998a) *Preventing Crime: What Works, What Doesn't, What's Promising: A Report to The United States Congress*, prepared for the National Institute of Justice, Maryland: University of Maryland.

Sherman, L. W., Gottfredson, D., MacKenzie, D., Eck, J., Reuter, P. and Bushway, S. (1998b) 'Preventing Crime: What Works, What Doesn't, What's Promising', *National Institute of Justice Research in Brief*, Washington, DC: National Institute of Justice.

Simmons, J. (2002) *Crime in England and Wales 2001/2002*, London: Home Office.

Simon, H. (1956) 'Rational Choice and the Structure of the Environment', *Psychological Review*, Vol. 63, pp. 129–138.

Single, E., Christie, P. and Ali, R. (2000) 'The Impact of Cannabis Decriminalisation in Australia and the United States', *Journal of Public Health Policy*, Vol. 21(2), pp. 157–186.

Skaperdas, S. (2001) 'The Political Economy of Organized Crime: Providing Protection When the State Does Not', *Economics of Governance*, Vol. 2, pp. 173–202.

Skaperdas, S. and Syropoulos, C. (1995) 'Gangs as Primitive States', in Fiorentini, G. and Peltzman, S. (Eds.) *The Economics of Organised Crime*, Cambridge, UK: Cambridge University Press, pp. 61–82.

Slovic, P. (1966) 'Risk-Taking in Children: Age and Sex Differences', *Child Development*, Vol. 37(1), pp. 169–176.

Smith, A. (1759) *The Theory of Moral Sentiments* (6th Edition published 1790), London: A. Millar.

Smith, A. (1776) *An Inquiry into the Nature and Causes of the Wealth of Nations* (5th Edition published 1904), London: Methuen & Co., Ltd.

Smith, D. (1980) 'Paragons, Pariahs, and Pirates: A Spectrum-Based Theory of Enterprise', *Crime and Delinquency*, Vol. 26, pp. 358–386.

Smith, D. (2007) 'Crime and the Life Course', in Maguire, M., Morgan, R. and Reiner, R. (Eds.) *The Oxford Handbook of Criminology* (4th Edition), Oxford: Oxford University Press.

Smith, D. C. (1994) 'Illicit Enterprise: An Organized Crime Paradigm for the Nineties', in Kelly, R. J., Chin, K.-L. and Schatzberg, R. (Eds.) *Handbook of Organized Crime in the United States*, Westport, CT: Greenwood Press.

Smith, M. D., Devine, J. A. and Sheley, J.F. (1992) 'Crime and Unemployment: Effects Across Age and Race Categories', *Sociological Perspectives*, Vol. 35, pp. 551–572.

Smith, P., Goggin, C. and Gendreau, P. (2002) *The Effects of Prison Sentences and*

Intermediate Sanctions on Recidivism: General Effects and Individual Differences, Saint John: University of New Brunswick.

Solivetti, L. M. (2001) *Drug Use Criminalization v. Decriminalization: An Analysis in the Light of the Italian Experience*, Swiss Federal Office of Public Health. Available from: http://w3.uniroma1.it/DCNAPS/solivetti/swissho.pdf#search=%22italy%20decriminali zation%20drugs%22 (accessed 11 November 2010).

Song, F. M. and Wu, Y. (1998) 'Hysteresis in Unemployment: Evidence from OECD Countries', *The Quarterly Review of Economics and Finance*, Vol. 38, pp. 181–192.

Sparks, R. F. (1980) 'A Critique of Marxist Criminology', in Morris, N. and Tonry, M. (Eds.) *Crime and Justice: An Annual Review of Research*, Vol. 2, Chicago, IL: University of Chicago Press.

Steinberg, L., Cauffman, E., Woolard, J., Graham, S. and Banich, M. (2009) 'Are Adolescents Less Mature Than Adults? Minors' Access to Abortion, the Juvenile Death Penalty, and the Alleged APA "Flip-Flop"', *American Psychologist*, Vol. 64(7), pp. 583–594.

Stern, N. (2007) *The Economics of Climate Change: The Stern Review*, Cambridge and New York: Cambridge University Press.

Stewart, M. (2004) 'The Impact of the Introduction of the UK Minimum Wage on the Employment Probabilities of Low Wage Workers', *Journal of the European Economic Association*, Vol. 2, pp. 67–97.

Storti, C. C. and De Grauwe, P. (2007) *Globalisation and the Price Decline of Illicit Drugs*, CESifo Working Paper No. 1990. Available from http://www.ifo.de/pls/guestci/download/CESifo%20Working%20Papers%202007/CESifo%20Working%20Papers%20May%202007/cesifo1_wp1990.pdf (accessed 11 November 2010).

The Sunday Times (2010) 'Forget the Nudge, David Cameron Will Need a Shove', 14 March.

Sung, H.-E. (2004) 'State Failure, Economic Failure, and Predatory Organized Crime: A Comparative Analysis', *Journal of Research in Crime and Delinquency*, Vol. 41, pp. 111–129.

Sunstein, C. and Thaler, R. (2003) 'Libertarian Paternalism is Not an Oxymoron', *University of Chicago Law Review*, Vol. 70, pp. 1159–1199.

Taleb, N. N. (2007) *The Black Swan: The Impact of the Highly Improbable*, London: Penguin.

Tarling, R. (1993) *Analysing Offending: Data, Models and Interpretations*, London: HMSO.

Tavares, L. V., Graça, P. M., Martins, O. and Asensio, M. (2005) *External and Independent Evaluation of the 'National Strategy for the Fight Against Drugs' and of the 'National Action Plan for the Fight Against Drugs and Drug Addiction – Horizon 2004'*, Lisbon: Institute for Drugs and Drug Addiction.

Thaler, R. (2009) 'Opting in vs. Opting Out', *New York Times*, 29 September.

Thaler, R. and Shefrin, H. (1981) 'An Economic Theory of Self-Control', *The Journal of Political Economy*, Vol. 89, pp. 392–406.

Thaler, R. and Sunstein, C. (2008) *Nudge: Improving Decisions about Health, Wealth, and Happiness*, New Haven: Yale University Press.

The Times (2007) 'Criminals "Must Have Terms Cut in Full Jails"', 5 November.

Toddington, S. (1993) *Rationality, Social Action and Moral Judgement*, Edinburgh: Edinburgh University Press.

Tozer, J. (2008) 'Highly-Paid Footballers are Openly Flouting Parking Laws – Because £70 Fines are Too Easy to Pay', *The Daily Mail*, 3 July, available at http://www.dailymail.co.uk/news/article-1031584/Highly-paid-footballers-openly-flouting-parking-laws--70-fines-easy-pay.html (accessed 2 April 2010).

Transform Drug Policy Foundation (2009) *A Comparison of the Cost-effectiveness of the Prohibition and Regulation of Drugs*, Bristol: Transform Drug Policy Foundation.

Triggs, S. (1997) *Interpreting Trends in Recorded Crime in New Zealand*, http://www.justice.govt.nz/publications/publications-archived/1997/interpreting-trends-in-recorded-crime-in-new-zealand-sue-triggs-ministry-of-justice-april-1997/publication (accessed 11 November 2010).

Tversky, A. and Kahneman, D. (1981) 'The Framing of Decisions and the Psychology of Choice', *Science*, Vol. 211, pp. 453–458.

United Nations (2004) *United Nations Convention Against Transnational Organized Crime and the Protocols Thereto*, Vienna: United Nations Office on Drug and Crime.

United Nations Drug Control Program (2000) *World Drug Report*, Vienna, United Nations.

United Nations Office on Drugs and Crime (2009) *World Drug Report 2009*, Vienna: United Nations Office on Drugs and Crime.

United States Department of Justice (2010) *National Drug Threat Assessment 2010*, Washington, DC: National Drug Intelligence Center.

United States Sentencing Commission (2009) *Federal Sentencing Guidelines Manual*, available at http://www.ussc.gov/2009guid/tabcon09_1.htm.

Vallone, R., Ross, L. and Lepper, M. (1985) 'The Hostile Media Phenomena: Biased Perception and Perceptions of Media Bias in Coverage of the "Beirut Massacre"', *Journal of Personality and Social Psychology*, Vol. 49, pp. 577–585.

van Dijk, J. (1991) *Future Perspectives Regarding Crime and Criminal Justice: Report for the Fourth Conference on Crime Policy*, Strasbourg: Council of Europe

van Duyne, P. C. (1996) 'The Phantom and Threat of Organized Crime', *Crime, Law and Social Change*, Vol. 21, pp. 241–277.

van Duyne, P. C. (2004) 'The Creation of a Threat Image: Media, Policy Making and Organised Crime', in van Duyne, P. C., Jager, M., von Lampe, K. and Newell, J. L. (Eds.) *Threats and Phantoms of Organised Crime, Corruption and Terrorism*, Nijmegen: Wolf Legal.

van Koppen, M. V., de Poot, C. J., Kleemans, E. R. and Nieuwbeerta, P. (2010) 'Criminal Trajectories in Organized Crime', *British Journal of Criminology*, Vol. 50, pp. 102–123.

Villettaz, P., Killias, M. and Zoder, I. (2006) 'The Effects of Custodial vs. Non-Custodial Sentences on Re-Offending: A Systematic Review of the State of Knowledge, A report to the Campbell Collaboration Crime and Justice Group', www.campbellcollaboration.org (accessed 21 September 2009).

Von Hirsch, A., Bottoms, A., Burney, E. and Wikstrom, P. (1999) *Criminal Deterrence and Sentence Severity: An Analysis of Recent Research*, London: Home Office, available at http://members.multimania.co.uk/lawnet/SENTENCE.PDF (accessed 20 July 2011).

Von Lampe, K. (2003) *The Use of Models in the Study Of Organized Crime*, paper presented at the 2003 conference of the European Consortium for Political Research (ECPR), Marlburg, Germany, 19 September.

Von Lampe, K. (2006) 'The Interdisciplinary Dimensions of the Study of Organized Crime', *Trends in Organized Crime*, Vol. 9(3), pp. 77–95.

Von Lampe, K. (undated) 'Definitions of Organized Crime', www.organized-crime.de/OCDEF1.htm (accessed 11 August 2010).

Walby, S. (2004) *The Cost of Domestic Violence*, London: Department of Trade and Industry.

Walker, A., Flatley, J., Kershaw, C. and Moon, D. (2009) 'Crime in England and Wales 2008/09', *Home Office Statistical Bulletin 11/09*, London: Home Office.

Warburton, H., Turnbull, P. J. and Hough, M. (2005) *Occasional and Controlled Heroin Use: Not a Problem?*, York: Joseph Rowntree Foundation.

Washington Post (2009) 'D.C. Man Fights Citation for Warning Other Drivers', http://www.washingtonpost.com/wp-dyn/content/article/2009/06/16/AR2009061603186.html (accessed 20 July 2011).

Weisburd, D. and Eck, J. (2004) 'What Can Police Do to Reduce Crime, Disorder, and Fear?' *The ANNALS of the American Academy of Political and Social Science*, Vol. 593, pp. 42–65.

Weisburd, D., Telep, C. W., Hinkle, J. C. and Eck, J. E. (2008) 'The Effects of Problem-Oriented Policing on Crime and Disorder', *Campbell Systematic Reviews 2008*, p. 14.

Welsh, B., and Farrington, D. (1999) 'Value for Money? A Review of the Costs and Benefits of Situational Crime Prevention', *British Journal of Criminology*, Vol. 39, pp. 345–368.

Welsh, B. and Farrington, D. (2001a) 'Assessing the Economic Costs and Benefits of Crime Prevention', in Welsh, B., Farrington, D. and Sherman, L. (Eds.) *Costs and Benefits of Preventing Crime*, Oxford: Westview Press.

Welsh, B., and Farrington, D. (2001b) 'A Review of the Research on the Monetary Value of Preventing Crime', in Welsh, B., Farrington, D. and Sherman, L. (Eds.) *Costs and Benefits of Preventing Crime*, Oxford: Westview Press.

Welsh, B. and Farrington D. (2002) *Crime Prevention Effects of Closed Circuit Television: A Systematic Review*, Home Office Study 252, London: Home Office Research, Development and Statistics Directorate.

Wilber, C. K. (2004) 'Ethics, Human Behavior and the Methodology of Social Economics', *Forum for Social Economics*, Vol. 33(2), pp. 19–50.

Williamson, O.E. (1985) *The Economic Institutions of Capitalism*, New York: Free Press.

Wilson, D., Mitchell, O. and MacKenzie, D. (2006) 'A Systematic Review of Drug Court Effects on Recidivism', *Journal of Experimental Criminology*, Vol. 2 pp. 459–487.

Wilson, H. (1980) 'Parental Supervision: A Neglected Aspect of Delinquency', *British Journal of Criminology*, Vol. 20, pp. 203–235.

Wilson, L. and Stevens, A. (2008) *Understanding Drug Markets and How to Influence Them*, Oxford: The Beckley Foundation Drug Policy Programme.

Winter, H. (2008) *The Economics of Crime: An Introduction to Rational Crime Analysis*, London: Routledge.

Witt, R, and Witte, A. (2000) 'Crime, Prison, and Female Labor Supply', *Journal of Quantitative Criminology*, Vol. 16, pp. 69–85.

Young, J. (2003) 'Merton with Energy, Katz with Structure: The Sociology of Vindictiveness and the Criminology of Transgression', *Theoretical Criminology*, Vol. 7, pp. 389–414.

Zedlewski, E. W. (2009) 'Conducting Cost Benefit Analyses in Criminal Justice Evaluations: Do We Dare?', *European Journal of Criminal Policy Research*, Vol. 15, pp. 355–364.

Zoutendijk, A. (2010) 'Organised Crime Threat Assessments: A Critical Review', *Crime Law and Social Change*, Vol. 54, pp. 63–86.

Subject index

Author index